WHERE ANGELS TREAD LIGHTLY

THE ASSASSINATION OF PRESIDENT KENNEDY
VOLUME 1

John M. Newman

Original Publication 2015; revised 2017
Copyright © 2017 John M. Newman
All rights reserved.

ISBN-10: 1478302410
ISBN-13: 9781478302414
Library of Congress Control Number: 2014922513
CreateSpace Independent Publishing Platform
North Charleston, South Carolina

I dedicate this book
to the many good men and women
in our government and armed forces
who refused to look the other way
and willingly paid the price
for telling the truth.

TABLE OF CONTENTS

Acknowledgements vii
Prelude: Where Angels Tread Lightly. xi
Prologue: Dark Operations. xiii
Introduction. xvii
List of Acronyms xxv

Chapter One: The Cold War and the American
    Failure in Cuba—1958 1
Chapter Two: Mayhem in Havana January 1-5, 1959. 21
Chapter Three: The Directorio Revolucionario and
    the Genesis of the Anti-Castro Movement. 27
Chapter Four: The CIA'S Early Recruitment of Manuel
    Antonio Varona 41
Chapter Five: The Herter-Hoover Luncheon and the Story of
    Catherine Taaffe 57
Chapter Six: Taaffe's January 1959 Trip to Cuba. 71
Chapter Seven: Frank Sturgis and the First Plot to
    Assassinate Fidel Castro. 81
Chapter Eight: June Cobb and Narcotics Traffickers in
    Ecuador and Colombia. 97
Chapter Nine: June Cobb, Rafael Herran and the Girlfriends
    of Don Juan 111
Chapter Ten: June Cobb and the Federal Bureau of Narcotics 129
Chapter Eleven: Castro's April 1959 Visit to the U.S. 141

Chapter Twelve: Cuba Invades the Caribbean................161
Chapter Thirteen: The Flight of Frank Sturgis and
    Pedro Luis Diaz Lanz..179
Chapter Fourteen: Castro's Agrarian Reform Program 189
Chapter Fifteen: The Exfiltration of Marcos Diaz Lanz 201
Chapter Sixteen: The Dominican Republic Invasion of Cuba......211
Chapter Seventeen: The Complete Victory of Castro in Cuba......229
Chapter Eighteen: The CIA Decision to "Remove"
    Castro from Power..243
Chapter Nineteen: The Exfiltration of Artime and the
    End of Catherine Taaffe and "The Dragon Lady"..............259
Chapter Twenty: Rolando Cubela, Juanita Castro
    and Tony Sforza..277
Chapter Twenty One: The Recruitment of Rolando Cubela 297

Afterword...309
Appendix One: Selected CIA Cryptonyms.........................313
Appendix Two: Selected CIA Pseudonyms.........................335
Appendix Three: The Pseudonyms of Tony Sforza................349
Appendix Four: Earl J. Williamson, Wallace A. Growery,
    and Alfonso L. Rodriguez....................................355
Appendix Five: The Pseudonyms of E. Howard Hunt: Walter C.
    Twicker, Terrence S. Crabanac, and Edward J. Hamilton.......367
Appendix Six: Al Cox and Robert Reynolds 393
Appendix Seven: The Psychological and Paramilitary
    Operations Staff...401
Appendix Eight: Research Methodologies........................403
Bibliography...411
Index..419

ACKNOWLEDGEMENTS

I want to thank my long time friend and research associate, John, "Jay," C. Harvey, Jr. Jay has been a tremendous help to me for more than twenty years. He lived fairly close to where I lived in Maryland. After reading my book *JFK and Vietnam*, he picked up the phone and called me. After that call, we spent innumerable hours doing research in the National Archives and Records Administration (NARA) and on the Mary Ferrell Foundation (MFF) once it came online.

I want to thank my wife and best friend, Sue Newman. Sue has been a true soldier and has tirelessly helped me with my research for nearly forty years. She is a great editor, and her determination to ask tough questions improved the quality of the manuscript, *Quest for the Kingdom—The Secret Teachings of Jesus in the Light of Yogic Mysticism*, and this volume too. I want to thank my children, Alexandra Kahler, Mary Singer, and John Newman III for their continuing support and understanding.

The mistakes in this book are mine.

Peter Dale Scott is a role model—certainly my role model—for researchers of any subject. His works have profoundly impacted mine. Malcolm Blunt has a sharp eye for detail and has shared an enormous amount of documents with me for several years. During that time I have had the benefit of meeting and discussing the case with Malcolm, meetings that often took place in the cafeteria at NARA in College Park. I thank the many prolific researchers whose published works have helped shape my views on the JFK case, including Gaeton Fonzi, Anthony Summers, Tink Thompson, Jefferson Morley, Dave Talbot, Jim DiEuginio, Lisa Pease, Warren Hinckle and William Turner, Michael Canfield and A. J Weberman, and, more recently, Bill Simpich.

I extend my gratitude to Fabian Escalante, who shared his sharp insights on the JFK case with me personally. His important work on the CIA's operations against Cuba has stood the test of time and proved valuable in my research for the present volume.

I extend a special thanks to Rex Bradford. His many years of hard work on the MFF data base and website have made it possible for so many of us to work on this case. I want to thank several of the members of Assassination Archives Research Center (AARC), including Dan Alcorn and Brenda Brodie and, especially the president, James H. Lesar. Jim and I have spent countless late nights picking over the details of discoveries, large and small. Jim's Freedom of Information Act requests have led to the release of many gigabytes of documents on Cuba without which several of the chapters in this volume would not have been possible.

I am very grateful to a new associate of the AARC, Dan Hardway, who has shared his thoughtful insights on this case with me. And although it is not a recent work, I want to extend a hardy thank you to Dan Hardway and Eddie Lopez for their trenchant work for the House Select Committee on Assassinations (HSCA) on Oswald and Mexico City, aka "The Lopez Report." It is hard for me to imagine where we would be today without their work then—and the great work of their close associate, Gaeton Fonzi.

I want to thank Debra Conway, Sherry Fiester, Alan Dale and their associates of the JFK Lancer organization; and Cyril Wecht, Gary Aguilar, John Judge, and Bill Kelly and their associates for their work and support of the former Coalition on Political Assassinations (COPA). Lancer and COPA have helped a great many researchers hone their skills and share their works with others over the past two decades.

I thank Alan Dale for his generous help and outstanding work as a reader of this manuscript. I am especially grateful to the many JFK soldiers who, instead of writing books, help the authors that do. For

ACKNOWLEDGEMENTS

me, that began with Mary Ferrell and includes Malcolm Blunt, Larry Haapanen, Alan Rogers and many others over the years. I would also like to thank my good friend Steve Brown, who was an excellent discussant as the manuscript developed. I want to express my gratitude to two researchers with whom I have collaborated for more than three years on a large number of possible multiple identity cases. For now, they will remain anonymous in order to protect serious and valuable ongoing work.

And, finally, as I begin a new attempt to move the chains down the sidelines of this case, I reflect back to acknowledge and thank two people who gave me an opportunity to run with the ball: Oliver Stone and Eric Hamburg.

PRELUDE:
WHERE ANGELS TREAD LIGHTLY

April 24, 1961: New York City

"My dear Mr. Kennedy," the type written letter began. It had been placed in a plain white envelope and addressed, "Mr. Robert Kennedy, Attorney-General of U.S., Department of Justice, Washington D.C., (Personal Correspondence)." Writing exactly seven days after the disastrous failure of the CIA's Bay of Pigs operation, the author of this letter used what may have been a pseudonym. Whether or not it was her true name, it had, with very few exceptions, vanished from U.S. intelligence files since the summer of 1960. The name was "Catherine Taaffe." This name appeared often in the government's files as far back as the Korean War. It had disappeared in the wake of its association with a murder and kidnapping plot of a former Cuban Senator from the Batista regime in Cuba.

Taaffe was unhappy with U.S. policy in Cuba and the Bay of Pigs failure had lit her fuse. She intended to blast her message to the top of the U.S. government. Taaffe knew full well that letters arriving at the Department of Justice (DOJ) addressed to the Attorney General (AG) did not arrive on the chief's desk unopened. She had anticipated that the AG's staff would check the name Taaffe against the DOJ's files, and she knew what they would find. She understood that this would ensure that her letter would be read by Robert Kennedy, along with many of her voluminous FBI files. By April 1961, those files were bursting at the seams. Much of them remain classified in 2015 but what has been released so far exceeds a thousand pages.

"My letter may be presumptive," Taaffe told Kennedy, "but I have heard of women being forgiven for tramping where angels tread lightly." This turn of phrase was her adaptation of the phrase *Where Angels Fear to Tread*, a line originally from **An Essay on Criticism**, written by the British poet Alexander Pope (1688-1744)—the third-most frequently quoted writer in **The Oxford Dictionary of Quotations**, after Shakespeare and Tennyson. Two hundred years later it became the title of E. M. Forster's novel **Where Angels Fear to Tread**.

Taaffe's use of the adjective "presumptive" to describe her letter to Kennedy was an understatement. To tell the Attorney General that where she was "tramping" would, by inference, strike the fear of God in men, was outrageously immodest. But it was also true. The president's brother would understand this once he began to leaf through her files.

PROLOGUE:
DARK OPERATIONS

A popular Government, without popular information, or the means of acquiring it, is but a *prologue* to a Farce or a Tragedy; or, perhaps both. Knowledge will forever govern ignorance: And a people who mean to be their own Governors, must arm themselves with the power which knowledge gives. James Madison, *Letter to W.T. Barry*, 4 August 1782.

The right of freely examining public characters and measures, and of communication among the people thereon . . . has ever been justly deemed the only effectual guardian of every other right. James Madison, *Virginia Resolutions*, 21 December, 1798.

A fondness for power is implanted in most men, and it is natural to abuse it when acquired. This maxim, drawn from the experience of all ages, makes it the height of folly to entrust any set of men with power which is not under every possible control. –Alexander Hamilton, *The Farmer Refuted*, 5 February 1775.

The above trenchant thoughts of our founding fathers informs us today about how we should approach learning from our recent past. This is especially true with regard to the American failure in Cuba (1958-1963) and the history of the Cold War (1946-1991). The lessons of these events cannot be ascertained from the study of publicly released State Department and White House records alone. Access to those documents is undeniably important. Yet, we also need access to CIA, FBI, and military records that are still being withheld behind the wall of official secrecy—records that should have been released a long time ago.

Physicists need access to information about *dark energy* and *dark matter*—together they account for ninety-six percent of the universe. Without this information they cannot understand how visible matter behaves. All too often, in our society, what lies behind that wall of secrecy is information connected to the *dark* dimension of political, military and economic power. Lack of access to this information distorts our understanding of what is taking place in our world. And this makes us more vulnerable to manipulation.

The dark contours of our society are formed by the nexus of political, economic and military interests in which shifting alliances of individuals— with personal stakes in the outcome—determine how events play out. Although the details about these interests and alliances are unseen, they shape, alter and even undermine presidential policy and larger American interests. They are not unlike "black holes." They cause the normal laws of social order to break down. They can be so weighty that they "curve" the political and economic paths of our history and our destiny.

Presidents are no more immune to manipulation than the common man on the street. The power of the presidency renders the person wielding it even more vulnerable. In the discussion of the unanticipated and dramatic American failure in Cuba in 1958 (in Chapter One), we will observe how President Eisenhower was kept in the dark about matters he should not have been. He was told no more than what a few senior officers in the government—particularly in the CIA—decided that he should know about Castro and communism. He was upset when he found out that the *main elements* of the Cuban situation had been withheld from him.[1] President Kennedy found himself on the horns of ex-

---

1   FRUS, 1958-1960, volume VI, Cuba, document #191, editorial note.

actly the same embarrassing dilemma in Cuba two years later. He, too, was kept in the dark about important information. As the moment for the planned invasion at the Bay of Pigs neared, the CIA was not as forthright as it should have been with the president about the long odds for the success of the operation.

Peter Dale Scott gave us the term, "Deep Politics,"[2] and the late Gary Webb gave us the term, "Dark Alliance."[3] I would like to add "Dark Operations" to our vocabulary. What I mean by that term is related to a remark that Dan Hardway made to me the first time we met. Hardway was a young lawyer in a very important place at a very important time: in 1978 he was an investigator for the House Select Committee on Assassinations (HSCA), looking into the deaths of President Kennedy and Martin Luther King, Jr. I did not meet Dan Hardway until 2014. We were at a meeting, and when we stepped aside to speak, the first thing he said to me was that under many of the CIA's operations, there is another operation in play. That is a very good way of describing what I mean by "dark operations."

CIA operatives use pseudonyms when they handle their sources. The Agency also uses cryptonyms for people and for operations. The original intended use of these methods was not merely to keep the American public in the dark. The CIA's pseudonyms and cryptonyms have been and still are also *used internally at the secret level*. The internal use of cryptonyms and pseudonyms was designed to protect CIA operations. Their use makes it difficult for moles to piece together sensitive operations generally. It is the foundation of what is called "compartmentalization" and the "need to know."

However, keeping cryptonyms and pseudonyms secret forever is unnecessary and even harmful. It can undermine the faith of the people in their institutions of government—especially if something goes wrong with intelligence operations. And something did go terribly wrong with

---

2   "A deep *political system or process* is one which habitually resorts to decision-making and enforcement procedures outside as well as inside those publicly sanctioned by law and society. In popular terms, collusive secrecy and law-breaking are part of how the deep political system works." Peter Dale Scott, ***Deep Politics and the Death of JFK*** (Berkley: University of California Press, paperback ed., 1996), Preface, Deep Politics: Some Further Thoughts.
3   Gary Webb, ***Dark Alliance: The CIA, the Contras, and the Crack Cocaine Explosion*** (New York: Seven Stories Press, 1999)

WHERE ANGELS TREAD LIGHTLY

American intelligence operations before, during, and after the assassination of President Kennedy.

There is no darker story in our recent history than how the American struggle with Fidel Castro became entangled with the assassination of President Kennedy. I am not arguing that it necessarily involved a lot of people in the CIA, the FBI, or in other U.S. national security organizations. But I am arguing that without unmasking the CIA's pseudonyms, cryptonyms, and multiple identities that were in use over half a century ago and were related to this case, it will not be possible to find out, let alone prove beyond a reasonable doubt, who was behind the assassination in Dealey Plaza and how they got away with it. We not only have the right to find out, but also, the duty to find out.

The president's murder happened fifty-three years ago. The CIA's continued withholding of records is still being justified based on the flawed premise that it is protecting sources and methods from foreign intelligence services. Those sources and methods have been known around the world for decades. This justification lacks credibility today. The continued withholding of this information now functions only to hide these operations from those to whom they belong: the American people. Our congress agrees. That is why they passed the JFK Assassination Records Act in 1993.

INTRODUCTION

The present volume is the first in a series about the assassination of President John F. Kennedy. This series will eventually comprise four or perhaps five volumes. Each volume will have one or more principal foci relative to time. Around those foci we will arrange clusters of people, events and operations. Each volume will also contain sections that look backward, as well as sections that leap forward. Looking forward and backward will help establish a baseline of the major boundaries and interstitial periods for the recurring themes and characters that came to dominate this case.

The political geology that led to that tragic event in Dealey Plaza extends back to WWII and even before. We will need to look there to find the first footsteps taken by many of the characters that became entangled in this case. It begins a few years before the epochal boundary that marks the start of the Cold War, ushered in around 1946. It ends just twenty years into the Cold War epoch that would continue for another quarter century. Two events mark a substratum of this epoch: Fidel Castro's assumption of power in Cuba on 1 January 1959, and the assassination of President John Kennedy on 22 November 1963. I believe that the first event led inevitably to the second one. But I do not believe that Fidel Castro was behind the president's murder in Dallas, Texas. The series of volumes that will make up the present work reaches only a little past the assassination in Dallas into the next substratum—the most active phase of the Vietnam War (1964-1974).

The main lens for the entire series of volumes is the period 1959-1963—perhaps the most seismically active period of the Cold War. The struggle between Fidel Castro and John Kennedy cannot be understood outside of the context of the Cold War any more than the Cold War can be understood apart from the struggle between Castro and Kennedy.

THE ORGANIZATION OF VOLUME I

We begin (Chapter One) with this cornerstone: the events of 1958. In this chapter we will look back into 1957, and even further back beyond that. However, we know that a major fault line is coming: the victory of Fidel Castro on 1 January 1959. The events of 1958 were every bit as much of an American failure in Cuba as the infamous Bay of Pigs invasion was in 1961. In a sense, the failure in 1958 created the fundamental conditions that inevitably led to the failure in 1961.

After a brief survey of the chaos that occurred in the first week in Cuba after Batista's flight (Chapter Two), we drop backward again (Chapter Three) to search for the roots of the anti-Castro movement that was already incipient when he seized power. Our lens will then focus on the CIA's early 1957 recruitment of Manuel Antonio Varona (Chapter Four), a Cuban who would play a major role in the Cuban-American conflict during the period between Castro's victory and the Bay of Pigs.

We will return to the beginning again, to the disorientation in Washington in the first month after Castro's victory (Chapter Five), and the strange tale of how Catherine Taaffe became the FBI's top informant on Cuban matters. We will follow her trail in Cuba, and then examine the plans of an American soldier of fortune in Cuba, Frank Sturgis, to assassinate Fidel Castro (Chapter 6). We will spend time to survey the narcotics trafficking activities of June Cobb in Chapters 8, 9, and 10—dropping well back in time to do so—and then end up back in the present to scrutinize her plan to penetrate Castro's inner circle during his trip to the U.S. in April 1959 (Chapter 11).

In the spring and summer of 1959, the Castro regime's invasions of Nicaragua, Guatemala, Panama, and the Dominican Republic all

INTRODUCTION

failed (Chapter 12). At that time the exodus of senior anti-communist leaders from Cuba began. We will examine the flight of Castro's air force chief, Pedro Diaz Lanz, and his sidekick, Frank Sturgis (Chapter 13). Castro's Agrarian "Reform" Program (Chapter 14) is the backdrop for the exfiltration of Pedro's brother, Marcos Diaz Lanz (Chapter 15) and the failed invasion of Cuba by the Dominican Republic (Chapter 16).

Castro's complete victory in Cuba (Chapter 17) is followed by the CIA decision to "remove" him from power in Cuba (Chapter 18). The exfiltration of Artime in December 1959 (Chapter 19) ended in disaster for the CIA's ace exfiltrator, Delia Failde, aka the "Dragon Lady" (AM-COO). Catherine Taaffe also overplayed her hand (also Chapter 19) and suffered a catastrophic end to her usefulness. Due to security concerns, Dave Phillips left Cuba too, at the end of 1959. This volume ends with a brief look ahead: Tony Sforza's recruitment of Castro's sister, Juanita, in 1961(Chapter 20), and the CIA recruitment of Rolando Cubela in 1962 (Chapter 21).

This volume also contains eight appendices. Appendix One is a list of the CIA cryptonyms related to the Cuban story—many of these identifications are new. Appendix Two is a list of pseudonyms used by CIA officers, operatives, and sources—again, many of these are new. Appendices Three, Four, Five and Six are detailed proofs for the multiple pseudonyms used by Antony Sforza, Earl Williamson, E. Howard Hunt, and Al Cox, respectively. Appendix Seven contains some preliminary data on the CIA's Psychological and Paramilitary Operations Staff (PP). Appendix Eight is a discussion about research methodologies that might be useful to researchers currently working on the case.

MAJOR WORKING HYPOTHESES

The following working hypotheses pertain to the entire series of volumes in the present work. The substance of Hypotheses Three and Four was presented in the 2008 edition of my previous work, ***Oswald and the CIA***. We will build upon them as the volumes of this series unfold.

- Hypothesis One: At some point in 1962, regardless of how much earlier someone might have wanted President Kennedy to be assassinated, the contours of the plot that eventually emerged began to fall into place: an American Marxist, Lee Harvey Oswald would assassinate JFK and *appear* to have done so for Fidel Castro with the assistance of the KGB.
- Hypothesis Two: The plot was also designed to make it *appear* that the Kennedy brothers' plan to overthrow Castro had been successfully turned around by Fidel, resulting in the assassination of President Kennedy.
- Hypothesis Three: Lee Harvey Oswald was sent by his agent handler to New Orleans in the summer of 1963 to build upon his pro-Castro Cuban legend that he had begun to establish in Dallas at the beginning of that year.
- Hypothesis Four: Oswald's CIA files were manipulated by CIA counterintelligence in the weeks before the assassination to support the design mentioned in Hypothesis One and Two. In this connection, Oswald (or an imposter) traveled to Mexico City (28 September-3 October 1963) and spent time in the Cuban Consulate and met with a Soviet diplomat, Valery Kostikov, who was known to U.S. intelligence to be the head of KGB assassinations (Department 13) for the Western Hemisphere.
- Hypothesis Five: An essential element of the plot was a psychological operation to raise the specter of WWIII and the death of forty million Americans.[4] This threat of a nuclear holocaust was then used by President Johnson to terrify Chief Justice Earl Warren and some of the other men who served on the Warren Commission to such an extent that they believed there was no alternative to writing a report stating Lee Oswald alone had assassinated the president.

---

4 See the discussion in David Talbot's **Brothers—The Hidden History of the Kennedy Years** (New York: Free Press, 2007), p. 252-253. Talbot discusses the threat of nuclear war, and also Castro's remark, "You watch and see, I know them, they will try to put the blame on us for this thing."

INTRODUCTION

FURTHER ASSUMPTIONS

- Neither Fidel Castro nor the Soviet Union was involved in the assassination of JFK.
- For the plot that was used in the JFK assassination to work, Castro had to be alive after the president's death. Rolando Cubela would have to be denied the means to easily kill Castro until after—several months at a minimum—the assassination in Dallas took place.
- Many of the post-assassination lies and cover-ups were carried out by people who had nothing to do with the pre-existing plot to assassinate the president. Many of these people mistakenly thought that what they were doing was in the best interests of the country.
- We would be mistaken to assume that just because there is no written evidence for an event that it never took place.

A NOTE ON CHAPTERS TWENTY ONE AND TWENTY TWO

The final two chapters of this volume leap forward into small slices of time in 1961 and 1962. The material in them will be expanded upon in forthcoming volumes. The critical moment in this Cuban-American drama may have occurred in the summer of 1962: A request from Cubela to defect to the U.S. arrived in the shadow of the forthcoming Cuban Missile Crisis. The intent here is to draw the reader's attention, at the outset of this series, to the history of the plots against Fidel Castro. Above, we have set forth the hypotheses and assumptions that address how those plots eventually led to the assassination of President Kennedy. And so, as we track through these plots, we will understand what is coming at the end: a very dark operation—the assassination of President John Kennedy. Many people in and out of the U.S. government believed then, as many do now, that the *false* scenario—of a Kennedy plot to overthrow Castro that was turned around by Fidel and used to assassinate President Kennedy—is true.

WHERE ANGELS TREAD LIGHTLY

The events described in the final chapter of this volume took place at a crucial juncture in July-August 1962: the CIA's recruitment of Rolando Cubela *and* the JMWAVE Station's discovery that the Soviet Union was up to something profoundly disturbing in Cuba.

In December 1959, the CIA had decided that Castro should be "removed" from power in Cuba (Chapter Eighteen). The Kennedy brothers were not in power in 1959 or in 1960. But they were in power when President Kennedy approved the exile invasion of Cuba in April 1961, and the subsequent plan to overthrow Castro, known as Operation Mongoose, in November 1961. The new Kennedy plan to overthrow Castro was only *part* of the context in which Cubela was recruited in July and August of 1962. When the CIA pitched him in Helsinki and Paris they were surprised to learn that he did not want to "defect." He agreed to be recruited, but he adamantly expressed his determination to return to Cuba to assassinate Castro.

The *other part* of the context surrounding Cubela's recruitment has been aptly described by JMWAVE Chief of Station Ted Shackley. In his autobiography, he described *an unexpected vectoring of events* that began in July 1962.[5] From its sources inside of Cuba, the JMWAVE Station detected a secret buildup of Soviet personnel, and this buildup continued in August. Shackley states that the JMWAVE Station knew that the Soviets were moving more of their equipment at night, and concluded that they were moving surface-to-air missiles (SAMs).[6] At the moment the JMWAVE Station first detected the Soviet plan to place missiles in Cuba, Cubela asked the CIA to provide him with the weapons he needed to assassinate Castro.

Looking ahead into the future, we see a bizarre snapshot at the very end of the line: the assassination of John Kennedy in Dallas occurred at the same moment a senior CIA officer was handing a pen—that could be weaponized to kill Castro—to Cubela in Paris.[7] And so, in this volume we will troll through the past to find out when the plots to overthrow Castro became intertwined with the plot to kill Kennedy. As we do that,

---

5   Ted Shackley, *Spymaster—My Life in the CIA* (Washington D.C., Potomac Books, 2006, paper ed.), p. 60.
6   Ted Shackley, *Spymaster—My Life in the CIA* (Washington D.C., Potomac Books, 2006, paper ed.), p. 62.
7   See the discussion in David Talbot's *Brothers—The Hidden History of the Kennedy Years* (New York: Free Press, 2007), p. 229. Talbot argues that the CIA tried to frame Robert Kennedy for the Cubela plot.

we glance *forward* from time to time, armed with a basic understanding about the nature of the plot, where it reached critical mass, and how it ended. Knowing something about the future better prepares us to go *back in time* to search for new clues. And, hopefully, we will find some long overlooked, low hanging fruit.

ABOUT THE FOOTNOTES IN THIS VOLUME

We will be using footnotes instead of endnotes. The majority of documents cited in the text are CIA and FBI records. I obtained some of these records before the Record Identification Form (RIF) system currently in use was created by the JFK Assassination Records Review Board.

Several important CIA records that do not have the new RIF numbers will have a long and annoying number such as this: 1993.07.02.10:57:45:030800. In most instances these older numbers can still be used to pull up the record from the Mary Ferrell Foundation (MFF) archives (if the colons are removed).

More than half of the FBI records cited in this volume do have the new RIF numbers. However, many citations do not have RIF numbers at all because they were released to a person who filed a Freedom of Information Act (FOIA) request. Attorney Jim Lesar has done more of these requests for JFK-related records than anyone I know, and he was kind enough to share them with me. One significant group of documents pertaining to Catherine Taaffe, more than 500 pages of records, was released to Lesar on 29 August 2008. In addition, Lesar's October 1994 request for the FBI HQS and New York FBI Office Cuban (109) files resulted in the release of tens of thousands of pages of records bginning around 2004. The AARC and MFF are currently discussing how to make these files available to the general public.

Most of the State Department records cited in this volume are from the Foreign Relations of the United States (FRUS) Cuba 1958-1960, Volume VI.

THE CRYPTONYMS AND PSEUDONYMS IN THIS VOLUME

A few of the cryptonyms (fully listed in Appendix One) and pseudonyms (fully listed in Appendix Two) used in this volume are not "hard" identifications. These are usually characterized as "possible" or "probable." As the series unfolds, we will carry an ongoing errata list if they need to be changed. This is the price of my decision to share what I know or suspect might be the case now, instead of waiting for years for complete proof. There has been enough waiting.

NOTE ON THE 2017 EDITION

The most substantive change from the original 2015 edition is the correction of the true name for the pseudonym Andrew F. Merton. It is Jack Stewart, not as I originally thought, Dave Phillips. Some of the reasons for that misidentification will be evident in Appendix Three to Volume II, which draws attention to a mistake in the State Department *Foreign Service Register*. It suggested, wrongly as it turns out, that Stewart was in Mexico at a time that Merton was actually still involved (for about three more months) in several important operations taking place in Havana. That matters less than getting the identification right. I want to acknowledge and thank Jerry Shinley for sharing his extensive data on Stewart, which made the oddity in the register irrelevant. It also enabled me to develop a very detailed life history of Stewart from civil records. I will continue to follow his story, including his continuing friendship with Earl Williamson. I have made some adjustments to other pseudonyms in Appendix Two: the most important (aside from Merton) is the discovery that Reichardt and Karnley are both pseudonyms for Ken Crosby—who was living only twenty miles from me in the Shenandoah Valley until a few years ago. The others are minor adjustments to the pseudonyms for Gerry Droller, Hernry Hecksher, Justin O'Donnell and William Harvey. I want to thank Alan Dale, and Jay Harvey for their valuable help on this new edition of volume I.

LIST OF ACRONYMS

ACU: Agrupacion Catolica Universitaria, a Cuban Catholic University Group
ADC: Accion Democratica Christiana, formed by Fabio Freyre
ASNE: American Society of Newspaper Editors
CI: Counterintellligence (CIA)
CNO: Chief of Naval Operations
COG: Cuban Operations Group (CIA)
COS: Chief of Station (CIA)
CRC: Cuban Revolutionary Council
CRM: Civic Resistance Movement, Manuel Ray, Cuban underground in Havana during Batista dictatorship
DCI: Director of Central Intelligence
DCOS: Deputy Chief of Station (CIA)
DDP: Deputy Director of Plans (covert operations)
DIER: Cuban Army Intelligence (G-2)
DOD: Department of Defense
DOJ: Department of Justice
DR: Directorio Revolucionario, a Cuban student-based revolutionary group
DRE: Cuban Student Directorate, formed in Miami JMWAVE Station in 1960
FBN: Federal Bureau of Narcotics
FEU: Federation of University Students (Cuba)
FI: Foreign Intelligence (CIA)

IAPA/SIP: Inter-American Press Association, aka Inter-American Press Society
ICBM: Intercontinental Ballistic Missile (ICBM)
INRA: Agrarian Reform Institute, created by Fidel Castro in 1959
INS: Immigration and Naturalization Service
IOC: Initial Operating Capability (usually referring to missile systems)
LAR: Legion of Revolutionary Action, formed by Manuel Artime
"Legat": The legal attaché, a cover for the FBI cover in U.S. embassies
MRP: People's Revolutionary Movement, formed by Manuel Ray
MRR: Movement of Revolutionary Rescue, formed by Artime and Sergio Sanjenis
NSC: National Security Council (U.S.)
OPC: Office of Policy Coordination (U.S., pre-CIA)
Organization of American States (OAS)
Office of Strategic Services (OSS—the forerunner of the CIA)
PP: Psychological and Paramilitary Operations Staff (CIA)
PPL: Partido del Public Libre, Free People's Party, formed by Carlos Marquez Sterling
PRC: Partido Revolucionario Cubana, Varona helped found the group in 1934
PRQ: Personal Record Questionnaire (CIA)
SAAG: Special Assistant to the Attorney General
SAS: Special Affairs Staff (CIA Cuban operations)
SFNE: Frente Nacional del Escambray, "Second Front" that fought with Castro against Batista
SIM: Servicio de Inteligencia Militar, Batista's Army Military Intelligence
SO: Security Office (CIA)
TFW: Task Force W (CIA, Cuban operations)
USIA: United States Information Agency
WHD: Western Hemisphere Division (CIA)

CHAPTER ONE:

THE COLD WAR AND THE AMERICAN FAILURE IN CUBA—1958

Since the spring of 1958, U.S. policy in Latin America favored the replacement of right-wing dictatorships with more progressive regimes. This was especially true in Cuba and the Dominican Republic, where increasingly corrupt and repressive dictatorships rendered them liabilities to the United States, which was then in a hostile Cold War contest with the Soviet Union. In keeping with this policy, *American weapons shipments to the Government of Cuba were precipitously suspended on 14 March 1958.*[8] During the following months, moderate Cuban leaders opposed to President Fulgencio Batista began seriously considering working with Fidel Castro to form a new provisional government.[9] U.S. policy in Cuba

---

8   FRUS, 1958-1960, volume VI, documents #36 and #37, telegrams between the State Department and the embassy in Havana discussing the cutoff.
9   FRUS, 1958-1960, volume VI, document #42, State Department memo, March 24, 1958, "Dr. Varona's Views on Civilian-Military Junta Membership."

therefore contributed to the conditions that led to the rise of Fidel Castro, who, at that time, was not unpopular in America. His popularity in the U.S. would be short-lived, particularly in the Pentagon and among U.S. corporations doing business in Cuba. During the summer of 1958, Castro's forces began harassing U.S. businesses and military interests with acts of sabotage and abductions of U.S. citizens, including sailors and marines.

As the revolution unfolded, real power gravitated to those who had paid attention to the development of military forces in the relative safety of the mountains and out of the reach of Batista's army. This was especially true for Fidel Castro. The enormously popular Jose Antonio Echevarria and his Directorio Revolucionario (DR) had been decimated after their bold assault against the Presidential Palace in 1957. Echevarria's death left Castro in a stronger political position. By the summer of 1958, Batista's lack of popularity and Castro's growing military strength meant that Cuban opposition leaders increasingly found no alternative but to accept Castro's central role in the revolution.

U.S. Government officials, including those involved with Cuba in the Central Intelligence Agency (CIA), were divided in their views toward Castro. Many were sympathetic toward him and many were not. "Unfortunately, some of the officers of the Havana Embassy continued to the end to believe," recalled U.S. Ambassador to Cuba Earl Smith, "that Castro was the salvation for Cuba."[10] According to the journalist Tad Szulc, between November of 1957 and the middle of 1958, the CIA delivered fifty thousand dollars to a half-dozen key members of Castro's 26 of July Movement in Santiago—Cuba's second largest city, located on the island's southeastern coast. A CIA case officer working under the cover of the vice-consul there, Robert D. Wiecha, handled these funds. The Santiago consul Park Fields Wollam told his State Department colleagues about the CIA's support for Castro in Santiago.[11] In August 1958, a senior officer in the CIA's Political and Psychological Staff (PP)

---

10   Earl E.T. Smith, *The Fourth Floor—An Account of the Castro Communist Revolution* (New York: Random House, 1962), p. 30.
11   Tad Szulc, *Fidel: A Critical Portrait* (New York: William Morrow & Co., 1986), pp. 427-429.

recommended that the CIA give Castro both arms and money (see more on this in Appendix Six).[12]

However, such pro-Castro sympathies were becoming more embarrassing and more difficult to defend after Castro's forces began kidnapping American citizens and raiding American business facilities. By the end of 1958, the CIA found itself in a desperate effort to derail the rebel leader's bandwagon as his moment of triumph drew near. By December, the CIA Station reported that Manuel Ray, one of the few remaining independent opposition leaders, had made his way up to Castro's Sierra Maestra base to discuss Fidel's suggestion that Ray "dissolve" his own opposition organization and incorporate it into Fidel's 26 July Movement.[13]

Time was running out for Batista and for any American effort to block Castro. His escalating attacks on U.S. interests in Cuba came at a crucial juncture in the history of the Cold War. The Eisenhower Administration came under increasing pressure to intervene in Cuba. The president might have done so were it not for two factors. First, Soviet Premier Nikita Khrushchev checked Eisenhower's freedom of action with a double-barreled bluff over Berlin and intercontinental ballistic missiles. Second, Eisenhower had not been told by his senior advisors that Communist penetration of Castro's movement was increasing and that the communists would be participating in a Castro regime. As a result, Eisenhower decided against giving any U.S. military guarantees to a successor regime in Cuba. This outcome gave Castro the time he needed to complete his drive to power.

U.S. INTELLIGENCE AND WEAPONS FOR CASTRO

Castro's forces got their weapons from various sources. They stole weapons from Batista's army and bought them from corrupt army offi-

---

12   8/25/58 Memo for Chief, PP STAFF by Alfred T. Cox, Chief, PP Paramilitary Division, Subject: U.S. Course of Action in Cuba; *CIA Official History of the Bay of Pigs Operations*, Volume III, pp. 8-9, and fn 15, p. 348. RIF 104-10301-10004.
13   12/15/58, HAVA 0693 to DIR CIA; RIF 104-10180-10062. On 26 July 1953, Castro and his brother Raul Castro led an attack on the Moncada barracks in Santiago, giving rise to the name Castro used for his movement thereafter.

cers. A major supplier was former Cuban President Prio Socarras, who had had fled Cuba with $140 million, which he later used to buy arms and ammunition and had it smuggled to the rebels in Cuba.[14] Prio's contraband activities ended in February 1958 when he was arrested and indicted in Florida.

U.S. intelligence knew that Castro also acquired significant amounts of weapons from American pilots, who were smuggling them from the U.S. and dropping them to Castro in the Sierra Maestra. In the summer of 1958, one of the better-known pilots, Charles Hormel, crashed his plane on his twentieth supply trip. The U.S. Navy rescued him and then "spirited" him to Havana so he could hide inside the U.S. Embassy, "where Batista's police could not get at him."[15] Hormel then illegally reentered the U.S.

Documents declassified in the wake of the 1993 JFK Records Act—some of which have since been reclassified[16]—contain details about why these pilots were protected. As the pattern of Castro's rebels' attacks against U.S. facilities dramatically increased in the fall of 1958, intelligence interest in Castro's forces intensified. A major intelligence opportunity presented itself at this time, when an American working in Castro's military supply effort agreed to become an American intelligence asset—an asset who would continue to work in the upper echelons of the rebel forces after the revolution.

"I've got garbage, muerdo shotguns, rifles that are rusted," Castro said in the fall of 1958, "and that idiot who is in Miami, who is head of the underground in Miami, doesn't know what he is doing."[17] Castro was complaining about "Bebe Hidalgo" to an American named Frank Anthony Sturgis. Sturgis was an ex-marine, who, disguised as a priest and using his birth name, Frank Fiorini, had made his way up into the Sierra

---

14   Earl E.T. Smith, *The Fourth Floor—An Account of the Castro Communist Revolution* (New York: Random House, 1962), see p. 48, p. 65, and p. 117.
15   Paul Bethel, *The Losers* (New York: Arlington House, 1969), p. 60.
16   For example, the first day of the Sturgis Deposition to *The President's Commission on CIA Activities*, 3 April 1975. The RIF for the original version, 178-10002-10238, is now classified in the National Archives. I copied it there before it was reclassified. Note: the NARA RIF audit trail does not show that it was ever declassified—although it was for a short while.
17   *The President's Commission on CIA Activities*, Sturgis Deposition, 3 April 1975, p. 92; NARA, RIF-178-10002-10238.

Maestra Mountains to seek out Castro's rebels.[18] In his 1975 testimony to the President's Commission on CIA Activities, Sturgis explained that he began by "going in and out of the mountains for Fidel as a courier for messages and money."[19] Castro said he needed equipment, and Sturgis told him he could get it. Castro gave him money and told him to get in touch with "Bebe Hidalgo" in Miami.[20] From weapons dealers in Alexandria, Virginia, Norborne, Missouri and elsewhere, Sturgis bought hundreds of thousands of dollars of M-1 rifles, Springfield rifles, Browning automatic rifles, bazookas, and other small arms and ammunition.[21]

Sturgis testified that he got "close to Castro" by smuggling guns and equipment to Cuba, "by air, by automobiles, and in Key West by the ferry."[22] CIA reports in August,[23] September,[24] and October 1958[25] reveal the close U.S. surveillance of Sturgis' arms smuggling for Castro and how, even when arrested by Batista's Army Military Intelligence (SIM), Sturgis always managed to wind up free. When Sturgis and two other rebel pilots, Pedro Diaz Lanz and Ricardo Lorie, met in San Francisco in October 1958, *everything*—their travel, hotel reservations, and even the license plates of the cars they used—was reported in detail by CIA field elements to HQS in Langley, Virginia.[26] The entire trip was monitored, including how it ended when they were caught with some of the loot in Cuba.[27] On 24 November 1958 Sturgis was caught in Cuba again,

---

18 *The President's Commission on CIA Activities*, Sturgis Deposition, 3 April 1975, pp. 32-34; NARA, RIF-178-10002-10238.
19 *The President's Commission on CIA Activities*, Sturgis Deposition, 3 April 1975, p.37; NARA, RIF-178-10002-10238.
20 *The President's Commission on CIA Activities*, Sturgis Deposition, 3 April 1975, p. 92; NARA, RIF-178-10002-10238. Bebe Hidalgo was a member of the 26 July underground in Miami; RIF 104-10221-10193.
21 *The President's Commission on CIA Activities*, Sturgis Deposition, 3 April 1975, pp. 93-98; NARA, RIF-178-10002-10238.
22 *The President's Commission on CIA Activities*, Sturgis Deposition, 3 April 1975, p. 91; NARA, RIF-178-10002-10238.
23 NARA, JFK files, see Russell Holmes computer pull on Sturgis, HM788, 9 June 1977; Box 2A, F16. CIA DBF-08393, August 21, 1959; the CIA file number is given as 100-009-012.
24 NARA, JFK files, see Russell Holmes computer pull on Sturgis, HM788, 9 June 1977; Box 2A, F16. CIA DBF-10987, September 23, 1958.
25 NARA, JFK files, see Russell Holmes computer pull on Sturgis, HM788, 9 June 1977; Box 2A, F16. The numbers of this report are still redacted except 2765 and the date, October 6, 1958.
26 NARA, JFK files, See IN 26114, November 13, 1958; IN 24954, 28 November 1958; IN 20551, 30 October 1958; and IN 21347, 31 October 1958.
27 NARA, JFK files, see Russell Holmes computer pull on Sturgis, HM788, 9 June 1977; Box 2A, F16. CIA TDCS-3/375,555, November 3, 1958.

and this time "three tons of Cuban rebel arms consisting of American-made bazookas, grenades, rifles, submachine guns and ammo [were] confiscated."[28] Again, Sturgis and his associates were released. In Mexico City in December, once again he was caught and released.[29] Sturgis said that while he was in Mexico he was able to speak with Castro using "one of the clandestine radio transmitters we had in Ecuador that would go directly into Cuba."[30]

Sturgis' luck betrays the importance that U.S intelligence placed on gathering information about Castro's arms supplies. Sturgis always made his way back to Castro's rebel army—in which he held the rank of Captain. We will return to his story in Chapter Seven.

THE MISSILE GAP AND EISENHOWER'S DECISION NOT TO INTERVENE IN CUBA

The Cold War was heating up in the summer of 1958. On 14 July, the King of Iraq, Faisal II, was assassinated in a military coup. The following day, President Eisenhower, fearing a similar coup in Syria would spill over into Lebanon, ordered U.S. Marines into Lebanon.[31] It was about this time that some U.S. intelligence analysts became alarmed by reports of communist influence among Castro's forces.[32] The cutting off of arms shipments to Batista sparked deep divisions within the Eisenhower Administration. Military leaders, most notably the Chief of Naval Operations, Admiral Arleigh Burke, complained bitterly that the Joint Chiefs had not been consulted about the arms cutoff.[33] This debate occurred amid a larger one—over the Soviet intercontinental ballistic missile (ICBM) program. The Soviet launching of the satellite *Sputnik*

---

28 CIA Havana station to HQ, 24 November, 1958, IN 30335; NARA, JFK files, CIA microfilm, Pedro Diaz Lanz, Vol/Folder 4/6/K. See also IN 29648, November 21, 1958, same location.
29 NARA, JFK files, see Russell Holmes computer pull on Sturgis, HM788, 9 June 1977; Box 2A, F16. CIA TDCS-3/330,304, December 5, 1958.
30 Sturgis interview in Michael Canfield and Alan J. Weberman, *Coup D'état in America* (New York: The Third Press, 1975), p. 243.
31 Richard Nixon, *RN* (New York: Grosset & Dunlap, 1978), pp. 194-195.
32 FRUS, 1958-1960, volume VI, document #85, State Department memo on Cuba, 8 July 1958; memo contains comments on CIA reporting of communist infiltration of Castro's movement.
33 FRUS, 1958-1960, volume VI, document #54, State Department JCS meeting, 2 May 1958.

the previous fall had had a traumatic impact on the U.S. and riveted American attention on the escalating missile race with Moscow.

The exploration of missile technology had been feverishly pursued since WWII, and *Sputnik* was alarming because it meant the Soviets might be able to launch intercontinental ballistic missiles (ICBMs) before—perhaps well before—the U.S. would be able to. This was the beginning of what became known as the "missile gap," an estimate that projected a "difference between the ICBM capabilities of the two countries so large as to put the United States in imminent peril."[34] Great arguments erupted throughout the summer and fall of 1958 over the numbers of Soviet missiles. It would not be known until two years later just how wrong everyone had been, including those who had argued for lower Soviet figures. The missile gap was a complete myth. Yet a top secret national intelligence estimate, "NIE 11-5-58: Soviet Capabilities in Guided Missiles and Space Vehicles," released on 19 August 1959, concluded that the Soviets would have available "10 prototype ICBM's" during 1959, with a possibility that this might occur almost immediately.[35]

The Cold War had thus reached a critical stage as the bearded rebel leader emerged from his Sierra Maestra mountain hideout to take Cuba by storm. Before long, this chain of events moved Washington to the brink of intervention. In the summer and fall of 1958, Castro's forces staged a series of incidents that exposed the weakness of the Batista dictatorship and tested the limits of American forbearance in Cuba. On 22 June, Raul Castro issued Military Order Number 30, calling for the abduction of American citizens in his area.[36] During the evening hours five days later, Cuban rebel forces kidnapped twenty-four U.S. naval personnel—including eleven marines—near Guantanamo Naval Base and refused to release them until the U.S. promised not to send arms to the ruling Batista regime and not to allow the Guantanamo base to be used for supplying Batista.[37] On 29 June, the American naval base command-

---

34 Wayne Jackson, CIA Historical Staff, *Allen Welsh Dulles as Director of Central Intelligence: 26 February 1953-29 November 1961*, Volume V, Intelligence Support of Policy, p. 41.
35 NIE 11-5-58, 19 August 1958, as quoted in Wayne Jackson, CIA Historical Staff, *Allen Welsh Dulles as Director of Central Intelligence: 26 February 1953-29 November 1961*, Volume V, Intelligence Support of Policy, p. 70.
36 Earl E.T. Smith, *The Fourth Floor—An Account of the Castro Communist Revolution* (New York: Random House, 1962), p. 140.
37 FRUS, 1958-1960, volume VI, documents #71 and #78.

er at Guantanamo, Admiral R.B. Ellis, ordered U.S. fighter aircraft to fly reconnaissance missions over the rebels, and Ambassador Smith sent Consul Wollam into the hills to demand the release of the hostages.[38]

"We are being humiliated," Chief of Naval Operations (CNO) Admiral Burke argued. He declared that "forceful measures are now required."[39] On 11 July, the Joint Chiefs appealed by memorandum to Secretary of Defense Neil McElroy to lift the ban on U.S. military aid to Batista. They also requested the immediate dispatch of a U.S. Marine Regimental Landing Team to Guantanamo Naval Base.[40] Members of Congress joined several military and civilian leaders—including Ambassador Smith—in calling for U.S. Marines to be sent in to free the hostages.[41] Eisenhower, for the moment, declined to do so or to take any of the actions requested by the Joint Chiefs.

The attacks against American interests in Cuba continued. On 20 October, Castro's forces kidnapped two Texaco employees near Santiago. On 23 October, rebel forces released these hostages and then promptly kidnapped two United Fruit employees and held them for a day. On 21 October, the rebels had seized the largest industrial complex in Cuba, the nickel plant at Nicaro, owned by the U.S. Government and run by the General Services Administration (GSA). This nickel plant at Nicaro had been built during the Second World War to ensure U.S. strategic supplies.[42] Castro's seizure of this facility led Eisenhower to raise the specter of U.S. intervention by dispatching warships to Cuba.[43] He ordered the U.S. attack transport *Kleinsmith* to Nicaro on Cuba's northeast coast to assist in the evacuation of American dependents from the

---

38 Earl E.T. Smith, *The Fourth Floor—An Account of the Castro Communist Revolution* (New York: Random House, 1962), p. 142-146.
39 FRUS, 1958-1960, volume VI, document #90, CNO memo to JCS, July 10, 1958; see note 1, which references a 10 July Finn memo to Murphy containing Burke's remarks.
40 FRUS, 1958-1960, volume VI, document #95, Memorandum From the Joint Chiefs of Staff to the Secretary of Defense (McElroy), subject: Cuba, Jul7 11, 1958.
41 Earl E.T. Smith, *The Fourth Floor—An Account of the Castro Communist Revolution* (New York: Random House, 1962), p. 144.
42 Thomas G. Patterson, *Contesting Castro* (New York: Oxford University Press, 1994), pp. 35-39.
43 Richard C. Thornton, "Exploring the Utility of Missile Superiority, 1958," 1979 unpublished manuscript, George Washington University, p. 44. See also *New York Times*, October 24, 25, and 27, and November 2, 1958.

THE COLD WAR AND THE AMERICAN FAILURE IN CUBA—1958

plant. The president also ordered the U.S. aircraft carrier *Franklin D. Roosevelt* to patrol nearby waters to back up the evacuation operation.[44]

Undaunted, Castro's forces began demanding "taxes" from American companies operating in eastern Cuba.[45] On 25 October, a representative of Castro's forces met with a Texaco representative and demanded either $500,000 in cash or $300,000 in arms.[46] Angry with the rebels and U.S. inaction, on 28 October officials from these American companies met in New York to discuss the problem. The following day in Washington, senior State Department officials listened to the heated complaints of several of these business leaders, including Kenneth R. Redmond, president of the United Fruit Company; Robert J. Kleberg, president of King Ranch; J. C. Carrington of the Freeport Sulfur Company; Harris F. Dodge of the Texas Company; and Mr. Hummel of the Lone Star Cement Company.[47] They were told that there was nothing the government could do except "carefully consider their comments."

Castro was gaining control of events in Cuba and this spelled dire trouble for American companies operating there. When his forces opened up a new military offensive and succeeded in cutting off Cuba's second largest city, Santiago de Cuba, American observers felt the situation had become critical. On 4 November, U.S. Ambassador Earl Smith cabled Washington, "It is essential…that our government learn beyond any doubt whether and to what extent Castro['s] movement is penetrated, supported, influenced or directed by international communism. Our information on this subject to date is dangerously inconclusive."[48] Frank Sturgis believed he had seen evidence of Castro's links to international communists, and he gave pictures related to this to Colonel Ericson Nichols, the U.S. air attaché at the American Embassy in Havana.[49]

---

44   Earl E.T. Smith, ***The Fourth Floor—An Account of the Castro Communist Revolution*** (New York: Random House, 1962), p. 149.
45   FRUS, 1958-1960, volume VI, document #145, Memorandum of a Telephone Conversation Between the Director of the Office of Caribbean and Mexican Affairs (Wieland) and Ernesto Betancourt, 8 October 1958.
46   FRUS, 1958-1960, volume VI, Editorial Note, citing State Dispatch 41 from Santiago, 29 October 1958.
47   FRUS, 1958-1960, volume VI, document #169, Memorandum of a Conversation, Department of State, Washington, 31 October 1958.
48   FRUS, 1958-1960, volume VI, document #152, cable from Havana embassy to State department, 4 November 1958.
49   It is possible that Nichols' true surname was "Severs." See RIF 104-10167-10057.

WHERE ANGELS TREAD LIGHTLY

President Eisenhower needed, but would not receive, this critical information before a series of events would doom American policy in Cuba.

On 4 November, the Republicans were hammered in the 1958 congressional elections. They lost 13 Senate seats and 46 House seats. The next day, 5 November, Eisenhower hinted publicly that protection of U.S. lives and interests in Cuba would be grounds for intervention, and he did so in language nearly identical to that which he used just before U.S. intervention in Lebanon earlier in the year.[50] Eisenhower might well have intervened in Cuba had Khrushchev not thrown the world into another major crisis five days later. In a 10 November speech, Khrushchev suddenly called on the Western powers to get out of Berlin. Eisenhower later said this Soviet challenge had transformed Berlin "into a tinderbox."[51] In a 14 November speech, Khrushchev further escalated the crisis by falsely declaring that the Soviet Union had begun production of inter-continental ballistic missiles (ICBM's). Whether by coincidence or by design, Khrushchev manufactured the Berlin crisis and his latest missile threat at the very moment that Castro began his final drive to seize power.

The Eisenhower Administration calculus for intervention in Cuba had to include an assessment of where things stood in the race to deploy ICBMs. The first deployments of American ICBMs were nearly two years away. U.S. intelligence knew that the Soviet ICBM test program had been inactive since April, but there was sharp disagreement over what this meant about Moscow's capability.[52] The CIA argued that the cessation meant the Soviet program was in trouble. The Air Force, on the other hand, argued that the cessation of the testing program meant the Soviets had entered the "mass production" stage and would begin deployments by the end of 1958.[53]

---

50 Richard C. Thornton, "Exploring the Utility of Missile Superiority, 1958," 1979, unpublished manuscript, George Washington University, p. 45. See also *New York Times*, 6 November 1958.
51 Eisenhower, *The White House Years: Waging Peace, 1956-1961* (New York: Doubleday, 1965), p. 329.
52 See James David Perry, *The Foreign Policy of John F. Kennedy, 1961*, George Washington University doctoral dissertation, 30 September 1996, p. 2; see also "Missiles: Ours and Russia's," *Newsweek*, July 13, 1959, p. 52; John L. Steele, "The Cold Hard Facts Just Don't Add Up," *Life*, February 8, 1960, p. 52; and "Washington Countdown," *Missiles and Rockets*, 3 August, 1959, p. 7.
53 See Lawrence Freedman, *US Intelligence and the Soviet Strategic Threat* (Boulder Colorado: Westview Press, 1977), p. 70.

President Eisenhower could not reject these threats out of hand, and the Soviet Premier kept the pressure on. In a 27 November note to the U.S. threatening to turn over Berlin access to East Germany, the Soviet Premier hinted that his ICBMs would be operational in six months.[54] Khrushchev was lying. He was carrying out a high-stakes gamble in order to back the Americans down. Khrushchev's statements on Berlin and missile production were beautifully timed, for they prevented Eisenhower from discarding the Air Force assessment that Soviet ICBM production had begun.

Khrushchev's gambit altered the American perception of the strategic balance of power at a crucial moment during the Cuban revolution. It was at this very moment that Castro's run for power led the Eisenhower Administration to review its options in Cuba. The choices Eisenhower made would give the Cuban revolution the breathing space it needed to become entrenched.

KHRUSHCHEV'S BLUFF AND THE TORPEDOING OF THE PAWLEY MISSION TO CUBA

The most creative U.S. scheme to prevent Castro from seizing power in Cuba was put in play by the CIA. The idea was to make use of the Justo Carrillo-led anti-Batista Montecristi Group. This group had been formed in 1952 by wealthy professionals and businessmen in opposition to Batista. Justo Carrillo had been president of the Agricultural Development Bank under former Cuban President Carlos Prio. Exiled in Miami in late 1958, Carrillo sought U.S. help for a plot to free Colonel Ramon Barquin in order to carry out a military coup designed to oust Batista and simultaneously block Castro.[55] Colonel Ramon was in jail because of his involvement in a 1956 plot organized by military officers against Batista. CIA analysts were interested in Carrillo's plan because Barquin's anti-Batista credentials could be expected to draw support away from Castro and help thwart his bid for power.[56]

---

54   Richard C. Thornton, "Exploring the Utility of Missile Superiority, 1958," 1979, unpublished manuscript, George Washington University, pp. 46-47.
55   Morris H. Morley, *Imperial State and Revolution: the United States and Cuba, 1952-1986* (Cambridge: Cambridge University Press, 1989 ed.), p. 65.
56   Morris H. Morley, *Imperial State and Revolution: the United States and Cuba, 1952-1986* (Cam-

WHERE ANGELS TREAD LIGHTLY

The Carrillo plan was still in the negotiation phase when the Pawley plan emerged suddenly in the final days of November. This situation was further complicated by the 3 November election of the Batista sycophant Rivero Aguero amid widespread perception of voting fraud. Not due to take office until late February, Aguero quickly sealed his and his country's fate by refusing to reform Batista's policies. Washington immediately abandoned any hope that Aguero might save the situation. Moreover, the CIA could only watch helplessly as Aguero's recalcitrance drove hundreds of thousands of Cubans to support Castro.[57] For the brief period of a few days in late November, the idea of freeing Colonel Barquin from jail in order to block Castro's rise was superseded by what appeared to be a better idea: a direct American request to Batista to step down and appoint a junta.

The idea of Batista arranging a junta acceptable to the Cuban people—that did not include Castro—had surfaced in March 1958, when Ambassador Smith discussed it with his contacts in Havana.[58] Smith pursued the idea for several months,[59] but eventually dropped it over concerns that Batista would have too many conditions. Now, with the regime near its end, the plan was resurrected by William Pawley, an influential man with a checkered past and many enemies in the State Department.

The arch-right wing Pawley had been American Ambassador to Peru (1945-1946) and Brazil (1946-1948) and had, at various times since WWII, worked closely with the CIA. Besides his two ambassadorial appointments, Pawley had served as an assistant to the Secretary of State in 1951 and as an assistant to the Secretary of Defense in 1952. He was also a member of the 1954 four-man Dolittle Committee, created by President Eisenhower to review and revise U.S. covert policy.

---

bridge: Cambridge University Press, 1989 ed.), pp. 65-66. According to Morley, "Carrillo was invited to a November meeting with William H. Carr (president of Carr Aluminum and a close friend of DCI Allen Dulles), who apparently was there on behalf of the CIA. After discussing the plan to free Barquin, Carr sent two people (whom Carr believed were CIA operatives) to assess the quality of the weapons and explosives, together with a plane, that Carrillo's group had already purchased for use in the commando-type raid.

57   Mario Lazo, ***Dagger in the Heart: American Policy in Cuba*** (New York: Twin Circle Publishing Co., 1970 ed.), p. 169.
58   Earl E.T. Smith, ***The Fourth Floor—An Account of the Castro Communist Revolution*** (New York: Random House, 1962), pp. 79-80.
59   Paul Bethel, ***The Losers*** (New York: Arlington House, 1969), p. 62.

THE COLD WAR AND THE AMERICAN FAILURE IN CUBA—1958

Pawley was influential in Cuban affairs and on good terms with Batista. Pawley's business ventures included holdings in Cuba—he was the founder of Cubana Airlines and had taken over the Havana Trolley Company in 1949. By the early 1950s, Pawley had also become firmly entrenched in Republican Party politics. In 1952, Pawley had raised substantial contributions for Eisenhower's presidential campaign and he did so again in 1956.[60] These campaign contributions and his Latin American experience resulted in access to Eisenhower personally and to broad influence in administration policy toward Cuba. Pawley was also on close terms with the Director of Central Intelligence, Allen Dulles, and the CIA's Western Hemisphere Division Chief, J. C. King.

Eisenhower explained that he realized "Mr. Pawley was a zealot,"[61] but that he nevertheless often used Pawley "as a private citizen, for chores of different kinds during my two Administrations."[62] U.S. officials at the CIA and the Bureau of Internal Revenue had concerns about the president's associate. Their files contained derogatory information about black market activities, income tax difficulties, possible misuse of lend lease material, questionable money transactions, and "attempted bribery."[63]

The December 1958 Pawley mission to Cuba was a complicated affair from the start. The plan called for Pawley to ask Batista to appoint a military junta that would then undertake the task of "setting up a provisional government excluding Castro, and later would hold general elections."[64] In the meantime, the U.S. would immediately recognize

---

60 Thomas G. Patterson, *Contesting Castro* (New York: Oxford University Press, 1994), p. 206.
61 FRUS, 1958-1960, volume VI, Cuba, document #613. Memorandum of a Meeting With the President, 29 November 1960.
62 Michael Beschloss, *The Crisis Years: Kennedy and Khrushchev, 1960-1963* (New York: Edward Burlingame Books, 1991), p. 94.
63 In 1954, CIA Security Director, Sheffield Edwards, wrote about the CIA's derogatory information on Pawley: about black market activities, income tax difficulties, possible misuse of Lend-Lease material, and questionable money transactions. NARA, JFK files, CIA January 1994 five brown boxes release, Memorandum from Director of Security, Sheffield Edwards, to Director of Central Intelligence, 13 July 1954. A 1944 Bureau of Internal Revenue investigation of Pawley's business dealings included his associates like General Claire Chennault, with whom Pawley founded the "Flying Tigers"—an airline that later became the CIA's airline, Air America. General Chennault reportedly said that Pawley's record in India and China was "questionable" and that he had been "involved in attempted bribery." NARA, JFK files, CIA January 1994 five brown boxes release, CIA memo from George O'Rourke to Mr. W. A. Osborne.
64 FRUS, 1958-1960, volume VI, Cuba, document #175, Editorial Note. This detail comes from Deputy-Under-Secretary of State Murphy, who used these words in describing it to Ambassador

WHERE ANGELS TREAD LIGHTLY

and support the Batista-appointed "caretaker" regime *with military assistance*. The scheme envisioned $10 million in U.S. arms for the caretaker junta and a place in Florida for Batista and his family.[65] As Pawley saw it, the "keystone of the plan" was the authorization for him to speak for Eisenhower. Pawley was right. Why would Batista step down for a junta composed of his own opponents unless the Eisenhower Administration would put the guarantee of American power behind it?

Yet virtually at the moment Pawley was set to depart for Cuba, the impact of Khrushchev's missile bluff reached its climax in Washington. To make sure that the Americans got the point, on 1 December Khrushchev told Senator Hubert Humphrey, then visiting Moscow, that the Soviets had an 8,700-mile ICBM that could hit anything in America. The Pawley plan's original assurances for Batista now had to be reviewed in the light of Khrushchev's strategic gambit and a possible showdown over Berlin. Unfortunately, that review did not include an assumption that the communists had so penetrated Castro's movement that they would occupy key positions in his government. None of Eisenhower's senior advisors had yet told him that such an outcome was likely.

It was in the context of Khrushchev's threats and the lack of candid advice from Eisenhower's advisors about Castro and the communists, that, during the first days of December, the Pawley mission was altered—to make it fail.

In his 1962 assessment, **Six Crises**, Nixon offered this interesting assessment of Khrushchev:

> Khrushchev has often been called a chess player in conducting his international policies—I suppose because chess is a favorite Russian game. I do not know chess, but I do know poker; and there is no doubt but that Khrushchev would have been a superb poker player. First he is out to win. Second, like any good poker player, he plans ahead so that he can win the big pots. He likes to bluff, but he knows that if you bluff on small pots and fail consistently to produce the cards, you

---

Smith on 10 December. Smith had returned to Washington on December 4 for consultations.
65 Thomas G. Patterson, **Contesting Castro** (New York: Oxford University Press, 1994), p. 208.

THE COLD WAR AND THE AMERICAN FAILURE IN CUBA—1958

must expect your opponent to call your bluff on the big pots.[66]

Nixon may have been thinking about the events of 1961, but his remarks were very relevant to the events that transpired in late 1958.

On 27 November, Thanksgiving evening, U.S. Ambassador Smith was playing bridge at the Havana Yacht Club, "when he felt a light tap on his shoulder." It was Mario Lazo, a Cuban lawyer educated in the U.S. who often slipped valuable information to the U.S. Embassy. Lazo whispered to Smith, "I have something important to tell you," and the two men stepped off to the side. Lazo told Smith that he was going to be summoned to Washington and that someone was going to replace Batista, who would be allowed to fly to his estate in Daytona Beach. Lazo also said he had heard that the ambassador was not to be told, "To protect you, so that if Batista asks, you can say you know nothing about it." Smith was stunned that a Cuban had just told him top-secret information which he, the ambassador, "knew nothing about."[67]

At the last moment, Ambassador Smith was recalled from Cuba and Pawley was directed to proceed to Havana *without permission* to use Eisenhower's name.[68] By the time Pawley arrived in Havana, he appeared to be no more than an emissary of American businessmen who, like himself, were eager to defend their own interests there. Eisenhower's decision to back away from an American military guarantee to a new junta was not given wide circulation inside the administration—and that was at the president's insistence. The result left the plan to block Castro from winning in Cuba hanging on the uncertain covert CIA-Carrillo scheme. These last minute changes caused confusion at the time and made it difficult for historians in later years to understand how and why the already secret Pawley mission had become even more secret.

Eisenhower's later comments support this interpretation of the alterations he made to the Pawley mission. During a 15 February 1960 National Security Council (NSC) meeting, President Eisenhower commented on what had happened to the Pawley mission. "He had," the

---

66 Richard Nixon, *Six Crises* (New York: Warner Books, 1979 ed.), p. 324.
67 John Dorschner and Roberto Fabricio, *The Winds of December* (New York: Coward, McCann & Geoghegan, 1980), pp. 71-72.
68 Thomas G. Patterson, *Contesting Castro* (New York: Oxford University Press, 1994), p. 208.

president said, "gone to Cuba as an emissary from civilians having an interest there, but with the knowledge of Mr. Dulles and Mr. Rubottom, to get Batista to abdicate in favor of a junta. Batista would have done this *had the U.S. guaranteed to keep the junta in power, but this could not be done.*"[69] [Emphasis added] Eisenhower's acknowledgment that official U.S. guarantees could not be given indicates that more than an anti-Pawley faction of State Department officials was behind the secret pullback from the Pawley plan in the first hectic week of December. The larger strategic calculus in the Cold War was the driving force behind a presidential decision to roll the dice in Cuba. Things were back where they had been before the Pawley mission: the CIA plan to spring Colonel Barquin from prison for a coup to oust Batista *and* simultaneously block Castro.

THE FAILURE OF THE CIA'S COVERT PLAN TO BLOCK CASTRO

Although Pawley did not know it, by the time he arrived in Havana, freeing Barquin was the Eisenhower Administration's last hope in Cuba. During Pawley's preparations in Washington, a list was put together of moderate opposition names that would become Cuba's leadership and would be acceptable to the U.S. Pawley was to show the list to Batista, who would be told to use it to select the junta. Once in Havana, the only other person privy to the list was the CIA station chief, Jim Noel.[70] On 9 December, when Batista asked Pawley who the U.S. wanted in the junta, Pawley showed him the list and the name at the top belonged to the imprisoned Barquin.[71] The mission then failed as it was supposed to. Batista was not about to give up his government to the opposition on the mere suggestion of William Pawley. Embarrassed and angry, Pawley returned to Washington to stew. Yet one important thing had been ac-

---

69   FRUS, 1958-1960, volume VI, Cuba, document #453. Memorandum of a Conference with the President, 15 February 1960.
70   Morris H. Morley, *Imperial State and Revolution: The United States and Cuba, 1952-1986* (New York: Cambraidge University Press, 1989 ed.), p. 65.
71   Earl E.T. Smith, *The Fourth Floor—An Account of the Castro Communist Revolution* (New York: Random House, 1962), p. 167.

THE COLD WAR AND THE AMERICAN FAILURE IN CUBA—1958

complished: Batista now knew that Washington did not want Barquin executed, an act Batista might have been expected to contemplate as Castro's forces tightened the noose around Havana.

The American plan now was for a coup carried out by a group of officers around Colonel Barquin. He was the key to the coup's ultimate success because he was still regarded as the one officer who could defeat Castro. The outlines of the coup plan emerged on 20 December.[72] General Cantillo, the commander of Cuban forces in Santiago, put the plan in motion. He took charge in specified regions of Cuba and confronted other officers with a choice of joining or being shot. Barquin was contacted and told of the plot. Barquin accepted, sending his graduation ring as a sign of his agreement.

Washington was still in the game, but time was running out. The problem was that Barquin was still in jail, Batista was still in power, and the rebels were closing fast. Another problem in Washington was also reaching critical mass: *no one had briefed Eisenhower on the extent of the potential communist problem in Cuba.* The president would not be told of the extent of this problem until plans for evacuating American dependents were underway.

At the 23 December meeting of the National Security Council, CIA chief Allen Dulles finally let the cat out of the bag with respect to the Castro-communist problem that was unfolding in Cuba. Dulles informed Eisenhower about the extent of communist penetration in Cuba.[73] Eisenhower was upset that he had not been properly informed. He explained his reaction to the news in his memoirs:

> During the rush of these last events in the final days of 1958, the Central Intelligence Agency suggested for the first time that a Castro victory might not be in the best interest of the United States.... "communists and other extreme radicals appear to have penetrated the Castro movement," Allen Dulles said. "If Castro takes over, they will probably participate in the government." When I

---

72   Hugh Thomas, ***Cuba, The Pursuit of Freedom*** (New York: Harper and Rowe, 1971) p. 1021.
73   FRUS, 1958-1960, volume VI, Cuba, document #188, Memorandum of Discussion of the 392d Meeting of the National Security Council, Washington, December 23, 1958.

heard this estimate I was provoked that such a conclusion had not been given earlier.[74]

Dulles stated flatly, "we ought to prevent a Castro victory." But by this time, events in Cuba were beyond the control of Washington.

Once in the saddle, General Cantillo played the game his own way. On 24 December, he met with Castro and other rebel leaders and promised Castro that the army would "prevent Batista's escape." Cantillo and Castro reportedly agreed to everything in the plan except for Castro's insistence that the Barquin group should be "held in prison." On 24 December, Cantillo returned to Havana and was summoned to Batista. Cantillo did not tell Batista of the promise to prevent his escape. Batista reportedly "told Cantillo he would be prepared to hand over power to a junta of officers headed by Cantillo as a gesture to the Cuban nation and that he (Batista) would leave on 26 February."[75]

On 26 December, Eisenhower held a restricted meeting with Allen Dulles, the White House Staff Secretary, Andrew Goodpaster, and the Special Assistant to the President for National Security Affairs, Gordon Gray. According to the minutes of this meeting, Eisenhower went on a tear.[76] He criticized the way Cuban policy had been handled and he ordered the unfolding CIA-Barquin covert plan to be very closely held. Eisenhower complained that, "for one reason or another the main elements of the Cuban situation had not been presented to him," and added that he intended to speak to Secretary of State John Foster Dulles about this. Eisenhower admonished those present not to go into the "the specifics of covert operations" in the NSC.

That same day, 26 December, the CIA informed Justo Carrillo that the Agency wanted to go ahead with the Barquin scheme. However, instead of a commando raid, the CIA proposed to bribe the Isle of Pines prison commandant with $100,000 to obtain Barquin's release.[77] On 30 December, Batista's army stacked arms and the final saga unfolded. The

---

74   Eisenhower, *The White House Years: Waging Peace, 1956-1961* (New York: Doubleday, 1965) p. 521.
75   Hugh Thomas, *Cuba, The Pursuit of Freedom* (New York: Harper and Rowe, 1971) pp. 1022-1023.
76   FRUS, 1958-1960, volume VI, Cuba, document #191, editorial note.
77   Morris H. Morley, *Imperial State and Revolution: the United States and Cuba, 1952-1986* (Cambridge: Cambridge University Press, 1989 ed.), p. 66.

THE COLD WAR AND THE AMERICAN FAILURE IN CUBA—1958

CIA dispatched an agent, Willard Hubert Carr, to the Isle of Pines where he successfully bribed the prison commandant and secured the release of Barquin.[78]

In Washington, the U.S. Joint Chiefs of Staff again requested that the embargo against U.S. military equipment transfers to Cuba be lifted.[79] Yet nothing more could be done except to wait and see what Cantillo and Barquin would do. Sometime before midnight on 31 December, a group of key U.S. leaders met in the Pentagon to watch the final minutes unfold. The participants included the Chief of Naval Operations Arleigh Burke, CIA chief Allen Dulles, and Deputy Undersecretary of State Robert Murphy.

Admiral Burke argued that "some action" needed to be taken to prevent Castro from capturing power.[80] The Pentagon meeting lasted until 2:00 a.m., almost the exact moment that Batista resigned. At 3:00 a.m., a plane left Havana for the Dominican Republic carrying forty passengers, including Batista, his family and various senior Cuban officials. A few hours later, Justo Carrillo's cousin, Colonel Carrillo, flew a plane from the Isle of Pines to Havana—and the passenger on board was Colonel Barquin.[81]

By the following noon, 1 January, in Havana, Barquin joined General Cantillo—the man to whom Batista had turned over power, designating him as "Chief of Staff." Cantillo quickly concluded he did not want to be the head of a new government so he decided to "turn over power to Barquin,"[82] including command of the substantial armed forces in Havana. Once Barquin was in control, however, the American plan to block Castro breathed its final breath. When Cantillo declined to leave Cuba

---

78 Richard C. Thornton, "Exploring the Utility of Missile Superiority, 1958," 1979, unpublished manuscript, George Washington University, pp. 49-52; see also Hugh Thomas, *Cuba, The Pursuit of Freedom* (New York: Harper and Rowe, 1971) p. 1028, see also note 36.
79 FRUS, 1958-1960, volume VI, Cuba, document #198, editorial note.
80 Hugh Thomas, *Cuba, The Pursuit of Freedom* (New York: Harper and Rowe, 1971) pp. 1025-1026.
81 Hugh Thomas, *Cuba, The Pursuit of Freedom* (New York: Harper and Rowe, 1971) p. 1028, see also note 35.
82 Robert E. Quirk, *Fidel Castro* (New York: WW Norton, 1993) p. 212. Other accounts vary: according to Morley, Barquin was not released until 1 or 2 January. See Morris H. Morley, *Imperial State and Revolution: the United States and Cuba, 1952-1986* (Cambridge: Cambridge University Press, 1989 ed.), pp. 65-66.

at Barquin's suggestion, the latter arrested Cantillo and proclaimed allegiance to Castro.

This turn of events ended the last American hope of influencing events in Cuba. It also paved the way for Castro to assume power without significant further bloodshed, contrary to the prediction of CIA chief Allen Dulles that, "Blood will flow in the streets of Havana."[83]

---

83 Victor Marchetti and John Marks, *The CIA and the Cult of Intelligence* (New York: A. A. Knopf, 1974), p. 306.

CHAPTER TWO:
MAYHEM IN HAVANA JANUARY 1-5, 1959

In the first days of January 1959 violence broke out in Santiago de Cuba, Cuba's second largest city, but lasted less than a week. According to a CIA Information Report (IR), there was shooting of automatic weapons in Santiago during the night of 2-3 January as remnants of former Senator Masferrer's followers were making last stands. The followers were accused of making "rapid attacks on rebels and civilians." The IR stated that the streets in Santiago were not entirely safe and that the Boy Scouts had been mobilized to direct traffic.

The IR also reported that on 2 January a special plane from Miami had arrived in Santiago with twelve men on board who would form the "pilot cadre" of Castro's new air force.[84] The situation remained fluid for a few more days. On 5 January, a CIA officer who was in Santiago, Nelson Raynock, reported that the situation there was rapidly normalizing. He said the streets were jammed with heavy trucks as they tried to

---

[84] 1/2/59, CIA IR 3 Jan 1959, Subject: Cuban Revolutionary Developments; RIF 124-90102-101431.

move food stuffs into the city. Raynock said there was occasional gunfire but it appeared that "law and order" had returned.[85]

In Havana, while blood did not flow in the streets after Castro's victory as Dulles had predicted, the events taking place there were extremely chaotic. Units of Castro's main forces had not yet arrived. News of Batista's 3:30 a.m. flight to the Dominican Republic on 1 January initially spread slowly throughout the capital. American mobsters running hotel casinos had a few precious hours before sunrise to grab as much money as they could and shove it into their suitcases. At dawn crowds began to form in the streets, cheering, honking their horns and making noise with buckets and sticks. Soon the jubilation turned into anger and violence. The rebel militia came out of hiding to take control of the city and encountered sporadic clashes with police. Then the militia encountered "Los Tigres," a guerrilla organization set up by Senator Masferrer to protect Batista:

> In Parque Central, across from the Plaza Hotel, a wild shoot-out ensued between the rebels and members of Los Tigres. The *Masferristas* were in a building on Manzana de Gomez Street and the rebels were firing at them, hitting balconies and windows on the second and third floors. People in the street ran for cover."[86]

Soon crowds of people destroyed the parking meters with hammers, pipes and bats, and then came the slot machines:

> People stormed into the corner bodegas, cafes, and bars, uprooted the machines and dragged them into the street. They were beaten with clubs and sledgehammers. Most of the slot machines were in the casinos, and so the crowd separated into smaller groups and each made its way by car or on foot toward the greatest symbols of all, the hotel casinos that had sustained the Batista dictatorship.[87]

---

85   1/5/59, SACU 334 to DIR CIA; RIF 104-10221-10033.
86   T. J. English, ***Havana Nocturne: How the Mob Owned Cuba and Then Lost the Revolution*** (New York: Harper, 2008), p. 302.
87   T. J. English, ***Havana Nocturne: How the Mob Owned Cuba and Then Lost the Revolution*** (New York: Harper, 2008), p. 303.

More ad hoc units of the 26 July militia were quickly thrown together and sent into the hardest hit areas. It took the rest of the day and evening before some semblance of order had been restored. However, the sacking of homes of pro-Batista elements continued for several days.[88] Those Batista officials who did not flee or find asylum in foreign embassies were arrested.

On 2 January, the FBI "Legat" (the title of the embassy legal attaché was an FBI cover) reported that conditions remained "unsettled" in Havana and around Cuba. Ramon Barquin, now the provisional head of the military junta, kept the former army in its barracks. The Legat described the violence and shooting as having been led by "a group of the rowdy criminal element." He also reported that the 26 July militia units were still working to maintain order in Havana.[89] At this point the American Embassy decided to begin the evacuation of the more than 2,200 tourists who had been caught in Cuba by the crisis, a task that took four days to complete.[90] Wayne Smith, a U.S. consular officer who worked on the evacuation recalls the "sense of urgency" that gripped those who had been connected in any way to the Batista government.[91] By the evening of 4 January, 1,972 Americans had been evacuated.[92]

Having secured as much of their casino cash as they could, several American mobsters were eager to get out of Havana. Catherine Taaffe, whose sources always seemed to have information concerning the underworld of organized crime, told the FBI's New York Office that an anonymous source told her on 3 January that three plane loads of gamblers from Havana "hit the grass fields" in Florida and Georgia and then dispersed to various U.S. cities. Taaffe said her source informed her that Meyer Lansky, Joe Rivers, and the Clark brothers were going directly to Miami Beach, New York and New Jersey.[93]

---

88   1/15/59, From FBI Legal Havana to Director, Intelligence Survey—Cuba, Synopsis, Lesar FOIA Release, FBI HQS 109 File Vol. II.
89   1/2/59, Urgent Teletype from SAC Miami to Director FBI, Subject: Cuban Revolutionary Activities, FPM-Cuba, RIF 124-10306-10098.
90   1/15/59, From FBI Legal Havana to Director, Intelligence Survey—Cuba, Synopsis, Lesar FOIA Release, FBI HQS 109 File Vol. II.
91   T. J. English, *Havana Nocturne: How the Mob Owned Cuba and Then Lost the Revolution* (New York: Harper, 2008), p. 307.
92   FRUS, 1958-1960, volume VI, Cuba, document #215, Editorial note, 4 January 1959.
93   1/5/59 Urgent FBI Teletype from SAC NYO to FBI Director, Subject: Cuban Revolutionary Activities, FPM-Cuba, RIF 124-90036-10153.

Lansky was Batista's closest friend and business associate in the Mafia, to whom the Cuban dictator had offered, for kickbacks, control of Havana's racetracks and casinos. Joe Rivers was an alias for Joe Silesi, a gambling manager at the Deauville Hotel and at the Hilton, and a close associate of another powerful American mobster in Havana, Santo Trafficante.[94] The Clark brothers were probably Lansky's old associates in Broward Country, Florida. Broward County Sheriff Walter Clark accepted payoffs from Jake and Meyer Lansky; Sheriff Clark's brother, Robert, owned the armored truck company whose vehicles transported the Lansky payoffs to Clark and the Florida Sheriff's Association.[95]

A few American mobsters elected to stay in Havana to see how the situation would play out. Among them was Santo Trafficante, for whom things did not work out. He was put under house arrest in June 1959 and eventually released after making a deal with Raul Castro.[96] In Chapter Nine we will return to Lansky and the American mob who shared "the skim" from their casino profits and money from narcotics trafficking with Batista and his associates.

By 5 January, Castro's 26 July forces were in full control of Cuba's cities and countryside. When some of his troops reached Havana that day, they immediately requested that he expedite his arrival to the city because of the factional difficulties that had erupted there.[97] The FBI Legat in Havana reported that martial law had been declared at noon because of disagreement between followers of Faure Chomon's Directorio Revolucionario (DR)—a student-based revolutionary group that had joined the fight against Batista—and supporters of Castro's 26 July Movement. The Legat added, "The DR holds the Presidential Palace and as of this time refuses to give it up."[98] On 5 January, when Manuel Urrutia, who had already taken the oath of office as Provisional Presi-

---

94   T. J. English, *Havana Nocturne: How the Mob Owned Cuba and Then Lost the Revolution* (New York: Harper, 2008), see pp. 108 and 188.
95   T. J. English, *Havana Nocturne: How the Mob Owned Cuba and Then Lost the Revolution* (New York: Harper, 2008), see pp. 78-80.
96   T. J. English, *Havana Nocturne: How the Mob Owned Cuba and Then Lost the Revolution* (New York: Harper, 2008), see pp. 311-314.
97   1/5/59 Urgent FBI Teletype from Havana Legat to Director, Subject: Cuban Revolutionary Activities, FPM-Cuba, RIF 124-90089-10255.
98   1/5/59 Urgent FBI Teletype from Havana Legat to Director, Subject: Cuban Revolutionary Activities, FPM-Cuba, RIF 124-90089-10255.

dent on 2 January in Santiago de Cuba, arrived at the Havana airport to begin his "triumphal entry" into the city, he discovered he had no place to go.[99] Negotiations between the DR and 26 July leaders were eventually ironed out later in the day. The DR vacated the presidential palace and Urrutia established himself there that evening.

On 4 January, Washington ordered Ambassador Smith to return to the U.S., which he did on 6 January. In a 7 January memo to the president, Secretary of State John Foster Dulles asked for Eisenhower's "authorization to take the necessary steps to recognize the present Provisional Government of Cuba."[100] Ambassador Smith returned to Havana that same day. Two days later, on 9 January, Smith sent an uncharacteristically optimistic assessment to Washington stating that there was no danger of a dictatorship emerging in Cuba because a government only becomes dictatorial when it lacks the support of the people, "and this government has the support of all Cubans." Smith added, "This government, and the revolutionary movement, will be honest. They will never defraud the Cuban people."[101] On 11 January Smith received a cable from Washington stating that Eisenhower had ordered his removal.[102] The question of blame and consequent recrimination led to a "fair amount of panic" in the U.S. policy-making apparatus and intelligence community.[103] Moreover, things were going to get much worse.

---

99 Final FBI Briefing Package for Hoover's 1/29/59 luncheon engagement with Undersecretary Herter, FBI HQS 109 File, VOL 11.
100 FRUS, 1958-1960, volume VI, Cuba, document #217, memorandum from the Secretary of State to the President, January 7, 1959.
101 FRUS, 1958-1960, volume VI, Cuba, document #220, Telegram from the Embassy in Cuba to the Department of State, 802, January 9, 1959.
102 FRUS, 1958-1960, volume VI, Cuba, document #221, cable from State Department to Embassy in Cuba, January 9, 1959. Smith's cable to Washington was received at 7:27 p.m. EST, and this cable was received in Havana at 9:23 p.m. EST.
103 See, for example, Morris H. Morley, *Imperial State and Revolution: The United States and Cuba, 1952-1986* (New York: Cambridge University Press, 1989 ed.), p. 73.

CHAPTER THREE:

THE DIRECTORIO REVOLUCIONARIO AND THE GENESIS OF THE ANTI-CASTRO MOVEMENT

The genesis of the anti-Castro movement was driven by a fundamental question for which the answer remained elusive until it no longer mattered: Was Castro a communist? The communist stripes of Raul Castro and Che Guevara were not in question. The same was not true for Fidel Castro during the critical stage of the revolution in 1958 and for much of the first year, 1959, after he had been in power. In November 1958, American Ambassador Earl Smith warned Washington that information was "dangerously inconclusive" on the subject of communist penetration of Castro's movement.[104]

---

104 FRUS, 1958-1960, volume VI, document #152, cable from Havana embassy to State department, November 4, 1958.

Once Castro assumed power on 1 January 1959, the threat of communist penetration in his new government soon became the dominant issue in American Cuban policy. Eisenhower's admonishment of the State Department for its failure to understand this threat loomed especially large over those officers who had earlier argued that there was no such threat. As we will see in Chapter Five, Undersecretary of State Herter turned to FBI Director Hoover for help. The embarrassing failure of the CIA's plan to block Castro's rise to power left senior CIA officers nervous about this threat too. According to the Deputy Director for Operations, Richard Bissell, "The general feeling in intelligence circles when Batista fell was that, although Castro's brother Raul was a dedicated communist, Castro himself was not. It became critically important to confirm or disprove this assessment."[105]

The point that needs to be emphasized is that Castro *understood and nurtured* the uncertainty that swirled around his potential communist leanings. Journalist Tad Szulc believed that Castro, "in the interest of a higher cause," was applying the Marxist concept of "historical justification" to conceal his true purpose until the "right moment."[106] In this chapter we will turn first to the task of explaining the character and details of Castro's secret plan. Against that backdrop we can then begin an examination of the movement that was already incipient against Castro when he took power. That examination begins with the history of the Directorio Revolucionario (DR).

CASTRO'S SECRET PLAN TO COMMUNIZE CUBA

How Castro succeeded in projecting a false image of himself as an opponent of communism while he was secretly planning to take Cuba communist was not well understood at the time. American observers on both sides of the Castro-communist question often saw what they wanted to see. Many who had been sympathetic naturally hoped they would be proven right, just as many on the other side wanted to see their view

---

[105] Richard M. Bissell, *Reflections of a Cold Warrior: From Yalta to the Bay of Pigs* (New Haven: Yale University Press, 1996), p. 152.
[106] Tad Szulc, *Fidel: A Critical Portrait* (Perennial, 2002 Ed.) p. 432.

THE DIRECTORIO REVOLUCIONARIO AND THE GENESIS...

vindicated. Such over simplistic handling of this crucial question played into Castro's hands. It helped him conceal a far more complex plan that he intended to implement in stages. Fidel used the same multi-stage strategy to implement his Agrarian Reform Program.

Batista was gone, but his army was not. For the moment, Castro was in charge, but other political leaders had ambitions too. Castro needed time to neutralize the armed forces and isolate his political rivals. These two objectives required that he publicly and persuasively distance himself from communism *and* the Cuban Communist Party (PSP). Castro understood that there were *two* issues in play: on the one hand, there was the issue of Castro and communism; and, on the other hand, there was the issue of Castro and the PSP. This distinction was not prominent in the meetings, memoranda and cables of the American establishment at the time. The significant difference between these two issues was lost by framing the question thus: "Is Castro a communist?"

The truth was that Castro disliked the PSP *and* intended to take the island communist. His attitude toward the PSP had been shaped by their opportunistic alliance with Batista. They had not played a significant role in the revolution and had not backed Castro until it was clear he was going to win. Castro's first Treasury Minister, Rufo Lopez-Fresquet, described this state of affairs incisively in his landmark book in 1966.[107] Castro intended to replace Cuba's economic structure with a socialist system, without the interference of the Cuban communists. He intended to dominate them and manipulate their party machinery to suit his own ends. He intended to seek an alliance with the Soviet Union to counter the threat of intervention by the U.S. For their part, the Cuban communists and Soviets favored a slow socialization of Cuba:

> They were convinced that a brusque change in the political and economic structure would precipitate American intervention. In the first months of 1959, the Communist Party in Cuba wanted only to regain the influence it had had with Batista.[108]

---

[107] Rufo Lopez-Fresquet, *My Fourteen Months With Castro* (New York: World Publishing Company, 1966).

[108] Rufo Lopez-Fresquet, *My Fourteen Months With Castro* (New York: World Publishing Company, 1966), p. 162.

The Soviet Union and the PSP understood the delicacy of the moment and stayed quiet. There was every reason to expect that if they followed this strategy, Castro would clean out the anti-communists while the aggressive Americans would eventually drive Castro into an alliance with Moscow.

JOSE ECHEVARRIA, ROLANDO CUBELA, CARLOS TEPEDINO AND THE DIRECTORIO REVOLUCIONARIO (DR)

Cuba has a long record of student opposition to dictators. The formation of the DR was an important chapter in the history of this activism at the University of Havana. During the early 1930s a splinter group of the Federation of University Students (FEU) formed a secret organization to overthrow the Machado dictatorship. They called it the University Students' Directorate.[109] Dr. Manuel Antonio Varona happened to be one of the original organizers of this organization and we will return to his history in the next chapter.[110] It was in this tradition that, at the University of Havana in 1956, Jose Antonio Echevarria founded the secret organization known as the Directorio Revolucionario (DR) to overthrow Batista. Rolando Cubela was also a founding member of the DR, and he became its second in command and military leader. Carlos Tepedino financed the group through the profits from his jewelry business.

By 1956, Echevarria, Cubela, and Tepedino had become very close. How this tight knit threesome later became entangled with a fourth Cuban, "Pancho" Varona (no relation to Manuel Antonio Varona), is worth mentioning due to its relevance to the CIA's anti-Castro activities. Tepedino was the oldest, born in Havana in 1924, as Carlos Lopez Gonzales. After his father, Ignacio Lopez, died in 1950, his mother, Amada Gonzalez, married Francesco Antonio Tepedino, a jeweler from Salerno, Italy, whose family had immigrated to New York in 1901. After the marriage, Carlos' name was changed to Carlos Tepedino Gonzalez.

Francesco Tepedino built his jewelry business in New York and Havana. Since the late 1930s, he had been, along with Carlos' mother,

---
109 3/27/58, FBI Miami Office Report on the Directorio Revolucionario, RIF 124-10296-10180.
110 2/13/51 CIA Biographic Report on Manuel A. Varona Loredo, RIF 104-10168-10447.

close friends with a Cuban family with the last name of Ugarizza. By chance, a daughter of that family, Norma Ugarizza, ended up married to one Francisco Wilfredo "Pancho" Varona, who got caught up with Carlos Tepedino, Echevarria and Cubela in the DR. We will have much more to say in this volume about Pancho Varona, whose CIA cryptonym was AMCONCERT-1, Rolando Cubela, whose CIA cryptonym was AMLASH-1, and Carlos Tepedino, whose CIA cryptonym was AMWHIP-1.

Echevarria was born in Cardenas, Cuba in 1932. Cubela was born in Cienfuegos, Cuba in 1933, and attended secondary school in Cardenas, where his friendship with Echevarria began.[111] According to CIA reports, Cubela became very attached to Echevarria's parents.[112] Echevarria entered the University of Havana in 1950—the same year Castro did. Popular and with strong organizational skills, Echevarria was elected president of the Federation of University Students (FEU)—a post Castro aspired to but never attained.[113] Cubela also attended the University of Havana and was elected representative of the school of medicine on the FEU Council.[114] Although Tepedino graduated from a grammar school, he refused to continue studying and decided instead to devote himself to the jewelry business of his step-father.[115]

Fulgencio Batista, facing certain defeat in the 1952 Cuban presidential election, seized power by staging a coup d'état. He revoked the 1940 constitution and aligned himself with Cuba's wealthiest landowners. His dictatorship contributed significantly to a widening gap between the rich and poor. Batista's policies helped to create a corrupt, repressive gangster state in which he and his wealthy friends lined their pockets by negotiating lucrative relationships with large American multinational corporations and by taking a significant "skim" from the American mafia's gambling, prostitution, and narcotics interests in Cuba.[116]

Echevarria's FEU quickly began to conduct demonstrations and riots. As early as 1952, Carlos Tepedino began assisting Antonio Eche-

---
111   November, 1960, CIA Biographic sketch of Rolando Cubela Secades, RIF 104-10244-10355.
112   6/18/62, JMWAVE 4746 to CIA DIR, RIF 104-10215-10107.
113   Robert E. Quirk, *Fidel Castro* (New York: W. W. Norton, 1993), p. 102.
114   6/18/62, JMWAVE 4746 to CIA DIR, RIF 104-10215-10107.
115   6/17/62, Biographical Data Sheet on Carlos Tepedino by AMCONCERT-1 ("Pancho" Varona Alonso), RIF 104-10183-10073.
116   For instance see the work of Jack Calhoun, *Gangsterismo: The United States, Cuba, and the Mafia: 1933-1966* (New York: O/R Books, 2013).

varria's anti-Batista activities by using the family jewelry business location as a safe house for Echevarria, Cubela and their associates.[117] It was through Echevarria that Tepedino was introduced to Cubela, after which their close friendship began. According to a 1962 CIA report, Tepedino and Cubela "became such close friends that they were like brothers," to the "extreme" point that Tepedino became the person who exerted the most influence over Cubela.[118] Throughout the six years of anti-Batista student agitation (1952-1958), only one political leader emerged who was a serious rival to Castro—Antonio Echevarria.

Castro, too, was engaged in anti-Batista activities, organizing weapons training for students at the University of Havana. Intent on doing something more spectacular than a demonstration, Castro decided to carry out an attack on a military target of the Batista regime. The attack took place on 26 July 1953, a date responsible for the name of Castro's organization, the "26 July Movement." Castro selected the Moncada Barracks because it was not near Havana and was not as well fortified as Camp Columbia.[119] However, as Quirk has observed:

> [Castro] had never seen the Moncada Barracks. He had never been inside any barracks. The drawing he had made to guide his men resembled a page full of haphazard doodlings. ...the larger part of Castro's contingents ...had become lost in the labyrinthine streets of the city. Recognizing the futility of continuing the assault, Castro ordered a withdrawal. Eight attackers had been killed and twelve wounded. No one in Castro's car was hurt. The leader had stayed well back.[120]

Batista imposed martial law throughout Cuba and initiated a widespread suppression of civil liberties. In his trial afterward, Castro's famous statement to the court, which he later expanded, "History Will Absolve Me," ended up giving him what he really wanted—some recognition.

---

117 6/28/65 CIA Contact Report, Subject: Meeting of Carlos Tepedino and Harold P. Swenson, RIF 104-10183-10424; this report has a useful bit of history on Tepedino, Cubela, and Antonio Echevarria.
118 6/17/62, Biographical Data Sheet on Carlos Tepedino by AMCONCERT-1 ("Pancho" Varona Alonso), RIF 104-10183-10073.
119 Robert E. Quirk, *Fidel Castro* (New York: W. W. Norton, 1993), p. 51.
120 Robert E. Quirk, *Fidel Castro* (New York: W. W. Norton, 1993), p. 52.

THE DIRECTORIO REVOLUCIONARIO AND THE GENESIS...

Despite Batista's ban against public meetings, on 27 November 1955, Cuban youths assembled throughout Cuba to commemorate the memory of students killed by Spanish authorities in 1871. After the police brutalized the demonstrators in Havana and Santiago, the FEU carried out a number of strikes and bombings. Echevarria and hundreds of others were arrested, while Batista cleverly appealed for "moderation and reconciliation."[121] This episode led Echevarria to change strategy. Instead of continuing public demonstrations, he founded the DR at the University of Havana on 26 February 1956, and began forming clandestine groups for assassinations and sabotage. Meanwhile, Castro, in exile in Mexico with his brother Raul, Che Guevara, and other 26 July members, was planning to land a military force in Cuba to begin a military revolution against Batista.

In the second half of 1956, Echevarria and Castro met twice in Mexico City to discuss how to reach a common position in the fight against Batista that might be acceptable to Castro and the 26 July Movement *and* to Echevarria and the DR. In the first meeting at the end of August, Castro proposed that the DR disband itself and join the 26 July Movement. Echevarria refused. Then they compromised and agreed to remain independent but mutually supportive of each other, and to coordinate their actions. Upon his return to the University of Havana, Echevarria was unable to convince his student and faculty supporters there to support the compromise. Echevarria went back to Mexico City in October only to fail again to find a satisfactory solution with Castro.

On 28 October 1956, the DR carried out an assassination in a Havana nightclub. Rolando Cubela, accompanied by Juan Pedro Barbo, shot and killed Colonel Antonio Blanco Rico, chief of Batista's Military Intelligence Service (SIM). Cubela later told the CIA how he got away with the assassination:

> According to his own account, he succeeded in fleeing the authorities by getting aboard a cargo ship bound for Charleston, South Carolina. He had joined a colony of Cuban exiles in Miami by February 1957. A month later he was back in Havana, where with Echevarria and the

---

121 Robert E. Quirk, *Fidel Castro* (New York: W. W. Norton, 1993), p. 103.

student-spawned Directorio Revolucionario he took part in the 13 March assault on the Presidential Palace.[122]

Before Cubela had made his way back to rejoin Echevarria, Castro's yacht, the *Granma*, with 82 men aboard, landed on Cuba's southern coast in Oriente Province in December 1956.

Echevarria and his DR were thus already active on the ground in Cuba when Castro's *Gramma* expedition landed. While Castro and his 26 July supporters were running for their lives in the swamps and jungle of Oriente, Echevarria and the DR were already planning and carrying out assassinations of high-level leaders in Batista's regime. Echevarria was on the verge of launching his boldest plot yet: to assassinate Batista and topple his regime. Echevarria chose not to endanger the security of this operation by becoming involved in Castro's group at the time of the Oriente landing. Castro mistook this as cowardice:

> Castro could neither forget nor forgive the reluctance of the university students in Havana to support the *Granma* landing. In late December, he sent Echevarria a letter by way of Faustino Perez, accusing the Revolutionary Directorate of treachery. "Especially you, Jose Antonio," he wrote, "who promised me you would join in the uprising." The students were cowards, he said.[123]

Echevarria was reportedly furious over Castro's insult and sent a strongly worded reply that did not reveal the planned attack on the Presidential Palace to Castro.

Fate did not favor Echevarria. Batista was not in his office when the attack took place and Echevarria was gunned down in the streets, gaining him martyrdom but not much else. Castro shed no tears over the outcome of the 13 March. He was reportedly relieved that the plot had failed:

> Thereafter no new student leader appeared who could deal with him as an equal. Had the attack succeeded in eliminating Batista and setting up a government, there would have been no place for him or for the 26 July move-

---

122 November, 1960, CIA Biographic sketch of Rolando Cubela Secades, RIF 104-10244-10355.
123 Robert E. Quirk, **Fidel Castro** (New York: W. W. Norton, 1993), p. 134.

ment. He condemned the venture as a "useless spilling of blood."[124]

This cold-hearted dismissal betrays Castro's envy of Echevarria's popularity. In the view of several CIA officers responsible for Cuban operations, during the revolution against Batista, Echevarria and Cubela had as much, if not more, prestige than Castro.[125] In Quirk's judgment, "until February 1957 Castro had not been much more than a name to the Cuban people."[126]

After Echevarria's death, Faure Chomon was made the secretary general of the DR.[127] Rolando Cubela remained as the second in command and head of the DR's military Escambray mountain front during the final twenty months of the revolution. The DR's forces played an important role in the military success of the revolution. Castro continued to look askance, now even more so, at Cubela's enduring popularity.

After Batista fled from Cuba, Castro maneuvered himself into control of Cuba at the expense of other revolutionary leaders who had played key roles in the struggle against Batista. Cubela accepted Castro's leadership only at first. Soon, however, Cubela became disenchanted with Castro's neglect of other key leaders. Cubela suspected that Castro was planning to turn Cuba toward communism.[128]

HOW CASTRO'S HANDLING OF THE DR CREATED THE DRE

We return now to that moment in Havana on 5 January 1959, when members of the DR seized control of the Presidential Palace and refused to give it up to the July 26 elements. The DR was holding out for new posts in the new Provisional Government to which they felt they were en-

---

124   Robert E. Quirk, *Fidel Castro* (New York: W. W. Norton, 1993), p. 137.
125   6/28/65, CIA Contact Report, Subject: Meeting of Carlos Tepedino and Harold P. Swenson, RIF 104-10183-10424; this report has a useful bit of history on Tepedino, Cubela, and Antonio Echevarria.
126   Robert E. Quirk, *Fidel Castro* (New York: W. W. Norton, 1993), p. 134.
127   3/27/58, FBI Miami Office Report on the Directorio Revolucionario, RIF 124-10296-10180.
128   6/28/65, CIA Contact Report, Subject: Meeting of Carlos Tepedino and Harold P. Swenson, RIF 104-10183-10424; this report has a useful bit of history on Tepedino, Cubela, and Antonio Echevarria.

titled.[129] However, after extensive negotiations, the DR agreed to vacate the Palace and, later that evening, Manuel Urrutia Lleo was installed in the Presidential Palace to announce the members of his Cabinet.[130] With this matter settled, Fidel Castro was ready to enter Havana. He did so on 8 January and held a mass rally at which he asked everyone to back the Provisional Government.[131]

It is likely that whatever deal was struck between the 26 July organization and the DR before Castro's arrival in Havana was done on his orders. At this early stage of the game, accommodating the DR and publicly stiff arming the Cuban Communist Party (PSP) were crucial tactics in Castro's strategy to capture and consolidate the reins of power in Cuba. Well informed sources inside Cuba knew that Castro "loathed and despised" both Faure Chomon and Rolando Cubela at this time.[132] But Castro had no practical alternative other than offering both men positions in the new regime.

Chomon would prove more useful to Castro and easier to handle than Cubela. Chomon did not share Cubela's disgust for the communists. Within weeks of Castro's victory, an American spy with extraordinary access to Cuban sources, Catherine Taaffe, was reporting that Chomon was "acting independently and is definitely with the communists."[133] Castro reportedly saw an opportunity to use Chomon to direct attention to himself and maintain his popularity with his Cuban supporters while continuing secretly to cultivate his power with the communists.[134] We will return to Catherine Taaffe in Chapters Five and Six.

From Castro's perspective in 1959, Cubela was more dangerous than Chomon and therefore had to be handled more cautiously. Tepedino was obviously familiar with Chomon and Cubela because he

---

129 1/5/59, Urgent FBI Teletype from Havana Legat to Director, Subject: Cuban Revolutionary Activities, FPM-Cuba, RIF 124-90089-10255.
130 Final FBI Briefing Package for Hoover's 1/29/59 luncheon engagement with Undersecretary Herter, FBI HQS 109 File, VOL 11.
131 1/15/59, FBI Legat in Havana to Director, Subject: Intelligence Survey—Cuba, Synopsis, Lesar FOIA Release, FBI HQS 109 File Vol. 11.
132 4/6/64, FBI Memorandum From SAC Miami to Director, Subject: Foreign Political Matters-Cuba, RIF 124-10290-10090.
133 3/10/59, FBI Memorandum to State Department, Subject: Caribbean Revolutionary Activities, RIF 124-10221-10339.
134 4/6/64, FBI Memorandum From SAC Miami to Director, Subject: Foreign Political Matters-Cuba, RIF 124-10290-10090.

THE DIRECTORIO REVOLUCIONARIO AND THE GENESIS...

had supported them during the DR's fight against Batista. It was Cubela, however, and not Chomon, that Tepedino sought to introduce to the CIA in Havana. According to CIA records, Tepedino had made tentative arrangements to introduce Cubela to CIA officer named Jack Stewart at an early date, "but these arrangements fell through at the last minute."[135] These arrangements were probably made in the weeks immediately following Castro's victory, by which time Cubela had become alienated by Castro's movement toward communism. The reason these arrangements fell through was due to Castro's rather sudden appointment of Cubela to be Cuba's Military Attaché to Spain in March 1959.[136]

According to FBI sources, prior to his acceptance of the attaché assignment, "Cubela privately told intimates that he was so disgusted with Castro that if he, Cubela, did not get out of the country soon he would kill Castro himself."[137] FBI Director Hoover shared this threat with the CIA.

Castro appointed Chomon as Cuba's first Ambassador to the USSR. In April 1959, a "fairly reliable" FBI source commented that Castro was taking advantage of internal dissentions within the DR to isolate its leaders and split the organization.[138] This FBI report provides more details about Castro's strategy:

> [Castro] allegedly sent him [Chomon] to Moscow for two reasons. One reason was that he had promised Chomon, when fighting in the mountains, that if and when Cuba established relations with Russia, Chomon would be Cuba's first Ambassador to Russia. The second reason allegedly was to get rid of Chomon. MM T-2 [the FBI informant] stated that Castro has nothing but disdain and contempt for Major Rolando Cubela. It is, of course, a

---

135 6/28/65, CIA Contact Report, Subject: Meeting of Carlos Tepedino and Harold P. Swenson, RIF 104-10183-10424.
136 00/3/59, CIA Havana Dispatch HKH-1855, from Andrew F. Merton, Subject: Rolando Cubela Secades, New Cuban Military Attaché to Spain, RIF 104-10215-10443.
137 6/2/59, FBI Memorandum from SA Thomas H. Errion, Subject: Directorio Revolucionario, RIF 104-10215-10442; For Hoover's 7/20/59 Note and Letterhead Memorandum to the CIA, see RIF 124-10244-10108..
138 6/2/59, FBI Memorandum from SA Thomas H. Errion, Subject: Directorio Revolucionario, RIF 104-10215-10442.

> matter of common knowledge that Chomon and Cubela are widely regarded, by Cubans in a position to know them well, as perverts and as having no moral or political scruples.[139]

Cubela's homosexuality was not news. For example, there are these allegations from a 1964 CIA history of "weaknesses" and "derogatory information" on Cubela. This is an entry for 29 November 1956: "Dr. Armando de Cardenas y Aranguren, a pathologist at the University of Havana ... admitted under pressure that he was a homosexual and that Cubela was his intimate friend."[140]

With its mission to oust Batista gone, the DR began drifting into a void. Cuban informants were reporting to the FBI that the DR was not engaged in any activity in Cuba and was only quietly watching and observing the new government:

> ...many of those who had belonged to the DR at the time of the revolution while the University of Havana was closed, had now left the ranks of the DR to concern themselves with the reopening and reestablishing of the University of Havana. ...the DR is losing its individuality. Members are entering the service of the government of Cuba which is operated essentially by the 26 July organization. ...this is possibly a means of assimilating the more important people of the DR into the present government set up.[141]

On the other hand, there were many DR members who believed that Castro was just another dictator and that he was taking Cuba Communist. They became embittered as they watched the DR become communist controlled and dominated.

This remnant of the DR began to organize clandestine opposition to the Castro regime. Before long, matters came to a head as this CIA report describes:

---

139 4/6/64, FBI Memorandum From SAC Miami to Director, Subject: Foreign Political Matters-Cuba, RIF 124-10290-10090.
140 10/24/64, CIA Memorandum RE Weaknesses and Derogatory Information on Rolando Cubela. RIF 104-10215-10235.
141 6/2/59, FBI Memorandum from SA Thomas H. Errion, Subject: Directorio Revolucionario, 104-10215-10442.

THE DIRECTORIO REVOLUCIONARIO AND THE GENESIS...

...by the autumn of 1960, the steady mounting resistance to communist domination of student affairs erupted in violence at ceremonies in honor of Soviet visitor Mikoyan. Leaders of DR clandestine groups chose this occasion to come out into the open and did so by violently attacking Mikoyan during the ceremony. The leaders were Alberto Muller Quintana, Manuel Salvat Roque, Miguel Garcia Armengol and Ernesto Fernandez Travieso, who later fled to PBPRIME [the U.S.] as political refugees. Here, they were met by Oliver H. Corbuston as "Douglas Gupton" [true name William M. Kent] and Harold R. Noemayr [true name Ross L. Crozier] as "Roger Fox."

After a series of meetings, the group was reconstituted as the Cuban Student Directorate (DRE), conceived and approved by CIA Headquarters as a JMWAVE [the CIA Station in Miami] unilateral psychological warfare asset. For its part, the DRE immediately accepted the CIA's "direct support, guidance and control."[142]

In 1963, Lee Harvey Oswald would become involved with the DRE cells in New Orleans and Dallas. We will get to that story in a later volume of this work.

---

142 8/14/62, CIA Dispatch From Chief, Task Force W to Chief of State JMWAVE, AMSPELL Progress Report, see "Attachment A: Background and Status of Internal and Exile Elements," 104-10171-10334.

CHAPTER FOUR:

THE CIA'S EARLY RECRUITMENT OF MANUEL ANTONIO VARONA

The Directorio Revolucionario (DR) was not the only problem for Castro at the time of his victory. While the DR and 26 July groups were locking horns over access to the Presidential Palace, a less noticeable group was secretly meeting in Havana. Where they were meeting is not clear, but it was probably not in the Presidential palace. We know it took place before the DR-26 July impasse was resolved on 5 January. The only FBI source with information on this secret gathering was Catherine Taaffe. What she said about it to the FBI's New York Office is preserved in two small segments of a 5 January 1959 urgent teletype from the New York Office to FBI HQS:

> Mrs. Catherine Taaffe, who is in a position to furnish reliable information, advised she received information from Mrs. Garcia Beltran, who had received a telephone

> call from her husband, Marcelino Garcia Beltran, in Havana... ...Taaffe also stated that she learned from Mrs. Garcia Beltran that her husband was called to Havana to take part in a political meeting prior to Urrutia's taking over the office of the president. Present at this meeting *among the opposition* was Dr. "Tony" Varona. Mrs. Garcia told Taaffe that Carlos Prio attempted to sit in on this meeting but was excluded.[143] [Emphasis added]

The political "opposition" to Batista had traditionally been considered to include the Ortodoxo party—a nationalist-populist party with a distinctly anti-corruption platform (1947-1952). It had also included a breakaway faction of another nationalist-populist party, the old Autentico party (1934-1953). A U.S. Embassy officer in Havana at the time, Wayne Smith, recalls that the breakaway Autentico faction "looked mostly to Tony Varona for leadership and to ex-President Prio Socarras for financing."[144]

The group meeting described in Marcelino Beltran's phone call appears to have been the breakaway Autentico faction described by Wayne Smith. The exclusion of Prio at this stage is interesting. Castro's strategy of neutralizing all potential political opponents included anybody who had opposed Batista in Cuba's elections from 1948 until his coup d'état just before the 1952 elections. In that election, Batista was running well behind Roberto Agramonte, the Ortodoxo candidate, and Carlos Hevia, the Autentico candidate, in all of the polls. Castro now decided to simply exclude these men and their parties from participation in any new government with his "decree of the Sierra." It banned anyone who had participated in any of Batista's elections from public life for a period of thirty years.[145] During the first months immediately following Batista's flight, some observers were hoping that Castro's Sierra decree would not hold up. Excluding Prio from the secret meeting in Havana suggests that the "opposition" group meeting there saw Varona as the logical exception to the Sierra decree and a viable alternative to Castro.

---

143 1/5/59 Urgent Telegram from SAC New York to SAC Miami and Director FBI, Subject: Cuban Revolutionary Activities, FPM-Cuba, RIF 124-90036-10153.
144 Wayne Smith, ***The Closest of Enemies*** (New York: W. W. Norton & Co., 1987), p. 19.
145 Hugh Thomas, ***Cuba: The Pursuit of Freedom*** (New York: Harper and Row, 1971), p. 1046.

THE CIA'S EARLY RECRUITMENT OF MANUEL ANTONIO VARONA

On 2 January 1959, the Miami Herald reported that "Varona had ended his exile following the downfall of Batista and had returned to Havana, Cuba."[146] According to Taaffe's sources, Castro was to be deposed by the end of March 1959, and a new coalition government would choose Antonio Varona as the new Cuban president:

> Mrs. Taaffe learned from Roy Preston of New York that a testimonial dinner is being planned for Varona in New York during the last week of March 1959 to coincide with the overthrow of the Castro Government; and that invitations were sent to about 40 U.S. Congressmen; and that some replies have been favorable.[147]

Of course, Castro was not deposed in March and the "testimonial" dinner was quietly canceled. Yet the secret group meeting in Havana and Taaffe's story about their plans prompt us to look at who might have been behind the early positioning of Varona to replace Castro.

Why would Marcelino Garcia Beltran have been called to Havana to attend the meeting? Beltran had been handling financial transactions for the Cuban sugar firm, Czarnnikow-Rionda Company, in New York City.[148] During the second half of 1958, he had also been helping Alberto Fernandez collect "tribute"—a sugar tax levied by Castro on Cuban and American sugar companies. In late November, the U.S. Justice Department began searching for witnesses to testify against Fernandez for this activity.[149] When the owner of King Ranch, Robert Kleberg, heard about this investigation and that Fernandez "might be in trouble," he told CIA chief Allen Dulles that this might not be a good thing for U.S. relations with the new Castro government. Dulles replied he would take up the matter with the State Department.[150] The Justice Department's

---

146 3/11/59 FBI Memo from A. H. Belmont to S. B. Donahoe, Subject: Antonio de Varona, RIF 124-90055-10062.
147 3/9/59 FBI Memo from S. B. Donahoe to Mr. Belmont, Subject: Antonio de Varona, RIF 124-90055-10063.
148 2/25/59 Memorandum from CIA Deputy Director of Plans to Director FBI, Subject: U.S. Banking Transactions by Marcelino Garcia Beltran, Friend of Former President Batista of Cuba, RIF 124-10200-10184.
149 11/25/58, Memorandum from Acting Assistant Attorney General, J. Walter Yeagley, to FBI Director, Subject: Alberto Fernandez, Registration Act. RIF 124-10200-10155.
150 1/12/59, FBI Memorandum from S. B. Donahoe to A. H. Belmont, Subject: Alberto Fernandez Casas, Internal Security, Cuba. RIF 124-10200-10158.

Internal Security Division, citing the Dulles-Kleberg objection to prosecution, quashed the investigation on 21 January 1959.[151]

In other words, Allen Dulles buried the case against what Fernandez and Beltran had been up to. The man Beltran was secretly meeting with in Havana, Varona, had been working, for quite some time, as a field agent for the CIA.

VARONA'S PRE-CASTRO CIA RECRUITMENT

The failure of the CIA plan to install a junta led by Colonel Barquin that excluded Castro left the Agency and the Eisenhower Administration looking for other ways to handle the Castro problem. As a former Cuban Prime Minister and long time opponent of Batista, Varona had political legitimacy. He was also working for the CIA. As of 2015, the CIA is still withholding important information about its early relationship with Varona. What has been released in full about this early period is a profile of Varona that was created at the end of October 1960. That was after Eisenhower had approved the CIA's "Covert Action Plan for Cuba" and Varona had become the choice to lead a Cuban government-in-exile until Castro was overthrown. It was also just days before the 1960 U.S. presidential election.

That CIA profile was at best ill-informed. Some of it was very misleading. The following is a recapitulation of its highlights:

> Manuel Antonio de Varona Loredo was born in Camaguey, Cuba, on 25 November 1908. He was jailed and exiled for his activities against the Cuban dictator Gerrardo Machado, who was finally overthrown in 1933. Varona helped found the Partido Revolucionario Cubana (PRC) in 1934; he graduated with his law degree from the University of Havana in 1938. Varona was elected to the House of Representatives in 1940; eventually he became that body's minority leader; in 1944, he was elected to the Senate and became chairman of the executive committee. During the presidential elections of 1948, a power

---

151 1/12/59, FBI Memorandum from S. B. Donahoe to A. H. Belmont, Subject: Alberto Fernandez Casas, Internal Security, Cuba. RIF 124-10200-10161.

struggle erupted between Carlos Prio Socarras and President Ramon Grau San Martin. As a result, the PRC split into two groups. Varona allied himself with Prio, and their faction became the Partido Autentico, also known simply as the "Autenticos."

To secure the nomination, Varona prevented Grau's representatives and supporters from attending the party's provincial assembly. He had them kidnapped and held. Varona was nominated easily, and in the national election he was reelected to the senate and Prio was elected president. Prio rewarded Varona's loyalty by appointing him Prime Minister, a post he retained for two years. He helped Prio carry out a number of long-needed reforms. This CIA profile states that "Unfortunately, the record of Prio's administration has been subjected to many charges of corruption and graft, and Varona's name is closely associated with this image."

Varona was appointed president of the senate in October 1950. As the 1952 national elections approached, Varona became the president of the executive committee of the Autenticos. However, the national election never took place as Fulgencia Batista staged a coup d'état on 10 March 1952. While Prio and many of his supporters went into exile, Varona refused to leave Cuba and decided instead to assume the leadership of the Autentico opposition to Batista. Varona went to Miami to confer with Prio and his group of exiles. Varona's strong protest against Prio's delay in moving against Batista fell on deaf ears and, over the next several years, Varona and the Autenticos continued to oppose Batista's government in Cuba.

On 18 September 1957, Varona was arrested for complicity in a proposed revolt of naval personnel and briefly imprisoned:

On 19 September, the Cuban Consul General in New York City, Alfredo Hernandez Valdez, told the FBI that

Varona was alive and "well kept." How long Varona was in prison is unknown, but by mid-December he was living in exile in Miami.

Castro repudiated Varona's attempt to forge unity among opposition groups to Batista and many of Varona's supporters defected to Castro's 26 July Movement. Varona spent 1958 in unfocused activities, mostly speech-making as he traveled in Latin America, and returned to Cuba immediately after Castro deposed Batista.

Varona's first "official" contact with the CIA Havana Station was not made until 1957. In May of that year a request was made to accept Varona as an agent to provide information about the political opposition to Batista, and operational approval was granted on 20 January, 1958.[152]

This flattering profile of Varona was composed at a time—27 October 1960—when the CIA was grooming Varona to become the principal leader of a new Cuban government in exile. The graft in Prio's administration was very serious and Varona's kidnapping of politicians placed him in a negative light by his own doing.

Moreover, this politically suitable CIA profile of Varona was penned at a time when he was negotiating, through a Washington public relations consultant, with mob representatives of two of the largest gambling casinos in Cuba. The mob knew about the CIA's plan to overthrow Castro and saw a regime under Varona as an opportunity. The mob had offered Varona four million dollars (this amount varies depending on the source), with the understanding that they would receive privileged treatment "in the Cuba of the future."[153] The Pentagon had learned of the mob's scheme to finance Varona's anti-Castro activities in the hope of restoring their "gambling, prostitution, and dope monopolies" in the event Castro is overthrown.[154] The Pentagon informed the FBI about

---

[152] 10/27/60, "Manuel Antonio de Varona Loredo—A Biographic Sketch, by E. W. Londregan, Jr., CIA, WH/4/PA, RIF 104-10167-10339.
[153] 5/23/67, CIA *Report on Plots to Assassinate Fidel Castro*, p. 30. RIF 1994.03.08.14:54:36:690005, pp. 29-31.
[154] 12/21/60, Hoover letter to Director CIA, Subject Manuel Antonio Varona, Internal Security—Cuba. RIF 124-90055-10230.

THE CIA'S EARLY RECRUITMENT OF MANUEL ANTONIO VARONA

this financing scheme on 13 December, and Hoover passed on the details to CIA on 21 December.[155] We will return to this matter below.

The above CIA profile of Varona was authored by E. W. Londregan, who was working in the Political Action (PA) Section of the CIA's Cuban Branch (WH/4) in the Western Hemisphere Division (WHD). It leaves out some important details. Varona's CIA 201 file (196435) indicates that before his so-called "official" contact with the CIA Havana Station in May 1957, he "was in contact with the Station for at least two years before this through Frau Masal (sp?)."[156]

This name might indeed be a misspelling of "Marsal." The present author discovered that the full name of Varona's early CIA Station contact, "Frau" Marsal Barbaressa Lorenzo, had been compromised when someone scribbled her name on top of the cryptonym AMGOSH-1 in a 1961 CIA cable. That cable was from Nelson Raynock, then at the CIA Station in Quidad Trujillo—the name the Dominican Republic capital before it was changed to Santo Domingo in 1962. Raynock said that Lorenzo had been a former Havana Station contact who, at one time, had taken asylum in the Ecuadorian Embassy in Havana.[157] AMGOSH-1 was associated with another interesting woman—Margot Pena. She had been the head of the Sierra Maestra terrorist group during the revolution against Batista.[158]

Varona's CIA 201 file, which is well over a half century old, remains heavily redacted today. Nevertheless, the present author has been able to fill in several of the redactions by consulting other documents that have been mostly or fully declassified. The present author was able to locate part of Varona's 1957 PRQ (Personal Record Questionaire) Part II. It indicates that he was "first introduced to James R. Palinger and Wallace A. Growery by a contact of Palinger in May 1957."[159] These two men were, respectively, the chief and deputy chief of the CIA Station in Havana. Although the name "Palinger" appears at the bottom of several

---

155   01/18/61, Hoover letter to the CIA, Subject: Manuel Antonio Varona, Internal Security—Cuba. RIF 124-90055-10134. See also 5/23/67, CIA *Report on Plots to Assassinate Fidel Castro*, p. 29. RIF 1994.03.08.14:54:36:690005.
156   00/00/00, House Select Committee on Assassinations, From CIA, Subject: De Varona, Manuel Antonio, 201 File, RIF 180-10142-10305.
157   6/16/61, TRUJ [0814 to CIA HQS, RIF 104-10226-1016
158   8/29/61, GAYA (Guayaquil, Ecuador) 1879 to CIA HQS. RIF 104-10296-10003
159   00/00 (probably circa 1960), CIA PRQ-II for AMHAWK. RIF 104-10167-10346.

CIA Havana Station documents at the time, the initials "SPR" are clearly visible at the top of several of them. Those initials very likely stood for Sherwood P. Rochom, whose name also appears in a 1959 PRQ-II as a case officer for Manolo Ray.[160] The identities and pseudonyms for these CIA officers are discussed in Appendix Four.

A few notes from Varona's May 1957 PRQ Part II were placed in his CIA 201 file. They indicate that after his "official" contact with the Station, he was "under development ever since." His mission at the time was to supply "information concerning political opposition plans including conspiratorial movements to overthrow the Government" [of Cuba] to his Case Officer.[161] The Londregan profile is apparently incorrect about the date of the Havana Station's request for approval to use Varona operationally in Cuba. Documents show that the request was not made at the time suggested in the profile—May 1957.

The present author's investigation of that date has turned up the other CIA documents pertaining to both the request and approval for using Varona in Cuba. On 8 August 1957, the Havana Station submitted Varona's PRQ Part I (Biographic Information)[162]; on 13 August, the Cuban section at CIA HQS requested a 201 file on Varona to be opened, noting that his PRQ Part II would be submitted upon receipt of the 201 file number.[163] Finally, on 15 August, the Havana Station forwarded the PRQ II and requested that operational approval for the use of AMHAWK, the CIA cryptonym for Varona, be granted.[164]

Five months later, on 20 January 1958, CIA HQS granted approval (No. C-64244) for the operational use of Varona as an "Indigenous Field Agent" in Cuba.[165] Why the delay? The answer can be found in Varona's

---

160 5/29/59, Havana Dispatch from COS Havana, Woodrow C. Olien, to Chief, WHD, Subject: AMBANG PRQ Part II. RIF 104-10179-10087.
161 00/00/00, House Select Committee on Assassinations, From CIA, Subject: De Varona, Manuel Antonio, 201 File, RIF 180-10142-10305.
162 8/8/57, Havana COS, HKH-A-3799 to Chief WHD, Subject: Manuel Antonio de Varona y Loredo, RIF 104-10260-10424, and, for the PRQ Part I attachment see RIF 104-10260-10425.
163 8/13/57, Personality (201) File Request, from Hugh O. MacAuley, WH/3/Cuba, to RI/Analysis Section, RIF 104-10260-10422; see also 104-10260-10423.
164 8/15/57, Havana COS, HKH-A-3819 to Chief WHD, Subject: AMHAWK, Ref: HKH-A3799, 8 August 1957, RIF 104-10261-10024.
165 00/00/00, House Select Committee on Assassinations, From CIA, Subject: De Varona, Manuel Antonio, 201 File, RIF 180-10142-10305; and for all of the pertinent memoranda concerning this see the following RIFs: 104-10130-10165, 104-10130-10167, and 104-10260-10415.

THE CIA'S EARLY RECRUITMENT OF MANUEL ANTONIO VARONA

true story during that delay—a period during which the Londregan profile claimed the CIA did not know how long Varona had been in prison and did not know until mid-December that he was living in exile in Miami.[166] The Londregan profile again leaves out important details. Two months *before* mid-December 1957, Varona was already in Miami and the CIA knew all about his activities there.

On 19 November 1957, a newspaper in Miami, Florida reported this about a large seizure of men and weapons:

> A Cuban rebel expeditionary force, consisting of 31 heavily armed men, was captured by federal agents on isolated, tree-fringed Big Pine Key early Tuesday. A 33-foot yacht, heavily loaded with munitions and medical supplies, in which they planned to take off for Cuba at dawn, was impounded, in addition to other arms still being loaded. "This is the largest expeditionary force apprehended or prevented since the revolutionary activities started in Cuba," a customs agent said.[167]

Another article captioned, "It's All News-De Varona," in the same newspaper that day reported this:

> Dr. Antonio M. De Varona, former president of the Cuban senate and a leader in the revolutionary junta in Miami today denied any knowledge of the expeditionary force seized by federal officials. Dr. Varona said he knew several of the men who were seized in the Keys, but had not been aware of their activities.

Obviously, Varona had arrived in Miami much earlier than mid-December 1957 and a lot more was known about the dates surrounding his imprisonment and exile than the Londregan profile suggested.

A side bar comment seems appropriate here. We need to take a step back and marvel at the gross incongruity between the Londregan profile, a document that comes from the CIA's Cuban branch (WH/4), and other CIA records on Varona. One month *before* the seizure of the rebel expeditionary force on 19 November, CIA HQS had already launched

---

166 10/27/60, "Manuel Antonio de Varona Loredo—A Biographic Sketch, by E. W. Londregan, Jr., CIA, WH/4/PA, RIF 104-10167-10339.
167 11/29/57, "Weapons-Loaded Yacht Impounded In Prize Catch," *Miami Florida News*.

49

an investigation into Varona's activities. Obviously, the CIA knew that Varona was already in Miami. The Londregan profile's claim that the CIA had only learned of Varona's presence there in mid-December was at best, sloppy, and, at worst, deliberately disingenuous. Inaccuracies such as this one are not uncommon in CIA reports and cables, and we will discuss how researchers can learn from such inaccuracies in Appendix Eight (Research Methodologies).

Back on 22 October 1957, the Washington Field Office of the CIA's Investigative Division was assigned to lead the Varona investigation.[168] The Resident Agent in Miami, James E. Mackey, Jr., "was in Miami on this and other cases" when the above story broke in the newspaper on 19 November 1957. At that time, Mackey had only completed police and credit checks on Varona. As a result, on 25 November 1957, the Washington Field Office decided to suspend its investigation and wait for CIA HQS to figure out how to proceed with the case:

> In view of the above *increased activity by other government agencies, coupled with an alleged link-up by Subject* [Varona] with the above arms cache, we are deferring further investigation at Miami, Florida, on the [Varona] case pending evaluation of the enclosed material [i.e. newspaper clippings] by Headquarters.[169] [Emphasis added]

On 3 December 1957, CIA HQS told its Washington Field Office to discontinue the investigation into Varona's activities, and on 16 December the Field Office forwarded what it had learned up to that point and closed the investigation.[170]

The Londregan profile left a significant hole—from mid-October to mid-December 1957—in Varona's record. Here are some of the items that this hole effectively omitted: 1) Varona's early arrival in Miami and his immediate assumption of a leadership position in the "junta" and the

---

168 See 12/16/57, CIA Memorandum for Chief, Investigative Division from Washington Field Office, George P. Loker, Special Agent in Charge, Subject: De Varona (Y Loredo), Manuel Antonio, RIF 104-10130-10172.
169 11/25/57, CIA Memorandum for Chief, Investigative Division from Washington Field Office, George P. Loker, Special Agent in Charge, Subject: De Varona (Y Loredo), Manuel Antonio, RIF 104-10130-10177.
170 See 12/16/57, CIA Memorandum for Chief, Investigative Division from Washington Field Office, George P. Loker, Special Agent in Charge, Subject: De Varona (Y Loredo), Manuel Antonio, RIF 104-10130-10172.

developing movement for "Cuban Liberation" there; 2) the public exposure of Varona's links to the largest armed rebel expeditionary force assembled for insertion into Cuba to date; 3) a CIA security investigation of Varona by its Washington and Miami field offices, resulting from the federal seizure of that expeditionary force in the Florida Keys; and, 4) the termination of the Varona investigation at the direction of CIA HQS.

It is implausible that the CIA was unaware of the publicity surrounding Varona's ties to the Cuban rebels in Miami at the very time they were considering approving him for operational use in Cuba. It is also improbable that, as the Londregan profile claims, the CIA had no idea how long Varona was in prison. He was only in prison for a few days, as the FBI Legal Attaché in Havana reported to FBI HQS at the time:

> Legat, Havana, reported Varona was arrested by Batista Government on 9/17/57. He had been accused by the Government of having been one of the leaders of a conspiracy which resulted in an abortive uprising against the Batista Government in Cienfuegos. Because of the *public uproar* caused by his arrest, the Cuban Government, in accordance with a *prearranged plan*, went through the formality of a presentation of Varona in court. The court *immediately released him* pending a further hearing. Varona took asylum in the Chilean Embassy, Havana, on 9/23/57 and subsequently departed into exile.[171] [Emphasis added]

It is unthinkable that the public uproar against the arrest of a Cuban political leader of Varona's stature, who had been in contact with the CIA Station for more than two years, went unnoticed by the Havana Station. Furthermore, the CIA Station—perhaps all of the sections in the U.S. Embassy in Havana—likely knew the details of the prearranged plan for Varona's court appearance, his immediate release, asylum in the Chilean Embassy, and departure for exile in Miami.

Here again, another side bar is in order. Why would the 1960 Londregan profile of Varona—an internal CIA document—feign this kind of ignorance? One possible reason for omitting so much about this pe-

---

171   3/11/59, FBI Memorandum from S. B. Donahoe to A. H. Belmont, Subject: Cuban Revolutionary Activities, Internal Security-Cuba, RIF 124-90055-10062.

riod of Varona's history may be that the CIA wished to distance itself from the planned rebel operation. Another possible reason might have involved the dark details of Varona's association with the mob *at the time that the Londregan profile of Varona was created*—27 October 1960.

As stated above, the CIA was grooming Varona to replace Castro as the leader of Cuba. It must have been unwelcome news when, seven weeks later, on 16 December 1960, the CIA received a report from the FBI passing on information it had received from George J. Gould at the Office of the Secretary of Defense. The report observed that U.S. "racketeers" were making "efforts to finance anti-Castro activities in the hope of securing gambling, prostitution, and dope monopolies in the event Castro is overthrown."[172] Another FBI letter to the CIA on 18 January 1961, linked Varona to the financing scheme and inquired what the CIA knew about "any extensive financial backing of Varona."[173]

The 1967 CIA Inspector General's (IG) report on plots to assassinate Castro contained this account of the scheme to finance Varona:

> Varona had hired Edward K. Moss, a Washington public relations counselor... Moss' mistress was one Julia Cellini, whose brothers represented two of the largest gambling casinos in Cuba. The Cellini brothers were believed to be in touch with Varona through Moss and were reported to have offered Varona large sums of money for his operations against Castro, with the understanding that they would receive privileged treatment "in the Cuba of the future."[174]

The amount offered to Varona, according to the 21 December 1960 FBI letter, was four million dollars. The IG said that "attempts to verify these reports were unsuccessful." Peter Dale Scott characterized this feigned ignorance as a "pretense."[175] There is a noticeable pattern to the Agency's alleged ignorance: The 1967 CIA IG report was as disingenu-

---

172 12/21/60, Hoover letter to Director CIA, Subject Manuel Antonio Varona, Internal Security—Cuba. RIF 124-90055-10230.
173 01/18/61, Hoover letter to the CIA, Subject: Manuel Antonio Varona, Internal Security—Cuba. RIF 124-90055-10134. See also 5/23/67, CIA *Report on Plots to Assassinate Fidel Castro*, p. 29. RIF 1994.03.08.14:54:36:690005.
174 5/23/67, CIA *Report on Plots to Assassinate Fidel Castro*, p. 30. RIF 1994.03.08.14:54:36:690005.
175 Peter Dale Scott, *Deep Politics II: Essays on Oswald, Mexico, and Cuba* (Skokie, Illinois: Green Archive Publications, 1995), p. 60.

THE CIA'S EARLY RECRUITMENT OF MANUEL ANTONIO VARONA

ous about Varona's 1960 activities as the 1960 Londregan profile was about Varona's 1957 activities.

Antonio Varona's activities included direct participation in the CIA-Mafia plots to assassinate Fidel Castro. The first attempt to use poison pills to assassinate Castro failed in early March 1961, about six weeks before the Bay of Pigs invasion. The poison pills were delivered to Castro's secretary, Juan Orta Cordova, but he lost his nerve and sought asylum in the Venezuelan Embassy in Havana.[176] It was then that Santo Trafficante brought in his long-time associate Antonio Varona to handle the job of poisoning Castro. Varona was *already* involved in the above-mentioned scheme to help the mob restore its former gambling, prostitution and narcotics activities in Cuba, once Castro was overthrown.[177]

Varona sent word in late February 1961 to the head of his Rescate Movement in Cuba, Alberto Cruz Caso, asking him to send someone trustworthy to Miami. The man selected was Varona's old friend Rodolfo Leon Curbelo.[178] On 12 March 1961, the CIA provided Trafficante with the poison capsules. Subsequently, just under five weeks before the Bay of Pigs, Varona gave the capsules to Curbelo, along with instructions for using the Rescate team in Havana to carry out the plot. Curbelo returned to Havana and delivered the capsules to Cruz Caso and Maria Leopoldina Grau Alsina (the niece of former Cuban President Ramon Grau San Martin). These two put a plan in motion to assassinate Castro at a restaurant that he frequented. However, the plan failed because Varona was physically unable to give the "green light": he and other senior exile leaders had been sequestered and were unable to communicate in order to ensure the security for the Bay of Pigs invasion.[179]

---

176 The CIA Inspector General's (IG) *Report on Plots to Assassinate Fidel Castro*, 23 May 1967, RIF 1994.03.08.14:54:36:690005, pp.27-28. *Alleged Assassination Plots Involving Foreign Leaders*, United States Senate, Interim Report of the Select Committee to Study Governmental Operations (Washington DC: US Government Printing Office, 1975), pp. 80-81.
177 The CIA Inspector General's (IG) *Report on Plots to Assassinate Fidel Castro*, 23 May 1967, RIF 1994.03.08.14:54:36:690005, pp. 29-32.
178 Escalante, Fabian, *The Secret War: CIA Covert Operations Against Cuba, 1959-62* (New York: Ocean Press, 1995), pp. 84-86.
179 *Alleged Assassination Plots Involving Foreign Leaders*, United States Senate, Interim Report of the Select Committee to Study Governmental Operations (Washington DC: US Government Printing Office, 1975), p. 82. Escalante, Fabian, *The Secret War: CIA Covert Operations Against Cuba, 1959-62* (New York: Ocean Press, 1995), p. 85.

In April 1962, at the instigation of the CIA's Task Force W Chief William Harvey, Varona sent a new set of poison capsules to a Spanish diplomat in Havana, Alejandro Vergara.[180] Varona directed Vergara to deliver the capsules to a Rescate contact in Havana. Again, it was Maria Leopoldina Grau Alsina, aka "Polita." Her CIA cryptonym was AMCOG-2. Polita and the Rescate chief in Havana, Alberto Cruz Caso, devised a plot to poison Castro in the Hotel Havana Libre. The opportunity to poison Castro did not arise until March 1963. That attempt also failed when a waiter accidentally broke the capsules before he could slip them into Castro's chocolate milkshake.[181]

This dark side of the CIA-Varona-mob triangle provides a suitable lens through which we may inquire as to why, as early as December 1957, the CIA halted its investigation of Varona's activities in Miami. Stopping that investigation, however, still left the sensitive question of whether or not to grant an approval for Varona's operational use in Cuba. Varona's political stature and visible public profile pushed the review of such an approval to a high level in the Agency. On 28 August 1957, the Chief of Counterintelligence/Operational Approvals (CI/OA) requested guidance as to whether or not Varona should be used "as an informant in Cuba by WH (Western Hemisphere) Division." On 13 January 1958, one week before the official approval finally moved through the normal mid-level security channels, the CIA's Deputy Director of Security weighed in, sending a firm memorandum about the situation directly to the Chief, CI/OA."[182] The memo made clear that the Deputy Director felt that using Varona was risky. The Deputy Director admonished the CI/OA Chief to take precautions:

…attached information indicates that the Subject is a "Cuban Liberation leader." *It is assumed… that if the Subject is utilized suitable controls will be established to prevent*

---

180 The CIA Inspector General's (IG) **Report on Plots to Assassinate Fidel Castro**, 23 May 1967, RIF 1994.03.08.14:54:36:690005, pp. 46-49. **Alleged Assassination Plots Involving Foreign Leaders**, United States Senate, Interim Report of the Select Committee to Study Governmental Operations (Washington DC: US Government Printing Office, 1975), p. 84. Escalante, Fabian, **The Secret War: CIA Covert Operations Against Cuba, 1959-62** (New York: Ocean Press, 1995), p. 132.
181 Escalante, Fabian, **The Secret War: CIA Covert Operations Against Cuba, 1959-62** (New York: Ocean Press, 1995), pp. 132-135.
182 1/13/58, Memorandum from Deputy Director of Security (Investigations and Support), to Chief, CI/OA, Subject: C-64244, 201 # 163681, RIF 104-10130-10166.

THE CIA'S EARLY RECRUITMENT OF MANUEL ANTONIO VARONA

the possibility of his becoming a source of embarrassment to the Agency. ...In view of the certification set forth in your request, no CIA files other than those of the Office of Security have been searched in connection with this case. It is assumed that all pertinent information concerning Subject ... has been furnished. [Emphasis added]

It is ironic that after only three months—during which all of these events took place *in the U.S.* –that on 20 January 1958 the CIA granted approval for the operational use of Varona *in Cuba.*

With Varona's use in Cuba approved, the ball bounced back into the CIA's Operations Directorate. On 3 February 1958 the Chief of the Western Hemisphere Division, Colonel J. C. King, cabled the CIA Station in Havana with this message: "Since Subject is presently in exile, HQS would appreciate being advised as soon as he returns to Cuba, and is contacted by Station Havana."[183]

The above information on Varona's early years with the CIA brings us full circle to the first FBI New York Office report from Catherine Taaffe after Castro's victory in January 1959. Recall that Taaffe told the FBI about Varona's attendance at the clandestine "opposition" meeting that took place in Havana just before Manuel Urrutia assumed the office of provisional president.[184] In a later report, Taaffe told the FBI that Alberto Fernandez was also connected to Varona's "opposition group" and that Cuba's wealthiest sugar producer, Julio Lobo, was financing the group.[185] In January 1959, however, many Cubans still hoped that Varona would replace Castro as Cuba's leader. By April those hopes had disappeared. For the rest of the year, Taaffe tried, unsuccessfully, to convince Varona to get out of Cuba.

---

183   2/3/58, HQS CIA, cable to Chief of Station, Havana. RIF 104-10260-10418.
184   1/5/59, Urgent Telegram from SAC New York to SAC Miami and Director FBI, Subject: Cuban Revolutionary Activities, FPM-Cuba, RIF 124-90036-10153.
185   See 7/27/59 FBI New York Office LHM, Re: Foreign Political Matters-Cuba, Anti-Fidel Castro Activities, RIF 124-90130-10068.

CHAPTER FIVE:
THE HERTER–HOOVER LUNCHEON AND THE STORY OF CATHERINE TAAFFE

JANUARY 1959—AN EMBARASSING SITUATION IN CUBA

"The Department of State is embarrassed as a result of the Cuban situation," the FBI was "advised confidentially" on 16 January 1959. E. Tomlin Bailey, Director of the Department of State Office of Security, and his Deputy, Otto Otepka, divulged that their department was embarrassed because "they did not know that the Batista Government was to be thrown out" on 1 January 1959, and added, "apparently some of the top State officials felt that they were not briefed on the Cuban situation as they should have been during the past several months." This news was immediately passed to A. H. Belmont, Director of the FBI's Domestic Intelligence Division.[186]

---

[186] 1/16/59 FBI Memo from R.R. Roach to A. H. Belmont, Subject: Dissemination of Information to Department of State, FBI HQS 109 File, VOL 10, p. 68. In June 1961, Belmont would become Hoover's Assistant Director.

57

This confidential disclosure from the State Department's Security Office to the FBI Liaison Section was directly related to something that had happened just a week earlier that the FBI was eager to learn more about. On 9 January, Belmont had learned that "Under Secretary of State Herter might call on the Director [Hoover] to discuss the Cuban Situation."[187] This development was all the more significant not only because of President Eisenhower's anger at being left out of the loop on Cuba, but also because Secretary of State John Foster Dulles' two-year fight with abdominal cancer had taken a sharp turn for the worse. At the end of 1958 and, by mid-January, he had only four months to live. Undersecretary Herter, the number two man at the State Department, knew how quickly he would be in the hot seat.

The frenzy in Washington went beyond Batista's fall. As discussed previously, it was only in the final days of 1958 that CIA chief Allen Dulles surprised President Eisenhower with the news that a Castro victory was a problem because communists had penetrated his 26 July Movement and would participate in the Castro government. The president was upset that he had not been informed about such a conclusion earlier.[188] On the ground in Cuba, the CIA had been slow to perceive who Fidel Castro really was. This passage from a CIA Havana Station officer, Frank J. Belsito, describes how late that perception was to change in the waning months of 1958:

> When I arrived in mid-1958, the situation was becoming nasty. ...Unfortunately, the CIA Station was not unsympathetic to Castro. It soon became clear that such "agents" as [we] inherited were Castro propagandists. In any case, the departing Chief of Station had belatedly become aware of the problem... ...The CIA Station underwent an almost complete change of personnel in mid and late 1958, and while my efforts to penetrate the revolutionary movements were a failure, open sources, not so-called controlled and paid sources, soon changed the

---
187 See the 1/14/59 Memo to Belmont, Subject: Cuban Political Situation, FBI HQS 109 File, VOL 10, pp. 8-10.
188 Dwight D. Eisenhower, *The White House Years: Waging Peace, 1956-1961* (New York: Doubleday, 1965) p. 521.

THE HERTER-HOOVER LUNCHEON...

thinking of the new Station officers to the extent that, to a man, the Station's opposition to Castro led the new Chief of Station to say on that frenetic day of Castro's victory, 1 January 1959, that he was pleased to see that we were "all of one mind" in deploring a new dictatorship worse than Batista's, and potentially very antagonistic to the United States.[189]

The same was true for several U.S. diplomats in Cuba. "Unfortunately, some of the officers of the Havana Embassy continued to the end to believe," recalled U.S. Ambassador to Cuba Earl Smith, "that Castro was the salvation for Cuba."[190] On 7 January, just six days after Batista's flight, the U.S. extended diplomatic recognition to the new regime in Cuba. On 11 January, President Eisenhower ordered Ambassador Smith to be removed from his post.[191]

This anxious atmosphere in Washington was the context in which Under Secretary Herter decided to find out what FBI Director Hoover knew about the events that had just transpired in Cuba. At FBI Headquarters on 16 January, the news arrived that Hoover had been invited by Undersecretary Herter to his private dining room for a luncheon and discussion about the Cuban situation on 29 January.[192] Hoover was probably ecstatic at this opportunity. He decided not to wait until the 29th to impress Herter. On 19 January he phoned Herter to accept the luncheon invitation and to offer the Undersecretary an hors d'oeuvre of his own. Hoover confided that he had the inside track on the Cuban situation due principally to the accurate intelligence coming through his New York FBI Office from an informant with extraordinary connections in Cuba.

On 21 January, Hoover followed up his 19 January phone call to Herter with a memorandum, delivered by courier, "regarding the Cuban situa-

---

189   Frank, J. Belsito, *CIA: Cuba and the Caribbean—CIA Officer's Memoirs* (Reston VA: Ancient Mariner Press, 2002, pp. 44-46.
190   Earl E.T. Smith, *The Fourth Floor—An Account of the Castro Communist Revolution* (New York: Random House, 1962), p. 30.
191   FRUS, 1958-1960, volume VI, Cuba, document #221, cable from State Department to Embassy in Cuba, January 9, 1959. Smith's cable to Washington was received at 7:27 p.m. EST, and this cable was received in Havana at 9:23 p.m. EST.
192   1/16/59, FBI Memo from Roach to Belmont, Subject: Cuban Political Situation, FBI HQS 109 File, VOL 10, p. 2.

tion and *particularly* concerning information we have been receiving from Mrs. Catherine Taaffe." [Emphasis added] Hoover told Herter, "I thought you would be interested in knowing she called our New York Office from Havana, Cuba, on 19 January 1959, and stated she had spent eight hours at the Sugar Institute and two and one-half hours at the Presidential Palace but had not been in contact with the American Embassy in Havana."[193] We will return to the subject of who Taaffe wanted to see in Cuba in Chapter Six.

J. EDGAR HOOVER—THE KEY GUEST AT UNDERSECRETARY HERTER'S LUNCHEON ON THE SITUATION IN CUBA

After Hoover's office confirmed that he would be able to attend the luncheon, Undersecretary of State Herter's office sent another note stating Hoover should come directly to Herter's office for the engagement. At the bottom of this note Hoover scrawled, "See that I have a brief (complete) promptly."[194] The final typed briefing package that Hoover's subordinates prepared for him was ready by 24 January. It was nearly 175 pages in length with a Table of Contents four pages long, and five major sections subdivided into more than 60 subsections. The second largest single section concerned "Coverage of the Cuban Situation," which comprised 15 pages of material. Only two informants were highlighted. One was a man close to the Castro regime that had been developed by the Miami FBI Office—the section on him comprised three and a half pages. By far, the person to which the most space in the report was devoted was Catherine Taaffe. The importance of her information earned her two sections in Hoover's briefing package—a 6-page highlights section up front (Section I-B) and a 21-page appendix (A) devoted entirely to her reporting. Hoover's briefing package and several memoranda relating to the Herter luncheon were included in the FBI Cuba 109 files released to attorney James Lesar in 2004 as a result of his FOIA request submitted to the FBI in October 1994.

---

193 1/21/59, Letter, from Hoover to Herter, FBI HQS 109 File, VOL 10, p. 58.
194 Note to Hoover RE his 1/29/59 luncheon engagement with Undersecretary Herter, FBI HQS 109 File, VOL 11, p. 7.

THE HERTER-HOOVER LUNCHEON...

The luncheon event was attended by Undersecretary Herter, half a dozen other senior State Department officers, and several officers from other government agencies. While no record of the discussion that took place at the luncheon has been released, it is probably safe to say that given his billing as the "key guest," Hoover was the star of the show.

From the treatment of Taaffe's reports in Appendix A we cannot ascertain how many reports she submitted to the FBI, but we know that she reported almost daily—sometimes several times in a single day—on numerous topics arranged into these categories:

1. Cuban Feeling Against Former U.S. Ambassador Earl E. T. Smith
2. Persons Considered for U.S. Ambassador to Cuba
3. Attitude of Cuban Government to Offer of Soviet Aid and communism
4. Feeling of Cuban Government to Nomination of Phillip W. Bonsal as Ambassador to Cuba
5. Rumors Concerning Possible Overthrow of Cuban Government by Batista Followers
6. Cuban Government's Desire for Removal of U.S. Military Missions
7. Executions by Castro in Cuba
8. Cuban Government's Desire for U.S. Assistance
9. 26 July Movement
10. Miscellaneous
11. Information Furnished by Catherine Taaffe Since Her Return to U.S. From Cuba on 24 January 1959.[195]

As Hoover spoke about what his informant was learning from her sources in Havana, the U.S. officials attending this luncheon were likely impressed with how much she was able to find out so quickly.

Back on 9 January, the very day Hoover had learned that the Herter luncheon might be in the works, a veritable missile from Taaffe had landed on the FBI Director's desk.[196] In this report, Taaffe said that she had received a phone call in New York the previous evening from John P. Booth in Miami. He was a lawyer with whom she was familiar and who

---
195   Final FBI Briefing Package for Hoover's 1/29/59 luncheon engagement with Undersecretary Herter, FBI HQS 109 File, VOL 11.
196   FBI Memo from D. E. Moore to A. H. Belmont, Subject: Cuban Revolutionary Activities, FBI 8/29/2008 FOIA Release to Jim Lesar, pp. 38-39.

61

happened to be closely associated with the Republican Party in Florida. Her report to the FBI included some very sensitive details:

> Taaffe stated that Booth related that the Republican Party in Florida ascertained that Democratic Senator George A. Smathers, Robert Thompson, an attorney from south Miami, Fnu [first name unknown] Smiley [Note: this surname should be Smuley, an attorney for Senator Smathers] and Fnu [first name unknown] Rebozo (phonetic), both from Miami, Florida, had investments in Cuba and the profits were too lucrative to have Smith replaced as Smith is taking care of their investments. Booth stated that the Republican Party in Florida ascertained in the beginning that Senator George Smathers was sympathetic toward the revolutionary movement, but was induced to visit Cuba and was given shares and interests in business down there for lending his name and for visiting Cuba and talking to former President Batista. Booth advised that the business interests included mining and cement plants and in some way the sugar industry. Booth also stated that Thompson fronted for these investments and that Fnu Rebozo fronted for the Italian money and was also influential at the Presidential Palace in business ventures between Ambassador Smith and former President Batista.

It was after learning this much from Booth that Taaffe had called the FBI New York Office on the evening of 8 January. However, the next day she called the New York Office again after receiving another call from Fort Lauderdale from a very nervous John Booth. Now he had this to say:

> ...she should be extremely careful with the information he furnished her on 1-8-59. Booth stated they further ascertained that Rebozo is identical with Bebe Rebozo who was in the United States Navy during World War II with Vice President Nixon, together with Robert Thompson. Booth stated that they have also ascertained that Vice President Nixon is also in on investments in Cuba and

THE HERTER-HOOVER LUNCHEON...

that all individuals involved have benefited financially. Booth also advised that when Vice President Nixon visits Miami, Florida, he stays at the home of Bebe Rebozo. Mrs. Taaffe also requested the NYO not to disseminate this information outside the Bureau. The NYO made no commitments to her.

At the bottom of this hot potato, Hoover scrawled, "We certainly can't sit on this information." But then, after mulling over the matter further, Hoover penned an additional remark: "Now that [Ambassador] Smith has resigned <u>this seems to be resolved</u>."[197] [Emphasis in original] The FBI Director's thinking was seconded a month later by his subordinates in a 10 February memo discussing Taaffe's "data" about the exceptional situation concerning Ambassador Smith, Vice President Nixon and Bebe Rebozo. This memo explained that inasmuch as the 10 January announcement of Smith's resignation "served to resolve this situation, no dissemination was made of the foregoing data."[198]

And so, whether or not the logic of Hoover's formula for burying Taaffe's revelations about Nixon, Rebozo and Smathers was sound, only a few of these sensitive details were included in Hoover's final briefing package for the 29 January Herter luncheon. Of course, exactly what Hoover said at the luncheon about this scandal cannot be determined. He probably disclosed what was necessary to alert his interlocutors that he had politically sensitive information about people in high places in Washington.

Taaffe had no intention of letting the details of this story fade. On 9 February, an FBI New York Office teletype to Hoover reported that Alberto Fernandez, head of the Sugar Institute in Havana, told Taaffe that "Cuban authorities have verified information concerning alleged investments in Cuba on part of Smathers, Nixon and others," and that this investigation was instigated by former Cuban President Carlos Prio Socarras who was under indictment in the U.S. for conspiracy to violate the Neutrality Statue (Section 960, Title 18). Fernandez said that "Prio

---

197 1/9/59, FBI Memo from D. E. Moore to A. H. Belmont, Subject: Cuban Revolutionary Activities, FBI 8/29/2008 FOIA Release to Jim Lesar, pp. 38-39.
198 2/10/59, FBI Memo from S. B Donahue to A. H. Belmont, Subject: Cuban Revolutionary Activities, FBI 8/29/2008 FOIA Release to Jim Lesar, pp. 137-138.

will publicize information regarding financial connections Smathers, Nixon, et cetera, and Batista regime in order to embarrass U.S., if necessary." Fernandez, Taaffe added, had reported to her that he was "doing everything in his power to prevent this information from becoming public but he does not know how long he can have information withheld." If Taaffe's information was accurate, the New York Office observed, "this represents a subtle form of blackmail." Consequently, the New York Office recommended that Hoover approve, which he apparently did, a letter "to the Attorney General setting out the pertinent information furnished by Mrs. Taaffe concerning this matter."[199]

CATHERINE TAAFFE'S INFORMATION ON "OTHER MATTERS"

We now turn to the contents of Hoover's briefing package. There are two documents, an early (14 January) shorter version of the Hoover briefing package and the final (24 January) lengthier version. The introductory details about Taaffe's identity and her curriculum vitae appear in one location in the shorter version and in two locations in the longer version. All three are heavily redacted. However, it is possible to fill in the majority of these deletions with certainty and to make reasonable estimates for most of the rest. The following inset material is a composite from both versions about Taaffe's background in Hoover's briefing package:

> Catherine Taaffe, *who had been providing information to our New York Office voluntarily with regard to other matters*, contacted us on 1 January 1959, following the downfall of Batista. Since that time she has provided considerable information concerning the Cuban situation as set forth hereinafter. [Emphasis added]
>
> [more than 5 lines redacted, but we know the expanded version of the story from other contemporaneous FBI records, see FBI 8/29/08 FOIA release to Lesar,

---

199 1/9/59, FBI NYO Teletype to HQS, Subject: Cuban Revolutionary Activities, FBI 8/29/2008 FOIA Release to Jim Lesar, pp. 137-138.

THE HERTER-HOOVER LUNCHEON...

p. 57:] Taaffe stated her mother had attempted suicide on several occasions and on one occasion after an unsuccessful operation for cancer, shot herself in the mouth but recovered from this wound. Mrs. Taaffe advised that her grandmother had accused her father of attempting to kill her mother and in a gun fight with sheriffs he was killed. Mrs. Taaffe advised that when her mother recovered she made a statement that her husband did not try to kill her and within three months after this accident, she herself died of cancer. As a result of this publicity, Mrs. Taaffe advised that she and her two brothers left South Carolina. Mrs. Taaffe was first married to [½ line redacted, but we know the details, see FBI 8/29/08 FOIA release to Lesar p. 57:] Huley Perry of South Carolina. She is presently married to [1 line redacted, but we know the details, see FBI 8/29/08 FOIA release to Lesar p. 57:] William Francis Randall Dunne Taaffe of San Francisco. Since January, 1956, she resided at Hotel Bretton Hall in New York City. She was formerly [1/2 line deleted, but we know the details, see FBI 8/29/08 FOIA release to Lesar p. 59:] a licensed arms dealer engaged in the import-export business, the bulk of her activities being in Latin America. In two investigations it was found that her information was reliable. In the past she has worked with the ["Central Intelligence Agency"; note: this is redacted but the CIA is the only organization that fits perfectly into the space]; the Office of Special Investigations, Department of the Air Force; and U. S. Customs Service.

Mrs. Taaffe claims to be personally acquainted with Generalissimo Trujillo of the Dominican Republic and former President Batista, and to have contacts with Senators Wayne B. Morse and Hubert Humphrey. She also claims to be on friendly terms with former Secretary of State James F. Byrnes and the former New York [2/3 line redacted, but we know the details, see FBI 8/29/08 FOIA release to Lesar, p. 59:] Cuban Consul General," "she has been very close to" "Mr. Alfredo Hernandez Valdez." In November 1958, Mrs. Taaffe was contacted [1/2 line redacted, but we know the details, see FBI 8/29/08 FOIA release to Lesar p. 59:] by Jose Llanusa, Secretary of Organization of] the 26 July Movement in the United States, who requested her advice on various problems facing the Movement. In addition to [1/3 line redacted, but it is almost certainly: "Jose Llunasa, Mrs. Taaffe"] was also in constant contact with other pro-Castro individuals with the July 26 Movement such as [3/4 line redacted, but possibly "Jose Sanchez and Julio Medina] both mentioned in 3/9/60 FBI NYO report, RIF 124-10206-10255] the July 26 Movement in the United States; [1/4 line deleted] a Havana real estate man; [1/4 line redacted, but possibly Rosita Preston] reportedly related to provisional President Urrutia; [1/2 line redacted] and [1/2 line redacted], wealthy sugar plantation owners in Cuba.

On 18 January 1959, she left the United States to go to Havana at the request of [1/2 line redacted, but possibly Alberto Fernandez] an official in the Cuban Government, to exert her influence in stopping the executions in Cuba and try to set up a Nuremburg trial system.

The Hoover briefing package's details about Taaffe's past are important for several reasons. For example, Appendix A discloses that she had been voluntarily providing the New York FBI Office information "with regard to other matters." The present author has located more information pertaining to several of these "other matters." One of the "other matters" concerned a man named Joseph Arthur Zicarelli, aka "Bayonne Joe," the head man in the numbers lottery and gambling operations in Hudson County, New Jersey, headquartered in Bayonne, New Jersey. According to a 16 March 1959 Newark FBI Office report on the Bureau's investigation of racketeering, Zicarelli told the FBI that he had been active in purchasing guns for the Cuban revolution, gambling activity in Mexico, kickback contracts and the possible assassination of a political leader in Venezuela. The Newark FBI Office added that "Another

Government Agency has furnished information that Zicarelli has been authorized to purchase $1,000,000 of rockets and machine guns for the Dominican Republic.[200]

That Newark report on Zicarelli included some interesting information about Taaffe's history, including this passage:

> On 24 November 1958, Mrs. Catherine Taaffe, Bretton Hotel, 86th Street and Broadway, New York City, was *recontacted* by SAs Alun Jones Whilding and James W. Skelley at which time she was shown a photograph of Joseph Arthur Zicarelli, and, after viewing it she stated *she met him in 1949 at the Warick Hotel, New York City, in connection with gambling in Caracas, Venezuela, where she (Taaffe) had a gambling concession.* Mrs. Taaffe stated she again saw Zicarelli in Cuba in approximately 1953 or 1954; however, she added she has not seen him since that time and does not have any knowledge of his activities. [Emphasis added]

Furthermore, the Newark report also contained this illuminating paragraph about Taaffe, her husband, and a man named Jesse Vickers:

> Review of Miami files regarding Jesse Vickers reflects Vickers has been an associate of G. L. Hollaway in the H. V. Salvage Sales Company, whose Miami address was 472 South Drive, Miami Springs. *He became associated with Catherine Taaffe to utilize her contacts as wife of Colonel W. Randall Taaffe. Since the departure of Vickers and Catherine Taaffe for Washington, D. C., Colonel Taaffe has been advising the Miami [FBI] Office of their activities and reported that they were working on a large arms order, for which they had already secured State Department export licenses and complied with other Government requirements.* [Emphasis added]

That Catherine Taaffe had a gambling concession in Venezuela during 1949 is, by itself, an intriguing detail. Even more noteworthy is that her Venezuelan gambling concession existed at a time when she was connected to the manufacture of crooked gambling equipment. We know about this detail from a 10 August 1950 Miami FBI Office report. Ac-

---

200 3/16/59 Newark FBO Office Report on Anti-Racketeering activities of Joseph Arthur Zicarelli et al, NARA RIF 124-90110-10031.

cording to the Miami FBI Office, in 1949 and 1950, Colonel and Mrs. Taaffe were associated with an individual (whose name was redacted) of a company named Monterey Woodcrafters, Inc., of Miami, Florida. The report stated that this company manufactured "crooked gambling equipment" and, that while associated with this person, the Taaffes "were considered by the Miami Office as prospective criminal informants" until such time as they severed their relationship with this person.[201]

Moreover, the Taaffes' activities in Venezuela went beyond gambling. According to a 10 July 1947 Miami FBI report, both Taaffes were "active in endeavoring to procure arms on behalf of the Lopez Contreras faction, which group was attempting to overthrow the Venezuelan Government of Romulo Betancourt."[202] The 10 July FBI report was captioned, "[21 letters redacted] et al, Organizing a Military Expedition Against a Friendly Power."[203] According to FBI documents, in 1950 Catherine Taaffe allegedly bragged that she was a "very close friend of an influential man in the Miami FBI Office," and that she had been successful in using his influence to get an investigation discontinued.[204] That investigation was probably about the Taaffes' connection to the 1947 Contreras arms deal. When Hoover heard about this boast on 9 August 1950, he fired off this urgent order to the Miami FBI Office: "Advise Bureau at once of facts involved and any basis for [Taaffe's] allegation."[205] Furthermore, Hoover ordered the FBI's Washington Field Office to "Institute any necessary investigation immediately concerning the allegation."[206]

On 10 August 1950 the Miami FBI Office sent an urgent reply to FBI HQS. The reply explained that they had no indication that "Catherine Taaffe ever influenced any official," and said that no prosecution of the Taaffes had taken place in connection with their investigation of the

---

201 8/10/50, Miami FBI Office Urgent Telegram to Director FBI, FBI 8/29/2008 FOIA Release to Jim Lesar, pp. 26-28.
202 8/10/50, Miami FBI Office Urgent Telegram to Director FBI, FBI 8/29/2008 FOIA Release to Jim Lesar, pp. 26-28.
203 This detail was included in a 1959 FBI memo about the past activities of the Taaffes: 1/12/59, SAC New York to Director FBI, Cuban Revolutionary Activities; see the FBI 8/29/2008 FOIA Release to Jim Lesar, p. 53.
204 8/2/50, SAC Guy Hottel, FBI Washington Field Office to Director, Subject: Catheran [sic] Taaffe, Neutrality Act, Espionage, FBI 8/29/2008 FOIA Release to Jim Lesar, pp. 8-16.
205 8/9/50, Hoover to Miami FBI Office, Subject: Catheran [sic] Taaffe, Neutrality Act, Espionage, FBI 8/29/2008 FOIA Release to Jim Lesar, p. 6.
206 8/11/50, Director FBI to SAC Washington, FBI 8/29/2008 FOIA Release to Jim Lesar, p. 7.

Taaffe-Lopez Contreras arms deal "*because* [the] *Department would not authorize same.*"[207] [Emphasis added] In other words, it was the Department of Justice, not the FBI Office in Miami, which had stopped the investigation of Catherine Taaffe and her husband for their role in the attempted coup in Venezuela.

What we learn from these memoranda is that Taaffe and her husband appear to have enjoyed protection from high places in Washington. Where there were arms deals and coups in Latin America, the Taaffes were often involved. Not surprisingly, they were also involved in the CIA's 1954 coup against Guatemalan President Jacobo Arbenz Guzman. This 1954 PBSUCCESS (the CIA cryptonym for the coup in Guatemala) Project Report by the CIA project chief, Jacob Esterline, makes the Taaffes' involvement abundantly clear:

> Mrs. Catherine Taaffe, an American arms dealer, appeared in Guatemala and talked with President Abenz and Lt. Col. Medina. She subsequently wrote a letter to her husband in New York instructing him to purchase aircraft from Sweden for a dissident group of Guatemalan Army leaders, headed by Col. Sanchez, Guatemalan Minister of Defense, and Medina, both of whom are reportedly planning to overthrow the Guatemalan Government and eliminate the communists. The FBI has been alerted to note all contacts made by Col. Taaffe in the U.S.[208]

In other words, for the previous nine years Taaffe had been providing the FBI with information on many "other matters."

---

207 8/10/50 Miami FBI Office Urgent Telegram to Director FBI, FBI 8/29/2008 FOIA Release to Jim Lesar, pp. 26-28.
208 5/4/54, CIA Memorandum, from Jacob D. Esterline, Subject: Progress Report—PBSUCCESS for the Period 27 April—3 May 1954; from CIA Web Site.

CHAPTER SIX:
TAAFFE'S JANUARY 1959 TRIP TO CUBA

Taaffe had done some extra-curricular digging around during her January visit to Havana. After her return to the U.S., she began a crusade to bring agents of several U.S. Government agencies to Cuba to examine files of certain people who had been working in Havana during the Batista regime. Singled out for special attention in her campaign were "dope peddlers and smugglers." Yet her campaign soon ran into a brick wall at the Justice Department, the FBI, and the Immigration and Naturalization Service (INS).

At that very moment another American woman decided to make a trip to Havana that concerned narcotics. June Cobb, so her story goes, wanted to present a "project" to the Cuban Minister of Public Health, Martinez Paez. She wanted Paez to help, along with some doctors from Peru and Bolivia, fix the cocaine problem in Cuba. Later, in June 1960, she told the CIA that her reason for pursuing this endeavor was the cocaine addiction of her Colombian ex-fiancé Rafael Herran Olozaga. Cobb had helped Raphael and his twin brother Tomas smuggle heroin into Cuba and Mexico. We will deal with Cobb's story in Chapters Eight, Nine, Ten, and Eleven.

MORE AMERICAN SKELETONS DANGLING IN CUBAN CLOSETS

Former Ambassador Smith, Vice President Nixon, Bebe Rebozo and Senator Smathers were not the only old American skeletons hanging around in Cuban closets after Batista's departure (see Chapter Five). Taaffe began an entirely new stream of reporting immediately after she returned to New York from her trip to Havana. This time her information was coming from the files of Cuban Army Military Intelligence (SIM).

Taaffe's reports to the FBI during her 18-24 January 1959 trip to Cuba alleged that she had no contact with the U.S. Embassy while she was there. Yet a 21 January FBI memorandum captioned "Relations with Cuban Army Military Intelligence (SIM)," suggests that this may not have been entirely true:

> Cablegram 1/20/59 from Legal attaché, Havana, indicates the Legal attaché had been advised by an embassy official that one Catherine Taaffe, who claimed she was from the "Washington office of security" and was "undercover" in Havana, had stated *she would see that officials issued identification cards by SIM were removed from their positions.*[209] [Emphasis added]

Whether or not Taaffe actually set foot inside the U.S. Embassy, it appears that she told or got word to an Embassy officer that she was an undercover security officer from Washington.

This *personal threat* issued by Catherine Taaffe to have U.S. Embassy officers removed from their jobs is odd. FBI HQS did not learn about it from her phone calls to New York. They found out instead through their Legat in Havana, James T. Haverty, who had learned about Taaffe's threat from a U.S. Embassy official. According to Haverty's report, Taaffe heard from a Havana news source that the former FBI Legal Attaché in Havana, John Wachter, and four other Americans had identification cards allowing them entry into SIM headquarters.

Haverty's cablegram landed like a missile, and instantly precipitated a "pink memorandum" from Hoover's office about the matter. By 6:30 pm that evening, new details from Havana were relayed to Hoover's

---

[209] 1/21/59 FBI Memorandum From S. B. Donahoe to A. H. Belmont, Subject: Relations with Cuban Army Military Intelligence (SIM), FBI 8/29/2008 FOIA Release to Jim Lesar, p. 51.

TAAFFE'S JANUARY 1959 TRIP TO CUBA

deputy, Clyde Tolson, as Wachter's replacement, Jim Haverty, quickly attempted to put the story to bed.[210] Taaffe's news source apparently worked for the *U.S. News and World Report* in Havana, and Haverty called their desk in order to tell them that he had heard about the story and to advise the desk of the following:

> …that all this amounted to was a building pass to Cuban Intelligence [head] quarters… …this was perfectly normal and would have been expected of American Embassy personnel to have entrée into areas of the government in whose country they were serving.

The *U.S News and World Report* desk then checked out the matter further and called Haverty back with this report:

> [redacted name of the reporter] had turned the story down, that what had happened was that a Cuban newspaperman had planted the story that there were five American spies for Batista who had entrée into Cuban intelligence and that [redacted name of reporter] had checked it out, found it to be a phony planted story and, accordingly, had turned it down.

At this point we encounter a two-week hole in the publicly available documentary record of this Taaffe episode that lasts until 4 February. However, documents obtained under the Freedom of Information Act in 2008 by attorney James Lesar dated 4 and 5 February 1959, allow us to reconstruct what happened during this interlude.

After her return to New York on 24 January, Taaffe offered the FBI the opportunity to check Cuban Army Military Intelligence (SIM) records that she had been shown in Havana. The FBI declined this offer and told her they would not get involved in checking SIM records.[211] That rebuff did little to stop Taaffe, who then managed to convince Assistant U.S. Attorney Marvin Segal to go to Cuba to "assist" in a review of the SIM files.[212] Taaffe then made "all the arrangements" with Alberto

---

210   1/20/59, FBI Memorandum From G. A. Nease to Mr. Tolson, Subject: Political Matters-Cuba, FBI NYO 109 File, Vol. 9, serial 402.
211   2/5/59, FBI Memorandum from Mr. S. J. Papich to Mr. R. R. Roach, Subject: Catherine Taaffe, Internal Security-Cuba, FBI 8/29/2008 FOIA Release to Jim Lesar, p. 61.
212   2/4/59, FBI Memorandum from A. Rosen to Director, Subject: Information Furnished by Catherine Taaffe re Cuban Matters, FBI 8/29/2008 FOIA Release to Jim Lesar, pp. 40-41.

73

WHERE ANGELS TREAD LIGHTLY

Fernandez in Cuba for Segal to help a Mr. Manners conduct the review of "all files in Havana." Both men worked for the Justice Department's racket squad, a unit subordinate to Milton R. Wessel, Special Assistant to the Attorney General (SAAG). Segal worked out of New York City, and Manners was Wessel's representative in Miami.

Taaffe was not yet finished in her effort to mobilize U.S. Government agencies to examine the Cuban Army Military Intelligence files. Since Castro's victory she had been supplying information about the developing situation in Cuba to the Immigration and Naturalization Service (INS). Apparently, she had been doing this anonymously. After her return from Cuba, she contacted the INS and again, without revealing her name, made this offer:

> ...she was in a position to make available the records of Cuban Military Intelligence (SIM). She indicated that these records contained the identities of *dope peddlers, smugglers and possibly communists.*[213] [Emphasis added]

Taaffe's news was sufficiently interesting to induce the INS to develop plans to send two Spanish speaking agents to Havana to review the materials that she claimed existed.

When the INS decided it might be a good idea to notify the FBI before sending their agents to Cuba, Taaffe's plans began to fall apart. On 28 January 1959, the INS contacted FBI Liaison Agent Sam Papich and told him that the above INS story came from "a woman in New York City." The officer said that the INS was following this situation closely and was interested in sending agents to Cuba to check the SIM files. The INS officer asked if the woman was Catherine Taaffe. He was told, in a call made shortly afterward to the New York FBI Office, that in fact the woman was Taaffe. Papich told the INS officer that Taaffe had been in touch with the FBI and other agencies about the SIM files and he suggested that the "INS not get involved in any project without first making certain that the interests of other agencies were not being jeopardized." The INS agent thanked Papich for this suggestion and added that he would make certain that INS did not get "fouled up."[214]

---

213 2/5/59, FBI Memorandum from Mr. S. J. Papich to Mr. R. R. Roach, Subject: Catherine Taaffe, Internal Security-Cuba, FBI 8/29/2008 FOIA Release to Jim Lesar, p. 61.
214 2/5/59 FBI Memorandum from Mr. S. J. Papich to Mr. R. R. Roach, Subject: Catherine Taaffe, Internal Security-Cuba, FBI 8/29/2008 FOIA Release to Jim Lesar, p. 61.

The FBI did not let this matter hang fire. After Papich's talk with the INS, FBI Assistant Director Alex Rosen contacted Milton Wessel at the Justice Department and told him that Marvin Segal was interested in going to Cuba to check the SIM records. Wessel's response then lowered the boom:

> Wessel informed Mr. Rosen that any plans which Segal had to go to Cuba were out and that he, Wessel, was not getting involved in the matter nor was Segal. Wessel made it clear that as far as he was concerned, none of his men would be going to Cuba.[215]

Once the Justice Department removed itself from Taaffe's files quest, the INS followed suit on 2 February 1959, and told Papich that INS personnel would not be checking into the SIM records in Cuba. At the bottom of Papich's memorandum of this story Hoover penned this statement: *"Just how many agencies is this Taaffe woman 'informing'?"*

On 4 February a disappointed Taaffe called Assistant Special Agent in Charge Bryant at the New York FBI Office. She had spoken with Marvin Segal the day before and she told Bryant that Segal's "attitude was completely different" than it had been before. In a memorandum about the Taaffe-Bryant conversation to the FBI's Domestic Intelligence Division Chief, Alan Belmont, Alex Rosen stated that it was his understanding that the FBI would not review the SIM files. Rosen then added this:

> If this is correct, I suggest I again call Manners and indicate to him that this information has come to our attention and that as far as the FBI is concerned, we are not participating in such a matter. Secondly, it is my understanding that neither Segal nor Manners nor anyone else out of the New York office plans to go to Cuba. This, of course, relates to *gambling matters* in Cuba. However, I understand that *the files which have been offered also refer to other matters of a subversive nature.* Consequently, this memorandum is being brought to the attention of the Domestic Intelligence Division.[216] [Emphasis added]

---

215 2/5/59 FBI Memorandum from Mr. S. J. Papich to Mr. R. R. Roach, Subject: Catherine Taaffe, Internal Security-Cuba, FBI 8/29/2008 FOIA Release to Jim Lesar, p. 61.
216 2/4/59, FBI Memorandum from A. Rosen to Director, Subject: Information Furnished by Catherine Taaffe re Cuban Matters, FBI 8/29/2008 FOIA Release to Jim Lesar, pp. 40-41.

After receiving Rosen's memo, Belmont attached this addendum to it:
> We have previously told New York to advise Taaffe to keep the FBI <u>out</u> of any arrangement to examine files in Havana. We have no knowledge of alleged subversive files being offered for examination and, regardless, we would not want to examine such files *at this time.* In fact, we have told the Legal attaché he is to refrain from making additional contacts with the Cubans solidifying existing contacts *at this time, until we see how the situation jells in Cuba.* We agree that Wessel should be informed that the Bureau is not going to become involved in the examination of files in Cuba *at this time*, and suggest that New York be instructed to advise Taaffe again that she should keep the FBI out of this matter.[217] [Emphasis added]

The Servicio de Inteligencia Militar (SIM) was not just military intelligence for the army. It was also Batista's personal protective service and the glue holding together the entire fabric of the corrupt alliance between his regime and the American mobsters and corporations. Along with the covert squad of the National Police and Masferrer's *Tigres*, the SIM was dreaded throughout Cuba for its terrorist tactics of arrests, disappearances, and assassinations. According to a former U.S. Embassy officer in Havana, torture was widespread and hundreds were killed, innocent and guilty alike. The bodies of rebels "were left hanging from trees along roadways."[218]

February 1959 was still a time when expectations were high that Castro's power would be short lived. It was therefore not a good time for snooping around a potential hornet's nest like the SIM files—at least until, as Belmont reasoned, the post-Batista leadership situation became clearer.

---

217 2/4/59, FBI Memorandum from A. Rosen to Director, Subject: Information Furnished by Catherine Taaffe re Cuban Matters, FBI 8/29/2008 FOIA Release to Jim Lesar, pp. 40-41.
218 Wayne Smith, *The Closest of Enemies: A Personal and Diplomatic History of the Castro Years* (New York: W. W. Norton, 1987), p. 16.

TAAFFE IN CUBA: YES FOR CAMILO, NO FOR FIDEL

The above brings us back to the questions: Who was Catherine Taaffe? For whom was she ultimately working all of those years? Recall Hoover's FBI briefing package for his January 1959 special luncheon with Undersecretary of State Herter. At the top of the list of Taaffe's true benefactors was the Central Intelligence Agency—followed by Air Force intelligence and U.S. Customs. The latter suggests a possible connection to drug smuggling. Air Force intelligence suggests a connection to aviation perhaps beyond the sale of aircraft—possibly counterintelligence. The CIA angle, however, is the most likely possibility for Taaffe's ultimate benefactor. This would cast an even more intriguing light on the oddest thing about her January 1959 trip to Cuba, specifically, the reason why Taaffe did not want—against the suggestions of just about everybody she talked with in the U.S. and Cuba—to speak with Fidel Castro.

A session with Fidel Castro in mid-January 1959 would have been, without a doubt, the biggest score in Cuba for anyone passing information to the U.S. Government. Castro's intention or lack of it to take Cuba communist was the number one concern in Washington. Preventing him from taking the island communist had become the CIA's top job after their plans to derail his ascendancy had failed in late 1958.

Both the CIA and the White House would jump at the chance to question Castro. Yet Taaffe, who had made such a concerted effort to be the fountain of knowledge with her reporting on the situation in Cuba, claimed that she really had no desire to be the person who could deliver the most important story of all. As we will see, this claim was a fairy-tale. The most plausible explanation of this seeming conundrum is that *Taaffe did not want Castro to see her*. Before turning to why that might have been the case, we will first review how we came to know about this fairy-tale.

We know about Taaffe's ludicrous claim—that she did not want to talk to Castro—principally from FBI records, especially from her late evening 19 January telephone call from Havana to the FBI Office in New York. Even before that call, Taaffe had already thrown cold water on any idea that she would speak to Castro. On 16 January, two days before her departure for Cuba, Taaffe told her New York FBI contact about what happened when a State Department official said he wanted her to speak with Castro:

> …he had agreed it would be advantageous for her to go to Cuba and consult with the new Cuban Government…
> …and [name redacted] also wanted Mrs. Taaffe to speak to Castro but she stated she would not go out of her way to speak to Castro as she desired to speak only to the civilian members of the new Cuban Government.[219]

The State Department officer was only asking Taaffe to do the most obvious thing. Unless she was ignorant of the critical importance such an opportunity would present, her puffed-up response was in all probability feigned in order to conceal her true motive for avoiding Castro.

In this case, the path of least resistance or "Occam's razor" if you like, is simply to change the focus from Taaffe seeing Castro to Castro seeing Taaffe. It stands to reason that the latter, not the former, was more likely to be the real problem. One thing is certain: even before she left for Cuba, Taaffe had already made up her mind that a meeting with Castro was out of the question.

Naturally, the prospect of such a meeting came up yet again during Taaffe's trip to Cuba. Again, she was asked to speak with Fidel Castro, only this time she said she was asked to do it by *everyone* she spoke with. The FBI learned about this from her late evening 19 January phone call. Hoover found out about it on 20 January, when the New York FBI Office sent him an urgent teletype about the call.[220] This was the same phone call (discussed previously) that excited Hoover so much that, on the next day, he sent a memorandum by courier to Undersecretary Herter to tell him about it. It is worth reviewing here which details of that call that Hoover chose to share with Herter:

> I thought you would be interested in knowing she called our New York Office from Havana, Cuba, on 19 January

---

219 Final FBI Briefing Package for Hoover's 1/29/59 luncheon engagement with Undersecretary Herter, FBI HQS 109 File, VOL 11; see p. 9 of Appendix A (A-9).
220 1/20/59, 1:22 AM, Urgent Teletype from SAC New York to Director FBI, Subject: Cuban Revolutionary Activities; FBI HQS 109 File, Volume 10, pp. 65-67.

1959, and stated she had spent eight hours at the Sugar Institute and two and one-half hours at the Presidential Palace but had not been in contact with the American Embassy in Havana.[221]

The urgent New York Office teletype to Hoover about Taaffe's phone call reveals that the FBI Director did not share some important details with the Under Secretary of State. Taaffe had reported that all of the people she had spoken with in Cuba had asked her "to speak with Fidel Castro, which she said she would do, but does not really desire to."

Moreover, Taaffe told the New York Office that the new civilian president of Cuba, Dr. Manuel Urrutia, was a "mere figurehead," had no power and that his only job was to reorganize the judicial system. Taaffe also said that she had "an appointment to speak with Commandante Camilo Cienfuegos at Camp Columbia" on the following day, 20 January. These details put the lie to her claim to the State Department that she would not speak with Castro because "she desired to speak only to the civilian members of the new Cuban Government."[222] Cienfuegos, an army officer and the third most powerful man in Cuba after Fidel and his brother, would shortly become the Commander of the Cuban Army.

In the weeks that followed, Taaffe claimed that Cienfuegos was not a communist. Setting aside that important observation for a moment, the most noticeable detail about her trip was that, according to her report, she had told all the people in Cuba urging her to see Castro that *she was willing to but did not want to.* Perhaps the truth was that Taaffe, and maybe others, *did not want Castro to see her.* It is not out of the question that Castro or someone in his entourage might have seen her before—in a situation in which she had been using a different name.

---

221 1/21/59, Letter, from Hoover to Herter, FBI HQS 109 File, VOL 10, p. 58.
222 Final FBI Briefing Package for Hoover's 1/29/59 luncheon engagement with Undersecretary Herter, FBI HQS 109 File, VOL 11; see p. 9 of Appendix A (A-9).

CHAPTER SEVEN:
FRANK STURGIS AND THE FIRST PLOT TO ASSASSINATE FIDEL CASTRO

In Washington D.C. the issue of Castro and communism had quickly become a hot issue. In Cuba it was *white hot.* A small but powerful group of Cuban military officers had discovered that Castro had, virtually from the moment he seized power, engineered a secret pact to turn Cuba communist. Well before it became known in Washington, these Cuban leaders knew that Castro had met secretly with the old-line leaders of the Cuban Communist Party (PSP) to negotiate the details of the plan. The super-secret negotiations were held under heavy rebel army guard at a hilltop house in the tiny fishing village of Cojimar—the same spot where Ernest Hemmingway wrote his magnum opus, **The Old Man and the Sea**.

In a landmark 1985 interview with journalist Tad Szulc, Blas Roca imparted the details of Castro's early negotiations with the PSP. Roca had been the secretary general of the PSP since 1934, and he represented the party at the Cojimar meeting with Castro. Roca told Szulc that both sides had agreed on the need for tight operational secrecy:

> ...the success [of the negotiations] was linked to the need of preventing the Americans from having a banner for an intervention, as they had done in Guatemala, and we had to go on maintaining the secret that had prevailed until then and had contributed to the success.[223]

The rank and file members of the PSP would not be told about the secret agreement of their party to accept Castro as Cuba's "principal revolutionary leader." They would not, for the time being, be informed that Castro was a "Marxist." PSP founder Fabio Gobart, also in a 1985 interview with Szulc, corroborated Roca's account of these clandestine consultations. Gobart explained that Castro's demands for a new communist party under his leadership would take time to prepare and that it was "impossible to state publicly in the first months of 1959 that *all these meetings* were occurring."[224] [Emphasis added]

Besides Fidel Castro, only four other leaders of the 26 July Movement were present at the secret Cojimar negotiations: Raul Castro, Che Guevara, Ramiro Valdes, and Camilo Cienfuegos. All were loyal to Castro except one. Castro had misread Cienfuegos, who would shortly become the commander of the Revolutionary Army. Cienfuegos was the Judas in this small group. This might explain why Taaffe wanted to see *him* instead of Castro during her trip to Cuba in late January 1959 [discussed in Chapter Six]. Castro's secret pact with the PSP was a fundamental betrayal of the revolution. We cannot be certain how much of this perfidy of the Cojimar pact that Cienfuegos shared with other anti-communist rebel commanders. He did not have to tell them everything. It is likely that he said enough to let them know that Castro had betrayed the revolution. Now ready to betray Castro, Cienfuegos secretly aligned himself with other key military officers who wanted to overthrow him. At the beginning of February 1959, Frank Sturgis joined this anti-Castro cabal.

---

223 Tad Szulc, **Fidel: A Critical Portrait** (New York: William Morrow and Co. Inc., 1986), pp. 473-474.
224 Tad Szulc, **Fidel: A Critical Portrait** (New York: William Morrow and Co. Inc., 1986), pp. 471-472.

THE CIA BASE AT SANTIAGO DE CUBA

During 1958, Frank Sturgis, using the alias "Frank Fiorini," [he had previously changed his birth name from Fiorini to Sturgis] was working with the U.S. Consular mission at Santiago de Cuba. He was smuggling weapons to Castro's forces at that time and, as discussed in Chapter One, American intelligence was interested in finding out what he had learned as a result of his activities with the rebel officers. According to Sturgis, the first person to openly approach him was Park F. Wollam. Wollam had replaced Oscar Guerra as the U.S. Consul in Santiago de Cuba in February 1958.[225] It was common knowledge in the city of Santiago that Guerra had been sympathetic toward Castro.[226] Sturgis later testified to the Rockefeller Commission that Wollam approached him in the Casa Grande Hotel, appealed to his American patriotism, and offered him a salary in exchange for intelligence information on "rebel movements, names of officers, strength, weapons, and so forth."[227] Sturgis agreed to serve as an intelligence asset for Wollam but declined the money.

Sturgis told the Rockefeller Commission that he assumed that Wollam and his colleague at the Santiago mission, "William Patterson," were CIA. Sturgis said that Patterson had gained the confidence of Castro's 26 July underground movement and was a "fixer" for Castro meetings with U.S. and foreign reporters.[228] Wollam was not CIA, but he did function as a cut-out to Sturgis. It was easier for Wollam to do this because, unlike his deputy, Wollam was not using his diplomatic status as a cover for covert work for the CIA.[229] However, the vice-consul, Robert D. Wiecha, was operating covertly for the CIA base at the mission.[230] During the period that Sturgis was smuggling arms to Castro and cooperating with the consul, Wiecha was financially supporting Castro.

---

225 In his Sturgis deposition to the Rockefeller Commission, he mistakenly used the name "Clark Wollin."
226 Paul Bethel, *The Losers* (New York: Arlington House, 1969), p. 59.
227 *The President's Commission on CIA Activities*, Sturgis Deposition, April 3, 1975, pp. 38-39; NARA, RIF-178-10002-10238.
228 *The President's Commission on CIA Activities*, Sturgis Deposition, April 3, 1975, pp. 38-39; NARA, RIF-178-10002-10238.
229 One wonders if "William Patterson" might have been a pseudonym for a colleague of Wollam used in contacts with Sturgis for consular cover. One candidate for the real person would have been Robert Wiecha himself, but it could have been someone else working for the CIA base.
230 Tad Szulc, *Fidel: A Critical Portrait* (New York: William Morrow & Co., 1986), pp. 428.

According to the journalist Tad Szulc, "between October or November 1957 and the middle of 1958, the CIA delivered no less than fifty thousand dollars to a half dozen or more key members of the 26 July Movement in Santiago." Szulc found this level of support surprising:

> The amount was quite large, relative to what the movement itself was able to collect in Cuba. ... These funds were handled by Robert D. Wiecha, a CIA case officer attached to the United States consulate general under the cover of vice-consul, who served in Santiago from September 1957 to June 1959. The late Park Fields Wollam, who was consul general and was Wiecha's superior in Santiago, had told State Department colleagues at that time of the CIA role in dealing with the Castro organization.[231]

After Castro assumed power, Sturgis had allied himself with powerful anti-communist military commanders. As a result, the value of the intelligence he could provide became even more important.

Frank Belsito joined the CIA Havana Station in mid-1958. As previously discussed (Chapter Five), in his biography he recalled how at that time the Station was "not unsympathetic" toward Castro. He also remembered how that perspective had become reversed by the time Castro assumed power. Belsito described the mood in the CIA Station on the day that it happened:

> ...the Station's opposition to Castro led the new Chief of Station to say on that frenetic day of Castro's victory, 1 January 1959, that he was pleased to see that we were "all of one mind" in deploring a new dictatorship worse than Batista's, and potentially very antagonistic to the United States.[232]

The details of how the CIA Base at Santiago had financially supported Castro have never been declassified. Yet there were also people in high places at CIA HQS who had wanted to arm and finance Castro (further

---

231 Tad Szulc, *Fidel: A Critical Portrait* (New York: William Morrow & Co., 1986), pp. 427-429.
232 Frank, J. Belsito, *CIA: Cuba and the Caribbean—CIA Officer's Memoirs* (Reston VA: Ancient Mariner Press, 2002, pp. 44-46.

FRANK STURGIS AND THE FIRST PLOT...

discussed in Appendix Six). That was a course of action that CIA HQS quickly wanted to be forgotten.

Wiecha had tried and failed for quite some time to arrange a meeting with Castro. While Wiecha had failed, Sturgis had succeeded—he had enjoyed complete access to Castro. The question now became how to best leverage Sturgis' access to Castro and other top Cuban leaders. Now that Castro was in power, Sturgis would become important at a high level in the Cuban military. This situation could rightly have been expected to produce an intelligence windfall, one which might even shed light on the issue on everyone's mind in Washington—Castro and communism. On 5 January 1959, the CIA Santiago Base cabled CIA HQS with a general situation update that included news from Sturgis, following contact with him in Santiago. Sturgis reported that he was under the command of Raul Castro and was waiting for orders to begin training a thousand militia in the Santiago area.[233] That same day the CIA Base sent an "operational" cable to HQS that said the Base would "try to develop" Sturgis.[234]

The next day, 6 January, the CIA Base sent HQS the results of a lengthier discussion with Sturgis.[235] He had said that he was the "chief 26 July arms buyer in Miami," and that he had the "confidence of Fidel Castro and other top commanders." He said he was a "personal friend" of the new rebel air force commander, Pedro Luis Diaz Lanz. Lanz, Sturgis reported, wanted to make him an "unofficial civilian advisor to the general staff of the new army." That plan changed into something even more significant once Sturgis was transferred to Havana."[236]

The 6 January cable from the CIA Santiago Base discussed the continuing prospects for the development of Sturgis:

> Subject [Fiorini] willing to cooperate 100 percent supplying info. [He is] Hesitant, however, to continue on and reveal all for fear of loss of [his] American citizenship. Known background [of] subject has made several trips to Sierras. ...Now circulating in good rebel circles. Possible

---
233 1/5/59, SACU 334 Priority to DIR CIA, NARA. RIF 104-10221-10033.
234 1/5/59, SACU 335 to DIR CIA, Operational REF SACU 334 CIA, 104-10221-10160.
235 1/6/59, SACU 337 to DIR CIA, Operational REF SACU 334 and SACU 335. 104-10221-10159.
236 *The President's Commission on CIA Activities*, Sturgis Deposition, April 3, 1975, p. 53; NARA, RIF-1781000210238.

he may lose value to rebels but [we] believe it worthwhile Kubark [CIA] *endorse his staying on.*[237] [Emphasis added]

The CIA HQS response to the Santiago Base proposal came on 13 January. Noting that Sturgis' smuggling activities were under investigation by the FBI, CIA HQS replied that the Santiago "*Base should deal with Subject [Fiorini] under strict consular cover* and not make any commitments which might later be construed as ODYOKE [U.S. Government] approval of his activities."[238] [Emphasis added]

The above cables establish these facts: 1) Sturgis was under CIA "development" by the CIA Base in Santiago from the moment of Castro's victory; 2) the Base asked HQS for permission to continue the relationship; and, 3) HQS approved the Base continuing to "deal with Fiorini" under consular cover. These facts undermine the veracity of the CIA's claim that Sturgis "never worked for the Agency."[239] That disclaimer shows how the Agency has made use of semantic nuances to twist the truth about what was really going on with Sturgis. His CIA 201 file, 242256, was opened on 1 December 1958.[240] From the moment of Castro's victory, the CIA made a decision to use Sturgis—even if very carefully. He did not have to complete a job application to "work" with them and for them.

In an interview with Michael Canfield, Sturgis explained that he never wanted to be an "employee" of the Agency.[241] Being an employee, he reasoned, meant that when the orders came, "you have to do it." Sturgis said that when he received orders from the Agency, "I made my own decision." If you're not an employee, you can "tell them to go to hell."

Sturgis' relationship with the Agency deepened when his training work for Raul Castro ended abruptly. Sturgis was quickly transferred to Havana to work for the Cuban air force. He reportedly "fell out" with Raul Castro over the inclusion of army officers into Raul's training program.[242] On 11 January, as he was preparing to leave Santiago, Sturgis

---

237 1/6/59, SACU 337 to DIR CIA, Operational REF SACU 334 and SACU 335. 104-10221-10159.
238 1/13/59, DIR 08002 to Santiago de Cuba, REF SACU 337. RIF 104-10221-10032
239 For example see 3/31/76, CIA Memorandum, Subject: Geraldine Isabella Shamma, with AKAs. JFK 1993.07.02.10:57:45:030800.
240 12/1/58, Personality (201) file Request on Frank Anthony Sturgis. RIF 104-10221-10162.
241 Michael Canfield and Alan J. Weberman, *Coup D'état in America* (New York: The Third Press, 1975), pp. 234-235.
242 01/30/59, SACU 364 (IN-13918) to DIR CIA. See CIA Various Sanitized Materials on Sturgis, JFK 1993.08.05.10:15:50:750052.

met a final time with the consul, Park Wollam. Sturgis told the Rockefeller Commission that Wollam "suggested I contact Colonel Nichols and a Major Van Horn" at the U.S. Embassy in Havana.[243]

STURGIS AND THE AMERICAN EMBASSY IN HAVANA

After arriving in Havana, Sturgis began working closely with the American military Air Attaché, Colonel Erikson S. Nichols. Sturgis' testimony to the Rockefeller Commission gave these details about how it started:

> Well, I met Colonel Nichols in various places… and he wanted to assist me from the American Government, and so forth, and again he offered me money, and I said no. And I told him that I would assist him as much as possible, that I felt the communists were trying to make contact with Fidel Castro. And I told him I had photographs that I had taken in the mountains of these people, and I gave him copies.[244]

Shortly before the revolution culminated, Sturgis had discovered that two of the men he knew in Castro's arms procurement effort were "Venezuelan communists." Sturgis said that when they had visited Castro, "they had secret documents with them in code."[245]

The various locations where Sturgis met Nichols included the U.S. Embassy and the Cuban air force base next to army headquarters at Camp Columbia (the name would soon be changed to Camp Libertad). Nichols had helped reconfigure the precise plan to insert Sturgis into the Cuban military. Pedro Diaz Lanz' original idea to make Sturgis an "unofficial civilian advisor" was changed to a much more powerful appointment—the chief of Air Force Security and Intelligence.[246] He held this position until his flight from Cuba six months later.

---

243   *The President's Commission on CIA Activities*, Sturgis Deposition, April 3, 1975, p. 50; NARA, RIF-178-10002-10238. It is possible that Colonel Nichols was a pseudonym for a Colonel "Severs." See RIF 104-10167-10057.
244   *The President's Commission on CIA Activities*, Sturgis Deposition, April 3, 1975, p. 52; NARA, RIF-178-10002-10238.
245   *The President's Commission on CIA Activities*, Sturgis Deposition, April 3, 1975, p. 44; NARA, RIF-178-10002-10238.
246   *The President's Commission on CIA Activities*, Sturgis Deposition, April 3, 1975, p. 53; NARA, RIF-178-10002-10238.

Sturgis' biography, written by his nephew Jim Hunt, states that Colonel Nichols and Major Van Horn were both "embedded CIA agents at the U. S. Embassy in Havana."[247] The CIA has denied that either of them "ever worked for the Agency."[248] Whether or not they were undercover agents for the CIA, they certainly worked closely with the CIA Station in Havana. They even received a letter of commendation from CIA Deputy Director Cabell for their help in CIA exfiltration work.[249] After Van Horn left Havana, he was assigned to an air attaché office in Miami that worked directly with the CIA's JMWAVE Station there. At that time, Sturgis was also in Miami and collaborating with Bernard Barker, who was assigned to William Kent's PW (Psychological Warfare) branch at the JMWAVE Station. Barker had been working in the Cuban police back when he was recruited by the CIA in April 1959.[250] It was for their help in Barker's exfiltration from Cuba in January 1960 that Colonel Nichols and Major Van Horn received their letters of commendation from CIA Deputy Director Cabell.

In his deposition to the Rockefeller Commission, Sturgis identified two other people that he had worked with at the American Embassy in Cuba in 1959 and that he believed were CIA: "Jack Stewart," and "Jim Knowles."[251] These men did work for the CIA. The latter's true name was James Noel and he was the chief of the CIA Station in Havana. Jack Stewart was a CIA officer who had been working at the Havana Station since 1955.

Sturgis also said that he had done some work for Dave Phillips. In his 1980 deposition during *Hunt V. Webberman*, Phillips was asked if Sturgis had worked with him in Havana during the period 1959 to 1961. Phillips replied that Sturgis "never worked with me" and "never worked for the CIA." This exchange then followed:

---

247 Jim Hunt and Bob Risch, **Warrior** (New York: Tom Doherty Associates Book, 2011), p. 307 and p. 310.
248 For example see 3/31/76, CIA Memorandum, Subject: Geraldine Isabella Shamma, with AKAs. JFK 1993.07.02.10:57:45:030800.
249 1/21/60 CIA DIR 11455 to Havana, RE "Action being recommended REF being handled by letter from General Cabell. RIF 104-10237-10088.
250 HSCA notes from Bernard Barker's CIA 201 file. RIF 180-10145-10362.
251 *The President's Commission on CIA Activities*, Sturgis Deposition, April 3, 1975, p. 4; NARA, RIF-178-10002-10238.

Q: In a previous deposition Mr. Sturgis indicated he had done some work for you in Cuba in the early 1960s. Do you know why he would make that statement?

A: It's quite possible because of the fact that during the period which led up to the Bay of Pigs, I was responsible for all sorts of different operations which involved a group perhaps. And if the group were large, perhaps someone would say, uh-huh, this is Phillips I worked for.

Q: On a one-on-one basis?

A: I might very well. I met a lot of people. I certainly don't recall.[252]

Later in his deposition Phillips said again, "It's my belief that Mr. Sturgis never worked for the CIA." Phillips was acutely aware of the official Agency position:

On many, many, occasions when I was CIA chief of Latin American operations at CIA, it was my job to answer inquiries from Congress, and people like that, about the affiliation of Sturgis—was he also Frank Fiorini? Yes—his connections with the Agency. And I recall quite vividly that the answer always came up that he had not been on our payroll.[253]

It seems fair to point out that were Phillips to hold his breath for a reading of the names of all the people who had worked with the CIA and who were "not on our payroll," he would have soon expired.

It is, of course, true that Sturgis had not been on the CIA payroll. On a CIA 1975 routing sheet about Sturgis, a senior CIA security officer scrawled what was just as true: "I am convinced from my review of the files that Sturgis never worked for us—*he did associate with people who did work for us.*[254] [Emphasis added] It is possible, as Sturgis claimed, that one of those people was Jack Stewart. This is the same Jack Stewart to

---

252 9/30/80, U.S. District Court, Southern District of Florida, Phillips deposition in Weberman V. Hunt. pp. 14-15.
253 9/30/80, U.S. District Court, Southern District of Florida, Phillips deposition in Weberman V. Hunt. p. 22.
254 6/10/75, Routing Sheet re Sturgis, Jerry G. Brown, Deputy Chief, Security and Analysis Group. JFK 1993.08.07.09:30:56:930063.

whom Tepedino had tried to introduce Cubela to in January or February 1959 (discussed in Chapter Three).[255]

Jack Stewart also also used the pseudonym "Andrew F. Merton." In October 1958, Stewart had a source who regularly visited the Segundo Frente Nacional del Escambray (SFNE) rebels and two other groups operating in the Sierra Escambray Mountains. The informant was Max Lesnick, a senior SNFE leader operating in Havana. Lesnick was providing exactly the same kind of order of battle intelligence on these Sierra Escambray forces to Stewart in Havana as Sturgis was providing about the forces with Castro in the Sierra Maestra to Wollam and Wiecha in Santiago: movements of forces, names of officers and their units, strength of forces, and weapons. Lesnick's report said that there was a well organized group of 1,400 men, mostly students from the Autentico party (including Emilio Ochoa); there were 100 students from Echevarria's DR under the command of Cubela; and there were 164 men under Che Guevara.[256]

Sturgis told the Rockefeller Commission that Colonel Nichols had asked him to "recruit military people." In the course of recruiting them, Sturgis learned that some were already in contact with Jack Stewart and Jim Knowles. Sturgis said that the Cubans understood that both of these men worked for the CIA.[257] Sturgis testified that the officers he recruited included the Chief of the Cuban Air Force, Pedro Diaz Lanz, and his brother, Marcos Diaz Lanz, Inspector General of the Cuban Air Force.[258] Pedro had worked for three years as a U.S. commercial airline pilot during Batista's reign and just before joining Castro's revolution had worked as a pilot for the Freeport Sulphur Company.[259]

At the airbase, Nichols attended some of the meetings with the Diaz Lanz brothers and other military officers such as Ricardo Lorrie and Huber Matos. A former rice grower, Matos joined Castro's forces in the Si-

---

255 6/28/65, CIA Contact Report, Subject: Meeting of Carlos Tepedino and Harold P. Swenson, RIF 104-10183-10424.
256 10/30/58, CIA Field Information Report, by Andrew F. Merton (Jack Stewart), Subject: Segundo Frente Nacional del Escambray. RIF 104-10220-10001.
257 *The President's Commission on CIA Activities*, Sturgis Deposition, 3 April 1975, p. 50; NARA, RIF-178-10002-10238.
258 *The President's Commission on CIA Activities*, Sturgis Deposition, 3 April 1975, pp. 69-70; NARA, RIF-178-10002-10238.
259 6/15/59, CIA Information Report, OO-B-3,132,514, Subject: Chief of Air Force's Confidential Statements About Need for Counter-revolution Against Castro; NARA, JFK files, CIA microfilm, Pedro Diaz Lanz, K6.

erra Maestra in March 1957, and brought the rebels their first significant reinforcements at that time.[260] Matos was now the military commander of Camaguey Province in eastern Cuba. Lorrie had flown supply planes for Castro, along with Sturgis and Lanz.

Pedro Lanz' CIA cryptonym was QDBIAS, Marcos Lanz' was QD-CHAR, and Ricardo Lorrie's was QDCOVE. These three cryptonyms appear in the handwritten "26 July Dissidents/Miami" chart constructed during Marcos Diaz Lanz' 28-29 July 1959 debrief, immediately after his exfiltration to Tampa.[261]

Sturgis testified that the focus of the airbase meetings was "communist infiltration into the military forces."[262] He stated that his recruitment targets also included the Army commander, Camilo Cienfuegos, and the National Chief of Police, Efigenio Ameijeiras.[263] Ameijeiras, according to Hugh Thomas' massive work on Cuba, had no ideology of his own and he blindly followed Castro, whose forces he had served with his two brothers who had died in the revolutionary war.[264] In June 1959, the CIA Station in Havana reported that Castro wished to "rid himself" of Ameijeiras as the chief of police.[265] Cienfuegos had been one of Castro's commanders from early in the revolution and, next to Castro himself, was "the man best loved in Cuba...the most loyal of the loyal."[266] Sturgis told the Rockefeller Commission that on one occasion when he met with Ameijeiras and Cienfuegos in the Capri Hotel, Cienfuegos gave him enough information to break into Army headquarters. Afterward, "I broke into their files," Sturgis continued, "and I did photograph and steal documents."[267] He testified that he turned over the documents from Cienfuegos' office to Colonel Nichols.

---

260   Hugh Thomas, *Cuba, The Pursuit of Freedom* (New York: Harper and Rowe, 1971) p. 934.
261   7/31/59, MFR, Subject: Debriefing of Jose Marcos Diaz y Lanz, 28-29 July 1959, Tampa Florida—hand-written chart attached to the typed debriefing. RIF 104-10167-10137
262   *The President's Commission on CIA Activities*, Sturgis Deposition, 3 April 1975, p. 55; NARA, RIF-1781000210238.
263   Sturgis badly garbled has name as "Commander Almejara."
264   Hugh Thomas, *Cuba, The Pursuit of Freedom* (New York: Harper and Rowe, 1971) p. 1071, p. 1321, and p. 1453.
265   6/13/59, CIA Havana station to HQ, IN 30622; NARA, JFK files, CIA microfilm, Marcos Diaz Lanz, Vol/Folder 4/6/J. He was expelled from the communist party in 1966.
266   Hugh Thomas, *Cuba, The Pursuit of Freedom* (New York: Harper and Rowe, 1971) p. 1247.
267   *The President's Commission on CIA Activities*, Sturgis Deposition, 3 April 1975, p. 80; NARA, RIF-178-10002-10238.

Sturgis had other important personal contacts, some in Castro's personal entourage. Among them was Castro's private secretary, Juan Orta, whom Sturgis testified was "a friend of mine."[268] Orta became involved with people connected to U.S. gambling interests in the Havana casinos. On 7 January 1959, Castro had closed the casinos and banned gambling. However, he reopened them for tourists and foreigners at the end of February.[269] Sturgis became involved because Castro asked him to act as a liaison to the casinos. Orta's gambling connections, however, did not result from any official duties but from the use of his privileged position as Castro's private secretary. CIA records indicate that Orta eventually wound up in a financial bind and took "kick-back payments from the gambling interests."[270] A year later Santo Trafficante recruited Orta to play a key role in a failed CIA plot to assassinate Castro using poison pills.[271]

STURGIS AT CAMP LIBERTAD

The idea to assassinate Castro sprang up shortly after he assumed power in January 1959. By early February, Sturgis was discussing assassination plots with some of Castro's top commanders—who wanted to get rid of him "because of the communist teachings that Fidel was forcing on the military."[272] In a news interview Sturgis explained his plan:

> I would arrange an important conference at Campo Libertad (Camp Liberty, the combined army-air force base and headquarters formerly known as Camp Columbia). All the top commanders would come to the base in their jeeps and cars. I was going to station gunners on the

---

268 Amazingly, the questioner cut off Sturgis who might have revealed more about this important person. See *The President's Commission on CIA Activities*, Sturgis Deposition, 3 April 1975, p. 66; NARA, RIF-1781000210238.
269 NARA, JFK files, CIA 1967 Inspector General's Report on Plotting Against Castro, May 23, 1967, JFK 1993.06.30.16:55:05:370140, p. 19.
270 NARA, JFK files, CIA 1992 Historical Review Program, D-000149; Memorandum for the Director of Central Intelligence, Subject: Johnny Roselli, December 9, 1970, p. 2; document ID # 1993.06.28.18:21:05:560310.
271 Ibid; NARA, JFK files, CIA 1967 Inspector General's Report on Plotting Against Castro, May 23, 1967, RIF-1993.06.30.16:55:05:370140, pp. 27-28.
272 *The President's Commission on CIA Activities*, Sturgis Deposition, 3 April 1975, p. 68 and p. 71A; NARA, RIF-178-10002-10238.

FRANK STURGIS AND THE FIRST PLOT...

roofs to set up crossfire. I would have wiped out Fidel, his brother Raul and all the top pro-communist military commanders in 30 seconds.[273]

In his interview with Michael Canfield, Sturgis said he did not trust many of the people in the U.S. Embassy, but he did trust Colonel Nichols and began talking to him about the plot in February 1959.[274]

Sturgis told the Rockefeller Commission that among the things he discussed with Colonel Nichols was "the attempted assassination on two occasions of Fidel Castro and all the top commanders that used to come to the Air Force base."[275] In the Canfield interview, Sturgis said he had asked Colonel Nichols for "the green light" to proceed:

> I said, look, pass the word upstairs. You want me to kill Fidel, I'll kill him, if he comes to the Air Force base. I'm here in control of the military police, of the security of all the Air Force bases in Cuba. I said, if he comes here with Che, if he comes there with all the top military people, with many of the ministers, I can kill him in two minutes. If you people want it done, I will do it with my people... and I'll just wipe the whole three jeeps right out, just taking two minutes to do it.[276]

Sturgis told Nichols he could do it "inside" too—meaning, inside a building. In a newspaper interview, Sturgis explained that if Castro and the other officers were not going to arrive at the same time, the best plan was to plant a bomb in the second-floor conference room at Air Force headquarters, and wait until they were all assembled around the conference table:

> The whole idea was to kill all of them at once. Unfortunately, if some of the anti-communist officers were in there at the same time, they would have to go too. The

---

273 4/21/75, Paul Meskil, "I Plotted Castro's Death, Sturgis Says," *The Miami Herald*, (New York News Service).
274 Michael Canfield and Alan J. Weberman, *Coup D'état in America* (New York: The Third Press, 1975), p. 258.
275 *The President's Commission on CIA Activities*, Sturgis Deposition, April 3, 1975, p. 73; NARA, RIF-178-10002-10238.
276 Michael Canfield and Alan J. Weberman, *Coup D'état in America* (New York: The Third Press, 1975), p. 258.

lives of some of the anti-communists commanders would have to be sacrificed in order to get Castro and his crew.[277]

A third option was to plant a bomb in Castro's office. Sturgis said he had access to the prime minister's office and could count on Castro's secretary, Juan Orta, whom he had recruited to work with the embassy.

One cannot help but wonder what went through Colonel Nichols' mind as he listened to Sturgis lay out the details of these different ways to assassinate Castro. Nichols "told me to stand by," Sturgis said, "don't do anything, stand by, stall." Sturgis told the Rockefeller Commission that he set up the exercise anyway:

> Yes sir, I would say the first attempt – and I set it up as an exercise, that if I was to get the green light – which I did not anticipate that I would, because there is such a thing as getting a green light – and there is another thing about doing something without a green light, in other words they do it – but don't get caught – but I did set it up as an exercise, stationed at the gate with me there, with men stationed on the rooftops on the homes – my excuse was for the protection of the entourage. Fidel and the military commanders he had with him. He had a hometown bunch with him when they came to the Air Force base, even with General Bayo.[278] And I felt that if I would get the nod to assassinate them, I could do it within 30 seconds, hightail it and everything.[279]

Sturgis did not follow through, he said, because he never got the green light from the Embassy.[280] By March 1959, there had already been two abortive plots to assassinate Castro.

---

277 4/21/75, Paul Meskil, "I Plotted Castro's Death, Sturgis Says," **The Miami Herald**, (New York News Service).

278 Alberto Bayo was an old Cuban-Spaniard who had fought in the Spanish Civil War, had led guerrilla expeditions in Castille, and later fought in the Moroccan Wars. Che Guevara spoke of Bayo as "el maestro" on matters of guerrilla warfare. See Hugh Thomas, **Cuba, The Pursuit of Freedom** (New York: Harper and Rowe, 1971) pp. 876-877, and p. 882. According to Marcos Lanz, Bayo was training guerrillas on Tarara Beach in Havana in 1959. 7/31/59, CIA Memo, RE 7/28/59 Marcos Lanz debrief. RIF 104-10167-10137

279 This portion of Sturgis' 3 April 1975 deposition is as quoted in Jim Hunt and Bob Risch, **Warrior** (New York: Tom Doherty Associates Book, 2011), p. 212.

280 **The President's Commission on CIA Activities**, Sturgis Deposition, 3 April 1975, p. 76; NARA, RIF-178-10002-10238.

FRANK STURGIS AND THE FIRST PLOT...

At a 26 March 1959 NSC meeting, CIA chief Allen Dulles said he was "disturbed" by the recent events in Cuba.[281] The minutes of the meeting indicate Dulles reported this to President Eisenhower:

> The Castro regime is now moving toward dictatorship and Castro already has practically all power in his own hands. ...Cuban business interests are very concerned about his actions, his wild statements continue, and *there is even some talk of a counter-coup.* ...communists were now operating openly and legally in Cuba. [Emphasis added]

Dulles added that communists had penetrated the armed forces. It is likely that he had learned through CIA channels about the coup plotting going on among Castro's military commanders. Eisenhower remembers this meeting with Dulles as the first occasion when the CIA reported that Castro's regime was becoming "an outright dictatorship."[282]

---

281 FRUS, 1958-1960, volume VI, Cuba, document #266, Memorandum of Discussion at the 400th Meeting of the National Security Council, Washington, March 26, 1959; pp. 440-442.
282 Eisenhower, ***The White House Years: Waging Peace, 1956-1961*** (New York: Doubleday, 1965), p. 523; see also FRUS, 1958-1960, volume VI, Cuba, document #266, Memorandum of Discussion at the 400th Meeting of the National Security Council, Washington, March 26, 1959; note 2, p. 440.

CHAPTER EIGHT:
JUNE COBB AND NARCOTICS TRAFFICKERS IN ECUADOR AND COLOMBIA

In Chapter Six we discussed Catherine Taaffe's January (18-24) 1959 trip to Cuba. We also closely examined her campaign in February to get the FBI, Assistant U.S. Attorney Marvin Segal, the Justice Department's Racket Squad, and the Immigration and Naturalization Service (INS) to investigate the identities of "dope peddlers and smugglers" in Cuba's Military Intelligence Service (SIM). There was another American woman with a narcotics agenda who went to Cuba at this time. In February 1959 a woman from Oklahoma, Viola June Cobb, traveled to Havana and tried to persuade the new Cuban government to join a cooperative effort with Peru, Bolivia, and Colombia to combat the cocaine problem.[283] The U.S. agencies with which Cobb had "connections" in-

---

283 3/30/62, June Cobb testimony during a hearing of the Senate Subcommittee to Investigate the Administration of the Internal Security Act and other Internal Security Laws, p. 5; RIF 104-10218-10384.

cluded the CIA and the Federal Bureau of Narcotics (FBN).[284] In this chapter, it will become evident that June Cobb had been involved in heroin and cocaine trafficking in Latin America since about 1949. A list of the principal documents from which this story is derived is provided below.

When researching the men and women of the CIA it is not uncommon to find that more than one character belongs to a single person in real life. Operational circumstances may require a single individual to actually play more than one character in the flesh, perhaps with the use of disguises. The circumstances may require only that different pseudonyms are used in documents that belong to the same person. For many years researchers have suspected that one or both of these circumstances might have been that case in the story of June Cobb. The Cobb story is very complicated and her CIA 201 file remains secret. To reach sound judgments about multiple identities in her case will take more time and we will need a lot more information. Many more Freedom of Information Act (FOIA) requests (some are currently under review) will be necessary. This volume does not purport to solve this task in the case of June Cobb. Rather, the intent is to frame the issues and share information with the research community about what has been found so far.

In Chapters Five and Six we began to peel back the layers that surround the Catherine Taaffe story. In this and the next two chapters, we will begin the process of doing so for Viola June Cobb. The full bibliographic citation material for the documents used in these three chapters will be located in the notes. There are several principal documents we will be using. There is June Cobb's June 1960 security interview with the CIA, along with the questionnaire she completed before the interview; we will refer to it in the text as her "June 1960 CIA interview," sometimes as her "CIA interview," and sometimes as the "Ralph True interview," as Ralph True was the interviewer. There is Cobb's March 1962 testimony to the U.S. Senate Subcommittee on Internal Security; we will refer to it in the text as the "Senate Subcommittee interview," her "subcommittee testimony, or the "Sourwine interview."

---

284   George H. Gaffney, FBN Deputy Commissioner, interview with Douglas Valentine, *The Strength of the Wolf: The Secret History of America's War on Drugs* (New York: Verso, 2004), p. 495.

JUNE COBB AND NARCOTICS TRAFFICKERS IN ECUADOR...

There are summary memoranda of Cobb's May 1960 interviews with a CIA recruiter using the pseudonym Harry Hermsdorf; we will refer to these as the "Hermsdorf interviews" or her "account to Hermsdorf." There is an August 1962 article in ***Parade*** magazine about Cobb written by Jack Anderson titled, *Meet June Cobb—She's A Soldier of Fortune*; in the text we will refer to this as the "Anderson interview" or "Anderson article." There is an informative 2008 book on narcotics trafficking and gambling in Cuba by Eduardo Saenz Rovner; in the text it will be referred to as the "Rovner account" or "Rovner's book." There are several Federal Bureau of Narcotics (FBN) records in the National Archives; in the text we will refer to these as "FBN records." There is also a lengthy hand-written critique by June Cobb about one of the above Hermsdorf memos that Cobb sent to the author of this work in 1995; we will refer to it as the "Cobb letter to Newman."

UNIVERSITY OF OKLAHOMA (1946-1947)

Viola June Cobb was born on 24 August 1927, in Ponca City, Oklahoma, to Jasper E. and Jesse Lois Cobb. She grew up with two brothers, Jasper E. Jr., and Arthur Tom. She graduated from Ponca City High School in 1944, and entered the University of Oklahoma in the fall of that year. "I spent my entire idyllic childhood in Ponca City," Cobb wrote in her 1995 letter to the present author, "My parents' home was my home through two years at the University of Oklahoma and the other year before I went off to Mexico City."[285] In early 1946, Cobb was attending the University of Oklahoma, and that is where the trouble begins in her CIA files. Cobb was allegedly *not* recruited by the CIA until May 1960 after being approached by a CIA man in Havana using the pseudonym Harry Hermsdorf. Hermsdorf's various memoranda about Cobb's history conflict sharply with other accounts.

In Harry Hermsdorf's description of his May 1960 interview of June Cobb in Havana, we find what appears to be, for the most part, an inaccurate story about Cobb's history, beginning with her attendance at the

---

285   1995 June Cobb letter to John Newman.

University of Oklahoma and her visit to Mexico. According to Hermsdorf, Cobb told him that after she *graduated* from the university she left Oklahoma and took a job with the Southeastern Oil Company in Texas.[286]

Cobb gave a different account to the CIA Security Office, the Senate Subcommittee, Jack Anderson, and to me. She said that she only attended one or two classes the entire time she was at the University of Oklahoma.[287] In her letter to me she said she had not graduated, and that she was "politely suspended" after her sophomore year.[288] In fact, Cobb did *just about everything but attend real classes.* She was involved in university organizations connected with politics, acting, media, French language, and the Civil Air Patrol—all at the same time. In her CIA security interview, Cobb said she had attended lectures with a group of intellectuals called "Student Citizens for Democratic Action," and that she had worked on the staff of the campus radio station, WMAD.[289] In her CIA pre-interview questionnaire, Cobb indicated that she had been an active member of the drama and French clubs on campus, and that she had also been in the Civil Air Patrol—"Specially commissioned 2nd Lt. of [the] squadron at the University of Oklahoma."[290]

When Cobb's CIA interviewer, Ralph True, noticed the questionnaire item regarding her participation in the Civil Air Patrol, he asked Cobb if she was "flying presently" (i.e. 1960). She responded, "*No. I never did fly. I was very dumb.*" [Emphasis added] She added that she had to get special permission to be in this unit and served with the adjutant.[291] Many years later, in August 1978, Dan Hardway, an investigator for the House Select Committee on Assassinations (HSCA), was interviewing David Atlee Phillips when the subject of June Cobb came up.

---

286 6/1/60, Memorandum by Harry Hermsdorf for Chief, Western Hemisphere Division, Subject: Contingent Recruitment of Viola June Cobb, RIF 104-10111-10148.
287 6/29/60, Attachment to CIA Memorandum to Chief, Security Support Division, Subject: June Cobb, Tape 1, p. 9. RIF 104-10174-10078
288 1995 June Cobb letter to John Newman.
289 6/29/60, Attachment to CIA Memorandum to Chief, Security Support Division, Subject: June Cobb, Tape 1, pp. 12-13. RIF 104-10174-10078
290 6/6/60, Questionnaire for Cobb's 6/3/60 CIA Security Office Interview, captioned "June Cobb Sharp," pp. 3-4. Note: A terrible copy is located at RIF 104-10111-10145; a clearer copy is located in the microfilm HSCA Segregated CIA Collection, Reel 10, Folder E.
291 6/29/60, Attachment to CIA Memorandum to Chief, Security Support Division, Subject: June Cobb, Tape 1, p. 9. RIF 104-10174-10078

JUNE COBB AND NARCOTICS TRAFFICKERS IN ECUADOR...

Phillips had worked with June Cobb during her assignment in Mexico City (1962-1963). When Hardway asked Phillips about Cobb in 1978, Phillips gave this extraordinary response: "Blond, flew an airplane; track record for hitting a lot of beds in Cuba; had a twin sister who was an aviator."[292] We will have more to say about Phillips' response in later volumes. For now I will leave it with this: it is unlikely that June Cobb had a twin sister, or a sister, or could fly. As a result of her father's remarriage in 1955, she gained two step-sisters, Joann and Lillian.

Cobb said nothing about going to Texas to work for the Southeastern Oil Company in her CIA interview, in her Senate Subcommittee interview, or in her letter to me. She told me that her association with that company began and ended during her subsequent visit to Mexico City.[293] She told the Senate Subcommittee that after she left the university in 1946 she took a job as "chief of continuity" for the radio station WBBZ in Ponce, Oklahoma.[294]

In January 1954, Cobb's mother, Jessie Lois Sharp, passed away. In August 1955 her father married Lucy Ann Bowles, whose husband had also died the previous year. The house June had grown up in at 1100 South Main disappeared in the remarriage, as Jasper Cobb moved into the Bowles home at 710 North Sunset. Cobb's letter to me recalls her reaction to this situation:

> In 1957, for about two months, when a visit to my recently remarried father became strained, I rented a room in a house in Newkirk and worked as a secretary of the county <u>attorney</u>, [Emphasis Cobb's] whom I had known since 1947 when I spent six month as staff reporter for two newspapers—the *Ponca City News* and the *Blackwell Journal Tribune*.[295]

Back in 1947, when Cobb left her "idyllic" life in Ponca City, her father, mother, brothers, and the house she grew up in were still in place as they had always been.

---

292 8/23/78, HSCA Interview of David Atlee Phillips by Dan Hardway, 180-10142-10078.
293 1995 June Cobb letter to John Newman.
294 3/30/62, June Cobb testimony during a hearing of the Senate Subcommittee to Investigate the Administration of the Internal Security Act and other Internal Security Laws, p. 2; RIF 104-10218-10384.
295 1995 June Cobb letter to John Newman.

WHERE ANGELS TREAD LIGHTLY

MEXICO (1947-1948)

In the 18 August 1962 edition of *Parade Magazine*, columnist Jack Anderson wrote this:

> June's adventures began when she became bored with her studies at the University of Oklahoma and sought a more glamorous curriculum at the University of Mexico. ...But in Mexico City she found romance. She fell in love with a dashing Colombian of good but poor family. He and a brother, in need of funds to support their expensive tastes, decided to find a hidden spot in the Jungle and start growing poppies for the opium trade. June and the brothers settled in the hot, steamy Ecuadorian jungle.[296]

The brothers were Rafael and Tomas Herran Olozaga, and Rafael became June's lover and fiancé. Rafael, a chemist, and Tomas, a pilot, were twin brothers from elite families in Bogota and Medellin. Their great-great-grandfather, Tomas Cipriano de Mosquera, and great-grandfather, Pedro Alcantara Herran, had served as presidents of Colombia during the nineteenth century.[297]

Between Oklahoma and Mexico City, the Hermsdorf account places Cobb in Texas and three Latin America countries, all while working for an oil company:

> She attended the University of Oklahoma and upon *graduating* left her native state for a job with the Southeastern Oil Company in Texas. This company was doing exploratory work in Colombia, Ecuador, and Peru. She traveled with the management staff and while in Colombia fell in love with the son of a wealthy Colombian family. They became engaged but his family would never sanction the marriage claiming the son would be marrying beneath his status. The romance continued on through the years

---

296 8/18/62, Jack Anderson, "Meet June Cobb: She's A Soldier of Fortune," Parade Magazine, *Washington Post*.
297 Eduardo Saenz Rovner, *The Cuban Connection: Drug Trafficking, Smuggling, and Gambling in Cuba from the 1920s to the Revolution* (Chapel Hill: North Carolina Press, 2008), p. 1.

JUNE COBB AND NARCOTICS TRAFFICKERS IN ECUADOR...

and *he followed her* to Peru, Ecuador, and Mexico. For a time she attended extension classes at the University of Mexico with him.[298] [Emphasis added]

This version of events is so off base that one is left wondering whether responsibility for the inaccuracies was Hermsdorf's or Cobb's or both.

The accounts that Cobb gave to the CIA, the Senate Subcommittee, Jack Anderson, and the present author oppose the above Hermsdorf version in three important ways. First, Cobb did not attend university classes in Oklahoma *or* in Mexico City, in spite of registering at both schools. Second, Cobb did not fall in love with Rafael in Colombia; rather, that took place in Mexico City. Third, the Mexico City episode occurred right after Cobb left Oklahoma, not well forward "through the years." Cobb told me that Hermsdorf's account was "Absolutely off the wall untrue," and that she met her fiancé, "Rafa," in Mexico City.[299] Rafael did not follow Cobb all over the Americas; rather, the opposite was true. It was not the Herran family who spurned Cobb; rather, it was her fiancé Rafael.

The subject of the Herran family's narcotics trafficking is missing from Hermsdorf's account. The only mention of narcotics is this:

According to June Cobb, because of family frustrations, she discovered one day that her fiancé was taking cocaine. June Cobb was then rather hazy about what happened but it seems that her fiancé's family came up from Colombia, sent the daughter home, and broke the relationship for once and for all.[300]

Yet Cobb claims that she told Hermsdorf about the narcotics story and was surprised that he had not told her CIA interviewer about it.[301]

Cobb told Jack Anderson that because the brothers were sampling their narcotics, she became a Narcotics Bureau informant to break her "sweetheart" of the habit. When Anderson checked with the Narcotics

---

298 6/1/60, Memorandum by Harry Hermsdorf for Chief, Western Hemisphere Division, Subject: Contingent Recruitment of Viola June Cobb, RIF 104-10111-10148.
299 1995 June Cobb letter to John Newman.
300 6/1/60 Memorandum by Harry Hermsdorf for Chief, Western Hemisphere Division, Subject: Contingent Recruitment of Viola June Cobb, RIF 104-10111-10148.
301 6/29/60, Attachment to CIA Memorandum to Chief, Security Support Division, Subject: June Cobb [Interview], Tape 2, p.1. RIF 104-10174-10078

WHERE ANGELS TREAD LIGHTLY

Bureau they told him Cobb found "her lover's affection straying and, in a fit of jealousy, squealed on him."[302] The CIA security interview of Cobb also indicated that she told the FBN about the twins' drug trafficking. However, what she said in that interview about their drug business and her work for the FBN was deceptive, and in several instances, false—especially on the most important part of the story in 1956, when she directly participated in trafficking heroin in Cuba and Mexico. We will examine that episode closely in the next chapter.

Cobb had another connection in Mexico City besides Rafael Herran. In 1962, the Subcommittee Chief Counsel, J. G. Sourwine, asked June Cobb to outline her employment history. After mentioning two small jobs in Oklahoma City, Cobb turned to Mexico City:

> In Mexico City *I was employed as public relations contact, you might say, for Southeastern Oil Co.*, which at the same time subsidized a little magazine called *Modern Mexico*, which as a matter of fact I have brought here, a little goodwill publication, that was founded 30 or 40 years ago by the Mexican Chamber of Commerce in the United States, and *at that time was published by an independent publisher*. I was representative, kind of editorial representative of this magazine, by way of the oil company, which subsidized the magazine to a certain extent.[303] [Emphasis added]

Sourwine wanted to know more about the magazine and its publisher. He asked Cobb to confirm that the edition of *Modern Mexico* that she had brought with her to the Subcommittee was actually published by the Mexican Chamber of Commerce in the United States. Cobb replied that the magazine had *not been at that time*. She explained, "At this time *it had been bought by a private publisher*, but it still had their endorsement." [Emphasis added] Looking at the edition of the magazine Cobb had provided to the Subcommittee, Sourwine realized something was amiss, and asked, "This issue is August 1948?" "Yes," she answered, "that was 1947 and 1948."

---
302 8/18/62, Jack Anderson, "Meet June Cobb: She's A Soldier of Fortune," Parade Magazine, **Washington Post**.
303 3/30/62 June Cobb testimony during a hearing of the Senate Subcommittee to Investigate the Administration of the Internal Security Act and other Internal Security Laws, p. 2; RIF 104-10218-10384.

Sourwine then asked Cobb a second time for the dates of her employment in Mexico City, and her answer again was 1947 and 1948. Sourwine invited Cobb to repeat for the record that she had *not* worked for the magazine while it was published by the Mexican Chamber of Commerce in the United States. Cobb reiterated what she had said before with a single word: "No."

Sourwine bored in: "Well," he observed, looking at the August 1948 edition of the magazine in his hands, "This issue purports to have been published by the Mexican Chamber of Commerce in the United States!" Cobb refused to yield. "I think not," she shot back. But it was no use. Sourwine was unrelenting: "It says 'A publication of the Mexican Chamber of Commerce of the United States.'" Cobb, unable to trump that simple fact, gave in and answered, "Perhaps it still was."

In this exchange with Sourwine, Cobb appears to have been avoiding the continuing role of the Mexican Chamber of Commerce in the U.S. with the magazine. Then she let slip, "I thought at that time it had changed, had been bought by Mr. Wallach. Perhaps not." We should not rule out the possibility that Mr. Wallach had bought *Modern Mexico* by that time (1948). If so, this would suggest that that the continued use of the name "Mexican Chamber of Commerce in the U.S." might have been an arrangement—to obscure the name of the real publisher for whom Mr. Wallach purchased the magazine with money from the oil company.[304]

Cobb told me that her "association" with Southeastern Oil ended in 1948, "when Rafa took me to the train and I left Mexico and spent a few months with my parents before taking the ship to South America to join the twins."[305] While riding on that train the man sitting across from her was Alfred Aufhauser. He noticed that she had a copy of the *Modern Mexico* magazine with her. It was the August 1948 edition, the same one she brought for

---

[304] The present author has indeed located a "Southeastern Oil Company, Inc." However, it was established in 1952 and incorporated in Dothan, Alabama, and was not operating in Texas in 1947. In addition, the present author has discovered that the publication named "Southeastern Oil Review"—founded in 1926—had "a loyal following of explorationists, operators, drillers, landmen and landowners in South Louisiana, Mississippi, Alabama and Florida." Recall that Cobb allegedly told Hermsdorf in 1960 that her Southeastern Oil Company in Texas was doing exploratory work in 1947 in Colombia, Ecuador, and Peru.
[305] 1995 June Cobb letter to John Newman.

her testimony before the Senate Subcommittee in 1962.[306] In her 1960 CIA security interview, Cobb said Aufhauser told her that he had been advertising in the magazine for some time but had never seen a copy of it. When she asked him if he wanted to see it, he said yes, and so she gave it to him. With that, they "made friends," she said, "and he has been very gracious to me."

ECUADOR, COLOMBIA, AND NEW YORK CITY (1949-1953)

After Mexico City in 1948, June Cobb returned for a "few" months to Oklahoma, probably sometime during the period June-August 1949. She told the Senate Subcommittee that she had done some temporary work for the Continental Oil Company—the company her father worked for.[307] After that, she was off to the jungles with the Herran brothers for a year—six months in Ecuador and six more in Colombia. In her letter to me, Cobb recalled, "In 1949 I took a ship from New Orleans to Ecuador to join him and his brother and go into the Amazon River Basin."[308] They went there, she told Jack Anderson, to grow opium:

> [Rafael], who had studied medicine, figured he could extract the drug from the poppy seeds. June and the brothers settled in the hot, steamy Ecuadorian jungle. With the help of Indian natives, they cleared and planted a few poppy patches, built a crude opium processing plant, and settled back to wait for the grim harvest.[309]

When Sourwine asked Cobb about this trip to South America, she offered a more opaque version of her story. Cobb said she had gone to Ecuador with her fiancé on a six month "expedition."[310]

---

306 3/30/62, June Cobb testimony during a hearing of the Senate Subcommittee to Investigate the Administration of the Internal Security Act and other Internal Security Laws, p. 2; RIF 104-10218-10384.
307 3/30/62, June Cobb testimony during a hearing of the Senate Subcommittee to Investigate the Administration of the Internal Security Act and other Internal Security Laws, p. 3; RIF 104-10218-10384.
308 1995 June Cobb letter to John Newman.
309 8/18/62, Jack Anderson, "Meet June Cobb: She's A Soldier of Fortune," Parade Magazine, *Washington Post.*
310 3/30/62 June Cobb testimony during a hearing of the Senate Subcommittee to Investigate the Administration of the Internal Security Act and other Internal Security Laws, p. 3; RIF 104-10218-10384.

The Ecuador-Colombia trip must have taken place approximately during the period August 1949-July 1950. It is possible that Cobb learned of the brothers' narcotics plans when she was with Rafael in Mexico. There is no doubt that she knew about it after she arrived in Ecuador. In her CIA interview she said, "I knew about it all along, and his mother did and his sister did." The brothers' plans to plant in the jungle did not work, she added, "It was a perfectly crazy idea. And then they came out and tried to plant opium in Colombia in the mountains."[311] There they soon switched to cultivating coca leaves. It seems fair to point out that what Cobb was doing was just as crazy. Why would a twenty two-year-old American woman allow herself to become associated with narcotics traffickers in South America for an entire year? Unless Cobb was an FBN informant, becoming Rafael's fiancé showed an extraordinary lack of judgment.

Cobb said that she went back to Oklahoma for ten months through the winter of 1951. Her year-long difficult experience in the jungles of South America did not dampen her desire to be with Raphael, so she went back to Colombia where the brothers had switched to making cocaine. While there, Cobb contracted tropical fever and was hospitalized. She returned to New York in approximately mid-1951 where she was again hospitalized, under the care of Dr. I. Snapper.[312] It was at this time in New York City that Cobb began to share, from "time to time," a "little studio apartment" with Monina, the youngest sister of the Herran brothers. After her husband died, Monina and her daughter had moved to the U.S.[313]

By 1952, Cobb was doing editing work for Dr. Snapper in New York. At some point, according to her CIA records, she became intimate with him. At the end of 1952, Cobb followed Snapper to the Cook County Hospital in Chicago. He became the Director of Medicine and she became his secretary.[314] Cobb left Chicago in February 1953 to visit her

---

311 6/29/60, Attachment to CIA Memorandum to Chief, Security Support Division, Subject: June Cobb, Tape 2, pp. 3-4. RIF 104-10174-10078
312 3/30/62, June Cobb testimony during a hearing of the Senate Subcommittee to Investigate the Administration of the Internal Security Act and other Internal Security Laws, p. 3; RIF 104-10218-10384.
313 1995 June Cobb letter to John Newman.
314 3/30/62, June Cobb testimony during a hearing of the Senate Subcommittee to Investigate the Administration of the Internal Security Act and other Internal Security Laws, p. 3; RIF 104-10218-10384.

father in Oklahoma. It was a short trip. In April, she went back to New York City and worked for just two weeks in the Editorial Department at Bantam Books filling in for someone who was away on a vacation. There followed more short duration fill-in jobs at places that she said were difficult to remember.

In April 1953, the "very gracious" Alfred Aufhauser reappeared in Cobb's life. He gave Cobb office space at 575 Madison Avenue to use however she pleased. There, she "invented" Intercontinental Counselors, a public relations firm for people visiting from Switzerland and Spain, but principally from South America. Cobb did translating and minor public relations work for clients recommended by the manager of the foreign department of the Waldorf Astoria—a Mr. Warren Broglie. She told her CIA interviewer that Broglie had since become a manager at a hotel in Mexico City.[315]

Cobb knew a lot more about Warren Broglie. She referred to him as a "Swiss boy." He managed hotels in strategic cities around the world. Later, in 1960, Cobb learned that Broglie had been the manager of the Hilton Hotel in Cairo, Egypt.[316] His Mexico City assignment was in 1962—at the very time that Cobb worked for the CIA Station there. Back when Broglie was referring foreigners to Cobb at the Waldorf Astoria in New York, around June-August in 1953, Cobb said she was living with "another friend" at 1192 Park Avenue.[317]

Obviously, Cobb was making almost no money from her fleeting jobs. In 1960, she explained to her CIA interviewer how she managed to live:

> I have a lot of wealthy friends. As I was telling Harry (Hermsdorf), no matter how I lived, I have some generous friends who know I don't work for money and say, June do you have any money? I say no. And they say, well here take this, you must be broke, take this money. Because they know I don't work for money, you know.

---

315 3/30/62, June Cobb testimony during a hearing of the Senate Subcommittee to Investigate the Administration of the Internal Security Act and other Internal Security Laws, p. 3; RIF 104-10218-10384.
316 6/29/60, Attachment to CIA Memorandum to Chief, Security Support Division, Subject: June Cobb [Interview], Tape 1, p. 21. RIF 104-10174-10078
317 6/29/60, Attachment to CIA Memorandum to Chief, Security Support Division, Subject: June Cobb [Interview], Tape 1, p. 20. RIF 104-10174-10078

JUNE COBB AND NARCOTICS TRAFFICKERS IN ECUADOR...

> Well, anyway, this is what my friends—are the type who pay hospital bills for me and give me tickets if I want to go to Mexico, or whatever, you know.[318]

Cobb's counseling company only lasted "for the summer" of 1953. In September of that year, she worked for World Films for three weeks. In her CIA interview with Ralph True, Cobb tried to make light of the many short jobs she had and how difficult they were to remember. She offered her CIA security interviewer this interesting metaphorical explanation: "This is going to be very hard to remember these places. It will be like some *Don Juan trying to remember his girlfriends*, you know."[319] [Emphasis added] With that statement she was putting herself in the role of Don Juan.

As we will see, however, it was June Cobb who felt like the forgotten girlfriend of Don Juan. And it had been about a year since Cobb had been with her Don Juan—Rafael. Not surprisingly, in October 1953 she went back to Colombia to see him.[320]

---

318 6/29/60, Attachment to CIA Memorandum to Chief, Security Support Division, Subject: June Cobb [Interview], Tape 1, p. 19. RIF 104-10174-10078
319 6/29/60, Attachment to CIA Memorandum to Chief, Security Support Division, Subject: June Cobb [Interview], Tape 1, p. 18. RIF 104-10174-10078
320 6/29/60, Attachment to CIA Memorandum to Chief, Security Support Division, Subject: June Cobb [Interview], Tape 1, pp. 20-24. RIF 104-10174-10078

CHAPTER NINE:

JUNE COBB, RAFAEL HERRAN AND THE GIRLFRIENDS OF DON JUAN

Before resuming the June Cobb narcotics story we will briefly examine how the narcotics problem developed in Cuba before, during, and after WWII. We will also review some of the missions that the Federal Bureau of Narcotics (FBN) sent to Cuba before and after Castro came to power.

NARCOTICS TRAFFICKING IN CUBA

The 1939 Nazi-Soviet Pact of 23 August 1939 cleared the way for the outbreak of WWII in Europe. As the war approached in 1940, communists in American unions supported the pact between Hitler and Stalin. In this "national security" context, American labor union leader Jimmy Hoffa emerged to take on the communists. He played a key role in the American Federation of Labor (AFL)-Teamster purge of the "reds" in a rival union in Minneapolis, which had defected to the Congress of Industrial Organizations (CIO). According to Peter Dale Scott, this event catapulted Hoffa toward national union leadership and "launched him into closer ties with mob elements in Chicago" and "elsewhere."[321] Hoffa persuaded several Teamster-associated mob leaders who had casino investments in Cuba to cooperate with the CIA. These mobsters included Russell Bufalino, Salvatore Granello, John La-Rocca, Gabriel Mannarino, and James Plumeri.

When WWII broke out, American mobster Meyer Lansky was the go-between for Charles "Lucky" Luciano and U.S. intelligence for matters concerning anti-Nazi counterintelligence operations, including the 1943 landing in Sicily.[322] During the war, the Office of Strategic Services (OSS—the forerunner of the CIA) used secret narcotics trafficking routes to insert their agents behind enemy lines. They were able to recruit drug smugglers and use the money to finance the liberation of these countries.[323]

According to Peter Dale Scott, the CIA collaborated with the underworld after the war to suppress communism in France and Sicily.[324] Douglas Valentine's study of American narcotics trafficking also describes how this dark trail continued after the war ended:

> America's spymasters would never sever the drug-smuggling connections they established during the war, nor could the FBN exert any influence over the situation. On the contrary, the FBN assumed a collateral role in narcotics-related espionage activities that was antithetical to its mandate.[325]

---

321 Peter Dale Scott, *Deep Politics and the Death of JFK* (Berkley: University of California Press, paperback ed., 1996), p. 173.
322 Jack Colhoun, *Gangsterismo: The United States, Cuba, and the Mafia: 1933-1966* (New York: O/R Books, 2013), pp. 10-11.
323 Douglas Valentine, *The Strength of the Wolf: The Secret history of America's War on Drugs* (New York: Verso, 2004), p. 46.
324 Peter Dale Scott, *Deep Politics II: Essays on Oswald, Mexico, and Cuba* (Skokie, Illinois: Green Archive Publications, 1995), p. 61.
325 Douglas Valentine, *The Strength of the Wolf: The Secret history of America's War on Drugs* (New York: Verso, 2004), p. 47.

JUNE COBB, RAFAEL HERRAN AND THE GIRLFRIENDS OF DON JUAN

After the war, as the underworld reorganized their drug smuggling and distribution operations, Santo Trafficante and Meyer Lansky acquired total control of the important drug route into the U.S. from Marseilles, France, through Cuba, and then to Tampa, Florida.[326] According to Peter Dale Scott, top international drug couriers like Giuseppe de Giorgio, traveling between Italy, France, the United States, Canada, and Cuba, helped turn Havana's casinos into "way-stations" for the transfer of large heroin shipments from Europe to the U.S.[327]

The roots of the gangster regime in Cuba had spawned from the early 1930s alliance between mobster Meyer Lansky and Cuban dictator Fulgencia Batista. Batista, and many corrupt political leaders and senior officers in the Cuban army and police, grew rich from their share of the profits from the casinos and nightclubs run by American gangsters. Those roots grew deeper in the 1940s as Lansky brought in "Lucky" Luciano and other mob bosses. Together, they used their infrastructure in Cuba to develop the island into a heroin distribution hub for the Western Hemisphere.[328]

In addition to the gambling rackets in Havana, there had long been a cocaine problem in Cuba. In 1945 the airline Aerovias Q began operating out of military airports. It was established so that the Mafia in Cuba would have its own airline to bring cocaine from Colombia and would not have to pass through local Cuban customs. The following account is taken from Enrique Cirules' examination of Mafia influence in Cuba:

> From early on, Aerovias Q made a weekly flight: Havana—Camaguey—Barrranquilla—Bogota. A powerful laboratory in Medellin produced "powder" destined for Santo Trafficante Sr.; but everything indicates that this intrigue involved the participation of certain figures of the Autentico party in Camaguey who were associated with pharmaceutical laboratories or drugstores. The Ca-

---

326 Douglas Valentine, *The Strength of the Wolf: The Secret history of America's War on Drugs* (New York: Verso, 2004), pp. 53-56.
327 Peter Dale Scott, *Deep Politics and the Death of JFK* (Berkley: University of California Press, paperback ed., 1996), pp. 180-181; see also Scott, *Deep Politics II: Essays on Oswald, Mexico, and Cuba* (Skokie, Illinois: Green Archive Publications, 1995), p. 59.
328 As cited in Jack Colhoun, *Gangsterismo: The United States, Cuba, and the Mafia: 1933-1966* (New York: O/R Books, 2013), p. 13.

maguey contacts were an essential link in the drug trade. The cocaine did not always reach the Cuban capital in a direct manner. Rather, the shipments were transferred at the Camaguey airport.[329]

By the late 1950s American narcotics agents viewed Cuba as the most important transit point in narcotics coming into the U.S., as trafficking was administered by organized, disciplined criminal gangs.[330]

In October 1946 Luciano organized a summit of mob bosses in Havana to reorganize the rackets under his command.[331] FBN agents learned about the summit from the transcripts of Luciano's phone calls from Cuba to major American cities.[332] Although Luciano's ability to physically remain in Cuba was thwarted by FBN Commissioner Harry J. Anslinger, Naval intelligence and FBN sources suggest that the CIA and military intelligence, working through the FBN, were still employing Luciano in the early 1950s. By this time, the CIA had well established international drug smuggling operations, including what FBN agent George White called the "CIA Avenue"—the Agency's protected drug route from the Far East, through Cuba, to the Mafia in New York.[333]

A substantial percentage of the "skim" from the mob's casinos in Havana went not only to pay off political officials but also to line the pockets of the military and police. Banks were used for laundering drug money and the under-the-table casino skim through a network of front companies. This was the perfect financial infrastructure that enabled Lansky, Trafficante, and other U.S. mobsters to build their criminal empire in Cuba. Protecting this infrastructure was, by itself, a lucrative business. One army general, Rafael Salas Canizarea, reportedly made $730,000 a month in "gambling protection income."[334] June Cobb told her CIA

---

329 As quoted by T. J. English, *Havana Nocturne: How the Mob Owned Cuba and Then Lost the Revolution* (New York: Harper, 2008), pp. 106-107.
330 Eduardo Saenz Rovner, *The Cuban Connection: Drug Trafficking, Smuggling, and Gambling in Cuba from the 1920s to the Revolution* (Chapel Hill: North Carolina Press, 2008), p. 122.
331 Douglas Valentine, *The Strength of the Wolf: The Secret history of America's War on Drugs* (New York: Verso, 2004), p. 66.
332 Jack Colhoun, *Gangsterismo: The United States, Cuba, and the Mafia: 1933-1966* (New York: O/R Books, 2013), pp. 11-12.
333 Douglas Valentine, *The Strength of the Wolf: The Secret history of America's War on Drugs* (New York: Verso, 2004), pp. 138-140.
334 T. J. English, *Havana Nocturne: How the Mob Owned Cuba and Then Lost the Revolution* (New York: Harper, 2008), see pp. 129-130 and p. 166.

interviewer that the Herran brothers had constantly been ripped off. They had learned the hard way that buying protection was a necessary part of narcotics trafficking.[335]

The arrangement between the American mobsters and Batista's regime allowed for most of the domestic Cuban cocaine trafficking money to go to the Cuban elite, such as the Italo-Cuban Amadeo Barletta Barletta and the Uruguayan Amletto Battisti y Lora. Drug arrests in Cuba were made, for the most part, against lower class people for marijuana possession. The Cuban police and judiciary did little to stop cocaine trafficking in and through Cuba.[336] Santo Trafficante once led his attorney, Frank Ragano, through the Sans Souci nightclub men's room and then through a locked door into a back room:

> ...in the rear was a wall filled with safety-deposit boxes. Inside the boxes, the rich Cubans kept their private stashes of cocaine. The mob boss explained to his attorney that the Cuban elite used cocaine as a way to sustain their prodigious nightlife.[337]

The Servicio de Inteligencia Militar (SIM) was the organization with the inside information, high-level political connections, and the muscle to help regulate the gambling and narcotics rackets. SIM was perfectly positioned to decide which establishments, boats, and airplanes would be searched and which would not, and to regulate the "skim" from the profits funneled to Batista and his associates.

FBN MISSIONS TO CUBA (1953 AND 1959)

In early 1953, the FBN Commissioner, Harry J. Anslinger, sent FBN agent George White to quietly investigate the Batista regime's handling of the narcotics trade. Douglas Valentine explains what he found there:

---

335   6/29/60, Attachment to CIA Memorandum to Chief, Security Support Division, Subject: June Cobb [Interview], Tape 2, p. 6, RIF 104-10174-10078.
336   Eduardo Saenz Rovner, *The Cuban Connection: Drug Trafficking, Smuggling, and Gambling in Cuba from the 1920s to the Revolution* (Chapel Hill: North Carolina Press, 2008), p. 122.
337   T. J. English, *Havana Nocturne: How the Mob Owned Cuba and Then Lost the Revolution* (New York: Harper, 2008), p. 208.

> White must have learned through his underworld connections what everyone else knew: that the Cuban dictator had renewed the illicit contracts that Meyer Lansky had entered into with his predecessors, and that narcotics were pouring through Cuba, into America, as never before. But the U.S. customs service had jurisdiction in Cuba, and FBN agents were not supposed to operate there unless the Treasury Attaché asked for their help...
> ...This situation left Batista in charge of drug law enforcement in Cuba, and as a result the only drug smugglers the FBN was allowed to pursue were those who hadn't paid Batista his required tariff.[338]

Sal Vizzini, an FBN agent who worked many undercover Cuban cases in the 1950s, told Valentine that Batista's tariff was 50 percent of the profits.

The U.S. Federal Bureau of Narcotics (FBN) was not immune from the hope that Fidel Castro might turn out to be a "good guy" after the revolution. Charles Siragusa recalls that the FBN thought that the overthrow of Batista "was our chance to chase the die-hard corps of dope peddlers from Cuba, an operating base less than 100 miles from our shores."

> For years we had tried without success to force the corrupt police of Batista's regime to clamp down on what was becoming the world's largest single source of cocaine. While much of this terrifying drug was finding its way to the Middle East and thence to the capitals of Europe, a substantial amount was coming to the United States, where once cocaine had become almost extinct.[339]

The dramatic increase in narcotics traffic between the United States and Cuba led FBN Commissioner Anslinger to dispatch an agent to Cuba quickly after Castro's victory.

Siragusa was given the assignment and he arranged to meet an informant, Juan Gonzalez, on 12 January 1959, at the Havana Hilton. Gonzalez took Siragusa to the Presidential Palace and, on the way, explained

---
338 Douglas Valentine, *The Strength of the Wolf: The Secret history of America's War on Drugs* (New York: Verso, 2004), pp. 130-131.
339 Charles Siragusa, The Trail of the Poppy: Behind the Mask of the Mafia (New Jersey: Prentice-Hall, 1966 ed.), p. 185.

that Siragusa would not be meeting Castro but would meet his "secretary," Senor De La Carrera.[340] Carrera said that Cuba was gratified that the U.S. wanted to rid the Western Hemisphere and Cuba of "cocaine racketeers." Siragusa gave Carrera an 18-page report critical of the Batista police and complained that "in many of the cases we had developed in Cuba, the cocaine peddlers had gotten only a day or two in jail—or had never been brought to trial."[341] Siragusa told Carrera that U.S. co-operation with Cuba required evidence of good faith first:

> Cuba must eject from the island as undesirables the American gangsters strongly suspected of being involved in dope smuggling behind the façade of their gambling operations, which had been legal under Batista. These men had strong ties with the Mafia, as did a number of French Corsican mobsters we also wished thrown out of the country. …Chasing them out would reduce the cocaine traffic into Cuba and help put a stop to the flow of the deadly drug into the United States.[342]

At the end of the meeting, Carrera promised that prompt and vigorous police action would be taken in Cuba. Afterward Siragusa mailed Carrera several dossiers to follow up on but De La Carrera never replied.[343] He, like many other people in the early days of the new regime, had quickly been replaced.

COBB IN COLOMBIA AGAIN (SEPTEMBER-OCTOBER, 1953)

At the end of September 1953, June Cobb went to work as a secretary for a refinery that the Foster Wheeler construction company was building in Colombia. When she told the Senate Subcommittee about the trip,

---

340 Charles Siragusa, The Trail of the Poppy: Behind the Mask of the Mafia (New Jersey: Prentice-Hall, 1966 ed.), p. 189.
341 Charles Siragusa, The Trail of the Poppy: Behind the Mask of the Mafia (New Jersey: Prentice-Hall, 1966 ed.), pp. 190-192.
342 Charles Siragusa, The Trail of the Poppy: Behind the Mask of the Mafia (New Jersey: Prentice-Hall, 1966 ed.), p. 185.
343 Charles Siragusa, The Trail of the Poppy: Behind the Mask of the Mafia (New Jersey: Prentice-Hall, 1966 ed.), p. 185.

she neglected to mention that her motive in taking this job had been to create an opportunity to make contact with her cocaine trafficking fiancé, Rafael Herran Olozaga.[344] This is what she told the CIA about it:

> I went to Colombia. I went down in the employ of a construction company, a very big one. *I wanted to go see my fiancé.* They were building a refinery in the jungle, and *I needed to go down to see my fiancé,* and *I couldn't go directly to his home town.* And so, I went over to this construction company and persuaded them to send me down. It's one of the truly biggest companies in the world.[345] [Emphasis added]

Besides her ardent need to see her fiancé, Cobb said nothing about his heroin and cocaine trafficking. Her CIA interviewer did not ask her why she could not go directly to his home town, as she had previously done.

On the other hand, Cobb once again mentioned the Don Juan simile to her CIA interviewer:

> I stayed about *three weeks* in the employ of the company and *then that's it. It's like a girlfriend of Don Juan.* …I was sick all the time I was there. I was an emotional—under *great emotional stress* while I was there and by mutual agreement I only stayed three weeks.[346] [Emphasis added]

In her testimony to the Senate Subcommittee about this trip, Cobb said nothing about how badly it had ended.

It seems probable that Cobb's emotional stress resulted from a failure to see her fiancé, Rafael Herran. This time in Cobb's use of the simile, Rafael was Don Juan and she was just one of his many girlfriends. Cobb did not tell her CIA interviewer whether or not she saw Rafael on this trip and her interviewer did not ask her about it. For the moment, she said only that she left in late October and returned to New York City. Once there, she went to work for "some lawyer" at 513 Madison Avenue.[347]

---

344 3/30/62, June Cobb testimony during a hearing of the Senate Subcommittee to Investigate the Administration of the Internal Security Act and other Internal Security Laws, p. 3; RIF 104-10218-10384.
345 6/29/60, Attachment to CIA Memorandum to Chief, Security Support Division, Subject: June Cobb [Interview], Tape 1, p. 24. RIF 104-10174-10078
346 6/29/60, Attachment to CIA Memorandum to Chief, Security Support Division, Subject: June Cobb [Interview], Tape 1, pp. 24-25. RIF 104-10174-10078
347 6/29/60, Attachment to CIA Memorandum to Chief, Security Support Division, Subject: June Cobb [Interview], Tape 1, p. 25. RIF 104-10174-10078

JUNE COBB, RAFAEL HERRAN AND THE GIRLFRIENDS OF DON JUAN

MEXICO CITY (APRIL-JUNE, 1954)

Cobb worked for the lawyer for one month and then spent Christmas with her father in Oklahoma. It was about that time that her mother, Jesse Lois, passed away. June returned to New York City in January 1954. She worked for Samuel Golden Motion Pictures and that job also ended quickly. She told the CIA that she did not work for a couple of months after that stint, and that she went to Mexico at the end of April or the first of May "*to visit my fiancé, who didn't arrive.*" [Emphasis added] She said she had waited for him for six weeks, much of it in the hospital, due to a relapse of her tropical fever. She said nothing about why Rafael failed to show up.[348]

Cobb told the CIA that she returned to New York City in the fall of 1954. There, after yet another relapse, she stayed in Northrup Hospital until Christmas. Cobb said that she then worked as a secretary for Specialty Papers of Dayton, Ohio, from January to mid-February 1955. "I was still convalescing," she explained, "you might say so…"[349] The pattern of Cobb's very short jobs and very long hospitalizations is remarkable. Just as striking is her non-stop effort to see Rafael Herran.

FLORIDA AND COLOMBIA (JUNE-DECEMBER, 1955)

In her CIA interview, Cobb's memory after February 1955 was convoluted in the extreme:

> Now, after that—I remember that February 14 *I was … in Colombia, but I didn't go.* So, it was from February until the next few months—until April, I didn't work. My father was sending me money, so I didn't work. *I don't recall what I did at all during that period.* Maybe once or twice someone who was referred by the Waldorf came … *I can't recall really.* No job at any rate. Now, then in –until June, that's

---
348 6/29/60, Attachment to CIA Memorandum to Chief, Security Support Division, Subject: June Cobb [Interview], Tape 1, pp. 26-27. RIF 104-10174-10078.
349 6/29/60, Attachment to CIA Memorandum to Chief, Security Support Division, Subject: June Cobb [Interview], Tape 1, pp. 27-28. RIF 104-10174-10078.

> right—from then until June. In June I went to Florida with a girl friend of mine, to Coral Gables, Florida. She had a house there, and I stayed with her until—*This is all fouled up what I'm saying because I was waiting for a cable, or I had my suitcase packed, you know, or something.* Anyway, I stayed with her until August of that year. [Emphasis added]

It seems likely that Cobb had her suitcase packed in anticipation for a cable from Rafael asking her to meet him in Colombia or Cuba.

Cobb's interviewer asked for the name of the girl friend in whose house she was staying. She replied:

> Mrs. Lee Barth. She lived in the same building as I did in New York. ...And she invited me down to Florida *which was close to Rafael.* ...she was going to Florida to look for a house, and she thought I could spend the summer with her. And, then, *I went to Colombia in the fall* of that year. That was just for a week or two. I know I didn't stay much longer because I came—in October of the same year, I was back in New York City.[350] [Emphasis added]

When asked if her fall 1955 visit to Colombia was to see her fiancé, Cobb answered evasively and quickly changed the subject:

> Well, all my trips to Colombia were always visits. I mean that one time I persuaded the construction company to send me was to visit Rafael just the same. I was back in October, and I worked for BBDO. I guess I started working for them in November or so. It's a big advertising agency, you know. It's one of the biggest. Batten, Barton, Durston and Osborne, in New York City. Then, from there, I went back to Florida.

The point is that her intentions to see Rafael did not come to fruition for years. As we saw during the September 1953 construction company trip, Cobb never said that she actually had succeeded in seeing Rafael. The same was true for her short fall 1955 trip to Colombia; although she

---

350 6/29/60, Attachment to CIA Memorandum to Chief, Security Support Division, Subject: June Cobb [Interview], Tape 1, pp. 28-29. RIF 104-10174-10078.

had intended to see Rafael, once again, she never said that she actually succeeded in doing so.

Cobb's return to New York in October 1955 and job with BBDO, once again, was very short-lived. She was back in Miami by December 1955, where she worked for Jackson Memorial Hospital for two weeks and then for just one week for an attorney.[351] In January 1956, Cobb went back to Cuba, *again*.

CUBA AND COLOMBIA (JANUARY-MAY, 1956)

Cobb said she had gone to Cuba because *she missed Rafael*. As she told CIA security about the visit she paused several times, seemingly struggling with her emotions and confusion about the sequence of events:

> True: Was that in January 1956? Cobb: Yes. *I missed Rafael.* He began … So, *he didn't come* and so …
> True: You went to Havana to meet him?
> Cobb: Yes, to meet him, and *he didn't come.* So, then, I went over to Key West to wait for him to arrive in Cuba, and I worked in Key West for the Key Wester Hotel as secretary to the manager for a few weeks. Then, after that, I went to—a few days or a couple of weeks before I worked for the Key Wester Hotel, I worked for a restaurant as a waitress, an Italian restaurant named Luigi's, and then for the Key Wester Hotel. And *Rafael never came to Cuba.* So, I left Key West and went back to Miami to my girl friend's house in Coral Gables. It was by now May of that year—no, was it 1955?[352] [Emphasis added]

Of course, it was not 1955. It was 1956. Just like Cobb's trips to Colombia and Mexico in 1953, 1954, and 1955—when her "Rafa" never came—it happened again in 1956. The "girlfriend of Don Juan" had struck out

---

351 6/29/60, Attachment to CIA Memorandum to Chief, Security Support Division, Subject: June Cobb [Interview], Tape 1, pp. 29-30. RIF 104-10174-10078.
352 6/29/60, Attachment to CIA Memorandum to Chief, Security Support Division, Subject: June Cobb [Interview], Tape 1, pp. 30-31. RIF 104-10174-10078.

yet again. For the moment, Cobb gave up. "I went back to Miami," she told the CIA. "I hardly remember myself."

COLOMBIA, CUBA, AND MEXICO (MAY-DECEMBER, 1956)

The final chapter in June Cobb's ten-year relationship with Rafael Herran Olozaga took place between May and December of 1956. Strangely enough, it began with a surprise: news from Rafael. It came in the form of a telegram from his brother, Tomas, who had come to Havana to collect Cobb and take her to Colombia "because Rafael was *sick*":

> And so, I went over to Havana from Miami, and from Havana to Colombia with the brother. And for a couple of months I was unemployed. And, finally, Rafael became *absolutely insane*, so I moved out of his brother's house into a hotel where I was living—*at that time I was hoping that it would go away, you know, that he would get well*. So I wanted to stay, so I worked—I taught the sixth grade at a school—the American School in Medellin, Colombia. And I also taught at the Colombian-American Culture Center—English. Until October. In October I came to Cuba with Rafael and his twin.[353]

Still, Cobb uttered not one word about narcotics trafficking. It is interesting that Ralph True did not ask for a clarification for what Cobb meant by *sick* and why this sickness would, after all the years of separation and waiting, justify a trip to Rafael's home town of Medellin, Colombia.

It also seems strange that Ralph True did not ask Cobb why she and the twins went to Cuba. Perhaps it was because she had yet to mention the subject of narcotics trafficking. True asked her only for a clarification of the word *twin*—asking in an unintelligent way, "The brother?" After a simple "Yes," affirming that the twin was the brother, the rest of Cobb's response was cleverly designed to avoid the incredible story of *what* she and the brothers were doing in Cuba and Mexico during the last months of 1956:

---

353 6/29/60, Attachment to CIA Memorandum to Chief, Security Support Division, Subject: June Cobb [Interview], Tape 1, pp. 31-32. RIF 104-10174-10078.

JUNE COBB, RAFAEL HERRAN AND THE GIRLFRIENDS OF DON JUAN

> Yes. In October—I have traveled I think fully. *We* went from Cuba to Mexico, back to Cuba, and then December of 1956 I came back to my girl friend in Coral Gables. And, from there I went back to Key West for two months—January and February of 1957 I was in Key West. I was visiting *my* … From there, I went to see my father in Oklahoma, in March of 1957 or February I guess— or March. When is Lincoln's birthday—Abraham Lincoln's—in February, right? OK from March—in March and April I worked as secretary to the County Judge—the county attorney …[354]

In a few mottled utterances, Cobb had raced though seven months of her life, asked her interviewer if Lincoln's birthday was in February, and then turned to small jobs in Oklahoma. The interview meandered through more small jobs in Oklahoma and then on to her activities in New York City. There she had been an editorial assistant for *MD Medical News Magazine* from September 1957 until August 1958, was subsequently unemployed for five months, and then began doing work for the Cuban revolution in 1959.[355]

At that point "Tape 1" of the CIA interview ends. The transcript of "Tape 2" begins some time after the interview resumed, so a part is missing from the record. The discussion in progress may have been about Cobb's friend in Key West. In her 1995 letter to me, she said it was "Monina."[356] Cobb now steered the interview to her February 1959 trip to Cuba to "present the project to the Ministry of Public Health about cocaine addiction."[357] Her interviewer took the bait and asked, "What gave you the idea to do this?"

That was the moment that Cobb was waiting for. She had been holding back the narcotics story, waiting for the subject of her February 1959 trip to Cuba to come up in the interview. Her response was lucid:

---

[354] 6/29/60, Attachment to CIA Memorandum to Chief, Security Support Division, Subject: June Cobb [Interview], Tape 1, p. 32. RIF 104-10174-10078.
[355] 6/29/60, Attachment to CIA Memorandum to Chief, Security Support Division, Subject: June Cobb [Interview], Tape 1, pp. 33-34. RIF 104-10174-10078.
[356] 1995 June Cobb letter to John Newman.
[357] 6/29/60, Attachment to CIA Memorandum to Chief, Security Support Division, Subject: June Cobb [Interview], Tape 2, p. 1. RIF 104-10174-10078.

[It was] because my fiancé was a cocaine addict and because I knew a great deal about the problem. I didn't mention it because it wasn't a job. But I felt maybe Henry (Hermsdorf) had spoken to you more than he did. I supervised a little mission for the Narcotics Bureau while I was working with an American magazine in Ecuador. *It was* ...But anyway, so I knew quite a bit about the problem. So I went over and proposed a project.[358] [Emphasis added]

There is nothing in any of the Henry Hermsdorf memos on Cobb that mentions her work for the FBN.

Cobb's interviewer was not ready to talk about Cobb's February 1959 trip to Cuba. She had not entered the FBN in the employment history section of the questionnaire. True asked Cobb when her "little mission" for the FBN took place. Cobb said it had taken place in October 1958 and then an argument ensued:

Ralph: *You skipped over it with me*, and I don't

June: I didn't put it down as a job because it wasn't a job.

Ralph: Were you paid for it?

June: I was given—something at the end of the mission, yes.

Ralph: Well, then you were paid for your services?

June: Yes. That was the $200 .... Income tax.

Ralph: But you were paid for services for doing

June: I received $1,000 on one of those—the Treasury Department has a reward provision to grant a reward. I was given $1,000 as a reward.

Ralph: Alright. Now that was in *October 1958* while you were working for the *MD Medical News Magazine*, you performed this service for the—

June: Treasury Department.

Ralph: For what?

June: I believe for the Bureau of Narcotics and Treasury Department.

---

358 6/29/60, Attachment to CIA Memorandum to Chief, Security Support Division, Subject: June Cobb [Interview], Tape 2, p. 1. RIF 104-10174-10078.

JUNE COBB, RAFAEL HERRAN AND THE GIRLFRIENDS OF DON JUAN

>Ralph: Alright. We'll just call it a mission in October 1958.[359] [Emphasis added]

In this rather pointed back-and-forth discussion, Ralph True had apparently forgotten what Cobb had told him earlier about the place and dates of her work for the *MD Medical News Magazine*. Whether by accident or design, Cobb's "story" about her 1958 work for the FBN took a wrong fork in the road. Earlier in the interview she had told Ralph that her job with the magazine was at "30 East 60th" in New York, not in Ecuador, and it *began in September 1957 and ended in July or August in 1958*.[360] That is the same thing she told the Senate Subcommittee.[361] Therefore, it follows that even if she was supervising "a little mission" for the FBN while working with an American magazine in Ecuador in October 1958, that publication could not have been the *MD Medical News Magazine*.

Cobb failed to remind Ralph True about the real dates of her employment with the *MD Medical News Magazine*. Apparently, he did not notice this divergence. Ralph was interested in obtaining more details about her "October 1958" FBN mission in Ecuador. Cobb simply let him continue:

>Ralph: Now what were the instructions—now what did you agree to do for them again?
>June: For the Bureau of Narcotics. Well, in the beginning someone was fired.
>Ralph: Fired in October?
>June: Yes. Someone was fired in October. I visited the [Narcotics] Bureau in New Orleans, and I told them about my ex-fiancé's laboratory.
>Ralph: What got you to visit them?

With this information, Cobb's "story" moved even further down the wrong road. The New Orleans FBN visit she had just described to Ralph True had nothing to do with 1958 and nothing to do with Ecuador. We

---
359 6/29/60, Attachment to CIA Memorandum to Chief, Security Support Division, Subject: June Cobb [Interview], Tape 2, p. 2. RIF 104-10174-10078.
360 6/29/60, Attachment to CIA Memorandum to Chief, Security Support Division, Subject: June Cobb [Interview], Tape 1, pp. 33-34. RIF 104-10174-10078.
361 3/30/62, June Cobb testimony during a hearing of the Senate Subcommittee to Investigate the Administration of the Internal Security Act and other Internal Security Laws, p. 4; RIF 104-10218-10384.

will establish in Chapter Ten that Cobb's visit to the FBN in New Orleans took place either in late 1956 (possibly October) or in early 1957. It was after her visit in February that George Gaffney led the mission to destroy the Herran brothers' laboratory on their estate in Medellin.

At this point, Cobb probably realized that she was caught in a snare of her own making. The "story" had strayed too far from the truth. So, Cobb chose not to answer Ralph's question. Rather, she changed the subject with this enticing statement: "Well, I'll tell you the *whole story*.[362] [Emphasis added] This tactic worked and then a lengthy discussion followed about her association with the Herran brothers and narcotics trafficking to Cuba, with Cobb doing most of the talking.

However, Cobb did *not* tell her CIA interviewer the *whole* story. She never told him who was fired and why. She did not report that she had been working for the FBN *since 1957*—a detail that she let slip during her 1962 Senate Subcommittee testimony.[363] Further, she never answered True's question about why she had visited the FBN in New Orleans in October 1958.

In Chapter Ten, we will return to the movement of the Herran brothers and Cobb, from Colombia to Cuba in October 1956, and their subsequent arrest during a heroin seizure in Cuba in late December 1956. We will entertain the possibility that after the group's arrival in October 1956, Cobb made a clandestine trip to New Orleans to visit the FBN and then rejoined the twins in Cuba. If that was not when she visited the Big Easy, then it would have to have been after she was released from jail and sent to Mexico in January 1957. We will return to that event below.

Meanwhile, in her CIA interview, Cobb continued to tell Ralph True the "story." She said that Rafael and Tomas had been producing narcotics "for a number of years," and that Rafael had eventually become a cocaine addict. She admitted that she had known about it all along, and explained how she had accompanied the twin brothers to plant opium in the Ecuadorean jungles in 1948 and coca plants in the mountains of

---

362 6/29/60, Attachment to CIA Memorandum to Chief, Security Support Division, Subject: June Cobb [Interview], Tape 2, pp. 2-3. RIF 104-10174-10078.
363 3/30/62, June Cobb testimony during a hearing of the Senate Subcommittee to Investigate the Administration of the Internal Security Act and other Internal Security Laws, p. 26; RIF 104-10218-10384.

Colombia.³⁶⁴ Cobb said that eventually they were paid for some shipments of cocaine to doctors in Havana. She continued, conveying that Rafael's brother, Tomas, became exasperated with the situation and decided to change to the production of heroin:³⁶⁵

> So *the twin brother went to Ecuador and got ten kilos of opium from which you make one kilo of heroin*, one dollar stick. And Rafael was the chemist, you know, so he processed this. So they took that—*I went with them in October* [1956] *when they went and took it up to Cuba.* When they got there, they discovered the realities of life—that it was worth about $30,000. ...no, it wasn't even worth—they couldn't sell it in Cuba, that's right.

"They didn't have a dime," Cobb recalled. In desperation, the group approached their Havana doctor friends for money. One doctor, the director of a hospital in Havana, gave them $1,500.

Ralph True hardly interrupted Cobb's soliloquy at all. Cobb said, "*And the brother and I went to Mexico* to see if he could sell the stuff there. And, there too, he was only offered $6,000. Well, anyway, *so we came back to Cuba.*"³⁶⁶ [Emphasis added] If True did not already know this "story," he should have been surprised—even shocked. June Cobb had just told him she had been an accomplice to smuggling a kilo of heroin into Mexico to sell it.³⁶⁷ The Cuba-Mexico-Cuba portion of the story must have taken place between late October and mid-November. Cobb said that after she and Tomas returned to Cuba, Rafael went "out of his mind," and may have been noticed by the police by "going down to Chinatown trying to sell it or something." Cobb's extraordinary performance ended with this:

> At any rate, *I finally left Havana and went over to see my girlfriend in Coral Gables because the whole thing was a nightmare.* Rafael hated me, he hated his mother. And 24 hours after I was

---

364 6/29/60, Attachment to CIA Memorandum to Chief, Security Support Division, Subject: June Cobb, Tape 2, p. 3. RIF 104-10174-10078.
365 6/29/60, Attachment to CIA Memorandum to Chief, Security Support Division, Subject: June Cobb, Tape 2, p. 6. RIF 104-10174-10078.
366 6/29/60, Attachment to CIA Memorandum to Chief, Security Support Division, Subject: June Cobb, Tape 2, p. 7. RIF 104-10174-10078.
367 6/29/60, Attachment to CIA Memorandum to Chief, Security Support Division, Subject: June Cobb, Tape 1, p. 32. RIF 104-10174-10078.

> *there, my fiancé and his brother were arrested in Havana.* Rafael was able to free himself on the grounds that he was innocent, but his brother, the twin, was arrested because he had narcotics in his apartment. And the brother said that Rafael was innocent and didn't have anything to do with it. He thought that maybe there was somebody on the outside who could help him out. So when that happened, I was in Coral Gables and when I heard about it, I went down to see the sister of Rafael (Monina) to see what I could do.[368] [Emphasis added]

After the last sentence of this quote, the text of Cobb interview with Ralph True has the following insert in capital letters: "REST OF STORY CAN BE FOUND IN THE BUREAU OF NARCOTICS REPORT."[369]

We should marvel at Cobb's CIA interview with Ralph True. We should also wonder at all the questions True should have asked but didn't. This story of narcotics trafficking sets like a Rosetta Stone at the base of June Cobb's supposed 1960 entry to the Central Intelligence Agency. We will return to Cobb's "whole story" about narcotics in the next chapter—because of its importance to her caper with Castro in New York City in April 1959.

---

[368] 6/29/60, Attachment to CIA Memorandum to Chief, Security Support Division, Subject: June Cobb, Tape 2, p. 7. RIF 104-10174-10078.
[369] 6/29/60, Attachment to CIA Memorandum to Chief, Security Support Division, Subject: June Cobb, Tape 2, p. 7. RIF 104-10174-10078.

CHAPTER TEN:
JUNE COBB AND THE FEDERAL BUREAU OF NARCOTICS

As we noted previously, the U.S. customs service had jurisdiction in Cuba and FBN agents were not supposed to operate there unless the Treasury Attaché requested their help.[370] Indeed, the story in this chapter begins with the Treasury representative in Cuba. Nevertheless, this chapter ends with June Cobb and the Federal Bureau of Narcotics (FBN) working together in Cuba and Colombia. There is also a sequel four decades later: a robbery at my mountain top home in West Virginia. The exchange of letters between FBN District Supervisor George Gaffney and June Cobb, which she had given to me, were stolen.

In this chapter we will deal with two reports that were authored by a U.S. Customs agent in Cuba named William Johnston. One of them is more detailed than the other. The differences between them are worth paying close attention to. To help the reader distinguish between the

---

[370] Douglas Valentine, *The Strength of the Wolf: The Secret history of America's War on Drugs* (New York: Verso, 2004), pp. 130-131.

two reports, we will refer to one as Johnston's "monthly activities report" and the other as Johnston's "more detailed report." The reader should also pay close attention to *how many* "Colombians" were actually arrested in the drug bust mentioned in both reports.

THE JOHNSTON REPORTS ON THE 1956 HEROIN BUST IN HAVANA

The U.S. Treasury Representative of the Customs Agency Service in the American Embassy in Havana was William W. Johnston. On 31 December 1956, he signed the Havana November-December monthly activities report and forwarded it to the Commissioner of Customs, Division of Investigations, in Washington D.C. Johnston's report covered all the activities of interest to the Treasury Department during that reporting period. One of the items he included was a "notable" seizure of almost one kilo of heroin. Here are the complete details that Johnston reported about the seizure:

> Local police officers apprehended *two Colombians and one Cuban* with 800 grams of heroin which was destined for the United States. For the past year information had been received by both this office and police relative to several Colombians engaged in smuggling narcotics and counterfeit money and traveler checks into Cuba and the United States. When it was learned that *a Colombian* was staying at a local hotel, his room was raided by police. That raid led to another raid on an apartment nearby occupied by *his brother* where the heroin was found. It was learned that they had let a Cuban trafficker have 100 grams the previous day, and the Cuban was also arrested and the 100 grams seized. This Cuban had been apprehended the previous May with one kilo of morphine which he was attempting to sell to an undercover agent posing as a United States buyer.[371] [Emphasis added]

---

371 RG 170, A1 Entry 9, Bureau of Narcotics and Dangerous Drugs: Subject Files, 1916-1970, Box 154 (Old Box 22), Folder 660-Cuba William Johnston Files. William W. Johnston Monthly Activity Report, December 31, 1956.

JUNE COBB AND THE FEDERAL BUREAU OF NARCOTICS

On 10 January 1957, the Deputy Commissioner of Customs, Chester A. Emerick, attached a courtesy copy of Johnston's report to a memorandum to the Commissioner of the Federal Bureau of Narcotics (FBN), Harry J. Anslinger.

Commissioner Anslinger was very interested in this heroin story from Cuba. On 16 January 1957, Anslinger wrote back to Emerick asking for more information:

> I have noted references in Mr. Johnston's report (page 3) to a recent large seizure of heroin in which *two Colombians and a Cuban* were involved, and to a prior seizure of morphine involving the same Cuban, in May 1956. I would be *very* interested in having a full report on these two seizures, and I would appreciate it if you would request Mr. Johnston to furnish detailed reports on them at his earliest opportunity.[372] [Emphasis added]

If Anslinger's letter to Emerick is to be taken at face value, it is apparent that the FBN Commissioner did not know that on the same date that Johnston issued the Havana monthly activities report, 31 December 1956, he had also issued a separate *more detailed* report devoted exclusively to the heroin and morphine seizures in Havana.

The story in Johnston's more detailed report was different. Apparently, at first he had only sent it to the Commissioner of Customs and to the Treasury Representative in Mexico City.[373] In this, more detailed, version of the story, Johnston said that in addition to the Cuban there had been *three Colombians* arrested. Moreover, Johnston said that all three of the Colombians were *important narcotics traffickers.* Johnston explained:

> They are identical twin brothers, Rafael and Tomas Herran Olozaga and Maria Cecilia Posada Franco. The Herran brothers came to Havana on 1 November 1956, from Colombia via Jamaica, and Maria Cecilia arrived in Cuba

---

372   1/16/57, Memorandum from H. J. Anslinger, Commissioner of Narcotics, to Mr. Chester A. Emerick, Deputy Commissioner of Customs, RE: Activities Report of Treasury Representative in Charge, Havana, Cuba, for November and December 1956. (Your memorandum of January 10, 1957)

373   RG 170, A1 Entry 9, Bureau of Narcotics and Dangerous Drugs: Subject Files, 1916-1970, Box 154 (Old Box 22), Folder 660-Cuba 1952-1958. William W. Johnston to Commissioner of Customs, December 31, 1956.

on 19 December 1956, to join Tomas Herran. *She came down from Philadelphia, Pennsylvania, where she is a student at a college there.*[374] [Emphasis added]

Johnston said it was "very likely the girl came to Cuba to act as a courier for the 700 grams seized." He added, "She will not be tried but merely deported, as the Herran brothers assumed all responsibility."[375] If, as Johnston had said, she was such an important narcotics trafficker, why was her story completely missing from the monthly activities report that he wrote the very same day?

Let us assume for the moment that Johnston's second, more detailed, report was a full accounting of what the Customs Service and Treasury Department knew about the case. Given what we know from June Cobb's CIA security interview we might suspect that she was the third "Colombian." And we would be wrong. Huge pieces of the story were missing from both of Johnston's reports.

On 1 November 1956, Rafael and Thomas Herran Olozaga arrived in Havana from Colombia via Jamaica with nearly one kilo of heroin.[376] *According to Cuban sources, a woman had helped bring the drugs into Cuba.*[377] That woman was June Cobb. She later told the CIA, "I went *with them* in October when they went and took it up to Cuba."[378] [Emphasis added] Cobb explained they were unable to sell it profitably in Cuba, so she and Tomas went to Mexico to try, "and, there too, he was only offered $6,000. Well anyway, so we came back to Cuba."[379] Cobb did *not* come from Philadelphia to join the Herran brothers on 19 December. On that date

---

374 RG 170, A1 Entry 9, Bureau of Narcotics and Dangerous Drugs: Subject Files, 1916-1970, Box 154 (Old Box 22), Folder 660-Cuba 1952-1958. William W. Johnston to Commissioner of Customs, 31 December 1956.
375 RG 170, A1 Entry 9, Bureau of Narcotics and Dangerous Drugs: Subject Files, 1916-1970, Box 154 (Old Box 22), Folder 660-Cuba 1952-1958. William W. Johnston to Commissioner of Customs, 31 December 1956.
376 RG 170, A1 Entry 9, Bureau of Narcotics and Dangerous Drugs: Subject Files, 1916-1970, Box 154 (Old Box 22), Folder 660-Cuba 1952-1958. William W. Johnston to Commissioner of Customs, 31 December 1956.
377 Eduardo Saenz Rovner, **The Cuban Connection: Drug Trafficking, Smuggling, and Gambling in Cuba from the 1920s to the Revolution** (Chapel Hill: North Carolina Press, 2008), p. 1.
378 6/29/60, Attachment to CIA Memorandum to Chief, Security Support Division, Subject: June Cobb, Tape 2, p. 6.
379 6/29/60, Attachment to CIA Memorandum to Chief, Security Support Division, Subject: June Cobb, Tape 2, p. 7.

a *fourth Colombian*, "Maria Cecilia," whoever she really was, joined the three who were already in Havana.

HOW MANY COLOMBIANS DID THE CUBAN POLICE ARREST?

By her own 1960 account [to the CIA] of the 1956 Havana heroin bust, June Cobb said that she had left Rafael and Tomas Herran behind in Cuba with the heroin and that she had returned to Florida the day before they were arrested. Eduardo Saenz Rovner conducted research for his book on drug trafficking in Cuba, ***The Cuban Connection***, using the two pertinent records groups (RG 170 and RG 59) in the U.S. National Archives and Records Administration. He also consulted nine collections at Cuba's National Archive. What Rovner's sources told him undermines Cobb's version of the arrest:

> At the end of December 1956, *two Colombian brothers*, Rafael and Tomas Herran Olozaga, were apprehended in Havana while holding a shipment of heroin valued at sixteen thousand dollars. …Arrested with them were *two Colombian women*, one of whom had helped bring the drugs into Cuba. The other, *Tomas' wife*, functioned as a courier, smuggling the drugs into the United States using her status as *a university student in Philadelphia*. A Cuban was also arrested along with the *four Colombians*.[380] [Emphasis added]

Rovner's sources for the arrest of, not two or three, but *four* Colombians were Cuban police records and Havana newspaper accounts created at the time of the arrest in late December 1956.

It was after the arrest that the brothers told the police they had sold 100 grams of the heroin to the Cuban, Antonio Botano Seijo, who was then arrested and the 100 grams seized.[381] In Johnston's monthly activities report, the Botano sale took place "the previous day"; in Johnston's

---

380   Eduardo Saenz Rovner, *The Cuban Connection: Drug Trafficking, Smuggling, and Gambling in Cuba From the 1920s to the Revolution* (Chapel Hill: University of North Carolina Press, 2008), p. 1.
381   RG 170, A1 Entry 9, Bureau of Narcotics and Dangerous Drugs: Subject Files, 1916-1970, Box 154 (Old Box 22), Folder 660-Cuba William Johnston Files. William W. Johnston Monthly Activity Report, 31 December 1956.

more detailed report, he said the Botano sale had taken place "recently." Another detail about the Cuban was different in Johnston's two reports: in the monthly activities report, Botano's arrest for the kilo of morphine took place in May 1956; yet Johnston's more detailed report indicates that Botano's arrest took place on 31 May 1955.

There is another subtle but interesting difference between Johnston's two reports. It concerns what prompted the police raid in the first place. That story is missing from Johnston's more detailed account. This time he put it in the monthly activities report. The Cuban police went to Rafael's hotel room first and from there to Tomas' apartment where the heroin was located.[382] The raid was prompted "when it was learned that a Colombian was staying in a local hotel." That hardly seems grounds for raiding Rafael's hotel room.

From the above, it is evident that the Cuban police had received a tip about Rafael, not Tomas. On Anslinger's copy of his letter to the Deputy Commissioner of Customs asking for more details about the heroin seizures, there is some interesting marginalia just above Anslinger's signature. He or someone wrote instructions to file this letter with the "report for Nov and Dec, OCX 0970, Rafael Herran Olozaga."[383] OCX 0970 appears to have been an FBN case file on Rafael Herran. Apparently, the FBN was more interested in Rafael than Tomas.

In his more detailed report, Johnston said that Botano's earlier apprehension with the kilo of morphine had been handled "by Cuban police officers in collaboration with this office and using one of the writer's [i.e. Johnston's] informers."[384] In his monthly activities report, Johnston said that Botano was "attempting to sell to an undercover agent posing as a United States buyer."[385] These different pieces of intelligence

---

382   RG 170, A1 Entry 9, Bureau of Narcotics and Dangerous Drugs: Subject Files, 1916-1970, Box 154 (Old Box 22), Folder 660-Cuba William Johnston Files. William W. Johnston Monthly Activity Report, 31 December 1956.
383   1/16/57, Memorandum from H. J. Anslinger, Commissioner of Narcotics, to Mr. Chester A. Emerick, Deputy Commissioner of Customs, RE: Activities Report of Treasury Representative in Charge, Havana, Cuba, for November and December 1956. (Your memorandum of January 10, 1957)
384   RG 170, A1 Entry 9, Bureau of Narcotics and Dangerous Drugs: Subject Files, 1916-1970, Box 154 (Old Box 22), Folder 660-Cuba 1952-1958. William W. Johnston to Commissioner of Customs, 31 December 1956.
385   RG 170, A1 Entry 9, Bureau of Narcotics and Dangerous Drugs: Subject Files, 1916-1970, Box 154 (Old Box 22), Folder 660-Cuba William Johnston Files. William W. Johnston Monthly Activity Report, 31 December 1956.

about informants and undercover work have a common thread: the U.S. was the intended destination of the heroin and the morphine. In his monthly activities report, Johnston stated that the remaining heroin seized in Tomas' apartment "was destined for the United States." Johnston did not say how he had learned this. And this brings us back again to Johnston's remark in his more detailed report about the Colombian girl from Philadelphia: she "came to Cuba to *act as a courier* ...she will not be tried but merely deported, as the Herran brothers assumed all responsibility." [Emphasis added]

So who was Maria Cecilia Posada Franco? According to Johnston's more detailed report, she was born on 6 December 1935, at Risaralda, Caldas, Colombia, and had thus just turned twenty one years old when she arrived in Havana. Her Colombian passport, No. 120822, had been issued on 11 February 1955. Her passport contained a student visa to the United States, issued by the U.S. Consul in Medellin, Colombia on 15 November 1955, probably in preparation for her to attend college in Philadelphia. Her passport next received a visa from the Cuban Consul in Philadelphia on 12 December 1956, in preparation for her trip to meet with the Herran brothers in Cuba. Johnston wrote, "Maria Cecilia arrived in Cuba on December 19, 1956 *to join Tomas Herran*."[386] [Emphasis added] Here we return to Rovner's account of the two Colombian women: one had helped the brothers bring the heroin into Cuba and the other one, Tomas Herran's *wife*, was going to smuggle the heroin into the United States.[387]

Rovner's sources apparently did not disclose the names of the two Colombian women. If Maria Cecilia was Tomas' wife, then Posada Franco would have been her maiden name. It would also seem unlikely that she came to Havana as an undercover agent to set up the bust of her husband and brother-in-law. On the other hand, her release after the arrest and deletion from the monthly activities report may have been in exchange for her agreement to provide information in the future.

---

386 RG 170, A1 Entry 9, Bureau of Narcotics and Dangerous Drugs: Subject Files, 1916-1970, Box 154 (Old Box 22), Folder 660-Cuba 1952-1958. William W. Johnston to Commissioner of Customs, 31 December 1956.
387 Eduardo Saenz Rovner, *The Cuban Connection: Drug Trafficking, Smuggling, and Gambling in Cuba From the 1920s to the Revolution* (Chapel Hill: University of North Carolina Press, 2008), p. 1.

Moreover, we cannot rule out the possibility that Maria was only posing as Tomas' wife.

It is June Cobb's role in this Cuban narcotics saga that is the most intriguing. There is *nothing at all* about her in either of Johnston's two reports or in Anslinger's query. Although Rovner's sources did not give up her name, Rovner learned from those sources that she had *helped bring the drugs* into Cuba—that *she actually had acted as a courier* for the brothers.[388] All of the rest of the information we have on Cobb's part in the 1956 Herran heroin case comes, directly or indirectly, from two sources: June Cobb and the FBN. The reader will recall from Chapter Eight that Cobb told Jack Anderson that because the brothers were sampling their narcotics she became a FBN informant to break her "sweetheart" of the habit. Yet when Anderson checked with his FBN sources they told him Cobb found "her lover's affection straying and, in a fit of jealousy, squealed on him."[389] We need not choose between these two versions of the story. One thing is certain: June Cobb, like Harry Anslinger, was more interested in Rafael than Tomas.

From Cobb's account to the CIA we know that she must have been one of the two "Colombian" women in the Herran group in Havana. It is important to note that the other Colombia woman and alleged wife of Tomas, Maria Cecilia, is missing in Johnston's monthly activities report but she does appear in his more detailed report. Cobb, however, is *completely missing* from the Customs Service and Treasury Department documents so far released. Cobb told the CIA she got out of Cuba the day before the arrest.[390] Rovner's Cuban sources indicate otherwise. From these sources Rovner found another unique and very important part of the story:

> The Herran Olozaga brothers confessed that they had brought drugs into Cuba before. *After their arrest, all of the parties except Tomas were released* on bail and traveled to Merida, Mexico. Tomas, evidently the gang's leader, re-

---

388 Eduardo Saenz Rovner, *The Cuban Connection: Drug Trafficking, Smuggling, and Gambling in Cuba From the 1920s to the Revolution* (Chapel Hill: University of North Carolina Press, 2008), p. 1.
389 8/18/62, Jack Anderson, "Meet June Cobb: She's A Soldier of Fortune," Parade Magazine, *Washington Post.*
390 6/29/60, Attachment to CIA Memorandum to Chief, Security Support Division, Subject: June Cobb, Tape 2, p. 7. RIF 104-10174-10078.

mained imprisoned in Cuba for a year. After gaining his freedom, he returned to Medellin.[391] [Emphasis added]

If this is true, then Cobb lied to the CIA about when she left Cuba. It was after they were all arrested and *not* the day before. Moreover, a major development had taken place in Medellin by the time Tomas returned in December 1957. And June Cobb was the reason behind it.

GEORGE GAFFNEY AND A "WOMAN" WITH CIA CONNECTIONS

As Rovner relates in his findings, "In February 1957, ...agents of the Colombian Intelligence Service, backed by an official of the U.S. Federal Bureau of Narcotics, raided the brothers' laboratory in a Medellin suburb, where they had been processing cocaine since at least 1952.[392] On 18 February 1957, the Assistant Deputy Commissioner for the FBN, Henry L. Giordano, wrote a memorandum about a trip to Medellin by the Atlanta FBN District Supervisor, George Gaffney:

> On 18 February 1957, District Supervisor Gaffney advised me by telephone that Commissioner Anslinger had instructed him to proceed to Medellin, Colombia, and attempt to arrange for the destruction of the reported clandestine laboratories in that city.[393]

Giordano took the necessary measures to ensure that Gaffney was furnished with the name of a secret agent of the Bogota police "in the event that he encountered difficulties with the local authorities in Medellin." The hand-written marginalia on Giordano's memo was almost identical with what was on Anslinger's letter: "OCX 0970, Rafael Olozaga."

According to Douglas Valentine's work on the history of American drug enforcement, George Gaffney had been working with a CIA officer,

---

391 Eduardo Saenz Rovner, *The Cuban Connection: Drug Trafficking, Smuggling, and Gambling in Cuba From the 1920s to the Revolution* (Chapel Hill: University of North Carolina Press, 2008), p. 1.
392 Eduardo Saenz Rovner, *The Cuban Connection: Drug Trafficking, Smuggling, and Gambling in Cuba From the 1920s to the Revolution* (Chapel Hill: University of North Carolina Press, 2008), p. 1.
393 RG 170, A1 Entry 9, Bureau of Narcotics and Dangerous Drugs: Subject Files, 1916-1970, Box 153 (Old Box 21), Folder 660-Colombia 1956-. Henry L. Giordano 'District Supervisor's Gaffney's Trip to Medellin, Colombia" 18 February 1957.

Robert Service, to develop a narcotics case on Tomas and Rafael Herran Olozaga. "The brothers had been in business since 1948," Gaffney explained in an interview with Valentine, "selling heroin and cocaine in Cuba. They had a lab on their estate." According to Rovner's account, both the Colombian and German police suspected that as early as 1939 Rafael was a drug trafficker trying to buy morphine for the Union Pharmacy he operated in Medellin.[394]

Valentine reports that, according to Gaffney, the case to take out the brothers' lab "began in New Orleans when *a woman with CIA connections* offered information to agent Arthur Doll."[395] That woman was June Cobb. The reader will recall (from Chapter Nine) the highlights of what Cobb told Ralph True about her "little mission" for the FBN in October 1958:

- She supervised this "mission" for the Narcotics Bureau while working with an American magazine, the *MD Medical News Magazine*, in Ecuador in October 1958.
- She neglected to enter this job on the employment section of her questionnaire for the interview.
- She visited the FBN in New Orleans in October 1958 and told them about her fiancé's laboratory.

As discussed in Chapter Nine, when asked why she had visited the FBN at that time, Cobb changed the subject and did not address the three items listed above. She promised to tell her interviewer the "whole story." However, she did *not* do so.

The above parts of the "story" that Cobb told her CIA interviewer bear no resemblance to her account of the period after she resigned from the *MD Medical News Magazine* (August 1958) and her trip to see Castro's Minister of Health (February 1959). During that time Cobb remained in New York on unemployment and was not in Ecuador.[396] On the other hand, the "story" about her visit to the FBN office in New Orleans bears an uncanny resemblance to a huge part of the real story that

---

394 Eduardo Saenz Rovner, *The Cuban Connection: Drug Trafficking, Smuggling, and Gambling in Cuba From the 1920s to the Revolution* (Chapel Hill: University of North Carolina Press, 2008), p. 1.
395 Douglas Valentine, *The Strength of the Wolf: The Secret history of America's War on Drugs* (New York: Verso, 2004), p. 205.
396 6/29/60, Attachment to CIA Memorandum to Chief, Security Support Division, Subject: June Cobb, Tape 1, p. 34. RIF 104-10174-10078.

JUNE COBB AND THE FEDERAL BUREAU OF NARCOTICS

took place *in 1956*, and that she carefully excluded from her account to Ralph True.

From Cobb's testimony to the Senate Subcommittee we know that *by 1957* she was *already* working as an informant for the Bureau of Narcotics.[397] Both Cobb and the FBN told Jack Anderson that she had "squealed" on the brothers.[398] We know from Gaffney's account that Cobb visited the New Orleans FBN office. And we know that her visit was *before* Gaffney's trip to Colombia to destroy the Herran brothers' Medellin lab in *February 1957*.[399]

Cobb wrote to me about a series of letters she exchanged with George Gaffney in early 1957. Cobb sent me copies of some of them. These letters were stolen from my West Virginia home in the 1990s. Fortunately, the thieves did not get an important piece of Cobb's correspondence with me—a long letter that I had accidentally misfiled among 20,000 pieces of paper.[400] Apparently, the thieves did not have enough time to look through all of the material.

I have wondered why those Cobb-Gaffney letters were taken from my home and what details were in them.[401] I suspect that the correspondence with Gaffney might have revealed important information on Cobb's movements during the heroin saga in October-December 1956, including the very elements of the real story she hid from her CIA interviewer in 1960. We know from Rovner's sources (see above) that Cobb was arrested with the rest of the group at the end of December 1956 and then released on bail—with Maria Cecelia and Tomas—to Merida, Mexico. Cobb must have met FBN Agent Arthur Doll in New Orleans either in October 1956, or in January 1957, after her arrival in Merida.

---

397 3/30/62, June Cobb testimony during a hearing of the Senate Subcommittee to Investigate the Administration of the Internal Security Act and other Internal Security Laws, p. 26; RIF 104-10218-10384.
398 8/18/62, Jack Anderson, "Meet June Cobb: She's A Soldier of Fortune," Parade Magazine, **Washington Post**.
399 Douglas Valentine, *The Strength of the Wolf: The Secret history of America's War on Drugs* (New York: Verso, 2004), p. 205.
400 1995 June Cobb letter to John Newman.
401 The letters from Gaffney were not all that was taken. Several more letters to me with newspaper clippings were included in the heist, as well as notes that I had made from an interview with Cobb and phone conversations with her. I had not yet had a chance to process all these materials as I was fully engaged in several time-sensitive projects.

WHERE ANGELS TREAD LIGHTLY

The circumstances surrounding Cobb's visit to the FBN in New Orleans, the heroin seizure in Cuba, and the destruction of the Herran brothers' laboratory in Medellin shed an entirely new light on why Cobb might have made so many concerted attempts to get to Rafael Herran. For years she had waited. Could she have ensnared her prey like a spider building a lair? When that moment finally arrived, she helped him transport the heroin to Cuba and she watched *and participated* as the game finally played out to its end.

But was this really the end? The following set of questions concern what is only a *hypothetical* possibility. The "story" might not have ended in Cuba. The heroin had been seized. But why stop there? Why wouldn't the FBN go to the next step: following the trail to where the heroin would lead them in the U.S. and in Mexico? Why wouldn't the FBN be interested in an opportunity to develop information on the drug trafficking networks in both of those countries? If so, their undercover informant, June Cobb, along with the school girl from Philadelphia, might have been useful as undercover couriers.

George Gaffney told Valentine that Cobb was connected to the CIA and that he was working the Herran case with another CIA agent at the time. While we cannot be certain, at least for now, about exactly when she went to the FBN in New Orleans, we can be certain about this: Cobb was no longer one of Don Juan's girlfriends.

And another point needs to be underscored. If George Gaffney is correct about the "woman" in New Orleans, then June Cobb had CIA connections well before she met Harry Hermsdorf in Havana in May 1960.

CHAPTER ELEVEN:
CASTRO'S APRIL 1959 VISIT TO THE U.S.

Planning for Castro's visit to the United States became public in late February 1959 when a delegation of the American Society of Newspaper Editors (ASNE) went to Cuba to personally invite the new Cuban leader to address its annual convention in April. The decision of ASNE President George W. Healy, Jr., to invite Castro to the annual convention—an event at which U.S. presidents were often the featured speaker—surprised the ASNE membership, many of whom were less than thrilled by the invitation. At a 28 February press conference in Havana for the visiting ASNE delegation, Castro said he hoped he could accept the invitation, but that he was concerned about his inadequate command of English.[402]

It is possible that Healy's decision may have been quietly brokered weeks before the ornamental ASNE trip to Cuba through the good offices of the head of the CIA-funded Inter-American Press Association (IAPA), Jules Dubois. This chapter will explore that possibility. We will also consider whether or not June Cobb's hurried translation of Castro's

---

402   3/5/59 FRUS, 1958-1960, Volume VI, DOCUMENT #258, p. 421.

speech, *History Will Absolve Me*, was a deliberate strategy to penetrate his inner circle.

LOPEZ-FRESQUET'S SUNDAY DRIVE TO COJIMAR

On 2 March 1959, Castro's Minister of Treasury, Rufo Lopez-Fresquet, and his wife went for an automobile ride toward the eastern beaches of Havana:

> As we passed the hills that environ the small fishing village of Cojimar, I spotted the house that Castro occasionally lived in, which had been built by a friend of mine 15 years before. The house, situated on the top of the highest hill, commanded a wonderful view; when I told this to my wife, she suggested we go visit it. We did not expect to see anyone but the military guards; however, the house was surrounded by automobiles. When I entered the house, I was met by Castro himself. "Hey, you guys got here pretty quick!" he said by way of greeting. Castro was hosting a large delegation of the American Society of Newspaper Editors; and only a few minutes before, he had ordered that we be invited to help entertain the visitors. By mere chance we had stopped at the house.[403]

Also, by chance, this was the same house overlooking Cojimar, where, just weeks before, Castro had made his secret pact with the Cuban Communist party (PSP). (See Chapter Seven).

There were more than thirty members of ASNE in Castro's living room, and Lopez-Fresquet became the translator for Castro and his guests. Lopez-Fresquet described the conference as pleasant but "at times difficult." He said, "Castro was in the best of moods. Because we were there, Castro had the idea of inviting *la Americana* (as he always called my wife) and me to accompany him on his trip to the U.S." Lopez-Fresquet accepted and convinced Castro to bring the other principal economic officials of his government on the trip. Lopez-Fresquet concluded, "The mission that escorted

---

403 Rufo Lopez-Fresquet, **My Fourteen Months With Castro** (New York: World Publishing Company, 1966), p. 100.

Castro on his tour of the U.S. in April 1959 was the result of a series of accidental events."[404] On 3 March 1959, the day after the ASNE delegates conferred with Castro at Cojimar, he officially accepted the ASNE invitation.[405]

JULES DUBOIS AND THE INTER-AMERICAN PRESS ASSOCIATION (IAPA)

The *formal* invitation for Castro's U.S. visit came from the American Society of Newspaper Editors (ASNE). As mentioned above, the President of ASNE at the time, George W. Healy Jr. of the *New Orleans Times-Picayune*, found it necessary to allay the concerns of ASNE members who were unhappy over the invitation. His rather perfunctory explanation was that he had a responsibility to "permit" ASNE members "as wide an opportunity as possible to see and hear" people who had made news or handled news in an outstanding manner.[406] The truth was that Castro had not handled "the news" well at all, although he had certainly made news. U.S. State Department and American intelligence records credit ASNE for arranging Castro's April 1959 trip to the U.S. However, Carlos Franqui, the renowned Cuban journalist, writer, and poet, tells a different story.

As a teenager Franqui joined a group of Cuban communists in Oriente Province and worked on the Cuban Communist newspaper *Hoy*. He subsequently broke with the communists and joined Castro's 26 July Movement against Batista. Franqui became one of Castro's most intimate associates. He directed the underground radio and press of the Movement during the campaign in the Sierra Maestra, and was the editor of the underground newspaper **Revolucion** which, after the victory over Batista, became the official newspaper of the new regime.

In his well-known book, **Family Portrait with Fidel**, Franqui suggests that Castro's April 1959 trip to the U.S. was the result of an under-the-table arrangement brokered by the American journalist Jules Dubois at Castro's request:

---

404   Rufo Lopez-Fresquet, *My Fourteen Months With Castro* (New York: World Publishing Company, 1966), p. 101.
405   3/5/59, FRUS, 1958-1960, Volume VI, DOCUMENT #258, p. 421.
406   ASNE News Bulletin, http://www.editorandpublisher.com/Article/U-S-Media-May-Operate-In-Cuba-p-11#sthash.KE3kkzKa.dpuf.

> Fidel's first trip to the United States (on 15 April 1959) demonstrated his intelligence. He neither requested nor accepted the classical official invitation; rather, he *had himself invited* by the press, the Press Club, through the good offices of a man of irreproachable credentials for the American Establishment, Jules Dubois. Dubois at the time was president of SIP (Inter-American Press Society, also known as the IAPA) and an opponent of Batista and of the censorship imposed by Latin-American dictators. He was the **Chicago Tribune's** correspondent in Cuba, a retired colonel, and a person to whom the State Department listened.[407] [Emphasis added]

Castro had succeeded in getting himself invited to give addresses to many organizations of the press—including two that carried the name "Press Club." His first major press event on the trip occurred on Friday, 17 April, when he addressed the annual ASNE convention in Washington D.C. Still in the U.S. capital on Monday, 20 April, Castro addressed a luncheon at the National Press Club,[408] and appeared afterward on the television show **Meet the Press**. On Tuesday, 21 April, Castro addressed the Overseas Press Club in New York City. It was the Overseas Press Club invitation to which Franqui was referring—the arrangement brokered by Dubois. It was there that Castro was greeted by baseball star Jackie Robinson. After being introduced by Jules Dubois, Castro received thunderous applause from an audience of international journalists working in the U.S.[409]

Dubois was among the many American journalists working in Cuba who had both opposed Batista and had become acquainted with Castro. Although Dubois was not a member of the Overseas Press Club, he had arranged that invitation and more. Franqui's point was that it was Jules Dubois' *irreproachable credentials with the American Establishment* that played a key role in arranging Castro's trip to the U.S. At the time of the trip, Jules Dubois was not only the *Chicago Tribune* Latin American correspondent in Havana, he was also the head of the CIA-backed Inter-American Press Association (IAPA), also known as the Inter-American Press Society (SIP). Dubois was a former U.S. Army Intelligence officer who had

---

407 Carlos Franqui, **Family Portrait with Fidel** (New York: Random House, 1984), p. 31.
408 4/22/14, http://www.press.org/news-multimedia/news/his-week-national-press-club-history.
409 Carlos Franqui, **Family Portrait with Fidel** (New York: Random House, 1984), p. 31.

CASTRO'S APRIL 1959 VISIT TO THE U.S.

served in WWII. He worked for many years in the Pentagon and had assignments in Panama, North Africa, and Europe. Dubois was close to Castillo Armas, the man installed by the CIA in Guatemala when it engineered the coup d'état in that country in 1954.[410] In 1977, the *New York Times* reported that Dubois was said to have been a CIA asset.[411]

In February 1959, for both Castro and the U.S., Dubois was the go-to man to design a trip as awkward as this one that both sides could live with. But Jules Dubois and the IAPA were too closely associated with the CIA and that is where ASNE came in. Unlike the Foreign Press Club, ASNE was made up of American journalists. Unlike the National Press Club in Washington, which oozed with the flavor of the Washington establishment, ASNE members were journalists from all over the U.S. In other words, ASNE provided a convenient independent American façade for the Castro invitation. That peg was exactly what Castro and American intelligence needed to hang the visit on.

As the planning for Castro's visit moved forward, the wheels of bureaucracy in Washington ground indecisively around the problem of Cuba policy—what to do about the U.S. military missions there; what to make of Castro's assumption of the premiership on 16 February; worry over what the communist party (PSP) was up to; and even whether or not the Castro trip should be prevented from taking place.

THE CIA TORPEDOES THE IDEA OF BLOCKING CASTRO'S VISIT

There was resistance at the highest levels of the U.S. government to Castro's impending visit. Acting Secretary of State Herter spoke out against it at the 26 March 1959 meeting of the NSC—the same meeting at which Dulles had reported Castro was becoming a dictator (see Chapter Seven). The Cuban leader had accepted the invitation without informing the State Department, and this, said the Secretary, "was singularly bad behavior." Eisenhower asked, "in that case could we not refuse

---
410   *Time*, 15 April 1957.
411   12/27/77, *The New York Times*, John M. Crewdson and Joseph B. Treaster, "CIA Established Many Links to Journalists in U.S. and Abroad," p. 40.

to give Castro a visa?" Deputy Secretary of Defense Quarles argued that "Castro had already behaved badly enough to provide us with very good reason for refusing him admission to the U.S." Special Assistant to the President for National Security, Gordon Gray, suggested that the newspaper editors might be persuaded to cancel their invitation to Castro.

The idea of blocking Castro's trip to the U.S. was torpedoed at the NSC meeting by the Director of Central Intelligence, Allen Dulles. He told the president that there was "a slow-growing movement against Castro in Cuba," and that a cancellation of the visit might "discourage the growth of that movement."[412] Apparently, no one at the meeting was willing to argue that a cancellation might actually *encourage* such a movement. In any event, there was another reason why the CIA wanted the Castro trip to take place. As CIA Deputy Director Richard Bissell noted in his autobiography, it had become *critically important* to confirm or disprove the assessment that Castro was not a communist, "and so a CIA representative was sent to meet with him on the occasion of his trip to the United States in 1959."[413] Castro would be approached overtly, although not publicly, to arrange a meeting during his trip. Castro would also meet with Vice President Nixon, but not in the White House.

There is another trail of evidence involving a famous Cuban journalist that suggests an operation to penetrate Castro's inner circle might have been put into play during his visit. The journalist, Luis Conte Aguero, was a long time friend of Castro and his top press person. Conte and an intimate girlfriend of June Cobb, Rosalba Roca, both played a crucial role in Cobb's strategy to bait and hook Castro into inviting her to work for him in Cuba.

JUNE COBB, ROSALBA ROCA, AND LUIS CONTE AGUERO

According to June Cobb's self-reporting to CIA security in 1960, at the end of February 1959 she was sitting outside of the office of

---

412 FRUS, 1958-1960, volume VI, Cuba, document #266, Memorandum of Discussion at the 400th Meeting of the National Security Council, Washington, March 26, 1959.
413 Richard M. Bissell, ***Reflections of a Cold Warrior: From Yalta to the Bay of Pigs*** (New Haven: Yale University Press, 1996), p. 152.

CASTRO'S APRIL 1959 VISIT TO THE U.S.

Castro's Minister of Health, Martinez Paez. Cobb told the CIA and the Senate Subcommittee on Internal Security that she had gone to Cuba for three days, for the purpose of convincing the Minister of Public Health to support the *Liga Anti Coca,* an organization in Peru and Bolivia that was trying to discourage the use of coca leaves.[414] While waiting to talk to Minister Paez, so Cobb's story went, a young doctor handed her an old Castro speech. At that very moment Cobb had an epiphany. She decided then and there that the speech needed to be translated into English in time to present it to Castro personally—and to have it ready for the ASNE newspaper editors who would be listening to his address at their annual convention in April.[415] This plan succeeded, and it landed Cobb a job in Castro's inner circle in Havana.

The Castro speech that the young doctor gave her had taken place during Castro's trial after his failed attack on the Moncada Barracks on 26 July 1953. It was eventually expanded and given the title, *History Will Absolve Me.* "So I read it," she said, "and I was very much impressed by it and decided that it should be translated before his visit to the United States."[416] After her visit to Cuba, Cobb checked with the Cuban Embassy in Washington and the Cuban Consulate in New York to see if there was already a translation of the speech that she could edit. No one had a copy anywhere and it was already March. She told her CIA interviewer, "Fidel was coming in April, so there was not very much time." Cobb found three translators to help, but said their work "was so miserable that I felt it should be done over."[417] At this point she asked a dozen friends to help and they worked "day and night" for several weeks and finished it just as Fidel came to New York.[418]

Cobb told her CIA interviewer about the critical role a girlfriend of hers had played in getting Cobb's work to Castro during his visit to

---

414 3/30/62, June Cobb testimony during a hearing of the Senate Subcommittee to Investigate the Administration of the Internal Security Act and other Internal Security Laws, p. 26; RIF 104-10218-10384.
415 6/29/60, Attachment to CIA Memorandum to Chief, Security Support Division, Subject: June Cobb, Tape 2, p. 3.
416 6/29/60, Attachment to CIA Memorandum to Chief, Security Support Division, Subject: June Cobb, Tape 2, p. 3.
417 6/29/60, Attachment to CIA Memorandum to Chief, Security Support Division, Subject: June Cobb, Tape 2, p. 11.
418 6/29/60, Attachment to CIA Memorandum to Chief, Security Support Division, Subject: June Cobb, Tape 2, p. 8.

New York City. Cobb said that Rosalba Roca, a twenty five-year-old girl from the Dominican Republic, "is my one intimate friend, and when I was involved in the narcotics thing, she was the one person that helped me write the letters and so forth."[419] Cobb said that Rosalba had gone to see Queen Elizabeth and President Eisenhower during the Queen's visit to the U.S. in October 1957 and that a newspaper convention of the Inter-American Society for the Press (SIP/IAPA) was going on in Washington D.C. at that same time. A Mexican magazine had given Rosalba a credential that enabled her to meet Queen Elizabeth and President Eisenhower. At some point during the gatherings associated with that IAPA convention, Rosalba met Luis Conte Aguero, "and they became friends."

According to Cobb, when Castro came to America in April 1959, Aguero, who was part of the entourage, called Rosalba "as a matter of course, as a friend he had made here before in the United States." Aguero made the phone call to New York while the entourage was still in Washington. As if on cue, Rosalba reportedly said to Aguero, "Oh you don't know, I have a friend that's working day and night for Cuba. Her apartment is like a Bohemian workshop, two or three typewriters going day and night."[420] Cobb said that Aguero told Fidel about it the next day. We will get to how this played out below.

THE CASTRO SHOW

On 14 April 1959, Castro and his entourage of eighty people arrived in two planes in Washington D.C.—two hours late. Castro showed up late at almost every occasion on the trip. The only event at which Castro wore a tie was at the Cuban Embassy in Washington, when he met with the Soviet ambassador.[421] Carlos Franqui, who accompanied Castro on the trip, said he was nearly always in his unpressed olive-green fatigues

---

419 6/29/60, Attachment to CIA Memorandum to Chief, Security Support Division, Subject: June Cobb, Tape 2, p. 12
420 6/29/60, Attachment to CIA Memorandum to Chief, Security Support Division, Subject: June Cobb, Tape 2, pp. 12-13.
421 Alan McPherson, "The Limits of Populist Diplomacy," *Diplomacy and Statecraft*, 2007, Vol. 18, p. 256.

and "wore his hair and beard shaggy so that he would seem older and more mature than his thirty-three years."[422]

Except for his meeting with Vice President Nixon, Castro's trip to the nation's capitol went splendidly. At the ASNE convention Castro's performance came off quite well, given the skepticism of the organization's membership. Out of the twelve ASNE members asked by the Associated Press to assess Castro, ten responded favorably. Most news editorials ended with calls to give the young leader time to prove himself.[423] Castro was well prepared with short and pithy sound bites. At the National Press Club luncheon, Castro said, "We didn't come here to get money. Many men come here to sell their souls. We want only understanding and sympathy."[424] On NBC's *Meet the Press* before a television audience of millions, Castro said, "We go first to the public opinion, and when public opinion supports our cause, it will be easier that the government support and understand our cause."[425] Castro's appearance on the *Ed Sullivan Show* was viewed by the largest audience ever for the show up to that point.[426]

CASTRO'S MEETING WITH NIXON

The meeting with Vice President Nixon took place on 19 April. Nixon claimed that his "considerable experience in dealing with Latin American problems" had led Ambassador Bonsal and Acting Secretary Herter to urge a Vice Presidential meeting with Castro.[427] Nixon accepted this assignment and former Secretary of State John Foster Dulles helped the

---

422 Carlos Franqui, *Family Portrait with Fidel* (New York: Random House, 1984), p. 31.
423 Alan McPherson, "The Limits of Populist Diplomacy," *Diplomacy and Statecraft*, 2007, Vol. 18, p. 250.
424 Alan McPherson, "The Limits of Populist Diplomacy," *Diplomacy and Statecraft*, 2007, Vol. 18, p. 246.
425 Alan McPherson, "The Limits of Populist Diplomacy," *Diplomacy and Statecraft*, 2007, Vol. 18, p. 249.
426 Alan McPherson, "The Limits of Populist Diplomacy," *Diplomacy and Statecraft*, 2007, Vol. 18, p. 249.
427 Richard Nixon, "Cuba, Castro and John F. Kennedy," *Reader's Digest*, November, 1964, p. 283.

vice president prepare for the meeting.[428] Nixon stipulated that he and Castro would have to meet alone, without members of each others staff present, and that no photos would be taken for publicity. Nixon was preparing to announce his decision to seek the presidency in the 1960 election and he was concerned that meeting Castro might somehow lessen his status as a thoughtful statesman.[429] The Cuban leader, anxious to increase his standing as a statesman, agreed to Nixon's conditions. On 19 April the two men talked alone for three hours, behind the closed doors of a room in the Capitol Building. They talked about international issues, Castro's "political views," and his "attitude" toward the U.S.[430] After the meeting, both men made cautious, noncommittal statements to the waiting reporters. Castro said the meeting had been "friendly, informal, and positive," and Nixon said the U.S. was "interested in helping the Cuban people in their economic progress in an atmosphere of freedom."[431]

Behind this show of public politeness, however, tension and rancor had marked the private dialogue between these two leaders. Barbs flew in both directions as each man attempted to size up the other, while giving away as little as possible. Castro complained afterward that Nixon had reprimanded him for supporting revolutionary activities in Nicaragua and Panama.[432] An acerbic exchange then followed. Nixon defended the Somoza regime in Nicaragua, singling out Somoza's preference for a democratic government over the dictatorship of his father. Castro countered icily, "Anyone interested in unseating the dictators need not look to the United States for assistance."[433] Nixon bluntly retorted that Cuba would likely not receive U.S. aid, and suggested Castro follow the example of Puerto Rican Governor Luis Munoz Marin, who had raised the standard of living of his people by attracting private capital. To this,

---

428 Nixon wrote a memo about the meeting to Eisenhower, along with a 24 April attachment to John Foster Dulles that reads: "Particularly since you were so helpful with suggestions for my talk with Castro, I thought you might like to see the enclosed copy of a memorandum I drafted of our conversation." FRUS, 1958-1960, volume VI, Cuba, document #287, FRUS Editorial note on Nixon's draft summary of his April 19 talk with Castro.
429 Robert E. Quirk, *Fidel Castro* (New York: WW Norton, 1993) p. 240.
430 Richard Nixon, *RN* (New York: Grosset and Dunlap, 1978, p. 201.
431 Robert E. Quirk, *Fidel Castro* (New York: WW Norton, 1993) p. 240.
432 Georgie Anne Geyer, *Guerrilla Prince: The Untold Story of Fidel Castro* (Boston: Little, Brown & Co., 1991), p. 235.
433 FRUS, 1958-1960, volume VI, Cuba, document #288, Memorandum by the Director of the Office of Mexican and Caribbean Affairs (Weiland), Washington, April 21, 1959.

Castro replied that Cuba would never again become a U.S. colony.[434] Still smarting after the exchange concluded, Castro reportedly told ***Bohemia*** editor Miguel Quevedo, "That son-of-a-bitch Nixon, he treated me badly and he is going to pay for it."[435] Beneath the bravado and swagger of the two men that afternoon, a great deal was at stake for their two countries.

In a memo to President Eisenhower afterward, Nixon concluded that Castro had not come for loans or economic help, but had come instead to win the support of American public opinion.[436] "He gave the *appearance* of sincerity," Nixon later wrote, "but what he said followed a pattern all too familiar to me. I had had conversations with many communist leaders abroad and in the United States."[437] In his assessment for Eisenhower, Nixon wrote, "The one fact we can be sure of is that he has those indefinable qualities which make him a leader of men. Whatever we may think of him he is going to be a great factor in the development of Cuba and very possibly in Latin American affairs generally."[438] In other words, the implications were significant for U.S. foreign policy. They were also significant for Nixon personally because a communist Cuba would spell trouble for his plans to be the next president.

On the all-important question of Castro and communism, Nixon inserted this derisive comment in his memo to the president:

> He is either incredibly naïve about communism or under communist discipline—my guess is the former, as I have already implied his ideas as to how to run a government or an economy are less developed than those of almost any world figure I have met in fifty countries.[439]

Underlying this remark was probably a conflict between hope and fear—hope that Castro was not a communist and fear of the likelihood that he was. Nixon glumly conceded, "because Castro has the power to lead ... we have no choice but at least to try to orient him in the right direction."

---

434   Robert E. Quirk, ***Fidel Castro*** (New York: WW Norton, 1993) p. 241.
435   Georgie Anne Geyer, ***Guerrilla Prince: The Untold Story of Fidel Castro*** (Boston: Little, Brown & Co., 1991), p. 235.
436   Georgie Anne Geyer, ***Guerrilla Prince: The Untold Story of Fidel Castro*** (Boston: Little, Brown & Co., 1991), p. 234.
437   Richard Nixon, "Cuba, Castro and John F. Kennedy," ***Reader's Digest***, November, 1964, p. 284.
438   Richard Nixon, ***RN*** (New York: Grosset and Dunlap, 1978, p. 202.
439   Richard Nixon, ***RN*** (New York: Grosset and Dunlap, 1978, p. 202.

During subsequent NSC meetings, Vice President Nixon was brutally critical of the Assistant Secretary of State for Inter-American Affairs, Roy Rubottom, for his early attempts to get along with Castro. Rubottom was removed after Nixon captured the Republican nomination in the summer of 1960.[440] "I wrote a confidential memorandum for distribution to the CIA, State Department, and White House" about the Castro meeting, Nixon wrote years later and added, "My position was a minority one within the Administration, and particularly so within the Latin American branch of the State Department."[441] Nixon elaborated, "Trying to 'get along with' and 'understand' Castro continued to be the State Department line despite my own strong recommendation to the contrary—one, incidentally, which was shared by J. Edgar Hoover and by two of our former Ambassadors to Cuba, Arthur Gardner and Earl E. T. Smith, as well as by William Pawley." In addition to these powerful men, another person who Nixon said had the same view of Castro was the Director of Central Intelligence, Allen Dulles. All of them thought that Castro was a communist. Nixon said he "sided strongly with Allen Dulles in presenting this view" in the National Security Council.[442]

THE COBB CAPER

We now return to June Cobb's "most intimate friend," Rosalba Roca, and her role in setting up a Cobb encounter with Castro. Probably as planned, Rosalba "insisted" that her friend Luis Conte Aguero should come and meet Cobb. Aguero obliged. Cobb said, "So when he did and saw how hard I was working, he was very much impressed by our interest." Moreover, Aguero even offered to write a prologue to Cobb's edition of the Castro speech. "So he did write the prologue," Cobb later told the CIA, "and I wrote the forward and he did exactly what I told him to do, it was very nice." The little book was ready—although not yet bound—by the time Castro arrived in New York City.[443]

---

440 Nixon was nominated on July 26, 1960, and Rubottom was sent off to be Ambassador to Argentina in August, 1960.
441 Richard Nixon, *Six Crises* (New York: Warner Books, 1979 ed.), p. 416.
442 Richard Nixon, *RN* (New York: Grosset and Dunlap, 1978, pp. 202-203.
443 6/29/60, Attachment to CIA Memorandum to Chief, Security Support Division, Subject: June Cobb, Tape 2, p. 13. RIF 104-10174-10078

CASTRO'S APRIL 1959 VISIT TO THE U.S.

In New York, Aguero introduced June Cobb to Fidel Castro and she presented him with her new book on his speech *History Will Absolve Me*. According to Cobb, Aguero told Castro about her background and that she had been "in the jungle and Andes Mountains, and all these things. So Fidel and Celia [Castro's private secretary] liked me and they were grateful for what I had done and the fact I had contributed money to it."[444] When Cobb's CIA interviewer asked her what had motivated her to do this, she replied:

> Because the Cuban Revolution was a very beautiful thing before it went to hell. ...at any rate, *History Will Absolve Me*, the self-defense speech, is one of the most beautiful documents you can imagine, with the most beautiful principles outlined and the most beautiful quotations from the best pamphlets from the beginning of time, you know, like Thomas Jefferson and Martin Luther and Calvert—the men, you know.[445]

Cobb told her CIA interviewer that from the time of her encounter with Fidel until the middle of the summer she was helping the 26 July Movement organize charity events in New York.[446] Cobb said that in August Cecilia Sanchez sent an aid of Fidel's, Pedro Perez Font, to New York to ask Cobb to come to Cuba to work on propaganda for Fidel. In her 1995 letter to me, Cobb said the same thing:

> I, of course, spent the rest of April, May and June, circulating the booklets I had published (*History Will Absolve Me*) and helping promote the 26 July banquet. In August Pedro Perez Font appeared (my phone was not working) with <u>Celia's</u> invitation on behalf of Fidel.[447]

---

444   6/29/60, Attachment to CIA Memorandum to Chief, Security Support Division, Subject: June Cobb, Tape 2, pp. 13-14.
445   6/29/60, Attachment to CIA Memorandum to Chief, Security Support Division, Subject: June Cobb, Tape 2, pp. 14-15.
446   6/29/60, Attachment to CIA Memorandum to Chief, Security Support Division, Subject: June Cobb, Tape 2, pp. 14-15.
447   1995 June Cobb letter to John Newman.

Cobb told her CIA interviewer that she went down to Cuba for a weekend in August, talked with Sanchez about Fidel's invitation, and agreed to come back in September.[448]

In other words, Cobb's story in the recorded interview with the CIA was that for more than four months she had stayed in New York doing "some things" for the 26 July Movement. She also said that during that period she needed money and so she did some editing work for her "dearest male friend," Dr. Snapper, who was writing a medical textbook. Her explanation about the money involved was contradictory:

> So he was giving me money, not on a salary basis, but he was giving me enough money …. I was helping him because I loved him, and I wanted him to … and he couldn't give me money because he didn't have any, you know. And I …. Well, so that was last summer.[449]

The confusion in her story strains its credibility and, at the most, her association with Snapper at this time appears to have been as insubstantial as "circulating booklets" and doing "some things" for the 26 July Movement for four months.

Even at face value, the account June Cobb gave to the CIA (and to me)—that she stayed in New York from late April through August and did not go to Cuba until September 1959—is odd.[450] But there are more reasons to question her version of where she was that summer. It is noteworthy that, on this particular point, Hermsdorf's account about a period in Cobb's history aligns with her own sworn testimony to the Senate subcommittee. Both of those accounts undermine the version she gave to the CIA and to me. Here is the relevant portion of her testimony to the Senate subcommittee:

> *In the spring of 1959, I went to Havana,* on the invitation of the Prime Minister, Fidel Castro, and his private secretary, Celia Sanchez, where I was in charge of English publications of the Prime Minister's office on behalf of

---

448 6/29/60, Attachment to CIA Memorandum to Chief, Security Support Division, Subject: June Cobb, Tape 1, p. 35 and Tape 2, pp. 21-22.
449 6/29/60, Attachment to CIA Memorandum to Chief, Security Support Division, Subject: June Cobb, Tape 1, p. 35 and Tape 2, p. 21.
450 6/29/60, Attachment to CIA Memorandum to Chief, Security Support Division, Subject: June Cobb, Tape 2, p. 47.

CASTRO'S APRIL 1959 VISIT TO THE U.S.

> the revolutionary government. This invitation was the result of voluntary activities in New York City, early in 1959, where I published an edition of Fidel Castro's defense plea after the Moncada attack, and certain other activities with the 26 July [Movement].[451] [Emphasis added]

This testimony is uncomplicated, without interruption, and it makes sense. Why wait more than four months to get started with Fidel in Cuba?

Hermsdorf's account is brief:

> After Castro's victory he met Miss Cobb on his triumphant tour through the States, was impressed with her, thanked her for her loyal service to the movement, and offered her a job in Cuba. *She went to Havana with him on his return* and was employed as an aide handling public relations.[452] [Emphasis added]

In her letter to me Cobb belittled the Hermsdorf account with this statement:

> Utter Confusion Harry! I have told you (referring to me, John Newman) the real story. I will type it out separately. [Re "offered her a job":] In the Statler his last night in N. Y., Fidel had just said to Celia they should bring me to Cuba and I had answered, "That's not necessary, I know the way."[453]

The explanation in this pushback seems curious too. Knowing the way to Cuba was hardly a good reason to turn down Castro's offer to take her back to Cuba with him.

Besides Cobb's sworn testimony to the Senate Subcommittee, there is another significant piece of evidence about where June Cobb was in the summer of 1959. It comes from the initial CIA Security Office check on Cobb during her "recruitment" in the spring of 1960. A CIA records officer, Joe Piccolo, was looking into Cobb's duties as a personal secretary to Fidel Castro. From *two FBI documents* that had been sent to the CIA by the FBI, Piccolo discovered that Cobb had made two trips in 1959. The first trip concerned her

---

451 3/30/62, June Cobb testimony during a hearing of the Senate Subcommittee to Investigate the Administration of the Internal Security Act and other Internal Security Laws, p. 4; RIF 104-10218-10384.
452 6/1/60, Memorandum by Harry Hermsdorf for Chief, Western Hemisphere Division, Subject: Contingent Recruitment of Viola June Cobb, RIF 104-10111-10148.
453 1995 June Cobb letter to John Newman.

"activities in [the United] States *while on vacation circa 6/59* [emphasis added], and the second trip concerned a "med[ical] RX in NYC in Sept/Dec '59."[454] The second trip would be consistent with Cobb's story that she began working in Cuba in September 1959. But the first trip destroys that story. It clearly indicates that Cobb—while working for Castro in Cuba—took a vacation back to the U.S. around June 1959.

---
454 CIA Office of Security File on Cobb, Viola June, p. 93 of 108 pages. 1993.08.02.10:27:46:250060.

CASTRO'S APRIL 1959 VISIT TO THE U.S.

```
                            SUPPORT BRANCH
                            (VERBAL REQUESTS)
                                              x 2971
                                              Barton Hall
                                              Rm 2011
    REQUESTOR         : Joe Piccolo
    DATE OF REQUEST   :
    IDENTITY OF RECIPIENT:
    TYPE OF REQUEST   :
    SUBJECT           :
    REMARKS           : (bouncing 927?)

              June COBB
         personal secretary to Fidel
         Castro
                         activities in States
                         while on vacation
                         circa 6/59
                                    Med Rx NYC in
    FINANCIAL         :
    DATE ASSIGNED TO FIELD OFFICE:   Sept/Dec '59
    DATE CONFIRMED BY FIELD OFFICE:
    DATE REQUESTOR NOTIFIED      :
                                     DBF 40107 dtd 8 Jan '60
    APPROVED FOR RELEASE 1993        DBF 44345 dtd 11 March 60
    CIA HISTORICAL REVIEW PROGRAM
```

Piccolo Request RE June Cobb activities in U.S. while on vacation [from Cuba]; circa 6/59 CIA Security File; FBI files: DBF 40107, DBF 44345.

The above two mentioned FBI records—that Joe Piccolo reviewed at the CIA—remain sealed. The continued withholding of these records conceals the truth about where Cobb was during the crucial months of May through August 1959. As most of the chapters in the present volume show, there was not much action in New York City at that time; rather, it was all taking place in Cuba, where Castro had offered Cobb a front row seat. The Piccolo memorandum and Cobb's sworn testimony suggest that Cobb might well have gone to Cuba right after Castro's trip to the U.S. We will return to this subject in more detail in Volume II of this series.

THE CASTRO-DROLLER MEETING [NYC 4/22]

As previously discussed, CIA Deputy Director Bissell said that the Agency sent a representative to meet with Castro during his visit to the U.S. First and foremost was the critical task of confirming or refuting the view that, unlike Che Guevara and his brother Raul, Fidel was not a communist. In addition, Bissell explained that the Agency briefed Castro "on communist penetration among his own supporters," hoping that once Castro realized its extent "he might take steps to combat it." Bissell further states that the Agency hoped giving Castro this information "might strengthen his own resolve not to espouse communism." That effort, Bissell concluded, had "proved futile."[455]

During Castro's visit, a CIA officer (unnamed) approached Castro's Finance Minister, Rufo Lopez-Fresquet, in an effort to establish communications regarding Castro's agenda in the U.S. and to set up a meeting between Castro and "Frank Bender," a reported "expert" on Latin American matters. Frank Bender was one of the many pseudonyms for Gerry Droller (see Appendix Two).

German born, Droller had worked with the Office of Strategic Services (OSS) and the *Maquis*—the rural French Underground—in France during WWII. Recruited by the CIA in 1949, Droller had assignments in Switzerland and Formosa (Taiwan), and was part of the Agency's operation

---

455 Richard Bissell, *Reflections of a Cold Warrior* (New Haven: Yale University Press, 1996), p. 152.

PBSUCCESS to overthrow Guatemalan President Jacobo Arbenz in 1954. Using the alias "Frank Bender," Droller would soon be in charge of the CIA's Cuban exile activities in Miami in preparation for the Bay of Pigs invasion. His reported expertise in Latin American affairs proved to be ineffective in that operation. One problem was his lack of any facility for Spanish.

In his book ***My Fourteen Months with Castro***, Rufo Lopez-Fresquet wrote about the strange three hour meeting between Castro and Bender. Rufo said that he had been contacted by a U.S. government official, whose name he did not want to reveal, about a meeting between Castro and "Mr. Frank Bender" [Droller]. Lopez-Fresquet said Bender was described as the "highest authority of American intelligence in Latin America." Lopez-Fresquet states that Castro avoided making a decision on a possible interview with Droller, but finally acceded because of Lopez-Fresquet's insistence to doing the interview in New York:

> Mr. Bender and Castro talked privately for more than three hours. When he had finished, Mr. Bender returned to my suite in a state of euphoria. He asked for a drink, and with great relief exclaimed, "Castro is not only not a communist; he is a strong anti-communist fighter." I remembered that, and when I told Castro of the fears in Washington about the communist question, he said, "Look Rufo, I am letting the communists stick their heads out so I will know who they are. *And when I know them all, I'll do away with them, with one sweep of my hat.*" Mr. Bender informed me he had arranged with Castro an exchange of intelligence information on the activities of the communists and that I was to be the Cuban contact. The following month, during a reception at the French Embassy in Havana, a high U.S. official approached me and gave me an oral message for Castro from Mr. Bender. At the next cabinet session, I gave Castro the intelligence. He didn't answer me, and he never gave me any information

to pass on to Mr. Bender, the "expert" on communists.[456]

[Emphasis added]

It is likely that Castro also told "Bender" the same lie about doing away with all of the communists with one sweep of his hat.

An informant in Castro's press entourage stated that Castro had said he was trying to "confuse" the Americans as to the "real objectives" of the revolution.[457] If there were communists in the Cuban government, Castro said on NBC's *Meet the Press*, then they had no influence.[458] Bender's euphoria and comment to Lopez-Fresquet that Castro was a strong anti-communist fighter was probably a ruse. Both men had been playing a mutual game of deception.[459] There would be no collaboration between the U.S. and Cuba against communism.

Meanwhile, in New York the Castro show went on. The poet Carlos Franqui said he tried to get Castro to go to the museum to see Picasso's *Guernica* and Wilfredo Lam's *Jungle*, but alas, his effort had failed. Instead, Castro went to the zoo and ate a hot dog.[460]

---

456 Lopez Fresquet Rufo, ***My Fourteen Months With Castro*** (New York, World Publishing Company, 1966 edition), p. 110. See also Hugh Thomas, ***Cuba, The Pursuit of Freedom*** (New York: Harper and Rowe, 1971) p. 1057 and p. 1211; see also Georgie Anne Geyer, ***Guerrilla Prince: The Untold Story of Fidel Castro*** (Boston: Little, Brown & Co., 1991), pp. 240-241.
457 FRUS, 1958-1960, volume VI, Cuba, document #288, Memorandum by the Director of the Office of Mexican and Caribbean Affairs (Weiland), Washington, April 21, 1959.
458 Robert E. Quirk, ***Fidel Castro*** (New York: WW Norton, 1993) p. 240.
459 Alan McPherson, "The Limits of Populist Diplomacy," ***Diplomacy and Statecraft***, 2007, Vol. 18, p. 245.
460 Carlos Franqui, ***Family Portrait with Fidel*** (New York: Random House, 1984), p. 32.

CHAPTER TWELVE:
CUBA INVADES THE CARIBBEAN

Once Castro's regime was ensconced in Havana many exiles from other Latin American countries went there to seek out contacts and make the case for support of revolutions in their own countries. Yet many of these so-called invasions were aborted soon after they began. Views differ on how many of them were fully backed by Castro. The United States Information Agency (USIA)[461] officer in Havana, Paul Bethel, was sharply critical of journalists—like Herb Matthews—who argued that the only invasion with Castro's official backing took place in the Dominican Republic:

> The innocence attributed to Fidel Castro again overlooks the truth. Through accounts published in the Cuban press it was clear that General Alberto Bayo and four members of Castro's government had been busy planning invasions of Cuba's neighbors in the Caribbean. Haitian exiles, Luis Dejoie and Daniel Fuguoli, transmitted calls for revolt in their country over radio stations in

---

461 The USIA CIA cryptonym is QKFLOWAGE.

Cuba which had to be known, and indeed sanctioned, by the Cuban government.[462]

Using the "extensive powers of the Cuban government," Bethel observed, General Bayo had opened and operated a guerrilla training camp at the beach of Tarara for use in these invasions. Hugh Thomas suggests that "perhaps" some of the attacks, such as those against Nicaragua and Guatemala, were done without the Cuban government's support.[463]

FRANK STURGIS' SECRET VISIT TO FBI HQS

Nearly two months before Frank Sturgis fled Cuba to save his life, he made a secret visit to FBI HQS in Washington. There, on 13 March 1959, Sturgis was interviewed by FBI agents, "upon referral" by Director Hoover's office. Anti-communist officers in the Cuban military, whose pleas had fallen on deaf ears at the U.S. Embassy in Havana, had approached Sturgis and asked him to go to Washington to explain the extent of the communist crisis in Cuba.[464] Sturgis specifically identified Pedro and Marcos Diaz Lanz as being among the Cuban military officers that had sent him with the news about the communist quandary.

Sturgis also told the Bureau about Cuban plans to invade other Caribbean countries:

> Fiorini (Sturgis) advised that there were various revolutionary groups in Havana, all of which were trying to contact Fidel Castro for assistance. He stated that these groups were having a difficult time contacting Castro as Castro was too busy with Cuban affairs to deal with them directly. Accordingly, representatives of these groups have been referred to other Cuban officials.[465]

Sturgis told the FBI that these plans called for the "elimination" of Nicaraguan President Somoza and the establishment of an "honest" gov-

---

462 Paul Bethel, *The Losers* (New York: Arlington House, 1969), p. 134-135.
463 Hugh Thomas, *Cuba, The Pursuit of Freedom* (New York: Harper and Rowe, 1971) p. 1228.
464 4/1/59, FBI Memo from M. A. Jones to DeLoach, Subject Frank Fiorini, AKA Frank Anthony Sturgis. RIF 124-10302-10238.
465 4/1/59, FBI Memo from M. A. Jones to DeLoach, Subject Frank Fiorini, AKA Frank Anthony Sturgis. RIF 124-10302-10238.

ernment there. The revolutionaries even hoped for help from the U.S. to overthrow the regime in Panama because it was not considered pro-American.

Sturgis explained that once these "hostile" Central American governments had been "neutralized," the revolutionaries' plan then called for the placement of guerrilla troops in the northern mountains of the Dominican Republic. This maneuver was expected to divide Trujillo's forces. The revolutionaries did not believe they could count on the peasants and assumed that only by dividing Trujillo's forces would they be able to succeed. And finally, Sturgis said, the revolutionaries hoped that success in the Dominican Republic would then enable them to overthrow the Government of Haiti.[466]

PANAMA

The Cuban incursion into Panama began on 22 April 1959, during Castro's trip to the U.S. Three days after Castro's meeting with Nixon and just two days after Castro's address at the United Nations, Cesar Vega lead a group of eighty-seven Cubans and Panamanians that landed at a remote beach on Panama's Caribbean coast. Panamanian President Ernesto de la Guardia, Jr. said that he had been "tipped off" that the landing would be near the town of Nombre de Dios, and that his source had indicated that two more invasion ships were on the way to Panama.[467]

Fidel Castro immediately dissociated himself from the invasion in a live "news conference," broadcast from on board his flight from Houston, Texas, to Buenos Aires, Argentina. Castro denounced the Cubans in Panama for violating his "Cuban revolutionary principles and ignoring direct orders to avoid any such involvements," and insisted that he had no interest in promoting revolutions elsewhere in Latin America.[468] He sent two Cuban officers to Nombre de Dios to negotiate the sur-

---
466 4/1/59, FBI Memo from M. A. Jones to DeLoach, Subject Frank Fiorini, AKA Frank Anthony Sturgis. RIF 124-10302-10238.
467 4/29/59, "Castro Officers Sent to End Cubans' Invasion of Panama," *The Cornell Daily Sun.*
468 4/29/59, "Castro Officers Sent to End Cubans' Invasion of Panama," *The Cornell Daily Sun.*

render of the invasion force. Bethel argues that had the invasion been successful, Castro's "story" would have been different.[469] On 1 May the Cuban invasion force surrendered to the Panamanian National Guard and to a team from the Organization of American States (OAS) that was sent to investigate the invasion.

According to Hugh Thomas, the Panama event helped bring the conflict between Castro and the anti-communists in Cuba to a head. By the time Castro returned to Cuba, Raul Castro had removed the chief of army intelligence (G-2), Sergio Sanjenis. Sergio had served in a rebel column in the Matanzas region during the revolution and Castro had appointed him as the Army G-2 in January. Sanjenis soon fell in with the growing group of officers disenchanted by communist penetration of the new regime. His firing by Raul Castro was the opening salvo in a campaign to purge the anti-communists in the Cuban military. In Sanjenis' place, Raul appointed his old friend, Ramiro Valdes, as the new Army G-2.[470] Valdes had, along with Camilo Cienfuegos, Che Guevara, Raul and Fidel, been part of the super-secret Castro-PSP agreement at Cojimar.

The fact that the Panama incursion occurred while Castro was in the U.S. was particularly offensive to Vice President Nixon. After his meeting with Nixon in Washington, Castro had complained that the Vice President had reprimanded him for supporting revolutionary activities in Nicaragua and Panama.[471] Nixon claimed that in the ensuing months he was "the strongest and most persistent advocate for setting up and supporting" a covert effort to remove Castro from power.[472] "Early in 1960, the position I had been advocating for nine months finally prevailed," Nixon said—referring to President Eisenhower's later approval of a covert plan of action to overthrow Castro.[473]

Apparently, the removal of Castro was also on Eisenhower's mind at the time of Castro's April 1959 visit to the U.S. The evidence for this

---

469   Paul Bethel, *The Losers* (New York: Arlington House, 1969), p. 134-135.
470   Hugh Thomas, *Cuba, The Pursuit of Freedom* (New York: Harper and Rowe, 1971) pp. 1031-1032, and p. 1213.
471   Georgie Anne Geyer, *Guerrilla Prince: The Untold Story of Fidel Castro* (Boston: Little, Brown & Co., 1991), p. 235.
472   Richard Nixon, "Cuba, Castro and John F. Kennedy," *Reader's Digest*, November, 1964, p. 288.
473   Richard Nixon, *Six Crises* (New York: Warner Books, 1979 ed.), p. 416.

comes from a discussion between Secretary of Defense Neil McElroy and Eisenhower that took place during Castro's trip. McElroy recalled these details:

> I remember clearly having a discussion with President Eisenhower about the threat to our country of having a communist island so close to our shores and expressed to the president the belief that if the Castro government turned out clearly to be communist oriented, we should have to take whatever action was necessary, to remove him and his group from their control of the Cuban government. It's my clear recollection that President Eisenhower agreed. This of course is not to say that we agreed on any specific action at that time.[474]

This early—spring 1959—White House determination to remove Castro if he moved Cuba into the communist camp foreshadowed what would take place at the end of the year.

NICARAGUA

Barely a month had passed after the Panama invasion when two more incursions took place: one in Nicaragua and another in the Dominican Republic. On 31 May 1959, a group of Cuban soldiers landed by plane in the mountainous area of Nicaragua. The Cuban air force commander, Pedro Diaz Lanz, told the FBI that the pilot, Roberto Verdaguer, flew the plane to Nicaragua on the "orders of Fidel Castro."[475]

The USIA officer in Havana, Paul Bethel, recalled that the Cuban newspapers contained many hints about the invasions. In his autobiography, **The Losers**, Bethel gives this account of the Nicaraguan incursion:

> The American Embassy in Havana was particularly aware of what was going on with regard to the invasion of Nicaragua. On 31 May, a group of Cubans landed in a plane

---
474 Neil McElroy interview, 1967, **The Eisenhower Oral History Collection**, Columbia University Library, p. 88.
475 7/8/59, Memorandum from SAC Miami to DIR FBI, RE LHM on Pedro Luis Diaz Lanz. RIF 124-10221-10252.

in the hilly country of Nicaragua and were joined by another group of Havana-trained Nicaraguans who had first gone to Honduras, there to cross over the border into Nicaragua in order to link up with the airborne units. An American adventurer, Leslie Bradley, was involved in the exploit, but to his astonishment he was arrested by Guevara and held in La Cabana Fortress.

In Bethel's scenario, the Nicaraguan episode was a Castro show all the way, and Che Guevara and Alberto Bayo cooked up a plot to use Bradley as an "insurance policy" to pin the blame on the U.S. in the event that the plot failed—which it did.[476]

On 28 June still another group of Havana-trained Nicaraguans was captured trying to cross the border from Honduras into Nicaragua. The OAS issued a finding that Che Guevara had trained the invaders at La Cabana fortress in Cuba—the same fortress where U.S. Embassy representatives were interviewing the imprisoned Bradley.[477] From that interview they concluded that Bradley's arrest was designed to lessen the blow of the failed invasion by getting him to testify—in return for his life—that the U.S. was behind the invasion.[478]

Yet it turns out that Bethel and his sources on the embassy staff were not aware of all that was going on with the Nicaraguan invasion. Leslie Bradley was one of several American adventurers in Cuba. There were others linked to this invasion too—such as Loran Hall and Gerry Hemming. Hemming was an American citizen who had left high school as a junior to join the Marine Corps in 1954, and had been discharged in October 1958. He arrived in Cuba on 19 February 1959.

According to the CIA Los Angeles Office, Hemming bluffed his way into the Cuban army "with no prior connections having been made in the U.S."[479] In October 1960, two months after Hemming had left Cuba, the chief of the Los Angeles office, Ernst Liebacher, received a phone call from Hemming. Liebacher's subordinate, Paul R. Hendrickson, interviewed Hemming on 12 October 1960, and again on 21 October.

---
476 Paul Bethel, *The Losers* (New York: Arlington House, 1969), p. 134-135.
477 Paul Bethel, *The Losers* (New York: Arlington House, 1969), pp. 134-135.
478 Paul Bethel, *The Losers* (New York: Arlington House, 1969), pp. 134-135.
479 10/12/60, Report of Ernst. Liebacher, CIA Field Los Angeles Field Office, RE Interview of Gerry Patrick Hemming. OO-A-3170536, RIF 1993.06.28.17:17:55:210360.

CUBA INVADES THE CARIBBEAN

According to Hendrickson's report, in February 1959 an American serving at the HQS of the General Staff at Camp Columbia, Captain Johnny Mitchell, befriended Hemming and obtained a pass for him to enter the camp. Hemming was then able to speak with several officers, including Major Camilo Cienfuegos. Cienfuegos assigned Hemming to Major Enrico Borbonet, a Fort Benning trained officer who was in command of a paratroop regiment:

> Major Borbonet reportedly did not like Hemming or want him in his unit, but Hemming obtained orders from "Camilo" detailing him to the paratroop regiment as an officer. Maj. Borbonet refused to accept him as an officer so he went into the unit as a sergeant about the end of February 1959. Hemming stayed with the unit until December 1959. He helped train paratroopers first at San Antonio de los Banos Air Force Base and later near San Jose do los Lajas, a small town about 35 miles southeast of Havana on the central highway.[480]

In a 1995 interview with the present author, Hemming claimed that he recruited Camilo Cienfuegos at this time.[481] Hemming confirmed what Alberto Fernandez and Frank Sturgis said about Camilo—he was anti-communist.

Hendrickson learned that while Hemming was in the Cuban army he had become involved with a number of Nicaraguans who were interested in invading Nicaragua from Cuba. Hendrickson said that the basic outline was "roughly" as follows:

> A Nicaraguan named Farfan contacted a number of troopers in the paratroop regiment to recruit volunteers for an expedition to Nicaragua. About fifteen of Hemming's troopers were involved. The expedition turned out to be well infiltrated with anti-Castro personnel and Batistianos, and the expedition appeared to have as its aim primarily the acquisition of arms for anti-Castro revolutionaries and also to embarrass Castro by tying him politically to a movement designed to overthrow President Somoza in Nicaragua.

---
480 10/12/60, E. Liebacher, Los Angeles CIA Field Office interview of Gerry Patrick Hemming. NARA JFK files, RIF 1993.06.28.17:17:55:210360.
481 Gerry Hemming, 6 January 1995 interview with John Newman.

Hemming told Hendrickson that the expedition never left Cuba and that Farfan's men were captured in Camaguey sometime during September 1959.[482]

The Los Angeles CIA office was not the first CIA source to interview Hemming about the Nicaraguan expedition. While still employed as a parachutist by the Cuban air force at San Julian, Hemming had slipped out of Cuba in February 1960 and was debriefed by his CIA contacts in Costa Rica—a journalist named "Bernie Godoy" and a "Mr. McGill."[483] McGill, Hemming recalls, was the one who debriefed him.[484] Hemming's information was compiled and disseminated in a "SECRET NO-FORN CONTINUED" CIA Information Report:

> Hemming was engaged in training Nicaraguans, and said that there were only twenty-five parachutists in Cuba, located in Baracoa, Caya Largo, Oriente, and San Antonio. All were willing to fight in Nicaragua, and would go well armed. Hemming, also a flier, was a marine in Korea and at the Guantanamo Naval Base, and had been warned when he was fighting with Castro that he could lose his citizenship, but this was not important to him. He said that the base at San Julian could be used as a location from which to fly food and arms to rebels fighting within Nicaragua. He knew of a number of 7.62 caliber Belgian automatic rifles that could be made available to Nicaraguan rebels. According to Hemming, a Mexican island one hundred and fifty miles from Cuba might be used as a base of operations for sending a plane or boat to Nicaragua, since it was poorly policed. He said he would furnish a C-46 aircraft when it was needed.[485]

Hemming's information supports Hugh Thomas' view about Castro's lack of enthusiasm for the Nicaraguan invasion. Hemming told his de-

---

482 10/12/60, Report of Ernst. Liebacher, CIA Field Los Angeles Field Office, RE Interview of Gerry Patrick Hemming. OO-A-3170536, RIF 1993.06.28.17:17:55:210360.
483 04/04/60, CIA Information Report CS-3/432,532, 4 April 1960; country: Nicaragua/Cuba/Costa Rica; field report number HPS-2280. RIF 104-10172-10034.
484 Gerry Hemming, 6 January 1995 interview with John Newman.
485 04/04/60, CIA Information Report CS-3/432,532, 4 April 1960; country: Nicaragua/Cuba/Costa Rica; field report number HPS-2280. RIF 104-10172-10034.

CUBA INVADES THE CARIBBEAN

briefers that the people associated with this invasion "practiced discretion to avoid having rumors reach Castro." Hemming had heard that Castro did not favor the "entire" movement for these invasions and had become particularly discouraged with the disagreements among Nicaraguan rebel leaders.[486]

In the spirit of due diligence, the present author searched for information on Hemming's "Mr. McGill," and did find a "Ralph M. McGill" in FBI and CIA records. FBI documents indicate that Ralph M. McGill was a publisher in the mid-1970s; and he had also been associated with the anti-Castro "White Rose" group and Mitchell L. Werbell.[487] [Werbell, possibly AMBOAR, had worked for Batista—see Appendix One.] FBI files also indicate McGill that had been a reporter for *The Evening Star* on Cuban matters in 1959 and 1960.[488]

In 1975 the CIA investigated a complaint that Ralph M. McGill was impersonating a CIA officer. Edward Lewis Bankston had called the CIA Security Office to report that he had been "flying individuals out of Cuba" from 1968 to 1974 for Ralph M. McGill." Bankston said that McGill led him to believe he was associated with the CIA. The CIA investigation concluded that no one by the name Ralph M. McGill had ever worked for the CIA or used that name as an alias.[489] Another CIA memo on the "McGill matter" stated, "Though McGill was not an Agency employee, the question is who was McGill working for?"[490] Whatever the answer to that question is, we can be certain of this much: The report Hemming claimed he gave to Mr. McGill *did find its way* into the above quoted CIA Information Report at the time and place indicated by Hemming—late February 1960 in Costa Rica. This lends credibility to Hemming's account.

There was another American soldier of fortune involved in the Nicaraguan invasion—Loran Hall. Hemming told the FBI that he first met Loran Hall, who liked to be called "Skip," in April 1959 when Hall

---

486 04/04/60, CIA Information Report CS-3/432,532, 4 April 1960; country: Nicaragua/Cuba/Costa Rica; field report number HPS-2280. RIF 104-10172-10034.
487 06/30/75, CIA Memo from Chief, Security Support Division to Deputy Director of Security. 1993.08.06.10:12:54:460015.
488 See 124-10291-10199.
489 00/00/74, CIA Memorandum for the Deputy Director for Administration, Subject: Ralph M. McGill. RIF 1993.08.05.15:16:44:840028.
490 06/30/75, CIA Memo from Chief, Security Support Division to Deputy Director of Security. 1993.08.06.10:12:54:460015.

was in jail at the army barracks at Camp Libertad near Havana (Camp Columbia became Camp Libertad in early 1959). Hemming said Hall had been arrested for being involved in preparations for the Cuban action against Nicaragua, and that he shared a Cuban jail cell with Miami gangster Santo Trafficante.[491]

Trafficante was not the only notable associate of Hall's during the Nicaraguan episode. U.S. Naval intelligence files reveal that in March 1959 Camilo Cienfuegos had contacted Loran Hall with respect to the invasion of Nicaragua.[492] The original source of that story was a 9 July 1959 report to the FBI from a Panamanian living in Miami, Ruben Miro Guardia. While in Cuba during April 1959, Miro had been detained by Cuban police and during his detention he met Loran Hall:

> Hall told Miro that he had arrived in Cuba in about March 1959, and had subsequently been contacted by Camilo Cienfuegos, a Cuban rebel army commander. Cienfuegos wanted Hall to participate in an invasion of Nicaragua. Hall claimed he trained a group of men on a farm known as La Lisa, located near Havana. Hall said the food for the trainees came from the Cuban Military Staff Headquarters, on the orders of Cienfuegos. Miro stated that Hall said he was arrested on 8 April 1959 by Cuban authorities, who alleged Hall was suspected of being an FBI agent.

Miro told the FBI that when he left Cuba on 7 July 1959, Hall was still in custody there.[493]

To understand why Leslie Bradley was in Bethel's account, while Camilo Cienfuegos and Loran Hall were not, requires looking deeper into what Camilo Cienfuegos was up to in the convoluted story of Cuba's invasions in the Caribbean.

---

491 8/14/64, Memorandum from SAC Miami to DIR FBI, RE Loran Hall, AKA Lorenzo Hall, AKA Lawrence Hall. "Skip." RIF 124-10216-10155.
492 NARA, JFK files, INS/ONI box 1; ONI report on Loran Hall, 15 January 1964, ONI routing slip GG134356.
493 8/14/64, Memorandum from SAC Miami to DIR FBI, RE Loran Hall, AKA Lorenzo Hall, AKA Lawrence Hall. "Skip." RIF 124-10216-10155.

CAMILO CIENFUEGOS' SECRET VISIT TO MIAMI

On 17 April 1959, forty-eight hours after the two planes carrying Castro and his entourage landed in Washington D.C., a Miami ship broker named Wallace A. Quinn contacted the New York Office of the FBI with peculiar news. Quinn was troubled by what he had to report. He told the Bureau that he had been "sent" by Alberto Fernandez and a *Castro opposition group* to "ascertain the course of action the U.S. would take re the Cuban government."[494] This was only a partial message, obviously presuming that an event was going to take place for which the U.S. would have to develop a course of action.

By 18 April the situation had become more apparent. Quinn told the FBI that "a Gomez Ochoa and a Miss Boyar were sent by Fernandez to Miami to see him." One might have ventured an educated guess as to why Fernandez wanted this Castro opposition group to approach Wallace Quinn, who was a ship broker:

> They were allegedly interested in obtaining two PT boats. On 4/18/59 Quinn advised he planned contact with these persons on 4/20/59 in Miami and would advise the Miami office of results. The New York office noted Quinn was upset over this matter fearing it may be attempt to implicate him in anti-Castro activities. Quinn plans to refer these people to Mrs. Catherine Taaffe, with whom he is familiar.[495]

Catherine Taaffe had established a long-standing relationship with Castro's head of the Sugar Institute, Alberto Fernandez, as well as with his father and family. Fernandez had introduced Taaffe to Wallace Quinn back in 1953.[496]

What made this story peculiar was its apparent anti-Castro dimension—that these individuals would risk being identified in a "Castro opposition group." And that was exactly why Quinn had cold feet about

---

[494] 4/21/59, FBI Memo from S. B. Donahoe to A. H. Belmont, Subject: Anti-Fidel Castro Activities, Internal Security—Cuba. RIF 124-90055-1074.
[495] 4/21/59, FBI Memo from S. B. Donahoe to A. H. Belmont, Subject: Anti-Fidel Castro Activities, Internal Security—Cuba. RIF 124-90055-1074.
[496] 4/29/59, Airtel, SAC New York to DIR FBI, Subject: Cuban Revolutionary Activities; IS—Cuba. FBI 8/29/2008 FOIA Release to Jim Lesar, pp. 123-125.

it. Apparently, Quinn did not know enough about Gomez Ochoa's background—at least for the moment—to proceed safely. It took only hours for a Miami FBI Office investigation to find the hotel where Gomez and Boyar were staying. They discovered a group of four people: Enrique Jimenez and Monica Boyar were registered in one room of the hotel and Gomez Ochoa and Ramon Ruiz in another. The FBI also quickly assembled what they knew about these four people and, presumably, shared these details with Quinn:

> Jimenez may be identical with Captain Enrique Jimenez, a Dominican revolutionary who served with Castro. Gomez may be identical with the 26 July Movement captain. Monica Boyar reportedly is a night club singer. Ruiz may be identical with Camilo Cienfuegos, Cuban army chief of staff, since Ruiz is the alias of Cienfuegos.[497]

These details had turned a peculiar story into an extraordinary one, and a senior FBI official, S. B. Donahoe, stated the obvious: "at first glance it would appear doubtful that Jimenez, Gomez and Cienfuegos would be involved in an anti-Castro movement."

Yet the FBI's investigation also turned up information indicating that these men might well have been involved in *Anti-Fidel Castro Activities*—which was the subject header for the Bureau's memorandum summarizing the group's bizarre meeting with Quinn in Miami:

> We have received allegations originating with Enrique Garcia, a registered Dominican agent, that Jimenez is actually a Dominican undercover agent working with Fidel Castro forces. Quinn reported that Gomez allegedly expressed disillusion with Castro revolution. Concerning Cienfuegos, Quinn has advised that Fernandez' father was supposed to have contacted Cienfuegos recently to ascertain his loyalty to Castro, *as it is felt that Cienfuegos is not completely behind Castro.*[498] [Emphasis added]

---

[497] 4/21/59, FBI Memo from S. B. Donahoe to A. H. Belmont, Subject: Anti-Fidel Castro Activities, Internal Security—Cuba. RIF 124-90055-1074.
[498] 4/21/59, FBI Memo from S. B. Donahoe to A. H. Belmont, Subject: Anti-Fidel Castro Activities, Internal Security—Cuba. RIF 124-90055-1074.

CUBA INVADES THE CARIBBEAN

Enrique Garcia had long been an FBI informant, and as such, Jimenez's alleged undercover status in Castro's forces was worthy of being taken seriously.

However, the above FBI memo provided little information about Gomez Ochoa's background beyond his rank as a captain in Castro's 26 July Movement. Gomez Ochoa had in fact gone to work for Castro in the Sierra Maestra in May 1957. According to Hugh Thomas' history of Cuba, Gomez Ochoa had become an *anti-communist* representative of the 26 July Movement in Havana in 1958.[499] Thomas' treatment underscored Ochoa's "almost violent manner" against any pact with the communists and added these details:

> Gomez Ochoa, who had left the Sierra on 23 May (that is, long before Carlos Rafael Rodriguez's [a communist] first visit to the hills), was an Ortodoxo student of diplomatic law at the University of Havana, the son of a landowner, and a passionate anti-communist and enemy of Raul Castro.[500]

By the summer of 1959, Gomez Ochoa had married Maria Witowska. She had previously been married to Rene Vallejo, a commander of Castro's forces in the Sierra and his personal doctor and aide-de-camp. Vallejo had served with the American Third Army in post-war Germany and had urged Castro, after his victory in Cuba, to make friends with the Americans. Maria had been a liaison between Castro's forces in the Sierra and Paul D. Wiecha, the chief of the CIA Base in Santiago.[501] She also facilitated meetings between Castro and journalists. In 1959 and 1960, Maria was one of June Cobb's closest associates in Cuba and an asset of the CIA's Henry Hermsdorf.

The big news was that Cienfuegos himself appears to have accompanied the group to Miami in search of boats for the Cuban invasion of the Dominican Republic. He was certainly the most senior military officer in this alleged "Castro opposition group." The FBI had known for some time that Alberto Fernandez had been reporting, through Taaffe, that

---

499 Hugh Thomas, *Cuba, The Pursuit of Freedom* (New York: Harper and Rowe, 1971) p. 1228.
500 Hugh Thomas, *Cuba, The Pursuit of Freedom* (New York: Harper and Rowe, 1971) p. 1006.
501 Tad Szulc, *Fidel: A Critical Portrait* (Perennial, 2002 Ed.) p. 428.

Cienfuegos was anti-communist. During the summer of 1959, Taaffe would work more directly with Cienfuegos during her trips to Cuba.

Cienfuegos remained in the background when Quinn met with Gomez, Jimenez and Boyar on 20 April. This time they gave Quinn a note from Fernandez asking him to assist Gomez to purchase the two PT boats. The note from Alberto Fernandez apparently allayed Quinn's doubts about remaining involved with this group. The FBI reported on 21 April that Quinn assumed that the boats were needed for the invasion of the Dominican Republic, that the Cuban government was supporting the deal, and that the group did not intend to defect from Castro. Quinn, now ready to play along, said he would make inquiries about the PT boats and keep the FBI informed.[502]

On 26 May 1959, an FBI letterhead memorandum was wholly devoted to intelligence developed by Catherine Taaffe during and since her 29 April-mid-May trip to Cuba. She reported the formation in Cuba of an "anti-Castro group composed of members of the 26 July Movement, the Autentico party and the Orthordox party." The group said Castro would have to come out publicly either in support of or in opposition to the communist party. Taaffe reported that Major Camilo Cienfuegos "is strongly anti-communist and is most resentful of certain individuals surrounding Castro." The opposition group told her they felt that they could get the support of Cienfuegos and members of the army "if it comes to the breaking point between democracy and communism in Cuba."[503]

THE DOMINICAN REPUBLIC

On 8 June 1959, six days before the invasion of the Dominican Republic, Sturgis visited the U.S. Embassy and reported that there were two Cuban air force planes at the air base at Camp Libertad from which Cuban insignia had been removed.[504] We might be forgiven for ignoring this

---

502 4/21/59, FBI Memo from S. B. Donahoe to A. H. Belmont, Subject: Anti-Fidel Castro Activities, Internal Security—Cuba. RIF 124-90055-1074.
503 5/26/59, FBI Letterhead Memorandum, RE Foreign Political Matters—Cuba. FBI 109, HQ 12-210, Vol. 16, pp. 24-28.
504 6/11/59, Legat, Havana to DIR FBI, Subject: Frank Fiorini, AKA Frank Anthony Sturgis. RIF 124-10302-10245. Sturgis had walked into the Air Attaché office at the embassy asking to speak with Ambassador Bonsal who had previous commitment. So Sturgis made this report to the Assistant Political Officer, William G. Bowdler, instead.

unfinished message from Sturgis, were it not for a detail from Pedro Diaz Lanz' FBI debrief right after his exfiltration from Cuba to Miami. Pedro Lanz recalled an event that had occurred just two weeks before Sturgis' report about the "two planes" at the airbase. According to Lanz, Castro had instructed him to have the Cuban air force fly two C-46s on an expedition to the Dominican Republic. Pedro said that because one of these two planes was under repair at the time he made no commitment to Castro and that "due to their subsequent differences" Castro did not ask him again.[505]

Pedro Lanz told the FBI that one of the aircraft used in the attack on the Dominican Republic was "a C-46 which had been painted grey with all the serials removed," and that it was commanded by Enrique Jimenez Moya and Delio Gomez Ochoa. According to Pedro Diaz Lanz' testimony before the Senate Internal Security Committee (SISC), Gomez Ochoa bought the C-46, that had been used in the invasion, in the U.S.[506]

On 14 June, the Cuban-led force invaded the Dominican Republic by air and sea. With Castro's approval, two hundred Dominicans and ten Cubans under a rebel army officer, Delio Gomez Ochoa, landed in two waves on the north coast of the Dominican Republic.[507] The naval force left Cuba on the morning of 13 June, and the airborne group left at 4:00 p.m. on 14 June. This attack was unquestionably the bloodiest venture among the various Cuban invasions of the Caribbean that summer.

Gomez Ochoa, Enrique Jimenez, and fifty-five other men, boarded a C-46 with false markings and flew from Oriente Province in Cuba to Costanza airport in the Dominican Republic, hoping to hide in the nearby mountains.[508] The C-46 was flown by Juan de Dios Ventura Simo, who remained with the expeditionary group while another Cuban pilot flew the plane back to Cuba.[509] Evidently, the other pilot was lucky: the plane returned with only eight holes in it.[510]

---

505   7/8/59, Memorandum from SAC Miami to DIR FBI, RE LHM on Pedro Luis Diaz Lanz. RIF 124-10221-10252
506   7/20/50, Pedro Luis Diaz Lanz testimony before the Senate Subcommittee on Internal Security, p. 36. RIF 124-10218-10362.
507   Hugh Thomas, *Cuba, The Pursuit of Freedom* (New York: Harper and Rowe, 1971) p. 1228.
508   Felix I. Rodriguez, *Shadow Warrior* (New York: Simon and Schuster, 1989), p. 39.
509   6/25/59, FBI Report by Daniel Brennan on the Cuban invasion of the Dominican Republic. 124-10279-10048.
510   7/8/59, Memorandum from SAC Miami to DIR FBI, RE LHM on Pedro Luis Diaz Lanz. RIF 124-10221-10252.

Fooled by the plane's markings, the airport guards were overcome,[511] but the invading group lost most of their men in the fight. A few, including Gomez Ochoa, struggled inland but never made it to the mountains. Trujillo dispatched about half of his "Legion" to mop up the Jimenez force—but most of the Cubans had already met a gruesome end.[512] Farmers and machete-wielding *guajiros* vigorously pursued and beheaded the invaders.[513] Trujillo had put a bounty on the bearded Cuban heads, which the farmers put into burlap bags and carried to army posts where they were paid U.S. $1,000 per head.[514] The invaders were all eventually captured. Most were tortured and shot, but not their commander, Gomez Ochoa. Ochoa was imprisoned.[515]

The other part of the invasion force consisted of two yachts—the *Carmen Elsa* and the *Tinita*. According to General Rafael Trujillo, Jr., son of the Dominican dictator, the nearly one hundred and fifty men aboard the two vessels never made it to shore. The *Tinita* got close to shore when it was sunk and the *Carmen Elsa* was intercepted about a quarter of a mile offshore.[516] A statement by General Rafael Trujillo said that the invaders had been "liquidated" and that Enriquez Jimenez was among those killed.[517]

Paul Bethel's memoir states that the military attachés at the embassy who had been watching preparations for the invasion for some months "were aghast at the openness with which they were carried out." Their agents knew everything that was going on, and reported that Raul Castro had personally taken charge of the departure of the invasion force. The army attaché, Samuel Kail, was able to give the ambassador's morning staff meeting "what amounted to a daily running account of the progress of the invasion force."[518] Bethel concluded that although "there was enough factual evidence for the United States to at least consider a military blockade of Cuba, if it were so disposed," nothing came of it.

---

511 Paul Bethel, ***The Losers*** (New York: Arlington House, 1969), p. 135.
512 Felix I. Rodriguez, ***Shadow Warrior*** (New York: Simon and Schuster, 1989), p. 39.
513 Paul Bethel, ***The Losers*** (New York: Arlington House, 1969), p. 135.
514 Felix I. Rodriguez, ***Shadow Warrior*** (New York: Simon and Schuster, 1989), p. 39.
515 Hugh Thomas, ***Cuba, The Pursuit of Freedom*** (New York: Harper and Rowe, 1971) p. 1228.
516 Paul Bethel, ***The Losers*** (New York: Arlington House, 1969), p. 136.
517 6/25/59, FBI Report by Daniel Brennan on the Cuban invasion of the Dominican Republic. 124-10279-10048.
518 Paul Bethel, ***The Losers*** (New York: Arlington House, 1969), p. 135.

Bethel's conclusion needs this modification: because the U.S. was *not* disposed to do anything about the invasion, something *did* come of it—a Dominican counter-invasion of Cuba.

Ochoa, and perhaps others, may have betrayed the Cuban forces that invaded the Dominican Republic, and for that reason Ochoa could not return to Cuba. Ochoa had become disillusioned with Castro before the expedition to the Dominican Republic.[519] During her 2-17 July 1959 trip to Cuba, Taaffe contacted Irving Davidson, a registered Dominican agent, to discuss the safe delivery of Ochoa to the U.S. Taaffe told the FBI New York Office that Trujillo would guarantee the safe exit of Ochoa if he could be diplomatically allowed to enter the U.S.[520] On 21 July, Taaffe visited the CIA in Langley, Virginia to deliver this report:

> Trujillo is anxious to send Delio Ochoa, the captured invader, to the U.S. She says Ochoa is ill and disillusioned with Castro. She believes Ochoa, properly exploited, could provide a greater propaganda and intelligence coup than Pedro Luis Diaz Lanz because Ochoa knows where all "the bodies are buried."[521]

Later, in November 1960, Alberto Fernandez and the CIA would succeed in securing the transfer of Ochoa to the United States.[522]

Could it be, as Bethel argued, that Che, Raul and Fidel were behind the Cuban attacks all the way? Had the Cubans planned all along to argue, *if their attacks failed*, that the participation of the American adventurers would be proof that the U.S. had instigated the attacks to justify a Dominican counter strike? Or as Fabian Escalante (who worked in Castro's State Security forces at the time) argues, was the opposite true? Had the U.S. planned all along to support and infiltrate the Cuban attacks *to ensure their failure* to justify a Dominican counter strike?[523] Beneath the surface this chess match was complicated. Understanding exactly how each side had

---

519 7/22/59, Memo from E. Ashcraft, Contact Division, to Chief/WH/FI, Subject: Mrs. Katherine Taaffe. RIF 104-10113-10267.

520 7/22/59, FB Letterhead Memorandum, RE Foreign Political Matters—Cuba. FBI 109, HQ 12-210, Vol. 18, pp. 10-12.

521 7/22/59, CIA Memorandum for Chief, WHD/FI from E. Ashcraft, Chief Contact Division, LA Branch, Subject: Mrs. Katherine (sic) Taaffe. RIF 104-10113-10267.

522 12/20/62, CIA PRQ-I on Alberto Fernandez. RIF 104-10172-10135.

523 Fabian Escalante, **The Secret War: CIA Covert Operations Against Cuba, 1959-62** (New York: Ocean Press, 1995), p. 18.

planned for the best possible scenario for its interests remains elusive. The irony in this chess match may be that both possible scenarios were in play. If it was not an "either/or" scenario but rather a "*both/and*" scenario, then Castro may have been walking into a trap, at least partly of his own making.

Apparently, Castro saw this trap coming after the collapse of his invasion of the Dominican Republic. With the Dominican attack on Cuba approaching, Castro decided to knock over his chess pieces and resign from this game of invasions. He sent a strong signal to Washington designed to dissociate himself from any further attacks on Caribbean countries. He gave a "confidential" interview to Tad Szulc and Herb Matthews of the *New York Times*, the details of which Castro expected would go straight to Washington. On 15 July, Tad Szulc made a telephone call from Miami to the State Department's Director of Caribbean and Mexican Affairs, William Wieland. Wieland's subsequent memorandum about the phone conversation includes this passage:

> Castro told the *Times* men that he was through with supporting revolutionary expeditions in the Caribbean area. He felt that he had complied with all commitments that he has assumed with revolutionary groups and from now on they would have to go ahead on their own with no further assistance from Cuba… Castro had given special assistance to the anti-Trujillo movement due in part to his hatred of dictators, his long-standing feud with Trujillo and to a "sentimental compulsion because of his close relationship with Captain Enrico Jimenez Moya."

The Dominican revolutionaries, Castro said, "will have to get along on their own from now on."[524]

One this is certain: Washington had advance knowledge of the invasions being planned both in Cuba and the Dominican Republic. And as such, the CIA had time to coordinate some sensitive and unpredictable exfiltration plans in June and July.

---

[524] FRUS, 1958-1960, volume VI, Cuba, document #334, Memorandum of a Telephone Conversation Between the Director of the Office of Caribbean and Mexican Affairs (Weiland) in Washington and Tad Szulc of the *New York Times* in Miami, 15 July 1959.

CHAPTER THIRTEEN:
THE FLIGHT OF FRANK STURGIS AND PEDRO LUIS DIAZ LANZ

After Castro returned to Cuba from his long trip to the U.S. and South America, he unveiled his agrarian "reform" program in mid-May 1959. The program established the Agrarian Reform Institute (INRA), in which communist penetration was especially strong. We will turn to that story in the next chapter. While the agrarian reform program and the Cuban invasion of the Caribbean unfolded together, Raul Castro began the purge of anti-communists in the military. This chapter is devoted to Raul's crusade and two air force officers that fled Cuba in its wake.

In the Dominican Republic, Trujillo was waiting for the expected attack to come from Cuba *and* preparing his "Legion" for a counter-invasion of Cuba. Meanwhile, in Cuba at the end of May 1959, Raul Castro fired the chief of army intelligence (DIER), Sergio Sanjenis. As previously mentioned, this was the opening salvo of a campaign to purge the anti-communists in the revolutionary armed forces. Raul replaced

Sanjenis with his old friend Ramiro Valdes, who would soon take over all of Cuba's political police.[525] The CIA's Havana sources reported that the purge would include "all majors who are members of the Directorio Revolucionario (DR) and probably DR officers of lesser rank."[526] In the ensuing foot-race, the only question was whether Castro could be overthrown before all of the anti-communists in the military were in prison, or dead, or out of Cuba.

Castro used the Cuban invasions to test his senior officers by ordering them to participate. Those who refused to perform were marked for quick elimination. According to a 27 April 1959 report from the CIA Station in Havana, Pedro and Marcos Diaz Lanz were among the first anti-communists who were scheduled to be "eliminated" by Raul Castro.[527] Three weeks after that report Fidel put Pedro in the hot seat. As discussed in the previous chapter, Castro ordered Pedro to fly two C-46s as part of an invasion into the Dominican Republic. At the same time, Castro told Pedro to promise "many people" he would fly them to safety in Miami while flying them instead to the fortress on the Isle of Pines to be imprisoned and "forgotten."[528] Realizing his days in Cuba were running out, Lanz refused both of Castro's orders and began preparations to exit Cuba with a bang.

Castro had to handle Camilo Cienfuegos and Huber Matos more delicately. Castro knew Camilo well enough to assume that he would remain outwardly loyal. Therefore, Castro could wait. He would force Cienfuegos to participate in the invasions, and then dispose of him after all the other anti-communists had been cleaned out of the armed forces.

CIA sources in Havana reported that Raul Castro planned to "eliminate all officers he considers to be rightists who are unsympathetic to him."[529] The purge continued through May. In the middle of June, twenty-five top air force officers, including the Lanz brothers, were dismissed.

---

525 Hugh Thomas, *Cuba, The Pursuit of Freedom* (New York: Harper and Rowe, 1971) p. 1213.
526 4/30/59, Havana Station Intelligence Report to CIA HQS RE: "Purge of Cuban Armed Forces." RIF 104-10261-10042. "Officers thought to have been friendly with Diaz Lanz were dismissed" and would be replaced with Venezuelans and Costa Ricans; see Thomas, p. 1230.
527 1/25/77, CIA Memo on Marcos Jose Diaz Lanz by Chris Hopkins. RIF 104-10167-10236.
528 7/8/59, Memorandum from SAC Miami to DIR FBI, RE LHM on Pedro Luis Diaz Lanz. RIF 124-10221-10252
529 4/30/59, CIA HAVANA IR TO DIR CIA, RE: Purge of the Armed Forces. RIF 104-10261-10042.

THE FLIGHT OF FRANK STURGIS AND PEDRO LUIS DIAZ LANZ

Raul Castro said that they were "politically unreliable."[530] This purge spurred plans for the exfiltration of Cuban military officers to the U.S.

THE FLIGHT OF FRANK STURGIS

Frank Sturgis told the Rockefeller Commission that Castro's program to infuse and steep the military in communist doctrine had generated a lot of scheming and intrigues between the communists and the anti-communist group, "and so naturally sides were being drawn up." Sturgis said that it was because of their distrust of the American Embassy that the military commanders in the anti-communist group had asked him to go Washington, D.C. to alert the FBI to the scope of communist infiltration into the Cuban military.[531]

At the time of Sturgis' visit to the FBI on 13 March 1959, the agents interviewing him appeared interested in staying in touch with him:

> Fiorini (Sturgis) obviously has excellent potential to furnish us valuable data and the door was left open for future contact. Since [the Havana] Legal Attaché Haverty has been in contact with him we are soliciting comments and recommendations of Haverty as to utilizing Fiorini to our advantage. With clear and present need for first-hand data out of Cuba it is not believed Fiorini's background should bar him but we must, of course, be careful.[532]

By 12 May, however, the tenor of the Bureau's view of Sturgis had completely changed—for the worse—as this FBI assessment shows:

> Past investigation of subject [Fiorini/Sturgis] indicates he is an opportunist who will seize upon any situation whereby his personal gain or self-glorification can be furthered. He has become involved with highly placed

---
530 6/13/59, HAVA 2289 to CIA HQS. IN 30622; NARA, JFK files, CIA microfilm, Marcos Diaz Lanz, Vol/Folder 4/6/J.
531 *The President's Commission on CIA Activities*, Sturgis Deposition, April 3, 1975, p. 71; NARA, RIF-178-10002-10238.
532 4/1/59, FBI Memo from M. A. Jones to DeLoach, Subject Frank Fiorini, AKA Frank Anthony Sturgis. RIF 124-10302-10238.

figures in the present Cuban government for these reasons and not, as he has stated in the past, in an effort to assist the U.S. government. Fiorini has made no effort whatsoever to cooperate with the FBI on an operational basis, his "cooperation" in the past having been for the sole purpose of attempting to avoid prosecution by the Federal Government.

The report concluded that no approach to Sturgis would be made since it was likely that such an approach would result in embarrassment for the Bureau.[533]

Once Raul's sycophant Ramiro Valdez replaced Sergio Sanjenis as the chief of military intelligence at the end of May, the new G-2's (DIER) attention quickly focused on Sturgis. Sturgis later told the Rockefeller Commission, "Well, the situation was getting very hot there."[534] As early as 7 April an FBI source in Miami reported that Raul Castro was believed to be investigating Sturgis for "anti-communist sympathies."[535] Sturgis told the Rockefeller Commission that he had become aware of the G-2's suspicions when a pro-communist American captain working in the G-2 named Devereau warned "that I was getting out of line; that I was with the wrong people." Devereau specifically mentioned Pedro Diaz Lanz, Captain Rolando Martinez, and Major Ricardo Lorie.

When pressed by the Commission for more details about his encounter with Devereau, Sturgis gave this reply:

> He must have overheard some things being discussed by Raul and Che Guevara about me, about my goings on between the military and the American Embassy. I had to request from the Chief of the Air Force a document naming me as liaison officer between the Cuban Air Force and the American Embassy. This was a cover for me be-

---

533   6/17/59, Memorandum from SAC Miami to DIR FBI, Subject: Frank Anthony Sturgis, AKA, Frank Fiorini; attached to 7/2/59 letter from Hoover to the Assistant Attorney General, Internal Security Division. RIF 124-10302-10247.
534   *The President's Commission on CIA Activities*, Sturgis Deposition, April 3, 1975, p. 71; NARA, RIF-178-10002-10238.
535   6/17/59, SAC Miami to DIR FBI, Subject: Frank Anthony Sturgis, AKA Frank Fiorini, IS-Cuba. RIF 124-10302-10247.

THE FLIGHT OF FRANK STURGIS AND PEDRO LUIS DIAZ LANZ

ing in touch with American officials and the American Embassy.[536]

Sturgis testified that he had a confrontation with Devereau and two of his bodyguards one night when they stopped him in his jeep. Sturgis added, "I told him mainly that he had better step lightly, that I would kill him right then and there."

Sturgis claimed he would have killed Devereau had Colonel Nichols not told him to leave Devereau alone. In spite of his bravado, Sturgis took the warning seriously enough to make some adjustments. He moved into the Ankara Hotel in Miami and from there made weekly trips to Havana to work at the air base. While there, he wore civilian clothes.[537] Sturgis flew the B-25 from the airbase at Camp Libertad to Miami, "ostensibly" for maintenance and repairs. He secretly took more than $700,000 in cash that he had stashed away from his work as Castro's gambling czar and deposited it in a Miami bank. While in Miami, Sturgis took out a lease on a house and contacted Carlos Prio to relay the news of the impending communist takeover in Cuba.[538]

On one of Sturgis' return trips to Cuba, a good friend, Sergio Sanjenis, approached him with a matter of grave concern. Sturgis had been working with Sergio Sanjenis since early 1958. On or about 18 June, Sergio told Sturgis that he was "finished." "He actually saved my life," Sturgis testified. "He told me that I had better leave because the G-2 was hot on my trail to capture me, and most likely if I was caught I would be executed."[539] Sturgis took Sergio's warning seriously. He started planning his escape immediately.

Recall that Sturgis had visited the U.S. Embassy on 8 June 1959 and at that time had told embassy officers that two planes located at Camp Libertad had had their Cuban insignia removed.[540] (Chapter Twelve) The C-46 was most likely one of the planes Castro had intended for Pe-

---

536 *The President's Commission on CIA Activities*, Sturgis Deposition, 3 April 1975, pp. 71-72; NARA, RIF-178-10002-10238. .
537 6/11/59, Legat Havana to DIR FBI, Subject: Frank Fiorini, AKA Frank Anthony Sturgis, IS-Cuba. RIF 124-10302-10245.
538 Jim Hunt and Bob Risch, ***Warrior*** (New York: Tom Doherty Associates Book, 2011), pp. 62-63.
539 *The President's Commission on CIA Activities*, Sturgis Deposition, 3 April 1975, p. 70; NARA, RIF-178-10002-10238.
540 6/11/59, Legat Havana to DIR FBI, Subject: Frank Fiorini, AKA Frank Anthony Sturgis, IS-Cuba. RIF 124-10302-10245. Possibly either Enrique Carreras Bolas or Enrique Jimenez.

dro Lanz to use in the invasion of the Dominican Republic. Those two planes might also have been the B-25 and the C-46 that Sturgis reported he and another Cuban pilot, "Enrique,"[541] flew to Opa-loca, Florida, a few days after getting the warning from Sergio Sanjenis.[542] On 24 June 1959, Sturgis told the FBI representative (Legat) in Havana that he would be returning to the U. S. within two days.[543] In fact, Sturgis arrived in Florida the very next day, 25 June.[544]

Sturgis claimed that he returned to Cuba on 1 July, rescued Marcos Diaz Lanz, and successfully brought him to Miami.[545] That was not true. Marcos was on the run in Cuba until the end of July and he was exfiltrated by the CIA, *not* Sturgis. We will return to that story in Chapter Fifteen.

Meanwhile, once he was permanently based in Miami, Sturgis would eventually work with Sergio Sanjenis' brother, Jose Joaquin Sanjenis, on "anti-Castro activities."

THE FLIGHT OF PEDRO LUIS DIAZ LANZ

Pedro Diaz Lanz's March 1959 dispatching of Sturgis to FBI HQS had failed to produce any significant results. But the air force chief did not give up his effort to bypass U.S. Ambassador Bonsal and report to U.S. intelligence his views on the disastrous circumstances unfolding in Cuba. By the end of May it was too dangerous to make direct contact with the CIA Station. So when an American businessman in the aircraft industry that the Lanz brothers trusted visited the air force headquarters at Camp Libertad for the final five days of that month, Pedro seized the opportunity to set up a meeting. The businessman (whose name remains classified) reported that the following took place on 31 May:

---

541 7/31/59, see CIA Memo, RE 7/28/59 Marcos Lanz debrief. RIF 104-10167-10137.
542 Jim Hunt and Bob Risch, ***Warrior*** (New York: Tom Doherty Associates Book, 2011), pp. 62-63.
543 6/17/59, Memorandum from SAC Miami to DIR FBI, Subject: Frank Anthony Sturgis, AKA, Frank Fiorini; attached to 7/2/59 letter from Hoover to the Assistant Attorney General, Internal Security Division. RIF 124-10302-10247.
544 7/6/59, Letter from Hoover to the Office of Security, Department of State, Subject: Foreign Political Matters—Cuba, Internal Security—Cuba. RIF 124-10302-10250. .
545 Jim Hunt and Bob Risch, ***Warrior*** (New York: Tom Doherty Associates Book, 2011), p. 63.

THE FLIGHT OF FRANK STURGIS AND PEDRO LUIS DIAZ LANZ

Pedro Diaz called me in my room at the Comadoro Hotel to meet him downstairs. Upon joining him, his wife and another brother (half brother), Sergio Diaz Brull, at the empty bar, he began almost immediately unburdening himself... ...One item, which stands out in my mind, is the statement that Fidel Castro is a trickster, who has succeeded thus far in convincing everyone in, and many outside, of Cuba of his sincere plans to set up a truly democratic regime in Cuba. ... [Pedro] is an individual who seems to be completely lacking in physical fear and he feels that there is a good chance that, if he can succeed in getting the backing of responsible elements, he is quite capable of organizing a counter-revolution. He stated frankly that this is his aim and that he wants support from the U.S. of a moral nature if and when the thing comes off. He casually admitted in his new wife's presence that he would probably not survive the event, but he seems to be unworried with regard to this.

Pedro said that he was under surveillance by the regime and that "enemies in the air force had recently tried to frame him, but he had managed to avoid the trap." His American friend told the CIA that the "sole purpose" of Pedro's request for the meeting was his hope that his story would reach the proper U.S. authorities.[546]

Barely a week had passed since the visit of the American businessman before the air force chief and Fidel Castro crossed swords. In a fierce argument Castro made derogatory statements about the air force and Pedro Diaz personally, calling him "insubordinate." Diaz shot back that his funds had been depleted due to his refusal to let Raul Castro "implant communist indoctrination classes" in the air force. Upon hearing this, Castro announced that he was going to place Juan Almeida in charge of the air force immediately "to inspect it and clean it up." A few days later, Pedro Diaz contracted typhoid fever when searching the swamps where Raul Castro had crash landed. Almeida placed Diaz un-

---

546 6/15/59, CIA Information Report, OO-B-3,132,514; Subject: Chief of Air Force's Confidential Statements About Need for Counter-revolution Against Castro. RIF 104-10260-10135.

der house arrest. The guards did not physically restrain Diaz, but they followed him whenever he left his residence.[547]

On 19 June 1959, the CIA Station in El Salvador sent a dispatch to HQS containing a list of ten documents and news clippings concerning communist activities in El Salvador to be delivered to Pedro Diaz Lanz and Andres Diaz Rojas [AMWARBLE] in Cuba.[548] The dispatch from El Salvador also referenced an earlier cable from Havana concerning Lanz. CIA HQS then cabled the Station in Havana, stating that they understood Diaz wished to pass documents to the air attaché and advised the Station to cooperate, "taking the usual precautions" to avoid exposing the U.S. to a "possible provocation."[549]

On 21 June 1959, the CIA Havana Station reported to HQS that Pedro Diaz "feels he is in disfavor with Fidel and is therefore anxious to leave the country clandestinely."[550] Sergio Diaz had relayed Pedro Diaz' plea for help to the air attaché, Colonel Nichols, the previous day. Understanding the magnitude of a defection by Castro's air force chief, the CIA Station immediately swung into action. A plan was made to acquire the help of a CIA-cleared American businessman, Jim Bryer, president of Aerodex Corporation. Bryer's yacht, the *Tangaroa*, would be used in an ostensible "fishing trip" to Cuba. After clearing Havana, the boat would pick up Pedro Diaz at a predetermined rendezvous point. The Station informed HQS that Sergio Diaz was returning to Miami the following day to arrange the final details, and also noted that the air attaché was "now of the opinion that Pedro Luis does not have documents to pass."[551] On 23 June, the air attaché, Colonel Nichols, traveled from Havana to Key West, Florida, to meet with Sergio Diaz and work out final arrangements with the Immigration and Naturalization Service (INS).[552]

With those arrangements set in place, Pedro Diaz Lanz began the final sequence. At 9:00 a.m. on 29 June 1959, he reportedly took over Radio Havana for a one-hour news broadcast in which he resigned his

---

547 7/8/59, SAC Miami to DIR FBI, Subject: Pedro Luis Diaz Lanz, and attached LHM. RIF 124-10221-10252.
548 6/19/59, Dispatch to CIA HQS. 104-10167-10297.
549 About 7/20/59, DIR 30694 (OUT 63841) to Havana. RIF 104-10260-10134.
550 6/21/59, HAVA 2301 to DIR CIA. RIF 104-10260-10134.
551 6/21/59, HAVA 2301 to DIR CIA. RIF 104-10260-10134.
552 6/22/59, HAVA 2304 to DIR CIA. RIF 104-10260-10133.

THE FLIGHT OF FRANK STURGIS AND PEDRO LUIS DIAZ LANZ

position, condemned Castro as a communist, and said that communists were infiltrating the Cuban government.[553] Diaz' statement received widespread distribution throughout the Cuban press, radio and television. At approximately 12:30 p.m., Castro summoned Diaz to appear before him. The two of them met for the last time. Castro harshly reprimanded Diaz for his unauthorized performance. Diaz then accused Castro to his face of being a communist and a dictator. Castro reportedly "became enraged" and ordered Diaz to return to his home and also ordered Almeida to assume complete charge of the Cuban air force.[554]

Almeida quickly launched a purge of anti-communist Air Force officers, but Diaz Lanz would not be among them. He had arranged for an unofficial automobile to be waiting after the confrontation with Castro. Pedro picked up his wife, his brother Marcos, his half brother Sergio Diaz Brull, and Carlos Echegoyen (another Cuban air force officer based in Miami.) In anticipation of being arrested and shot on sight, the group drove directly to a dock in west Havana without luggage or money, where they boarded Bryer's boat, the *Tangaroa*. Marcos and his wife and children stayed behind in Cuba and went into hiding. The rest of the group arrived in Miami at approximately 4:14 p.m. on 1 July 1959.[555]

The U.S. air attaché, Colonel Nichols, indicated that Lanz wanted the CIA to ensure that his entry into the U.S. was kept secret.[556] On 1 July these wishes were brushed aside by the CIA Havana Station. Hoping to embarrass Castro, the station recommended "maximum hemisphere-wide press and radio exploitation" of the defection.[557] HQS agreed with the Station and the next day sent a mass cable to many of its stations in the hemisphere, directing them to coordinate "maximum press and radio exploitation of the defection," and "to encourage Cuba to reaffirm her national respect and integrity by cleaning house and salvaging

---

[553] FRUS, 1958-1960, volume VI, Cuba, document #327, editorial note; see also 7/8/59, SAC Miami to DIR FBI, Subject: Pedro Luis Diaz Lanz, and attached LHM. RIF 124-10221-10252.

[554] 7/8/59, SAC Miami to DIR FBI, Subject: Pedro Luis Diaz Lanz, and attached LHM. RIF 124-10221-10252.

[555] 7/8/59, SAC Miami to DIR FBI, Subject: Pedro Luis Diaz Lanz, and attached LHM. RIF 124-10221-10252. See also 7/2/59, SAC Miami Urgent to DIR FBI, RE: Pedro Luis Diaz Lanz. 124-10221-10254. Note: a 6/30/59 Defense Intelligence Agency document states that the boat used was a 43-foot yacht named the *Bounty*. See RIF 124-10221-10250.

[556] 6/22/59, HAVA 2304 to DIR CIA. RIF 104-10260-10133. Nichols' true surname might have been Severs. See RIF 104-10167-10057.

[557] 7/1/59, HAVA 2350 to DIR CIA. RIF 104-10260-10129.

the good aspirations of the Cuban people."[558] The FBI found that they could only interview Lanz for a "limited period of time" due to a barrage of press inquiries. "Hampered" by so many reporters, the INS and FBI were forced to use "discretion" in their handling of Lanz.[559] Not surprisingly, Pedro Luis soon ended up testifying about his story before the Senate Subcommittee on Internal Security.

At first this spectacle was considered a windfall for the Eisenhower Administration, which considered Lanz to be "the best placed" and "most credible first hand witness" about communist infiltration in the Cuban Armed Forces and on Castro's support of expeditions to overthrow other governments.[560] Yet, for whatever the Lanz defection did for American public opinion, in the end, it did little to change what was happening in Cuba. Hugh Thomas has posed this trenchant argument:

> The "Diaz Lanz affair" had precisely the opposite effect to what Diaz Lanz probably wanted: the prevention of further radicalization of the regime. It gave Castro another opportunity to head leftwards with impunity. ...By this time at least Castro must have decided, whatever sentimental views he may have had earlier, that, as he told Herbert Matthews four years later, the Cuban communist party "had men who were truly revolutionary, loyal, honest and trained. I needed them."[561]

It still seems fair to point out that neither Pedro's exfiltration to the U.S. or his death in Cuba would have impeded Castro's relentless march to communism. At the very least, the anti-communists officers that fled Cuba could hope to live and make plans to fight another day.

---

558 7/2/59 DIR 88358 to many CIA Stations, subject: "PSYCH". RIF 104-10167-10290.
559 7/8/59, SAC Miami to DIR FBI, Subject: Pedro Luis Diaz Lanz, and attached LHM. RIF 124-10221-10252.
560 FRUS, 1958-1960, volume VI, Cuba, document #327, editorial note.
561 Hugh Thomas, *Cuba, The Pursuit of Freedom* (New York: Harper and Rowe, 1971) pp. 1232-1233.

CHAPTER FOURTEEN:
CASTRO'S AGRARIAN REFORM PROGRAM

As previously mentioned, while the Cuban invasions were taking place in the Caribbean, Castro's agrarian "reform" was simultaneously unfolding in Cuba. This program turned out *not* to be what Castro had promised in the Sierra Maestra: land redistribution to the peasants *and* the protection of the right to own property. Castro was using the same strategy with his agrarian reform program that he had successfully used with the question of communism. He had deliberately deceived everyone, except for a very small group, about his intentions to take Cuba communist, and did so only gradually—and in stages. The 1958 agrarian reform promised in the Sierra was only the first stage. The second stage took place when the May 1959 program was implemented during the summer of that year. Later on, it would be changed once more. Only in the end would the public understand that they had been fooled again. Castro had always planned to impose state ownership and political domination in Cuba.

COJIMAR AGAIN

Shortly after Castro returned from his trip to North and South America, on or about 7 May 1959, he assembled his cabinet at his house in Cojimar. Some of the events that took place in this house had turned out badly and this "cabinet meeting extraordinaire" was no different. Some non-cabinet members were present, such as Cuba's new ambassador to the People's Republic of China, Oscar Pino Santos.[562] Castro had a draft of the agrarian reform law with him and a mimeographed copy of the proposal was distributed. The law was more about changing the structure of land-holding than improving agriculture.[563] As Lopez-Fresquet described it, "This new law changed the emphasis from the creation of more private property to the curtailment of it."[564] Humberto Sori Marin opened the debate. He had served as Castro's Judge Advocate General during the final months of the revolution. Afterward, Sori Marin had become the Minister of Agriculture in the new cabinet.

The new draft law had been mainly written by Che Guevara's aide, the economist Nunez Jimenez.[565] None of the ministers had participated in its creation. At the Cojimar meeting Sori Marin complained that even he, the Minister of Agriculture and the author of the agrarian reform bill issued in the mountains, had not been consulted in the preparation of this new document. The reform law proposed in the Sierra Maestra had been signed by Fidel and Humberto on 10 October 1958. For Humberto, that version was the true objective for agrarian reform. But for Fidel, it was only a means to an end. Lopez-Fresquet explained that for Castro this version was a "sly political tool" that he had "carefully phrased" to please both peasant *and* landowner. In the earlier version, the right to own property was to be protected. Lopez-Fresquet argues that the prestige and time gained by Castro during his visit to the U.S. in April 1959 had enabled him to consolidate his political power. And with this power, he could well afford the luxury of enacting another law

---

562 Rufo Lopez-Fresquet, *My Fourteen Months With Castro* (New York: World Publishing Company, 1966), p. 114.
563 Hugh Thomas, *Cuba, The Pursuit of Freedom* (New York: Harper and Rowe, 1971) p. 1213.
564 Rufo Lopez-Fresquet, *My Fourteen Months With Castro* (New York: World Publishing Company, 1966), p. 115.
565 Hugh Thomas, *Cuba, The Pursuit of Freedom* (New York: Harper and Rowe, 1971) p. 1213.

CASTRO'S AGRARIAN REFORM PROGRAM

much more radical in its measures, at the expense of engendering a few enemies.

However, Lopez-Fresquet explains that even the May 1959 bill still did not represent Fidel's ultimate intentions:

> ...But this bill was also (later) set aside to make way for the agrarian reform that was finally effected; the unwritten one that Castro always had in mind; the one that dispossessed the landlords and gave nothing to the peasants; the one that destroyed the institution of private property and made the state the sole owner of all land; the one that gave no compensations. These two earlier "laws" were merely steps toward Castro's ultimate goal, carefully hidden to fool the public and lead it blindly toward state ownership and political domination.[566]

The reading of the version at Cojimar, proposed by Castro, droned on for hours, often interrupted by Sori Marin. He, Castro and Pino Santos were the principals in the debate and, according to Lopez-Fresquet, Che Guevara said nothing of importance.[567]

Castro appointed a subcommittee headed by Sori Marin to examine the new draft law. When the committee offered some amendments to the draft law, Castro rejected them on the grounds that Sori Marin was missing at the crucial moment.[568] On 17 May 1959, the agrarian reform law was promulgated where the first one was: in the Sierra Maestra. The first two casualties were Sori Marin and the stock markets. Humbarto resigned as minister and joined Manuel Artime, Antonio Varona, Carlos Prio and others to develop a subversive campaign to combat communist penetration of the government and armed forces. The other immediate consequence was a fall in the value of several large corporations traded on the New York Stock Exchange, and of many Cuban stocks as well.[569]

---

566 Rufo Lopez-Fresquet, *My Fourteen Months With Castro* (New York: World Publishing Company, 1966), pp. 113-115.
567 Rufo Lopez-Fresquet, *My Fourteen Months With Castro* (New York: World Publishing Company, 1966), p. 114.
568 Hugh Thomas, *Cuba, The Pursuit of Freedom* (New York: Harper and Rowe, 1971) p. 1215.
569 Hugh Thomas, *Cuba, The Pursuit of Freedom* (New York: Harper and Rowe, 1971) p. 1218.

INRA

The agrarian reform law called for the expropriation of the large tracts of land owned by foreigners. This land was to be turned over to agricultural cooperatives run by the new Institute of Agrarian Reform (INRA) or supposedly redistributed to Cubans in single sixty-seven acre lots. Sugar companies could no longer operate sugar plantations unless the shares in the companies were registered to and owned by Cubans. The new law mandated that only Cubans could buy Cuban land.[570] The FBI reported that the new law was a "distinct shock to the conservatives and to the large landowners."[571]

The cooperatives were largely unanticipated by those regular Cubans who had heard of Castro's promises in October 1958. According to Hugh Thomas, most people had expected a simple division of land among the landless, but from the start the word "co-operatives" was never what the word usually means. INRA appointed the "managers" of these cooperatives, sometimes from among the workers. INRA would also directly run farms that had come from the estates of Batista, his supporters, or those people who had either fled Cuba, or were dead or in prison. Cuba's future agricultural organization would be based on these state farms.[572]

Structurally, INRA became the de facto main agency of the new government. It was in charge of land redistribution *and all infrastructure projects in Cuba.* Castro was INRA's nominal president, but Nunez Jimenez directed its day-to-day operations.[573] Under INRA, Cuba was divided into twenty-eight zones, each commanded by an officer of the rebel army. The zone chiefs had considerable freedom in interpreting how to carry out the law in their respective zones. One of Sori Marin's final acts before his resignation had been to appoint Manuel Artime as the deputy chief of zone 0-22, a district in the Manzanillo region of Cuba. Just days before Batista's fall, Artime had taken his clandestine "Legion of Revolutionary Action" (LAR) group into the Sierra Maestra

---
570   FRUS, 1958-1960, volume VI, Cuba, document #306, Editorial Note.
571   5/19/59, FBI Letterhead memorandum, Subject: Intelligence Survey—Cuba. FBI 109 HQ 12-210, Vol. 15, pp. 27-28.
572   Hugh Thomas, *Cuba, The Pursuit of Freedom* (New York: Harper and Rowe, 1971) p. 1218.
573   Hugh Thomas, *Cuba, The Pursuit of Freedom* (New York: Harper and Rowe, 1971) p. 1217.

to join Castro—where they remained after the revolution to fight communism.[574] Artime's assistant in INRA was Roberto Varona, the brother of Antonio Varona. Artime and Roberto Varona would flee Cuba together in December 1959.

REACTION TO INRA ON WALL STREET AND IN WASHINGTON

The advent of INRA turned disbelief into dismay in Washington. The earlier optimism of several State Department officials about Cuba's prospects under Castro was now in full retreat. On 22 May the State Department told the embassy in Havana that the Agrarian Reform Law was causing great consternation in the U.S. Government and immediately recalled Ambassador Bonsal to Washington.[575] Before leaving for Washington, Ambassador Bonsal told the Department that representatives of thirty of the thirty-four U.S. sugar mills in Cuba had already visited the embassy in Havana. Bonsal said they were all "deeply concerned" about the adverse effect the law would have on their interests.[576]

That was exactly what Castro had in mind. He had been planning to use U.S. economic domination of Cuba as a tool to consolidate his power and the new law was calculated to anger the U.S. As Castro himself later explained, he needed an enemy to stir up nationalist sentiment in Cuba.[577]

U.S. corporations with large investments in Cuba appeared headed for disaster. Wall Street unmercifully hammered the stock values of these corporations.[578] In this manner, the pain broadened to include the vast numbers of shareholders in these companies. The pleas for help included standard bearers such as Texaco, Procter & Gamble, Borden, Goodyear, International Harvester, and Colgate-Palmolive. Yet

---

574 5/18/60, NARA, JFK files, CIA Investigative Action report on Manuel Artime, Joseph Piccolo signed for Jacob Esterline, Chief of WH/4; RIF 104-10163-10161. See also CIA microfilm, Artime, Reel 2, Folder J.
575 FRUS, 1958-1960, volume VI, Cuba, document #308; Telegram From the Department of State to the Embassy in Cuba, 940, May 22, 1959
576 FRUS, 1958-1960, volume VI, Cuba, document #309; Telegram From the Embassy in Cuba to the Department of State, 1425, 23 May 1959.
577 Hugh Thomas, *Cuba, The Pursuit of Freedom* (New York: Harper and Rowe, 1971) p. 1058-1059.
578 Hugh Thomas, *Cuba, The Pursuit of Freedom* (New York: Harper and Rowe, 1971) p. 1218.

the Eisenhower Administration saw little wisdom in taking actions that might further stimulate Cuban nationalism and help Castro. The old game in Cuba was over and everyone except Ambassador Bonsal knew it. Bonsal was still arguing that Castro was not a communist, that "Castro wasn't such a bad fellow," and that, "he, Bonsal, could handle him if he were left alone."[579] As Castro's intelligence officers saw it, Bonsal was impeding CIA activities because he thought smoother diplomatic relations would improve his own image.[580]

In Cuba, the Sugar Mill Owners asked Castro to postpone the enactment of the law, arguing that it would have "grave economic repercussions." Tobacco growers in Pinar del Rio also protested, as did the heads of the Francisco Sugar Co., the Veritientes Sugar Co., and the Manati Sugar Co. They sent letters to their shareholders in attempts to reassure them. The nature of land-holding in Cuba meant that the storm against the new law would be as intense in New York as it was in Cuba.[581]

On 24 June 1959, Robert Kleberg, owner of King Ranch in Texas and a $5.7 million 40,000 acre[582] cattle ranch in Camaguey Province, Cuba, told Secretary Herter that the new law would wipe out his entire investment and those of all American landowners in Cuba.[583] Kleberg predicted that Castro's "communist-inspired" reform "might well bring about a communist-controlled nation close to our shores."[584] The next day, Robert Kleberg went to the White House demanding to see Eisenhower "on the grounds that he could tell the president—and no one else—certain things." The president granted Kleberg's request, listened to him, and accepted a strongly worded letter. In it, Kleberg asked the president to suspend the sugar quota, seize all Cuban assets in the U.S., order the U.S. fleet on Caribbean maneuvers, and "announce that in 1898 we fought to free Cubans from tyranny—and we will not stand by

---

579   Hugh Thomas, ***Cuba, The Pursuit of Freedom*** (New York: Harper and Rowe, 1971) pp. 1206-1207.
580   Fabian Escalante, ***The Secret War: CIA Covert Operations Against Cuba, 1959-1962*** (Melbourne: Ocean Press, 1995), p. 21.
581   Hugh Thomas, ***Cuba, The Pursuit of Freedom*** (New York: Harper and Rowe, 1971) pp. 1218-1219.
582   Thomas G. Patterson, ***Contesting Castro*** (New York: Oxford University Press, 1994), p. 36.
583   Louis A. Perez, Jr., ***Cuba and the United States: Ties of Singular Intimacy*** (Athens: University of Georgia Press, 1990), p. 240.
584   FRUS, 1958-1960, volume VI, Cuba, document #324, Memorandum of a Conversation, Department of State, 24 June 1959, 2:40-3 p.m.; subject: Cuban Agrarian Reform Program.

CASTRO'S AGRARIAN REFORM PROGRAM

now and allow communism to permanently destroy this freedom." In a note afterward to Secretary of State Herter, Eisenhower wrote that he had "not thought it necessary to comment to Bob or reply to his communication."[585]

After discussing the unfolding Cuba nightmare in Washington, Ambassador Bonsal returned to Havana on 12 June to sit down with Castro. The Cuban leader told Bonsal that, while Cuba intended to compensate American landowners for the lands being "expropriated" from them, Cuba presently had no money. Bonsal alerted Washington to this new piece of unhappy news:

> He [Castro] said the difficulty was that the government lacked resources to pay promptly in cash and unless it could reach some financial arrangement with U.S. land reform could not wait, he said, until his government was able to pay in cash; it had to be undertaken everywhere once it was started. This is a matter of life or death, Castro stated.[586]

On 11 June, in a diplomatic note to Cuba, the U.S. demanded "prompt, adequate and effective compensation" for U.S. owners of Cuban land who had been promised only Cuban bonds for their loss.[587] On 15 June the U.S. received Castro's rejection in a diplomatic note. Castro replied that Cuba "does not accept and will not accept any suggestion or proposal that might in the least impair the sovereignty and dignity of the nation."[588]

On 22 May the Havana Legat sent an urgent Airgram to FBI HQS reporting that the Directorio Revolucionario (DR) had been informed by "sugar magnates" that if they did not receive relief from the effects of

---

585 FRUS, 1958-1960, volume VI, Cuba, document #329, Memorandum From the Secretary of State to the President, subject: Recommendations of Mr. Robert Kleberg on the Cuban Situation, 7 July 1959. The president's letter to Secretary Herter was on June 27, and Herter's reply to the president was not sent until July 7.
586 FRUS, 1958-1960, volume VI, Cuba, document #320, Telegram From the Embassy in Cuba to the Department of State, 1555, June 12, 1959.
587 See State Department *Bulletin*, 19 June 1959, pp. 958-959.
588 FRUS, 1958-1960, volume VI, Cuba, document #321, Note From Minister of State Roa to the Ambassador in Cuba (Bonsal), June 15, 1959, pp. 531-534.

the new agrarian reform program they would subsidize a counter revolutionary movement to protect their interests.[589]

U.S. EYES AND EARS INSIDE INRA

Castro's agrarian reform program worried wealthy Cuban landowners and government employees that were still in place—individuals that U.S. intelligence found useful for information. One particularly useful Cuban asset recruited by the CIA at this time was Bernard Barker, a sergeant in the Havana police department who worked as a liaison with U.S. agencies—including the FBI, the Treasury Department, the U.S. Post Office, and the U.S. Secret Service.[590] The CIA Havana station approached him in March 1959 and on 2 April processed him for a security clearance. The Agency wanted Barker to collect information from his Cuban contacts on communist penetration and control in the Cuban government and military forces.[591] One of Barker's closest associates in Cuba was Mario Lazo, a lawyer for the Freeport Sulphur Company.[592] Contemporary CIA records stated that Barker could also be used "to transport our agents to the harbor(s) for exfiltration."[593]

One of Barker's informants inside of INRA was Manuel Artime,[594] a senior INRA administrator of a cooperative in the Manzanillo region, a low-lying area beneath the Sierra Maestra, where his Legion of Revolutionary Action (LAR) remained organized. Not far from Manzanillo was Camaguey Province. Its commander, Huber Matos, had been scheming against Castro for months. By June, Humbarto Sori Marin had become

---
589 5/22/59, Airgram from Legat Havana to Dir FBI, RE Foreign Political Matters—Cuba. FBI 109 HQ 12-210, Vol. 16, pp. 3-4.
590 6/14/66, NARA, JFK files, Barker letter to Frank P. DeLay, CIA Barker microfilm, 3/B/B.
591 5/16/74, NARA, JFK files, CIA memo, "Chronology of Bernard L. Barker's Association With CIA," CIA Barker microfilm, 3/B/B.
592 5/16/74, NARA, JFK files, CIA Personal Record Questionnaire (standard form 1050), Bernard L. Barker, 500, 5126's Association With CIA," Barker microfilm, 3/B/B. Another person Barker knew previously in Havana from the time of Batista's secret police, was Orest Pena who, years later, as a bar owner in New Orleans, crossed paths with Lee Harvey Oswald.
593 6/21/72, NARA, JFK files, CIA Memorandum for the Record, Chris Hopkins; Hopkins' source was "Dave," possible David Phillips. CIA Barker microfilm, 3/B/B.
594 5/18/60, NARA, JFK files, CIA Investigative Action report on Manuel Artime, Joseph Piccolo signed for Jacob Esterline, Chief of WH/4; RIF 104-10163-10161. See also CIA microfilm, Artime, Reel 2, Folder J.

CASTRO'S AGRARIAN REFORM PROGRAM

so disenchanted with Castro that he joined Artime and Matos in clandestine plotting against him. Sori had arranged for Artime's appointment in INRA and his placement in Manzanillo to make it easier for the LAR to carry out its operations. But this secret cabal's activities did not escape the attention of Castro's intelligence agents.[595]

While on a trip to Cuba in early May, Catherine Taaffe reported that a source close to Humbarto Sori Marin had told her that Humbarto was disappointed with the leftist trend in the Cuban government and in Che Guevara's power in INRA.[596] The Director of INRA, Nunez Jimenez, had one of the busiest jobs in Cuba. He needed a staff to handle his extensive responsibilities and one of his aides, Enrique Cabre, was a mole who reported to Taaffe. The draft reform law that Castro presented at Cojimar on 7 May was authored by Nunez Jimenez. Catherine Taaffe arrived in Cuba on 29 April and had a copy of the draft law in her hands by 5 May. Taaffe obtained the draft plan from Cabre, whom she had recruited and put on a payroll of $500 per month for information.[597]

On 28 April, Taaffe told the New York Office of the FBI that she was going to Cuba, using "a legitimate cover of checking on mining interests in Cuba." She said Alberto Fernandez was financing her trip with his personal money. The urgent teletype from New York to FBI HQS said, "She plans to contact her other sources while in Cuba and is going to take detailed notes of names of communists and their positions in the Cuban government." Taaffe asked for the name of the FBI Legat in Havana so that she could contact and turn over her notes to him to avoid the risk of going through Cuban customs with them.[598]

Hours later on the same day FBI HQS sent an urgent cable to the Legat in Havana alerting him to Taaffe's impending trip. The cable said that she had been given the unlisted office number of the Legat and had been told to ask for a "David Green." The HQS cable also gave the Legat these instructions: "She has not been told this is the Bureau Representa-

---

595 Fabian Escalante, *The Secret War: CIA Covert Operations Against Cuba, 1959-1962* (Melbourne: Ocean Press, 1995), pp. 32-34.
596 5/13/59, Letter from DIR FBI to the State Department Office of Security; it mentions a 7 May communication from Taaffe during the course of her trip. RIF 124-90089-10290.
597 8/20/59, CIA memo of Meeting with Taaffe in the Tiptoe Restaurant, NYC, with Isaeff. RIF 104-10106-10535, and RIF 104-10106-10533.
598 4/28/59, Teletype from SAC NYO to DIR FBI, Lesar pp. 129-130.

tive. When [her] call is received, make arrangements to obtain data and notes from her. Promptly furnish Bureau the data received." The cable also noted that Inspector D. E. Moore at FBI HQS had ordered the situation to be handled in this manner.[599]

On 5 May Taaffe visited the Legat in Havana to tell him that Cabre had plans in his possession that could be furnished to the Legat.[600] Cabre wanted a favor in return: some letters that had been confiscated from him by the U.S. Border Patrol in 1957. Taaffe offered to introduce Cabre to the Legat. He refused on the grounds that such a contact might compromise his operations.[601] Cabre had approached the American Embassy in February about the return of the letters but had received no reply since then. The FBI New York Office had actually interviewed him during Castro's visit to the U.S., and told HQS that if the Bureau could do "anything to hasten the return of these letters requested by Cabre, he could prove to be of invaluable assistance to the Legat, Havana."[602]

Taaffe had other informants inside Castro's regime on her payroll too. She reported their names and the amount of their monthly payments to Rostislav G. Issaeff of the CIA's Manhattan Contacts Office.[603] The list included Enrique Cabre of INRA; Captain Yanez Pelletier, Fidel's aide-de-camp; "Peppy," a personal bodyguard of Fidel; and "Manuel," a personal bodyguard of Raul Castro.

Taaffe had other informants inside Castro's regime on her payroll too. She reported their names and the amount of their monthly payments to Rostislav G. Issaeff of the CIA's Manhattan Contacts Office.[604] The list included Enrique Cabre of INRA; Captain Yanez Pelletier, Fidel's

---

599 4/28/59, Cablegram from DIR FBI to Legat Havana, Subject: Fidel Castro, IS—Cuba. Lesar p. 126.
600 6/1/59 SAC NYO to DIR FBI, Foreign Political Matters—Cuba; IS—Cuba. FBI 109, HQ 12-210, Vol. 16, p. 29.
601 Cabre had approached the American embassy in February about the return of the letters, but had received no reply since. The FBI actually interviewed him during Castro's visit to the U.S., and the New York Office "feels that if the Bureau can do anything to hasten the return of these letters requested by Cabre, he could prove to be of invaluable assistance to the Legat, Havana."
602 5/26/59, FBI Airtel from SAC NYO to DIR FBI, RE Foreign Political Matters—Cuba; IS—Cuba; the Airtel mentions the 4/24/59 FBI interview of Cabre during the trip. FBI 109 Cuba, HQ 12-210, Vol. 16, pp. 22-23.
603 8/20/59, CIA memo of Meeting with Taaffe in the Tiptoe Restaurant, NYC, with Isaeff. RIF 104-10106-10535, and RIF 104-10106-10533.
604 8/20/59, CIA memo of Meeting with Taaffe in the Tiptoe Restaurant, NYC, with Isaeff. RIF 104-10106-10535, and RIF 104-10106-10533.

aide-de-camp; "Peppy," a personal bodyguard of Fidel; and "Manuel," a personal bodyguard of Raul Castro.

By the end of the summer of 1959 Castro's grip on power in Cuba had reached the tipping point.[605] The need to mask the influence of the communists was no longer as pressing as it had been. The head of the communist party (PSP), Blas Roca, had become the Minister of Labor. The PSP had continued its infiltration of the armed forces, the sub-cabinet posts in the government, the leading administrative posts in the agrarian reform program, and key positions throughout Cuba's provinces and municipalities.[606] It was simply a matter of time before the curtain was raised to reveal a fully communist Cuba. In fact, in just three months, at a meeting of INRA managers, Castro would announce his plan to communize all of Cuba in three years.[607] Manuel Artime, who was present at that meeting, would make it his mission to let the world know about it.

---

605   Georgie Anne Geyer, *Guerrilla Prince: The Untold Story of Fidel Castro* (Boston: Little, Brown & Co., 1991), p. 244.
606   Morris H. Morley, *Imperial State and Revolution: The United States and Cuba, 1952-1986* (New York: Cambridge University Press, 1989 ed.), p. 89.
607   *Anti-Castro Activities and Organizations*, Appendix to Hearings before the Select Committee on Assassinations of the US House of Representatives, Ninety-fifth Congress, Second Session, Volume X, (Washington DC: US Government Printing Office, March 1979), p. 7.

CHAPTER FIFTEEN:
THE EXFILTRATION OF MARCOS DIAZ LANZ

When we last discussed Jose Marcos Diaz Lanz (Chapter Thirteen), he had said goodbye to his brother Pedro Diaz Lanz, his half brother Sergio Diaz Brull, and Carlos Echegoyen. That was on 30 June 1959. The latter trio boarded Byers' yacht, the *Tangaroa*, and made their escape from Cuba. By early July 1959, friends of Marcos Diaz Lanz approached the U.S. Embassy in Havana and requested assistance in exfiltrating him from Cuba:

> [The CIA] Station established contact with [Marcos] Diaz Lanz and it was decided to exfiltrate him clandestinely via *a shipping line used by the CIA previously in several successful exfiltrations*, since his wife was obviously in danger and he had access to information of priority interest to CIA.[608] [Emphasis added]

The CIA Station in Havana had been using the Delfa Line for past exfiltrations; "Delfa" being a contraction of the name Delia Failde, the

---
608 3/30/60, CIA Memo for the DCI, Subject: CIA Involvement in the Case of Marcos Diaz Lanz. RIF 104-10260-10165.

woman who operated the shipping company.[609] Delia Failde's CIA cryptonym, AMCOO, can be established by close examination of the marginalia[610] and other hand-written notes on Agency documents. According to Manuel Artime, Delia Failde was also known as "the Dragon Lady,"[611] an ascribed moniker that somehow conveyed just how bold and intrepid the woman could be.

Whether the name Delia Failde is a pseudonym or a true name, the person using this name may possibly appear as one or more additional characters in the long history of female spies who worked for the CIA at its Havana and Mexico City stations. The person who worked most closely with AMCOO's exfiltrations at the Havana Station was Jack Stewart. In this role, Stewart's name in the CIA files was always Andrew F. Merton—a pseudonym also associated with his activities with Rolando Cubela and Cubela's friend Carlos Tepedino. Another Agency officer who helped out with Havana Station exfiltrations was David Morales. He had diplomatic cover, as he was an attaché at the embassy. Analysis of CIA cables and memoranda also establish that Morales used the pseudonym Stanley R. Zamka in Havana and later again at the JMWAVE Station in Miami.

PUTTING TOGETHER THE PLAN

Since the day of his brother's escape, Marcos Lanz had been on the run. He had to move from one safe house to another to avoid Castro's agents, who were desperately engaged in an all-out manhunt to find him before he could escape. When the news of the request for help reached CIA headquarters, the Havana Embassy air attaché, Colonel Ericson S. Nichols,[612] was there on temporary duty. On 8 July HQS cabled the Havana Station:

---

609 1/19/60, CIA Memo for Director of Security, Subject: Request for Assistance in the Case of Manuel Francis Artime Buesa and Manuel Antonio Varona [handwriting indicates the second name should be Roberto Blas de Varona]. RIF 104-10110-10254.
610 1/13/60, MEXI 4922 to DIR CIA. RIF 104-10240-10042.
611 No Date, CIA "OPS NOTES ON AMBIDDY" [Artime]. RIF 104-10162-10197.
612 It is possible that Nichols' true surname was "Severs." See RIF 104-10167-10057.

THE EXFILTRATION OF MARCOS DIAZ LANZ

Air attaché on TDY (temporary duty) at headquarters and says the Station has means to contact Marcos Diaz Lanz. If contact has not already been made, request it be established and headquarters be kept informed concerning his activities.[613]

Colonel Nichols suggested that the Station contact Captain Alfredo Guerra Aguiar, who was working in Castro's personal office, and who Nichols described as "somewhat pro-Fidel but anti-communist." Nichols believed that Castro had assigned Guerra to his office in order to keep an eye on him (Guerra) "in view of his close connections to the Diaz Lanz brothers."[614]

On the night of 11 July, Stanley Zamka (Morales), using the pseudonym "Delgado," contacted Guerra by phone.[615] Guerra told Morales that Marcos was hiding in a Catholic Monastery. Guerra indicated that although he was not in direct contact with Marcos, he could get messages to him. Guerra added that he was endeavoring to help Marcos leave Cuba clandestinely, but that no firm arrangement had yet been made.[616]

On 13 July, Marcos' wife applied for an American visa at the embassy. Her request was denied. Morales met with her afterward, in the office of the air attaché. She told Morales that she did not know where her husband was, except that he was hiding. Morales told her not to tell anyone—especially Guerra—about their conversation and then made arrangements for "future discreet contact with her."[617]

On 17 July, a newspaper reporter (the name of the reporter and newspaper are still redacted) contacted two American friends[618] of the Diaz Lanz brothers and gave them a note from Marcos Diaz addressed to Frank Fiorini (Sturgis). The note asked Sturgis and Sergio Diaz to "arrange his (Marcos) escape from Cuba." The names of the two Americans in the note are also redacted, but subsequent cables reveal they were Byers and Williams. The reporter gave Byers and Williams the note

---
613 7/8/59, DIR 34579 to HAVA. RIF 104-10167-10162.
614 7/15/59, HAVA 2396 to DIR CIA. RIF 104-10261-10040.
615 7/15/59, HAVA 2396 to DIR CIA. RIF 104-10261-10040.
616 7/15/59, HAVA 2396 to DIR CIA. RIF 104-10261-10040.
617 7/15/59, HAVA 2396 to DIR CIA. RIF 104-10261-10040.
618 The names of the two Americans are redacted, but they were Byers [sometimes written as "Bryer in these cables] and Williams.

from Marcos and some phone numbers. All of this was relayed to the CIA Station in Havana by HQS, which added that Marcos "has been moving from one hiding place to another, is now in a church, but running out of hiding places."[619]

The cable said that "HQS desires to assist Marcos' escape," and also indicated that Byers and Williams had agreed to withhold the note from Sturgis pending a CIA decision on the matter. HQS said Byers and Williams were both "cleared KUBARK (CIA) contacts," and proposed to send them to Havana on 18 July and have them, rather than Guerra, act as a "cut out" for the station on the exfiltration operation. They would register in the Hotel Nacional and wait for a station contact, using the identification phrase "Bernie sent me." HQS asked that Marcos be provided with "evasion and escape assistance."[620] Byers arrived on 18 July and registered at the Riviera Hotel, instead of the Hotel Nacional, to await contact.[621]

On 18 July, Morales made contact with Byers and Williams. The Havana Station reported that they would return to Miami the next day and then proposed the following plan to CIA HQS:

> A. Merton (Stewart) fly [to] Tampa 20 July to lay on exfiltration with AMCOO (Delia Failde) as in previous cases with target date of 25 July. B. Either AMCONCERT (Francisco Wilfredo Varona Alonso) or AMCLATTER (Bernard Barker) take delivery of body without knowledge of true identity and transport body to ship. C. HQS take whatever action necessary to prevent subsequent publicity in PBPRIME (U.S.) as this would seriously prejudice ODYOKE (U.S. government) interest in this area. D. HQS provide pseudonym for body use. E. Fiorini (Sturgis) not to be made witting under any circumstances as Station considers him untrustworthy.[622]

CIA HQS provided the pseudonym Mariano Jimenez Gomez for Pedro's use.[623]

---

619 7/18/59, DIR 36199 to HAVA. RIF 104-10167-10161.
620 7/18/59, DIR 36199 to HAVA. RIF 104-10167-10161.
621 7/18/59, DIR 36227 to HAVA. RIF 104-10261-10038.
622 7/19/59, HAVA 2437 to DIR CIA. RIF 104-10167-10159.
623 7/19/59, DIR 36250 to HAVA. RIF 104-10167-10160.

THE EXFILTRATION OF MARCOS DIAZ LANZ

On the night of 19 July, Byers and Williams made contact with Marcos Diaz. They reported that although he appeared to be in good shape he was a nervous wreck. He was scared, concerned about his wife's safety, and upset that the embassy had refused her request for an American visa. The Havana Station relayed this news on to CIA HQS and said that Byers and Williams had made contact arrangements to transfer Marcos to Bernard Barker, who would then take him to a station safehouse on the evening of 23 July. The Havana Station also asked HQS to send KURIOT (disguise and false documents specialists) to meet Morales in Miami, who would then use his diplomatic status to safely carry the kits and documentation to Havana. Byers and Williams also added that if CIA funds were not available to send Marcos' wife to Mexico, then they were "willing to pay" for her expenses.[624]

On 20 July, CIA HQS sent a cable to the Havana Station, mostly devoted to clarifying the situation regarding Marcos' wife—why her visa application was refused and how to handle matters pertaining her and her children going forward. The drafter of the cable, Martha Tharp of Branch 3 of the Western Hemisphere Division (WH/3), said that HQS assumed Stewart's planned trip to Tampa to "lay on the exfiltration" with AMCOO had been postponed while the Station awaited a response to their request for KURIOT assistance. Tharp added that an answer to the request would be forthcoming the next day. HQS also wanted to know if the target date for Marcos' exfiltration was still 25 July.[625]

On 21 July, the Havana Station answered all of HQS questions about Marcos' wife and children, including the cost of sending them all to Mexico to get visas. She had been denied the visa because of Marcos' "political exile status" and the high probability that Mrs. Diaz would not return to Cuba and would seek asylum in the U.S. Due to the secrecy surrounding the CIA exfiltration of Marcos, the U.S. Consulate was unaware that Marcos was still in Cuba. The Station also advocated strongly that CIA HQS intervene with the State Department to get the visas issued in Havana.[626]

---

624 7/20/59, HAVA 2441 to DIR CIA. RIF 104-10167-10158.
625 7/20/59, DIR 36427 to HAVA. RIF 104-10167-10155.
626 7/21/59, HAVA 2446 to DIR CIA. RIF 104-10261-10036.

The Station cable also allayed the concern at HQS that Stewart's trip to Tampa had been postponed. In fact, Stewart *had* gone to Tampa as scheduled on the evening of 20 July to "lay on" the final plan with AMCOO. The Station said the only foreseeable risk was the transfer of Marcos from the safehouse to the boat:

> KURIOT assistance is needed for the purpose of disguising the subject sufficiently so that he will not be recognizable during the transfer. Once on the ship, no risks are foreseen. Unless unforeseen problems arise, the target date is still 25 July.[627]

The situation became even tenser as this cable literally crossed on the wires at the same time (21 July) with an "urgent" HQS cable asking for the answers that were already inbound.

This new urgent cable from HQS also contained a plan to grant the Station's request for KURIOT assistance. It said that a male documents specialist and female disguise specialist would be prepared to meet Morales in Miami on the morning of 23 July to give him the kits to carry to Cuba. HQS directed the Station to cable the contact plan for the Miami rendezvous and to make hotel reservations for the KURIOT team in Havana. The Technical Services Division at CIA had put together a planned documents list that would work for Marcos prior to, and if necessary, during, embarkation.[628] A few hours later, the Havana Station followed up by referencing its previous cable that had answered all the HQS questions. The cable added just two brief items: Stewart had just returned to Havana during that afternoon, and AMCOO had agreed to exfiltrate Marcos on 25 July.[629]

On 22 July, the Havana Station sent HQS the Miami contact plan for the KURIOT team: Morales would register at the Columbus Hotel that night (22 July) and await contact from the team. The KURIOT team would use the identification phrase "Eugene sent me."[630] HQS also cabled the names of the two specialists (which are still classified), and said they would arrive in Miami early the next morning, traveling as

---

627 7/21/59, HAVA 2446 to DIR CIA. RIF 104-10261-10036.
628 7/21/59, DIR 36520 to HAVA. RIF 104-10167-10157.
629 7/21/59, HAVA 2447 to DIR CIA. RIF 104-10167-10156.
630 7/22/59, HAVA 2448 to DIR CIA. RIF 104-10261-10034.

THE EXFILTRATION OF MARCOS DIAZ LANZ

tourists. HQS also said arrangements were being made to meet the boat on which Marcos would travel to Tampa, and that it preferred Marcos' wife and children go to Mexico to get visas.[631]

At the end of what was already a busy day on 22 July, the Chief of WH/3, Robert K. Dahlgren, and the Acting Chief of WH Division, Rudolf Gomez, summarized the Marcos exfiltration operation for the Chief of WH Division J. C. King, who was away from CIA HQS at the time. Dahlgren also asked King for a decision on what to do with Marcos' family, laying out the Station position that CIA HQS intercede and get the visas issued in Havana versus the HQS position that it was preferable for the family to go to Mexico. Either way, the cable stated, it was necessary to get the family out of Cuba *before* the exfiltration of Marcos.[632]

The response from J. C. King came on the next day, 23 July. He sided with the HQS position and authorized the use of CIA funds for the family's travel to Mexico, as well as for subsistence. King also directed that the CIA Office of Security escort Marcos to Patrick Karnley (a pseudonym for Bernard Reichardt) on 26 July, who would then escort Marcos to Washington. A safehouse would be provided in Washington, where Marcos would be debriefed by interested agencies of the intelligence community.[633]

EXECUTING THE PLAN

On the night of 23 July, Bernard Barker transferred Marcos safely to the Station safehouse. That same evening, David Morales brought in the KURIOT supplies to the Station and the two technicians quietly checked into their Havana hotel.[634] On the evening of 24 July, Morales met and briefed Marcos on the plan for the following morning. He also relieved Marcos of all of his personal documents and said they would be copied at the Station and pouched to HQS.[635] On the morning of 25 July, Marcos was transferred to Port Mariel without incident, where he was placed

---

631 7/22/59, DIR 36618 to HAVA. RIF 104-10167-10154.
632 7/22/59, DIR 36688 to HAVA. RIF 104-10112-10007.
633 7/23/59, [16-7] 4671 to DIR CIA. RIF 104-10113-10378.
634 7/24/59, HAVA 2457 to DIR CIA. RIF 104-10167-10150.
635 7/25/59, HAVA 2464 to DIR CIA. RIF 104-10113-10301.

on board the *Roatan* at 9 a.m. Morales watched the boat as it left at 12:15 p.m. The CIA Havana Station cabled HQS that the *Roatan* would arrive in Tampa at 8:00 a.m. on 27 July. The cable also asked that whoever met Marcos in Tampa immediately repossess all of the false documentation furnished by the KURIOT team for return to CIA HQS.[636]

After Marcos arrived in Tampa, the plan to take him to Washington was scrubbed.[637] The problem was that making Marcos available to the intelligence community required a bit of explaining, that is, how to tell the State Department—which had been deliberately kept in the dark—about the exfiltration. That problem caused a delay in bringing Marcos to Washington, as the Director of Central Intelligence, Allen Dulles, had to be briefed on the situation and make the decision on how to handle the issue. Dulles ordered that the transfer of Marcos to Washington be put off for the time being.[638]

On the morning of 27 July, Morales called Marcos' wife to tell her of his safe departure and to make arrangements to see her that evening to discuss how she and the children would proceed.[639] To permit the early surfacing of Marcos, his family would have to leave Cuba first. Accordingly, on 28 July CIA HQS cabled the Havana Station and asked that they make arrangements for the family's travel to Mexico on 30 July, by which time the debrief of Marcos in Tampa by two HQS officers would be completed.[640]

That plan, too, quickly dissipated. This time it was due to a snag concerning Marcos' children. On 29 July the Havana Station sent HQS the bad news: only the wife had a passport and the children could not be issued their passports until Marcos sent a notarized statement authorizing his wife to apply for their passports and take them out of Cuba. Furthermore, the passports for the children could not be issued until seven days after the receipt of the notarized statement.[641]

---

636 7/25/59, HAVA 2464 to DIR CIA. RIF 104-10113-10301.
637 7/24/59, CIA Memo for Chief, Support Branch, Subject: Marcos Diaz Lanz. RIF 104-10113-10376.
638 7/27/59, CIA Memo from Rudolf K. Gomez, ACWH, Re: Telecon with the Director. RIF 104-10167-10146.
639 7/27/59, HAVA 2476 to DIR CIA. RIF 104-10167-10147.
640 7/28/59, DIR 37485 to HAVA. RIF 104-10167-10144.
641 7/29/59, HAVA 2486 for DIR CIA. RIF 104-10167-10141.

THE EXFILTRATION OF MARCOS DIAZ LANZ

The Havana Station cable asked how HQS wished to handle the "surfacing" of Marcos in light of this unanticipated development. The cable pointed out that surfacing Marcos while his family was still in Cuba might create problems with Cuban authorities and make it hazardous for the Station to contact Marcos' wife. Additionally, surfacing him in Tampa could endanger the station's future use of AMCOO because so few ships traveled between Havana and Tampa. The Station therefore recommended surfacing Marcos in Houston, Texas, or at some other point away from Florida.[642]

On 28 July, the CIA notified the FBI that Marcos Diaz Lanz had departed Cuba with the assistance of the CIA and had arrived in Tampa on 27 July with the assistance of the INS. The Agency said that Marcos would depart for Miami on 29 July or 30 July, where he would be available to the FBI for debriefing, and that because the Marcos family was still in Cuba, not to disseminate this information outside of the Bureau.[643]

The CIA debriefed Marcos for five hours on 28 July and for five more hours on 29 July.[644] On 3 August, the FBI debriefed Marcos Lanz in its Miami Office.[645] On 29 July, CIA HQS informed the Havana Station that AMCOO would be in Havana on 30 July and would call on Merton (Stewart) while there "to discuss ops."[646]

In spite of the challenges of keeping Marcos safely hidden during the complicated arrangements that had to be put together for his exfiltration, the exfiltration itself was carried out without incident or a breach of security. The CIA team on the ground in Cuba was as much at risk as the person being exfiltrated. This time they were lucky. As we will see in Chapter Nineteen, they would not be so lucky in December 1959.

---

642   7/29/59, HAVA 2486 for DIR CIA. RIF 104-10167-10141.
643   7/28/59, CIA Memo to Jane Roman for FBI from CI/OPS/WH, Subject: Marcos Diaz Lanz. RIF 104-10167-10139.
644   7/31/59, CIA MFR, Debriefing of Jose Marcos Diaz y Lanz, 28-29 July 1959, Tampa, Florida. RIF 104-10167-10137.
645   8/8/59, SAC Miami to DIR FBI, Subject: Marcos Diaz Lanz, IS-Cuba. RIF 124-10294-10266.
646   7/29/59, DIR 37757 to HAVA. RIF 104-10167-10142.

CHAPTER SIXTEEN:
THE DOMINICAN REPUBLIC INVASION OF CUBA

There is evidence that a full month before the Cuban invasion of the Dominican Republic Camilo Cienfuegos was passing detailed information to the FBI about Trujillo's plan to invade Cuba. On 13 May 1959, FBI Director Hoover informed the State Department Office of Security that during her recent visit to Cuba Catherine Taaffe had met with Camilo Cienfuegos. He had told her that Rolando Masferrer was behind a buildup of weapons for the planned Dominican invasion of Cuba. These weapons included 1,000 Enfield rifles and 150 Thompson machine guns. Cienfuegos told Taaffe that he wanted this information passed to the FBI "in the hopes that something could be done about it."[647]

By the time that the much anticipated Dominican attack materialized at the end of July 1959, the CIA had successfully coordinated the exfiltrations of Pedro and Marcos Diaz Lanz and their half brother, Sergio

---
647 5/13/59, Letter from Hover to State Department Office of Security, Subject Anti-Fidel Castro Activities. RIF 124-90089-10290.

Diaz Brull. Manuel Varona, Sergio Sanjenis, Sori Marin, Manuel Artime, Huber Matos, and Camilo Cienfuegos remained in Cuba. Only the last three remained at their positions in INRA and the army, but time was running out for all of them. Although Frank Sturgis had managed to escape in June, time was also running out for most of the American soldiers of fortune remaining in Cuba. Loran Hall and Leslie Bradley (see Chapter Twelve) were in prison. William Morgan, who played both ends against the middle during the Trujillo plot, would eventually be executed for scheming against Castro. Only Gerry Hemming, who apparently enjoyed the support of Camilo Cienfuegos, remained untouched by Cuban intelligence before, during, and after the Dominican attack on Cuba.

HEMMING AND THE CASTRO-TRUJILLO WARS IN 1959

Cuban intelligence officials claim that the U.S. Embassy was aware of the planned Cuban attack on the Dominican Republic and secretly "supplied some resources for the enterprise through its agents Frank Sturgis and Gerry Hemming." In his book *The Secret War: CIA Covert Operations Against Cuba*, Fabian Escalante (who worked in Castro's State Security forces and eventually became the chief of the Cuban State Security Department), argues that the American *objective* in aiding the plot against Trujillo was to help give the Dominican Republic grounds for retaliating.[648] If Escalante is correct, then Sturgis' role in the plot was very short-lived. Cuban intelligence was hot on his trail during the run up to the attack against Trujillo, and just ten days after the attack Sturgis fled Cuba. Hemming, on the other hand, *was* intimately involved in the plot to invade the Dominican Republic. Unlike Sturgis, Hemming *was not* in hot water. CIA reports confirm that Hemming did in fact "contact a number of Nicaraguans, Cubans, Dominicans, etc., who had as their primary aims the overthrow of established governments either in Nica-

---

648 Fabian Escalante, *The Secret War: CIA Covert Operations Against Cuba, 1959-1962* (Melbourne: Ocean Press, 1995), p. 18.

ragua or the Dominican Republic."[649] The question is whether or not U.S. intelligence was behind Hemming's involvement in these schemes.

The 1960 CIA reports from Los Angeles on Hemming (discussed in Chapter Twelve) and later CIA analyses of Hemming's association with the Agency[650] do not acknowledge a relationship with Hemming until after he exited Cuba in August 1960. However, a lengthy CIA Information Report (IR) establishes that his relationship with the CIA began earlier. Six months before his interview with the CIA's Los Angeles Field Office, Hemming was debriefed by Agency sources in Costa Rica.[651] In that debrief, Hemming provided details about the training of the Cuban forces that would invade Nicaragua and the Dominican Republic. That debrief, which was more fully described in Chapter Twelve, was still well *after* the attack on the Dominican Republic and does not establish how far back Hemming's association with Agency assets went. In a 1995 interview with the author of this volume, Hemming claimed to have been loosely associated with CIA counterintelligence as far back as 1954, at which time he says he was introduced by his uncle to James Angleton, the Agency's counterintelligence chief.[652]

Hemming described the *objective* for what he was up to *in general* in Cuba. That description is clearly relevant to any discussion of a possible American *objective* in secretly aiding the Cuba invasions of Nicaragua and the Dominican Republic. Hemming described *his* objective to the CIA's Los Angeles office in October 1960. In it, Hemming disclosed a "general thesis of intelligence operations connected with revolutionary movements" that he "and many others" subscribed to. These intelligence operations called for "special forces types" to do the following:

...to penetrate certain revolutionary movements at an early stage, attain positions of real influence within the

---

649 The CIA account varies slightly with the Cuban claim on timing, placing these contacts, and therefore the planned operations, in the fall of 1959. The CIA account also claims these groups were "well infiltrated" by anti-Castro men and that the Nicaraguan group never left Cuba and was captured in September.
650 See for example, NARA, JFK files, CIA, memorandum for Chief, Security Analysis Group, From: Jerry Brown; Subject Hemming, Gerald Patrick, 8 April 1977.
651 NARA, JFK files, CIA Information Report CS-3/432,532, 4 April 1960; country: Nicaragua/Cuba/Costa Rica; field report number HPS-2280. This document was one of the first released by the CIA after the passage of the JFK Records Act of 1992, and therefore has no RIF number. It is stamped, "Approved for Release 1992 CIA Historical Review Program."
652 Gerry Hemming, 6 January 1995 interview with John Newman.

organizations, and subsequently attempt to channel the movement's activities into areas which are most favorable, or at worst least detrimental to U.S. interests.[653]

Hemming's objective for rendering aid to the Cuban attacks on Nicaragua and the Dominican Republic was to *penetrate and steer the invasion plans* to maximize American interests. Even if his activities were not actually a part of U.S. intelligence operations, his objective was purposely designed to be parallel with them.

ADVANCE KNOWLEDGE OF THE DOMINICAN ATTACK

Just as American officials knew a lot about the invasion teams being readied in Cuba for expeditions into Panama, Nicaragua and the Dominican Republic, they also knew a lot about the plans for a Dominican attack on Cuba. In the months after Batista's January 1959 fall from power, remnants of his armed forces were reorganized into a rag-tag force in the Dominican Republic. About 100 Cubans, 150 Spaniards, and 50 Europeans of various nationalities were integrated into what Trujillo liked to call his "Foreign Legion."[654] Castro's intelligence officer, Fabian Escalante, claims that at the behest of Vice President Nixon, the CIA reportedly sent an agent, Gerry Droller (aka Frank Bender) to evaluate them:

> Toward the end of February 1959, CIA representative Frank Bender met with Trujillo and his intelligence chief Johnny Abbes Garcia to analyze the plans that they were preparing against Cuba. Bender considered that the Caribbean Legion—as the mercenary expedition was to be called—could be converted into a kind of police force to be used whenever necessary.[655]

Escalante also states that in early March William Morgan met with a Mafioso messenger of Trujillio, Fred Nelson, and told him that for a

---

653 10/12/60, Report of Ernst. Liebacher, CIA Field Los Angeles Field Office, RE Interview of Gerry Patrick Hemming. OO-A-3170536, RIF 1993.06.28.17:17:55:210360.
654 Felix I. Rodriguez, **Shadow Warrior** (New York: Simon and Schuster, 1989), p. 39.
655 Fabian Escalante, **The Secret War: CIA Covert Operations Against Cuba, 1959-1962** (Melbourne: Ocean Press, 1995), p. 17.

THE DOMINICAN REPUBLIC INVASION OF CUBA

million dollars he could turn the Second Front against the revolution and "bounce Fidel Castro from power!"[656] Morgan's accomplice was the Spaniard Eloy Gutierrez Menoyo, commander of the Second Front of Escambray that fought alongside Castro's 26 July Movement and the Revolucionario Directorio (DR) to overthrow the Batista dictatorship.

On 15 April 1959, Morgan went to the Du Pont Plaza in Miami to meet with the Cuban consul of that city, Colonel Augusto Ferrando. The consul explained that former Batista General Jose Eluterio Pedraza intended to invade Cuba with his "Foreign Legion." They wanted an uprising to be underway before the invasion arrived and thought this could be accomplished by the Second Front and the White Rose counterrevolutionary group. Morgan learned that another group in the conspiracy inside of Cuba would be led by Armando Cainas Milanes, president of the Ranchers Association of Cuba. On 21 April, Morgan returned to Miami to report that Eloy Gutierrez Menoyo and the other most important leaders had agreed to participate—but only if the U.S. government supported the plot. Ferrando gave the necessary assurances and said that operating expenses would be distributed in $10,000 installments to Morgan's emissaries, who were to travel to Miami periodically.[657]

Later, when Morgan met John Martino in a Cuban prison, Morgan said that he had told Fidel about Trujillo's plan "when the approach was made to me."[658] Escalante's version is different: it was the trips to Miami by Morgan and Gutierrez Menoyo that "began to arouse suspicion" and alerted Cuban intelligence to the plot. Sometime afterward, according to Escalante, Morgan and Menoyo began to fear that Fidel knew of their plans. So, Menoyo suggested to Morgan that they inform the Cuban leader. The next day Gutierrez and Morgan met secretly with Castro and reported the conspiracy. They told Fidel that they had remained silent until seeing "how serious" the plans really were. They said that the mercenaries planned to land at Trinidad and that a provisional government would be set up in the nearby Escambrey Mountains. They said

---

656 Fabian Escalante, *The Secret War: CIA Covert Operations Against Cuba, 1959-1962* (Melbourne: Ocean Press, 1995), p. 20.
657 Fabian Escalante, *The Secret War: CIA Covert Operations Against Cuba, 1959-1962* (Melbourne: Ocean Press, 1995), p. 20.
658 John Martino, *I Was Castro's Prisoner –An American Tells His Story* (Southlake, Texas, JFK Lancer Publications, 2008 ed.), pp. 138-139.

the plan called for them (Gutierrez and Morgan) to arrange uprisings in the mountains, cut communications, and then ambush the Cuban troops on their way to stop the invasion.[659] They did not tell Fidel about the money or their contacts with the American Embassy.[660]

WASHINGTON WARNS OF THE IMPENDING DOMINICAN ATTACK

As soon as Washington knew that Castro's forces had landed in the Dominican Republic, several American ambassadors were formally notified about the impending invasion from the Dominican Republic into Cuba. On 18 June, the State Department alerted all U.S. missions in Latin America with this message:

> Our information indicates that *for some time* a force has been gathering in the Dominican Republic for purpose of creating counter-revolution under leadership consisting largely of elements who fled Cuba following Batista's downfall... This force has attempted to obtain arms from various sources abroad, including this country, and has been reported to have infiltrated agents into Cuba for purpose of organizing internal support for counter-revolution.[661] [Emphasis added]

The cable also pointed out that Castro had sent a small invasion force into the Dominican Republic to topple Trujillo, and suggested that U.S. diplomatic posts publicly decry intervention from either side.

On the surface, the U.S. was assuming a neutral position in the conflict and State Department cables described the hostilities between the two countries as tit-for-tat.[662] However, at this point we must pose this question: Why had the U.S. said nothing at all about the Trujillo plan

---

659 Fabian Escalante, *The Secret War: CIA Covert Operations Against Cuba, 1959-1962* (Melbourne: Ocean Press, 1995), p. 20.
660 Paul Bethel, *The Losers* (New York: Arlington House, 1969), p. 191. Fabian Escalante, *The Secret War: CIA Covert Operations Against Cuba, 1959-1962* (Melbourne: Ocean Press, 1995), p. 20.
661 FRUS, 1958-1960, volume VI, Cuba, document #322, Telegram From the Department of State to All Missions in the American Republics, June 18, 1959.
662 See, for example, FRUS, 1958-1960, volume VI, Cuba, document #322, Telegram From the Department of State to All Missions in the American Republics, June 18, 1959.

to overthrow Castro until just *four days* after the Cuban invasion force landed in the Dominican Republic? The Americans were equally cognizant that preparations for invasions were underway in both countries. Yet there is no indication that the State Department notified its embassies of the impending Cuban attack before it took place.

The answer to that question is suggested by some clues in the sessions of the U.S. National Security Council (NSC) at that time. The 25 June NSC discussions covered Castro's expedition against the Dominican Republic at length but made no mention of the ongoing preparations in the Dominican Republic for a strike against Cuba. This passage from the meeting's minutes illustrates that imbalance:

> There had also been reports of four [Cuban] rebel landings in the Dominican Republic, some of which were still in being while others had been destroyed. Fidel Castro seemed to be determined to get rid of both Trujillo and Somoza [in Nicaragua]… It seems Castro thinks it is possible to repeat in the Dominican Republic and Nicaragua the success of his own movement in Cuba which began with very small forces. …Secretary [of State] Herter emphasized how seriously the Caribbean problem appeared to the Department of State… if we did not do something, the fire would spread very fast. Cuba was the center of unrest and presented, in itself, the most serious situation. U.S. business interests in Cuba were very frightened and were now clamoring for U.S. economic action against the Castro regime.

This seems more a call for action against Castro than a call for no invasions at all. The minutes indicate that Secretary Herter told Eisenhower that the State Department was working closely with the CIA "with respect to activities going on in Miami."[663] That was where the activities of the invaders were being synchronized with the activities of anti-Castro participants inside Cuba.

On 3 July the American Embassy in Mexico City reported that it had learned from Cuban sources in Mexico that an anti-Castro revolution might occur at the end of July. The embassy cable stated that opposition to Castro was reportedly gathering "final momentum" as a result of

---

663 FRUS, 1958-1960, volume VI, Cuba, document #325, Memorandum of Discussion at the 411th Meeting of the National Security Council, Washington, June 25, 1959.

increased communist infiltration of the armed forces, police, and the security apparatus.[664] When the U.S. Ambassador to Cuba, Phillip Bonsal, read the cable from Mexico City, he did not agree with its assessment of the opposition to Castro in Cuba. On 7 July he cabled the State Department to argue that Castro enjoyed the support of the "large majority of Cuban people," and added he believed any armed attempt to overthrow him "would both strengthen such support and would fail."[665]

The Director of Central Intelligence had another view. In a 9 July NSC meeting, Allen Dulles said that Fidel Castro was "facing increased domestic unrest in Cuba."[666] Dulles again deferred any comment about the imminent strike against Cuba from the Dominican Republic—even though he knew his agents were encouraging some anti-Castro leaders in Cuba to act in coordination with the invasion and encouraging others to defect to the U.S. Again, Dulles put the spotlight on Castro's attack against the Dominican Republic. The minutes contain this passage:

> Turning to the situation in the Caribbean, Mr. Dulles indicated that there were further reports concerning efforts based in Cuba against the Dominican Republic. These reports seemed to indicate that the attack might go through Haiti rather than be launched as a frontal attack on Dominican territory.[667]

Dulles did not reveal that a key trainer of the force was an American informant. On the other hand, the FBI *did* learn about that sensitive detail at the time. On the same day as this NSC meeting, the FBI debriefed a Ruben Miro Guaraia in Miami, who provided details on—among other things—the activities of Americans involved in training one of Castro's groups for an "invasion of Nicaragua."[668]

---

664 FRUS, 1958-1960, volume VI, Cuba, document #330, note 2, 3 July 1959 telegram from the Embassy in Mexico City.
665 FRUS, 1958-1960, volume VI, Cuba, document #330, Telegram From the Embassy in Cuba to the Department of State.
666 FRUS, 1958-1960, volume VI, Cuba, document #325, Memorandum of Discussion at the 412th Meeting of the National Security Council, Washington, 9 July 1959.
667 FRUS, 1958-1960, volume VI, Cuba, document #325, Memorandum of Discussion at the 412th Meeting of the National Security Council, Washington, 9 July 1959.
668 NARA, JFK files, INS/ONI box 1; ONI report on Loran Hall, 15 January 1964, ONI routing slip GG134356. The original source of this report was Ruben Miro Guaraia, who provided the information to the FBI in Miami on 9 July 1959. Miro Guaraia said he had been arrested by the Cuban Police in Havana in April, and that he met Loran Hall while in detention, and that Hall furnished him with the information about the planned Cuban attack against Nicaragua.

It was at this point—as discussed previously in Chapter Twelve—that Castro sent a signal to Washington, via Tad Szulc and Herb Matthews of the *New York Times*, designed to dissociate himself from any further attacks on Caribbean countries. Castro had a reason for sending this particular signal to the Americans. He was trying to discourage any further pretexts for a Dominican or American invasion of Cuba. His own role in the Cuban incursion into the Dominican Republic had increased this threat, and now he downplayed the issue by disowning whoever might be involved in any further attacks.

One reason why the activities of the Cuban conspirators in the Trujillo plot were coordinated in Miami was due to Bonsal's hands-off policy in Cuba. He had placed a number of obstacles to running CIA activities out of the embassy, arguing that they threatened to affect diplomatic relations. The U.S. Embassy would eventually conclude that Morgan had flipped completely and told Castro he was acting as a double agent.[669] A colleague of Morgan's, John Spiritto, tried to contact the CIA Station to report what he had learned about Morgan's activities. Spiritto's case officer, the station's deputy chief, Arthur Avignon, refused to meet him.[670] In the meantime, Morgan decided to make a triple play.

MORGAN—TRIPLE AGENT

Fabian Escalante revealed that Cuban intelligence was alert to the possibility that, in spite of telling Castro about their role in the Trujillo plot, Morgan and Menoyo might switch again once the invasion got underway.[671] They had only brought Castro into their part of the plot to save their lives.

On 29 June 1959, Morgan made a risky move. He lured the American press attaché, Paul Bethel, to his home by saying he needed to talk about a "life and death" situation. In his garden outside the house, Morgan told Bethel, "I have five thousand men willing and able to fight communism," and added that they were to be used in a counter-revolution

---

669 Paul Bethel, *The Losers* (New York: Arlington House, 1969), p. 191
670 Fabian Escalante, *The Secret War: CIA Covert Operations Against Cuba, 1959-1962* (Melbourne: Ocean Press, 1995), pp. 19-21
671 Fabian Escalante, *The Secret War: CIA Covert Operations Against Cuba, 1959-1962* (Melbourne: Ocean Press, 1995), p. 21.

against Castro. Morgan let drop that "he had been told" the U.S. government was willing to "get behind a move to oust Castro," and also that his plans were tied in with the Dominican consul in Miami. Then Morgan got to the point: he was seeking a visa for his pregnant Cuban wife to get her out of Cuba before the hostilities broke out. Bethel told Morgan that they would not meet again, and immediately returned to the American Embassy and wrote a memorandum to the CIA Station chief, Jim Noel. His deputy, Arthur Avignon, to whom Bethel handed his memo, said that the Station was not disposed to make contact with Morgan "just yet."[672]

The CIA Station's reaction to the news from Bethel suggests that they knew a lot more than he did about the Trujillo plot. It might also indicate that the attack was not expected right away and that when it got closer they might consider contacting Morgan for information. Bethel's memo to Noel survives today in the U.S. National Archives. It concluded with a remark that Castro made to Morgan about the firing of Pedro Diaz Lanz: Fidel said he had told off Diaz Lanz, and then boasted, "I have the only pair of gonads around here."[673] Morgan might have been thinking that about himself. He was an agent of Trujillo who had become a double agent for Castro. By telling the American Embassy he was with the conspiracy *after* he had betrayed his own role to Castro, Morgan was in fact working as a *triple agent*. Triple agents often end up playing both ends against the middle, and that, Morgan would discover, is as risky as it gets.

The same day that Morgan approached Bethel, the CIA Station in Havana disseminated a detailed information report on the forces gathering for the Dominican attack. Assembled by Jack Stewart, the report was based upon information from a female source in Bernard Barker's AMCLATTER net with "good opposition contacts."[674] Stewart' report said that around 25 June 1959 a military junta had been formed in Mi-

---

672 Paul Bethel, *The Losers* (New York: Arlington House, 1969), pp 186-189.
673 6/30/59, Memo from Paul Bethel to Mr. Noel, Subject: William Morgan. RIF 124-90136-10098.
674 7/2/59, CIA Field Information Report by Andrew F. Merton, Source Cryptonym: AMCLATTER; Source: Person with good opposition contacts (F); Subject: Organization of Military Junta to Overthrow Fidel Castro; Date/Place Acquisition: Havana, 29 June 1959. RIF 104-10069-10368.

ami by Cuban counter-revolutionary groups who hoped to overthrow Fidel Castro and hold immediate elections:

> The junta is headed by Jose Eleuterio Pedraza Cabrera, a Cuban Army general under former President Batista, and includes Nelson Carrasco Artiles, former Cuban Army colonel under Batista, and Roberto Melero Juvier, a Habana lawyer and secretary to Carlos Marquez Sterling, founder and head of the Partido del Public Libre (PPL, Free People's Party).

The report described several groups supporting the new junta. One was headed by Rolando Blanco Navarro, a captain of the Revolutionary Army, and his deputy, Regueiro, both in Cuba; their group coordinator, Angel Navarro (aka Armando Noval) was in Miami with Francisco Rordriguez Tamayo (aka "El Mejicano"), a recent defector from the Revolutionary Army. Another group, whose chief was Nelson Carrasco Artiles, had 800 men in training on a key off the Mexican coast. This group also included Santiago Alvarez, a former Cuban congressman, in Mexico, and Roberto Melero Juvier, in Cuba; Artiles functioned as the group's courier between Mexico and Miami.

Jose Eleuterio Pedraza Cabrera was training a group in the Dominican Republic. A former Havana gambling figure in Miami, Fredesvindo Bosque Cueto (aka "El Gordo"), was recruiting and sending men to Pedraza's forces. Pedraza was said to be counting on 3,000 men and 115 planes. Former Cuban senator Rolando Masferrer Rojas, in Miami, had already sent a group of 200 armed men to Las Villas at the beginning of June. There was also Francisco Batista Zaldivar (aka "Panshin"), former President Batista's brother and governor of Habana Province, who was giving money and food "to the cause." Stewart' report also stated that half a dozen instances of planes dropping revolutionary leaflets in Cuba may have been connected with Pedraza's "air force."[675]

Meanwhile, the more the planning for the Dominican attack against Cuba went forward, the more its operational security was compromised. In early July Cuban intelligence spotted a secret emissary of Trujillo—a

---

675   7/2/59, CIA Field Information Report by Andrew F. Merton, Source Cryptonym: AMCLATTER; Source: Person with good opposition contacts (F); Subject: Organization of Military Junta to Overthrow Fidel Castro; Date/Place Acquisition: Havana, 29 June 1959. RIF 104-10069-10368.

Spanish priest named Ricardo Velazco Ordonez—who had arrived in Havana to review the preparations for the uprising, for which Morgan and Menoyo were supposed to be gathering support. They were to knit together the political leadership that would assume power after Castro was overthrown. According to Escalante, Velazco met secretly with former Cuban senator Arturo Hernandez Tellaheche and Cainas Milanes and offered them the presidency and vice-presidency, respectively, of the future Cuban government.[676] Later in July, Dave Phillips found himself sitting across from Cainas Milanes in a clandestine meeting that he (Phillips) quickly realized he did *not* want to be in.

Velazco Ordonez completed his mission on 20 July and Cuban intelligence was certain that he left Havana unaware that his chauffeur throughout his visit was a Cuban intelligence (G-2) agent. This unfolding episode may have been related to a tirade on Cuban television delivered just two days before Velazco's departure, in which Castro accused the U.S. "of espionage" and of "treating Cuba like some minor United States municipality." Ambassador Bonsal nervously watched as the moment approached for the invasion from the Dominican Republic. In a cable to Washington, he drew attention to Castro's claim that some U.S. Senators were being paid by Trujillo.[677]

A CLOSE CALL FOR DAVE PHILLIPS

Toward the end of July 1959, the CIA Station in Havana instructed Dave Phillips to contact Michael P. Malone, Vice President of the Czarnikow Rionda firm, which controlled four of the major sugar companies in Cuba, and manager of Robert Kleberg's (King Ranch) $5.7 million 40,000 acre cattle ranch in Camaguey Province, Cuba. Phillips wrote down what happened as a result in a 6 August memo.[678] On 29 July, Phillips, as instructed, met Malone in his room at the Hotel Nacio-

---
676 Fabian Escalante, *The Secret War: CIA Covert Operations Against Cuba, 1959-1962* (Melbourne: Ocean Press, 1995), pp. 23-24.
677 FRUS, 1958-1960, volume VI, Cuba, document #338; Telegram From the Embassy in Cuba to the Department of State, July 18, 1959.
678 8/6/59, CIA memorandum by Michael H. Choaden, Subject: Meeting with Cuban Group re Public Relations Campaign. RIF 104-10267-10168.

nal in Havana. Malone said he had talked with several people at CIA HQS about his association with a group of Cuban landowners anxious to do something about Castro's Agrarian Reform program. CIA HQS had told Malone that Phillips would be able to act as an advisor in a public relations program. Malone told Phillips that the Cubans had approached him in the hope that he and the interests he represented would contribute to a fund being generated to prepare "a plan of action."

Malone then contacted the Cuban group and told them he would introduce them to a representative of a large, unnamed public relations firm in the U.S. who was experienced in "unconventional" propaganda techniques. The Cubans asked to meet Phillips that same day. Hours later, Phillips returned to the hotel room to meet Malone. Malone said that one of the Cubans, Martinez Conhill, was on his way to the room and that they would then go to meet Caines Milanes, President of the Cuban Cattleman's Association. Conhill told Phillips that Cainas was "the absolute leader of the group, and that the only thing to remember in talking with him was that he had strong political ideas." In the memo he wrote afterward, Phillips said he took "ideas" to mean ambitions.

Phillips had guessed right about Caines. But Phillips did not know at the time that Caines' group was one of two nuclei working inside of Cuba with the Trujillo plot and that Caines would become the new vice president of Cuba if the plot succeeded in overthrowing Castro. The three men drove to meet Caines at a large home in Miramar. Phillips assumed that the home belonged to Caines, but in fact it was the home of another Cuban, Gustavo de Los Reyes. An attorney for the Cuban Cattleman's Association also joined the meeting. In his memo, Phillips said that in view of being in this "sudden crowd" he was inclined to be "as discreet as possible."

Caines dominated the two-hour meeting from the beginning. The first thing Phillips told the group was that he would have to consult his "home office" before making any definite commitment. At length, this exchange took place between Caines and Phillips:

> After about an hour Caines said to me directly: "Look here—we were told you were an expert on this sort of thing. But so far you have contributed nothing. Can't

you give us one concrete idea of the sort of program you might provide? ...I suggested, that if they wanted to move at once and really do something, they should purchase a newspaper (or at least promise the owner of a paper complete financial repayment in the event of loss or closure), and that this newspaper should begin daily editorial attacks against the drastic aspects of the Agrarian Reform program and equally strong attacks against the growing communist activity in Cuba. Such a paper, I pointed out, would draw the immediate interest from the Cuban readers. One of three things would happen:
a. Castro would close the paper and if so all the world would see that freedom of the press did not exist in Cuba.
b. The mob would burn the paper—[meaning] even worse international propaganda against Castro's government.
c. Or nothing would happen—in which case the full story would be carried to the Cuban public in heavy doses, and other newspapers would find the courage to speak out against communism.

Caines and his group liked Phillips' idea. In fact, they liked it so much that they talked about which newspaper they might use. They spoke of starting their own weekly newspaper only to destroy it later. And they even said they would provide "the mob" if Castro did not.

At this point in the meeting it dawned on Phillips that this particular group of Cubans was less interested in publicity work than in *direct militant action to overthrow the Castro government.* They spoke of many other Cubans who were with them and discussed possible *paramilitary activities*—what would happen if *there was an invasion of Cuba from the Dominican Republic*; the possible effect of bomb throwing, and what would happen if *Castro were assassinated.* In his memo, Phillips wrote,

> *Things really became conspiratorial.* Malone was an enthusiastic supporter of the most militant ideas. Generally, he exuded a "give 'em hell" attitude. *I felt it was time to leave.* I promised to report back to the group two days later

with a plan of some kind. But I made it clear that I would
have to consult with my home office. [Emphasis added]

In his memo, Phillips wrote that the group was "undisciplined security-wise," and did not know exactly what they wanted except "Castro's head." Phillips concluded,

They would be willing to do almost anything—even supporting a Dominican invasion. They want to get out on the streets and fight, they claim, and they are having a hard time holding their people back. With the new death penalty in Cuba for anti-revolutionary activity, it is not hard to imagine that at least one member of this group might inform to the government.

Phillips was quite right that there was an informant in the Trujillo plot—and he might even have been thinking of Morgan.

Phillips was traveling to CIA HQS and to New York when the American Embassy in Havana learned that a Cuban government tape recorder in the home of Gustavo de Los Reyes had taped a prior conversation between Caines and a "non-Kubark [CIA] American Embassy official."[679] After much handwringing and exchanges of cables, the CIA eventually concluded that Phillips' meeting with Caines had not been recorded, and Phillips returned to Havana on 27 August.[680]

THE ATTACK FINALLY COMES

On 28 July, Morgan went to Miami to get a boatload of arms to deliver to various points in Cuba, including Trinidad. According to Escalante, Menoyo's cooperation increased at this time. Castro learned information from Menoyo during Morgan's absence that he and Menoyo had previously agreed not to reveal. This was the final plan:

The signal to set off the counter plan would be given by Morgan himself, without his knowing it, when he reported to Havana that he was headed for the island with the

---
679 8/18/59, HAVA 2573 to DIR CIA. 104-10267-10166.
680 See 8/21/59, HAVA 25898 to DIR CIA. 104-10128-10335; and 8/22/59, DIR 41198 to HAVA. 104-10177-10088; and HAVA 2603 to DIR CIA. 104-10267-10161.

arms shipment. At that moment the roundup of the conspirators began, dismantling the fifth column that was to have facilitated the invasions and capturing the men and weapons of the Foreign Legion.

Morgan arrived in Havana Bay shortly after midnight on 8 August, and in the morning Castro inspected the machine guns, rifles and ammunition on the boat.[681]

On or about 8 August, two dozen of Batista's former soldiers—what appears to have been the Dominican advance team—landed near Cienfuegos. There they found themselves in the middle of a much stronger Cuban force arranged by Camilo Cienfuegos. In the moments after their plane landed, the Dominican advance team was killed or captured and subsequently put in prison. Castro then directed the arrest of local Cubans suspected of anti-communist activities.[682] Escalante estimated that nearly a thousand counterrevolutionaries were rounded up.[683]

The Cubans then began their tactical deception operations. Still on 8 August, Menoyo radioed Trujillo that the battle against the communists had begun and that all was well. On 10 August Morgan radioed Colonel Johnny Abbes that the forces of the Second Front were preparing to take the city of Trinidad. Trujillo ordered an arms drop at Ingles Beach on 11 August, which Castro's forces recovered the next morning.

Press reports on 11 August about arrests inside Cuba threw a monkey wrench into the smoothness of the Cuban deception plan. A suspicious Trujillo demanded that Morgan come to the microphone. After whispering with Castro, Morgan (or perhaps Castro impersonating Morgan) assured Trujillo that Trinidad had just fallen. That night the Cubans shut off the electricity in Trinidad to make the show more convincing. On 12 August Trujillo sent Father Velazco to come and inspect the situation. He came, was successfully fooled, and returned to Trujillo with a false report of success.

The false story of success then backfired when Trujillo decided that he really did not need to send his Legion and radioed Morgan that the

---

681 Fabian Escalante, ***The Secret War: CIA Covert Operations Against Cuba, 1959-1962*** (Melbourne: Ocean Press, 1995), p. 25.
682 Felix I. Rodriguez, ***Shadow Warrior*** (New York: Simon and Schuster, 1989), pp. 42.
683 Fabian Escalante, ***The Secret War: CIA Covert Operations Against Cuba, 1959-1962*** (Melbourne: Ocean Press, 1995), p. 25.

Legion would be sent when conditions were "favorable." According to another version, the Legion was boarding their vehicles when their orders were canceled because Trujillo had learned the true fate of the advance team.[684] There were reports that the troops were not paid at all and were poorly fed; there were rumors that some Dominican officers had "skimmed money from the Legion's food budget."[685] In any event, the Cubans realized that the Foreign Legion was not coming. Castro decided to end the game and appeared on national television to tell the entire story.

The situation was delicate for both sides, and neither Castro nor Bonsal—who had warned Castro of an assassination attempt planned against him—wished to make public the fact that they had been discussing the event before it happened. Castro's denunciation gave himself and Washington cover—if only temporarily. There must have been hard feelings among the exiles that had participated, in one way or another, with this invasion plan. Trujillo, for one, must have felt very foolish to have fallen into such a trap. In this manner, the story ended, and the first attempt to invade Cuba and overthrow Castro ended in ignominious defeat.

In September, Cuban-American relations fell even further into a free fall that nothing could stop. On 4 September, Castro told Ambassador Bonsal that the $75 million Freeport Sulphur mining plant at Moa Bay and other "American private interests would come under review," meaning he was considering taking action against these companies."[686] In Washington, business leaders were visiting the offices of policy-makers more frequently. Robert Kleberg, Lyndon Johnson's neighbor in Texas, lost his huge ranch in Cuba. At a 24 September meeting with State Department officials, the heads of several U.S. sugar companies sought information on "what tactics we should employ" in Cuba. The United Fruit Vice President, Sam H. Baggett, said he feared Castro's actions would spread to other countries and would "force the United Fruit Company out of business."[687]

---

684   Felix I. Rodriguez, *Shadow Warrior* (New York: Simon and Schuster, 1989), pp. 42.
685   Felix I. Rodriguez, *Shadow Warrior* (New York: Simon and Schuster, 1989), pp. 39-40.
686   FRUS, 1958-1960, volume VI, Cuba, document #359, Telegram From the Embassy in Cuba to the Department of State, #571, September 4, 1959.
687   FRUS, 1958-1960, volume VI, Cuba, document #363, Memorandum of a Conversation, Department of State, Washington, September 24, 1959.

CHAPTER SEVENTEEN:
THE COMPLETE VICTORY OF CASTRO IN CUBA

By mid-October 1959, events had pushed Cuban-American relations into a further downward spiral. On 11 October, an aircraft flew from Miami to Pinar del Rio, where it dropped three bombs on the sugar mill operating there. The crew, 18 Cubans and two American pilots, were caught and detained in Cuba. The Eisenhower Administration denied that any official approval had been given to this mission.[688] While this incident grabbed the news headlines, Castro was quickly implementing the final phase of his transformation of Cuba's military and state structures. On 16 October, he abolished the Army, Navy, National Police, Joint Chiefs of Staff, and his Ministry of National Defense. He then reconstituted them into revolutionary organizations and merged them all into the Military Revolutionary Armed Forces (MRAF). Castro put his communist brother Raul in charge of the MRAF, and then ap-

---

688   Hugh Thomas, *Cuba, The Pursuit of Freedom* (New York: Harper and Rowe, 1971) p. 1243.

pointed another communist loyal to Raul, Augusto Martinez Sanchez, as the Minister of Labor.[689]

These actions solidified communist control over Cuba's key military and state organs, making Castro's victory in Cuba complete. On 17 October, a worried Ambassador Bonsal cabled Washington, "Raul Castro and supporters now confirmed in notably strong position, exercising control over all armed forces including police and investigative agencies." He added, "This is a disturbing development."[690] It must have been difficult for Bonsal to admit this, hanging perilously as he was on futile hopes that Castro might yet see the light. Cuba's "maximum leader" was a master of mixed signals, and he was particularly adept at feeding the hopes of the ambassador—desperate for any shred of good news. As late as September, Bonsal was still sending hopeful morsels to Washington. "Castro regrets some of his own statements against the U.S. Government," the ambassador reported after an evening with Castro on 4 September, and added, "I believe that some progress has been made in his thinking on this subject."[691] When the end came, it was cruel for Bonsal.

Castro now flaunted his victory openly. On 19 October, he delivered a television appearance so memorable that the American correspondents covering it judged it to be his "most violently anti-American performance in some time." The U.S. Embassy was predictably more defensive, saying Castro's performance was "illogical" and "unnecessary."[692] Nevertheless, now even the Ambassador understood that the game was over, and that there was a purpose to Castro's new invective. In making these displays, Castro sought to make it crystal clear that only he was in charge and that he was taking Cuba on a communist path. No one could stop him now. A December covert CIA analysis from Havana stated that the communists were "getting cocky due to their new power and influence."[693]

---

689 FRUS, 1958-1960, volume VI, Cuba, document #370, Telegram From the Embassy in Cuba to the Department of State, #848, 17 October 1959.
690 FRUS, 1958-1960, volume VI, Cuba, document #370, Telegram From the Embassy in Cuba to the Department of State, #848, 17 October 1959.
691 FRUS, 1958-1960, volume VI, Cuba, document #359, Telegram From the Embassy in Cuba to the Department of State, #571, 4 September 1959.
692 FRUS, 1958-1960, volume VI, Cuba, document #371, note 2, telegram 871from Havana, 20 October 1959.
693 12/31/59, CIA Havana to HQ, IN24556, see NARA, JFK files, CIA microfilm, reel 10B, at the same general location as Varona and many others, but the name of the person whose personnel file this is, is still protected.

THE RESIGNATION OF HUBER MATOS

A political crisis enveloped Cuba on the morning of 20 October 1959. The INRA captain in Camaguey Province, Enrique Mendoza Reboredo, denounced commander Huber Matos as a "traitor to the revolution."[694] In the army barracks at Camp Agramonte in Camaguey, Matos resigned his position and released a tape recording of a blunt letter he had written to Castro the day before. Matos had the letter given to the officers under his command. In the letter, Matos said that he had to speak clearly to Castro "about the problem of communism" and that in doing so he knew he would be branded as a traitor. Matos declared, "It is clear that the hour has arrived when all of those who are against communism must go as traitors."[695]

Matos, a former rice grower and Castro sympathizer, had joined the 26 July Movement in 1958 after arriving on an air mission from Costa Rica bringing arms for the revolution.[696] He became one of the principal rebel commanders and eventually led the advance into Santiago. After Batista's downfall, relations between Castro and Matos had begun on a strong note. Castro had rewarded Matos by appointing him as the military commander of the important Cuban province of Camaguey. As late as the end of April, Castro had given a yacht cruise for government economists and had included Matos. Castro reportedly stated, "Matos was with us because he was the only officer in the rebel army qualified to participate in our deliberations."[697]

The situation in Cuba had fundamentally changed during the hectic summer of 1959. The fact that Matos was anti-communist made conflict with Castro inevitable. Matos had gravitated toward Diaz Lanz, and they had begun working together in a losing battle to oppose communist control of Cuba.[698] Matos had become indiscreet about his views, mak-

---

694 FRUS, 1958-1960, volume VI, Cuba, document #372; see note 2, telegram 866 from Havana, 20 October 1959.
695 12/1/59, HAVANA Legat to DIR FBI, Subject Commandante Huber Matos.
696 Fabian Escalante, *The Secret War: CIA Covert Operations Against Cuba, 1959-62* (New York: Ocean Press, 1995), p. 32.
697 Rufo Lopez Fresquet, *My Fourteen Months With Castro* (New York: Wolrd Publishing Company, 1966), p. 130
698 Hugh Thomas, *Cuba, The Pursuit of Freedom* (New York: Harper and Rowe, 1971) p. 1213.

ing anti-communist remarks in public during June.[699] By early September, Matos had privately approached Lopez-Fresquet, the Minister of Finance, and suggested that there was a communist conspiracy underway in which Raul Castro was prepared to kill his brother Fidel, who knew nothing of the plot.[700] Before long, Lopez-Fresquet (who had not been included at the super-secret Cojimar negotiations) became persuaded of Matos' concerns and began working with this anti-communist group.[701] Matos was angry when his officers were required to attend classes at a school for communist indoctrination. He complained about the creation of the INRA "People's Stores" in Camaguey, which he saw as a front for communist penetration into the province.[702]

At the time of his resignation in October, Matos was enormously popular in Cuba. Castro decided to deal with the Matos problem permanently. Cuban officials claim Matos called for a general strike and that on 21 October Castro and the Rebel Army commander, Camilo Cienfuegos, traveled to Camaguey to arrest Matos. While they were en route, Cuba's national radio stations were linked to the local Camaguey city stations, as part of a broadside media attack on Matos.[703] Pedro Diaz Lanz disputes some of this story:

> Cienfuegos told Matos not to worry, "I will straighten this out with Fidel." Then he sent word to the radio station, ordering the broadcasts against Matos to be halted immediately. He was too late. Castro, who had flown to Camaguey, refused to listen to Cienfuegos, accused Matos of conspiracy with Major Diaz and ex-President Urrutia, charged him with treason and had him placed under arrest.[704]

According to the official version of the story, Cienfuegos, using the force of his own personality, arranged for Matos to abandon his plans.[705] There

---

699 Hugh Thomas, *Cuba, The Pursuit of Freedom* (New York: Harper and Rowe, 1971) p. 1230.
700 Rufo Lopez-Fresquet, *My Fourteen Months With Castro* (New York: The World Publishing Company, 1966), p. 130.
701 Hugh Thomas, *Cuba, The Pursuit of Freedom* (New York: Harper and Rowe, 1971) p. 1241.
702 Paul Bethel, *The Losers* (New York: Arlington House, 1969), p. 193.
703 Rufo Lopez-Fresquet, *My 14 Months With Castro* (New York: The World Publishing Company, 1966), p. 148.
704 7/64, Statement of Pedro Diaz Lanz to Walkenhut Security Reviwew, Vol. 4, No. 7. 124-10294-10123.
705 Fabian Escalante, *The Secret War: CIA Covert Operations Against Cuba, 1959-62* (New York: Ocean Press, 1995), p. 37.

THE COMPLETE VICTORY OF CASTRO IN CUBA

was confrontation and much street theater. The "Maximum Leader" entered and, in front of a crowd of 5,000 people, Castro denounced Matos as a "traitor and coward, afraid of Trujillo and the North American chancery."[706]

Bethel argues that Matos could not be allowed to "just resign, any more than communists can turn in their party cards and forget all about it." Because he had publicly differed with the regime, with Castro, and with his communist friends, "Matos had to be destroyed."[707] He was convicted of "treason and sedition" by the regime, and spent the next twenty years in prison (1959–1979).

The day Matos resigned, a B-25 bomber piloted by Pedro Diaz Lanz and Frank Sturgis flew from Florida and dropped leaflets from a very low altitude over Havana. They flew the aircraft straight down Linea Street and then pulled up over the Havana Hilton, where, from their balconies, hundreds of members attending a convention of the American Society of Travel Agents observed the spectacle. The Castro informants among the Americans at first explained the Matos incident with the line, "we revolutionaries still have some elements of the old order in our midst trying to steal money from the people, and Fidel of course has to see that they are brought to justice." The following day the Americans were told that it had been discovered that Matos had been working with Diaz Lanz on the "bombing" of Havana the previous day.[708]

This dare-devil flying stunt garnered a lot of attention, but achieved little of substance. Castro appeared on television to make the case that American aircraft had dropped bombs and had machine gunned the city, killing and wounding its citizens. Ambassador Bonsal sent a cable to Washington saying that the damages were "probably caused by aircraft with Cuban military markings, anti-aircraft fire from various Cuban military and naval installations, and bombs from Cubans on the ground."[709] The dropped leaflets denied that Lanz was a traitor, said Castro was know-

---

[706] FRUS, 1958-1960, volume VI, Cuba, document #372, Telegram From the Embassy in Cuba to the Department of State, #876, 21 October 1959. See also document #373, Telegram From the Embassy in Cuba to the Department of State, #886, 21 October 1959.
[707] Paul Bethel, *The Losers* (New York: Arlington House, 1969), pp. 193.
[708] Paul Bethel, *The Losers* (New York: Arlington House, 1969), pp. 193-196.
[709] FRUS, 1958-1960, volume VI, Cuba, document #377, Telegram From the Embassy in Cuba to the Department of State, #912, 23 October 1959.

ingly permitting the communists to take over, and claimed that Lanz had heard Castro discuss plans to deceive the Cuban people and introduce a "system like that in Russia."[710] Such a statement would have been a revelation six months earlier but, by October, the Lanz-Sturgis leaflets only said what many people in Cuba had already concluded—Castro was taking Cuba down the communist path.[711] Like the bombing of the sugar mill, however, these air raids did draw attention to Cuba's inability to repel intrusions into its airspace. This point would be important to the unfolding American plans for a political-military operation in Cuba.

THE RESIGNATION OF ARTIME AND DEATH OF CIENFUEGOS

Meanwhile, the next piece of the unfolding conflict occurred two days later, on 23 October. Manuel Artime resigned his position in INRA and circulated this news in an open letter to Castro in which he also accused the Cuban leader of surrendering to "international communism."[712] Artime had joined Castro's revolution late as a protégé of a rebel commander, Sori Marin, in the Sierra Maestra.[713] Marin had made Artime commander of the Rural commandoes; under Castro, Artime followed Marin into agricultural work[714] and, as discussed in Chapter Fourteen, Artime had become an INRA official. Like other anti-Batista leaders who were also anti-communist, Artime's time to break with Castro had arrived. After he resigned in October, he returned to Orient Province to recruit students and peasants and organize them to fight against Castro. Artime joined Sergio Sanjenis in founding the Movement of Revolutionary Rescue (MRR).

---

710   FRUS, 1958-1960, volume VI, Cuba, document #374, Telegram From the Embassy in Cuba to the Department of State, #887, 22 October 1959.
711   Felix Rodriguez, *Shadow Warrior: The CIA Hero of a Hundred Unknown Battles* (New York: Simkon and Schuster, 1989), p. 31.
712   Fabian Escalante, *The Secret War: CIA Covert Operations Against Cuba, 1959-62* (New York: Ocean Press, 1995), p. 37.
713   Fabian Escalante, *The Secret War: CIA Covert Operations Against Cuba, 1959-62* (New York: Ocean Press, 1995), p. 32.
714   Hugh Thomas, *Cuba, The Pursuit of Freedom* (New York: Harper and Rowe, 1971) p. 1275.

THE COMPLETE VICTORY OF CASTRO IN CUBA

As previously discussed, on 26 October at a huge rally in front of the presidential palace in Havana, Castro delivered an angry speech that the embassy described as "vehemently anti-American" as anything he had ever done. He listed virtually all local American interests as items which were "not in the interests of Cuba."[715] This effectively closed out any remaining hopes that American businesses could work with Castro, further accelerating the deepening vortex in U.S.-Cuban relations.

Finally, Cienfuegos himself died in an alleged plane crash on 28 October. The circumstances surrounding the death of the enormously popular Cuban army commander have been in dispute ever since. According to one view, it was an accident; according to the other view, Cienfuegos was assassinated. Cuban exile and American sources, while not uniform, have supported the view that Castro eliminated Cienfuegos and covered it up because of the latter's popularity. Official Cuban sources insist Cienfuegos death was an accident. Accident or not, at least two soldiers of fortune, Hemming and Sturgis, each thought that they had recruited Cienfuegos to work for the Americans. Recall Sturgis' claim that the Army commander had facilitated Sturgis' surreptitious entry to army facilities for the clandestine removal and photographing of military documents. The true circumstances about Cienfeugos' death may never be known for sure, but one thing is certain: his death removed the last remaining obstacle to the total communist control of Cuba's armed forces.

The imprisonment, death, or flight of the last remnants of the non-communists in the Cuban leadership consummated the second round of political struggle in 1959, one in which Castro had defeated his post-revolutionary opponents inside Cuba. The tumultuous events of October were the end of the line in Washington. There, the State Department was laying the policy groundwork for a new secret objective for Cuban policy: *the removal of Castro from power*. On 23 October, Assistant Secretary of State Rubottom summarized U.S.-Cuban relations in this way:

> …we have been giving Castro every opportunity to follow a course consistent with good U.S.-Cuban relations and have exercised in public great restraint in order to make it possible for him to modify his attitudes and policies if

---

715   FRUS, 1958-1960, volume VI, Cuba, document #379, Editorial Note.

he had any inclination to maintain the bonds of friendship and common interest which have linked this country to Cuba. To date, he has failed the "test" by which his intentions with respect to maintaining good relations can be judged.[716]

From here on, U.S. policy would be based on the judgment that Castro's regime was "inconsistent with the minimal requirements" of U.S. policy objectives. Only "Cuban opposition to Castro's present course and/or a change in the Cuban regime" could change this situation, the Assistant Secretary said. Such a change now became the "immediate objective" of the U.S. and it had to be accomplished "not later than the end of 1960," he added.[717]

Rubottom's call to overthrow Castro by the end of 1960 was set forth in a paper entitled, "Current Basic United States Policy Towards Cuba."[718] It concluded that Castro had to be removed *before* the next election, but Rubottom did not say exactly how Castro was to be removed. This policy change was important to presidential hopeful Richard Nixon, and it might have been seen as helpful to the Republican political campaign of 1960. It was, however, highly sensitive. Rubottom warned that wide distribution of this new policy paper might have "damaging consequences," and added, "It is my thought that it be distributed on a strictly 'need-to-know' basis." The need for official secrecy for Cuban policy would hamstring Richard Nixon in the 1960 campaign. Rubottom's "need-to-know" list in October 1959 included the CIA but, unwisely, excluded the Department of Defense (DOD). After some minor additions at the request of Secretary of State Herter and President Eisenhower, the new policy and the "need-to-know" restrictions were approved in early November. The exclusion of the Pentagon did not last and, after a series

---

716 FRUS, 1958-1960, volume VI, Cuba, document #376, Memorandum From the Assistant Secretary of State for Inter-American Affairs (Rubottom) to the Under Secretary of State for political Affairs (Murphy), Subject: Current Basic United States Policy Towards Cuba, 23 October 1959.
717 FRUS, 1958-1960, volume VI, Cuba, document #376, Memorandum From the Assistant Secretary of State for Inter-American Affairs (Rubottom) to the Under Secretary of State for political Affairs (Murphy), Subject: Current Basic United States Policy Towards Cuba, 23 October 1959.
718 FRUS, 1958-1960, volume VI, Cuba, document #376, Memorandum From the Assistant Secretary of State for Inter-American Affairs (Rubottom) to the Under Secretary of State for political Affairs (Murphy), Subject: Current Basic United States Policy Towards Cuba, 23 October 1959.

of queries and memoranda, DOD was brought into the loop by early January 1960.

By the end of October 1959, Castro had consolidated his power completely. He no longer needed to pretend he was something that he was not. "Castro seems to be burning all the bridges behind him," Secretary of State Herter wrote to British Foreign Secretary Selwyn Lloyd.[719] "Our bitter enemies, Raul Castro and Che Guevara are very much in the saddle," Ambassador Bonsal cabled Washington on 6 November, adding gloomily, "They can be counted on to speed up radical agrarian reform as well as measures designed to destroy or cripple U.S. mining, petroleum, and public utility interests."[720]

U.S. intelligence confirmed this prediction almost immediately. Covert sources reported that the nickel mining operations of the U.S. company, Freeport Sulphur, had become Raul Castro's next target. According to an 18 November State Department intelligence memo, two weeks earlier Raul had urged Fidel to intervene in the Freeport Sulphur's Moa Bay installations in order to take the eight million pesos a year they could earn from their operations.[721] The enormous investment in the Moa Bay project made this news particularly hard to swallow at Freeport Sulphur, where there were hopes that, somehow, Castro would spare this facility. U.S. diplomatic records contain this official statement on behalf of Freeport Sulphur:

> On 15 November Dr. Mario Lazo of Lazo and Cubas, attorneys for Freeport Sulphur, gave his opinion that Castro would not find intervention of this property advisable, since its concentrates can only be treated at Freeport's New Orleans plant and intervention would throw

---

719 FRUS, 1958-1960, volume VI, Cuba, document #386, Letter From Secretary of State Herter to Foreign Secretary Lloyd, 4 November 1959.
720 FRUS, 1958-1960, volume VI, Cuba, document #388, Telegram From the Embassy in Cuba to the Department of State, #1043, 6 November 1959.
721 FRUS, 1958-1960, volume VI, Cuba, document #395, Memorandum From the Director of the Office of Intelligence Research and Analysis for American Republics (Hall) to the Director of Intelligence and Research (Cumming), 18 November 1959, pp. 672-673. A relative of Luis Botifolls had witnessed a conversation in a restaurant between Castro and his brother, in which Raul urged Fidel to intervene in the Moa Bay.

1,500 Cubans out of employments, affecting 6,000 dependents.[722]

Lazo said these facts would be "communicated tactfully to Fidel this week by his senior partner Dr. Jorge Cubas." Tact would have been advisable indeed, as Castro was holding all the cards.

CUBAN POLICY AND THE "MISSILE GAP"

If Khrushchev had been clever in avoiding the appearance of interference in Cuba, Castro had been just as clever in avoiding the appearance of a communist takeover in Cuba. Both leaders had followed deliberately deceptive policies in order to diminish the chances for U.S. military intervention in Cuba—an act that might well have profoundly changed the course of events that followed. Castro needed to forestall U.S. action in order to survive; Khrushchev needed to preserve Cuba as a potential Soviet base—the value of which could be expected to increase as U.S. ICBM's came on line. Khrushchev had played the "missile gap" card at a propitious moment during Castro's seizure of power, after which Castro successfully stalled for time by making misleading remarks about his plans for Cuba.

During the period of power consolidation, Castro kept a question mark over the communist issue, orchestrating carefully the rate at which communist party (PSP) members moved into positions of power. Khrushchev played his part too and for the rest of 1959 took no action that could be construed by Washington as an indicator of international communist control of Cuba. Castro and Khrushchev achieved their objectives and by the latter part of 1959 many U.S. policy-makers appeared frustrated and embarrassed as Castro packed more and more communists into his regime while the Soviet missile threat turned out to have been a missile bluff all along. Angrily, the Chief of Naval Operations,

---

722 FRUS, 1958-1960, volume VI, Cuba, document #395, Memorandum From the Director of the Office of Intelligence Research and Analysis for American Republics (Hall) to the Director of Intelligence and Research (Cumming), 18 November 1959, p. 673, note 2.

THE COMPLETE VICTORY OF CASTRO IN CUBA

Admiral Arleigh Burke, said that Soviet submarines had been sighted in the Caribbean and that "the whole area was menaced by communism."[723]

In the U.S., the missile gap had taken on a political life of its own. The fact that it was a bluff was not welcome news to those whose military programs or political careers had profited from the gap. For example, the commanding generals of the Strategic Air Command—Curtis Lemay and Thomas Power—argued for higher estimates of Soviet ICBMs. Their arguments actually served Khrushchev's scheming. They may have believed that the Soviet generals would want as many missiles as they did, but they knew that a gap meant more U.S. resources for air force missiles. The news that it was a bluff had political implications for several Democratic senators like Anderson (D-New Mexico) and Symington (D-Missouri), who relentlessly attacked the Eisenhower record on the "missile gap." Democrats were, of course, looking forward to using this issue in the 1960 elections.

Symington, who had presidential ambitions, flatly accused the administration of lowering Soviet missile estimates because of budget constraints. Indeed, the CIA had lowered its estimate, but not due to budget considerations, as this 4 February 1959 testimony of Allen Dulles makes clear:

> We have changed our position in the CIA somewhat because of the fact that from May of 1958 until the present time, to the best of my belief and I feel confident about it, they haven't successfully tested any missiles, and I changed my views when I believed the basic evidence changed.[724]

Dulles was right—the evidence had changed. The Soviet missile test program had been down since May of 1958 and would not resume until March 1959. Dulles' confidence stemmed from the fact that the enormous blast pits from which the SS-6's had to be launched were easy to spot with U-2s—the CIA's overhead reconnaissance planes.

---

723 As quoted in Hugh Thomas, *Cuba, The Pursuit of Freedom* (New York: Harper and Rowe, 1971) p. 1241.
724 Wayne Jackson, *Allen Welsh Dulles as Director of Central Intelligence, 26 February 1953-29 November 1961*, CIA Historical Staff, Volume V, Intelligence Support of Policy, p. 76.

Eisenhower was not planning to deploy large numbers of the first-generation U.S. ICBMs, but he had approved modest increases for planned deployments of both the Atlas and Titan systems.[725] By March 1959, these U.S. missiles were still about 18 months away from initial operating capability (IOC). The president had decided to concentrate on the development of the next-generation of solid-fueled Minuteman and Polaris ICBMs. He paid for this politically by enduring a blistering attack from Democrats in Congress and their allies in the press. The most recent U.S. intelligence estimate had predicted IOC for the Soviet SS-6 in the latter half of 1959.[726] Journalists such as Joseph Alsop soon forgot about the Air Force prediction for the end of 1958, and charged that Eisenhower was committing "national suicide" and playing "Russian Roulette."[727]

During senate hearings in March 1959, Senator Symington made this imaginative forecast: "Now, I want to make this prediction to you. In three years the Russians will prove to us that they have 3,000 ICBMs. Let that be on the record."[728] That same month, the Soviets resumed testing of ICBMs at a rate of four firings per month.[729] There were still major problems with the oversized, clumsy missile. Many failed on the launch pad or in flight.[730] Less than half were successful, and even they were not accurate.[731] Nevertheless, the regular pattern of firings after March was taken to indicate that the SS-6 testing program "was at last in its terminal stages," and by July, Secretary of Defense Neil McElroy and the CIA were predicting that a few Soviet missiles would be operational by the end of the year. McElroy said that the U.S. and USSR were "neck and neck" in

---

725   John Prados, *The Soviet Estimate: US Intelligence Analysis and Soviet Strategic Forces* (Princeton: Princeton University Press, 1986 ed.), p. 80.
726   Memo, GMIC to Dulles, 9 October 1958, as quoted in Wayne Jackson, CIA Historical Staff, *Allen Welsh Dulles as Director of Central Intelligence: 26 February 1953-29 November 1961*, Volume V, Intelligence Support of Policy, p. 67.
727   1/24/59, Joseph Alsop, *New York Times*,
728   Wayne Jackson, CIA Historical Staff, *Allen Welsh Dulles as Director of Central Intelligence: 26 February 1953-29 November 1961*, Volume V, Intelligence Support of Policy, p. 81.
729   Lawrence Freedman, *US Intelligence and the Soviet Strategic Threat* (Boulder: Westview Press, 1977), p. 70.
730   John Prados, *The Soviet Estimate: US Intelligence Analysis and Soviet Strategic Forces* (Princeton: Princeton University Press, 1986 ed.), p. 84.
731   James Perry, *The Foreign Policy of John Kennedy, 1961* (Dissertation, Columbian School of Arts and Sciences, George Washington University, 1996), Part I, p. 2.

the missile race.[732] Senator Lyndon Johnson, like Symington, had his sights set on the White House, and had his own view. Johnson accused Eisenhower of ceding a 3-to-1 edge in ICBMs to the Soviet Union over the next three years.[733]

The approaching 1960 election became a big political factor in the "missile gap" debate. Democratic presidential hopefuls did not cease their emphasis on the issue even though the estimated IOC of Khrushchev's SS-6s kept slipping, month after month—a slippage that became more noticeable over the summer of 1959. In an August 19 memorandum to the president, Director of Central Intelligence (DCI) Dulles wrote that the consensus on the date for Soviet IOC was now estimated to be "in 1959 or in 1960."[734] In the midst of the drubbing it was taking for being weak on communism, the administration must have welcomed the fact that U.S. missile deployments were just a year away. American deployments would enable Washington to reassess its policy stands in Cold War hot spots such as Berlin, Cuba, and Laos.

By late 1959, when the American Administration was involved in this general policy reassessment, Cuban policy had grown in importance. From Washington's perspective, the previous year had seen an unbroken string of embarrassing disasters. Castro's dualism was particularly vexing because it pointed to a failure in judgment for the Eisenhower Administration. Like the missile gap issue, Castro's communization of Cuba was a politically explosive issue as the next presidential election approached in America.

Khrushchev's bluffing and Castro's cunning thus played a role in one of the worst defeats for the Eisenhower Administration and handed the Democrats a devastating issue for the upcoming elections. They would be able to criticize the Republicans for having stood idly by while a communist regime ensconced itself just 90 miles from U.S. shores. The continuing deterioration of the situation in Cuba during the fall of 1959 called for a serious reevaluation of Cuban policy at a crucial

---

732 Lawrence Freedman, *US Intelligence and the Soviet Strategic Threat* (Boulder: Westview Press, 1977), p. 70.
733 John Prados, *The Soviet Estimate: US Intelligence Analysis and Soviet Strategic Forces* (Princeton: Princeton University Press, 1986 ed.), p. 85.
734 John Prados, *The Soviet Estimate: US Intelligence Analysis and Soviet Strategic Forces* (Princeton: Princeton University Press, 1986 ed.), p. 86.

juncture of the missile race. During early October, the U.S. intelligence community was completing a fundamental revision of its "missile gap" estimate. U.S. analysts realized, by mid-October, that the SS-6's were not being deployed. NIE 11-5-59, dated November 3, 1959 concluded, "it is now well established that the USSR is not engaged in a 'crash program' for ICBM development."[735]

The secret conclusion that the estimate of Soviet missiles had been overdone did not end the public debate over the missile gap. That issue continued to gather steam as the 1960 election campaign neared. As it happened, in November 1959, Khrushchev decided against deploying large numbers of the first-generation Soviet missiles. This decision would not be known to the U.S. for several months, during which Khrushchev pulled yet another one of his missile bluff stunts. Pretending that he had already made large deployments of the SS-6, the Soviet leader publicly claimed he had stockpiled so many missiles that the USSR "could wipe from the face of the earth all of our probable opponents."[736]

The effects of Khrushchev's latest bluff were mixed. His remarks certainly helped keep the missile debate alive and provided the Democrats more ammunition for the upcoming election campaign. On the other hand, they did not convince the U.S. intelligence community or the president. At the classified level, it had become increasingly evident that much of Khrushchev's past saber rattling had been bluster, and this realization had important implications for US foreign policy. American decision-makers were no longer constrained by the imminent threat of a strategic imbalance. The time to get tough with Castro had arrived.

---

735 James Perry, *The Foreign Policy of John Kennedy, 1961* (Dissertation, Columbian School of Arts and Sciences, George Washington University, 1996), Part I, p. 10.
736 James Perry, *The Foreign Policy of John Kennedy, 1961* (Dissertation, Columbian School of Arts and Sciences, George Washington University, 1996), Part I, pp. 4-5.

CHAPTER EIGHTEEN:
THE CIA DECISION TO "REMOVE" CASTRO FROM POWER

Given the tumult that had accompanied the completion of Castro's victory in Cuba, Moscow was keeping a low profile in Cuba—perhaps too low. At a 1 December 1959 National Security Council (NSC) meeting Allen Dulles remarked, "The USSR was being very clever in not permitting its interest in Cuba to be openly identified." Secretary of State Herter added that Moscow did not want to give the U.S. an excuse to topple Castro's regime.[737]

Yet the star of U.S. action to overthrow Castro was already rising on the horizon. It was no longer a question of *if* the U.S. would attempt to overthrow Castro; it was merely a matter of *how* it would be undertaken. In the face of the coming elections in 1960, it was also a matter of *when*. No one with future political ambitions in Washington was more vulnerable on the issue of Castro and communism in Cuba than Vice President Nixon. Nixon wanted action on Cuba and he wanted it fast. He

---

737 FRUS, 1958-1960, volume VI, Cuba, document #402, Memorandum of Discussion at the 426th Meeting of the National Security Council, 1 December 1959.

demanded that the *routine fashion* of diplomacy be replaced by dramatic covert actions.

PAWLEY, THE EXILES, AND TRUJILLO

William Pawley had been a CIA conduit for many right-wing Cuban exiles in Miami. Pawley was also closely associated with Trujillo and his network of pro-Batista exiles operating in the Dominican Republic, including Pedraza, who was rebuilding forces to invade Cuba again. The secrecy around that plan had been thoroughly blown by a prominent Cuban exile leader who had found out about it—and that he was to be excluded from the plan. He was Emilio Nunez Portuondo, the Cuban Ambassador to the UN during the Batista regime.

In early November, Portuondo began making statements in Latin American countries that the U.S. was "on the point of intervening in Cuba." His statements quickly worked their way through diplomatic channels back to the State Department, which, as usual, was not totally up to speed about Pawley's subterranean maneuvering. Secretary of State Herter told the Latin American U.S. missions that the U.S. was not planning an intervention in Cuba and that any implication that Nunez Portuondo was closely associated with the State Department was false. Herter added that the Department assumed that Nunez' statements were motivated by his desire to advance his own political cause.[738]

Pawley and his Cuban confidant Fabio Freyre went to Washington on 30 November to prepare for a trip to the Dominican Republic. While in the Capitol they would seek out top officials who would be important bell weathers for their plan to invade Cuba.[739] Pawley was furious with Portuondo and intended to fix that problem in Washington too. A memo, apparently written by Freyre after the visit, said that in Washington they "had the impression that everyone there was most concerned

---

[738] FRUS, 1958-1960, volume VI, Cuba, document #385; Circular Airgram From the Department of State to Certain Diplomatic Missions in the American Republics, CG-308, 4 November 1959.
[739] 12/10/59, CIA Memorandum for the Record, Subject: Meeting on 6 December with William D. Pawley in Miami. RIF 104-10049-10356. The memo has two name lists identified as "Attachment A" and "Attachment B."

THE CIA DECISION TO "REMOVE" CASTRO FROM POWER

and very worried with the latest events that were developing in Cuba."[740] During the trip, Freyre assembled a list of nineteen Cuban exile leaders to present to General Jose Eleuterio Pedraza, head of the proposed invasion force—the name Foreign Legion having been dropped in favor of the Cuban Constitutional Army.[741] While in Washington, it is likely that Pawley met with his close friend J. C. King, Chief of the CIA's Western Hemisphere Division. If so, Pawley would probably have coordinated Freyre's list with King. One week later a fresh initiative at the CIA was underway to recruit and train a commando force to be used in Cuba.

Pawley and Freyre traveled to the Dominican Republic and met with Trujillo, Commander-in-Chief of the Dominican Republic Armed Forces, and General Pedraza, from 3-5 December.[742] Pawley learned more about the new invasion force Trujillo and Pedraza had put together and their plan for obtaining U.S. approval and support from Cuban exile groups operating in the U.S. Pawley showed his list of Cuban exile leaders to Pedraza and asked him if he would be willing to work with any of the people named on the list. Pedraza replied that he would have no objection to anyone on the list.

Pawley also showed Pedraza another list of seven persons made by a Cuban associate Pawley did not identify, and Pedraza reacted favorably to this list as well.[743] A description of the meeting, apparently prepared by Freyre, contains this passage:

> We had found that Generalissimo Trujillo was in a position more than willing to cooperate in all ways possible with him [Pedraza] so that the Cuban opposition would be organized to overthrow the present communist regime. We have found that General Pedraza had an organized army at his disposal of over 2,000 men of various nationalities including Cubans and that he was most will-

---
740 NARA, JFK files, CIA January 1994 five brown boxes release, CIA Memorandum for the Record, Subject: CIA record of 9 December 1959 meeting in Pawley's office. Handwritten at the top: "Recd: 16 Dec 59." This memo appears to be minutes prepared by Freyre.
741 12/10/59, CIA Memorandum for the Record, Subject: Meeting on 6 December with William D. Pawley in Miami. RIF 104-10049-10356.
742 12/10/59, CIA Memorandum for the Record, Subject: Meeting on 6 December with William D. Pawley in Miami. RIF 104-10049-10356.
743 12/10/59, CIA Memorandum for the Record, Subject: Meeting on 6 December with William D. Pawley in Miami. RIF 104-10049-10356.

ing to help any organized army that would start working in Cuba or its coast at any moment.[744]

Pedraza authorized Pawley to make commitments in his, Pedraza's, name to facilitate forming "the opposition block" against communist Cuba. He also offered to head the military force that would strike, or work in close cooperation with a group of army officers, such as General Tamayo, Colonel Corzo, Colonel Barquin and Colonel Borbonet. Pedraza "begged" Pawley and Freyre to contact the various exile groups in Miami and get them to begin organizing their forces and prepare themselves for his (Pedraza's) anticipated visit to Miami.

Apparently, Trujillo and Pedraza were impressed with Pawley's credentials and his ability to talk to the top American leaders in Washington. CIA agents learned about the details of the Pawley-Trujillo meeting from other Cuban informants with whom Trujillo spoke after Pawley's departure. One such informant was Francisco G. Cajigas, a former wealthy Cuban businessman turned political leader.[745] Trujillo told Cajigas that Pawley "promised that he would have information on the United States official position on the Cuban matter" by 15 December.[746] This date was an accurate prediction, for on that date Pawley would dine with the vice president, who was scheduled to preside over an important NSC meeting the following morning.

Meanwhile, Cajigas had also learned from Trujillo that he had given *his own* name list to Pawley, apparently a list of men to form a junta. Confirmation of this detail came two weeks later when Pawley told the CIA that he had asked Pedraza to make such a list, and that it was a list of men who would form a junta "if and when Castro was deposed."[747] After contacting the CIA in Miami on 6 December,[748] Pawley did as Pedraza

---

744   NARA, JFK files, CIA January 1994 five brown boxes release, CIA Memorandum for the Record, Subject: CIA record of 9 December 1959 meeting in Pawley's office. Handwritten at the top: "Recd: 16 Dec 59."
745   FRUS, 1958-1960, volume VI, Cuba, document #599; Memorandum From the Assistant Secretary of State for Inter-American Affairs (Mann) to the Secretary of State, 28 October 1960, Subject: President's Inquiry Regarding Cuban Opposition Groups.
746   NARA, JFK files, CIA January 1994 five brown boxes release, CIA Memorandum for the Record, Subject: Cuban Political Matters, date: 12, 15, and 16 December 1959. The Cuban source was Francisco G. Cajigas, who passed on the information to one "Jack Gillespie" who, in turn, relayed the information to the CIA.
747   NARA, JFK files, CIA January 1994 five brown boxes release, CIA Memorandum for the Record, Subject: Telephone Conversation with Mr. Pawley, 11:45 a.m., 31 December 1959.
748   NARA, JFK files, CIA January 1994 five brown boxes release, CIA Memorandum for the Record, Subject: Meeting on 6 December with William D. Pawley in Miami, 10 December 1959."

had asked, and, on 9 December, summoned to his Miami office the representatives of various organized Cuban opposition groups. In Pawley's office, the exile leaders heard what Pawley and Freyre had to say about their talks with Trujillo and Pedraza, and all that had been discussed about military preparations to overthrow Castro.[749]

On that day, however, Pawley had important news for his interlocutors. He mentioned that there was a possibility of preparing "two or three bases that would be training centers for the commandos that would ultimately work on the Cuban coast and inside Cuba." Pawley's comments about commando training centers were a reference to a new plan being developed at CIA HQS—a plan that would ultimately become the "Bay of Pigs" operation. Pedraza, however, was not part of the CIA plan.

THE SEARCH FOR AN OPPOSITION LEADERSHIP

In December 1959, the planners at CIA HQS were considering credible opposition leaders, such as former Prime Minister Antonio Varona, to form a government in exile. Varona had opposed Batista, but he was also openly critical of Castro's refusal to hold elections and failure to move Cuba toward democracy. Varona publicly criticized the Agrarian Reform Program. He stated that cultivated lands should not be redistributed, and added that state lands should be distributed first. Varona and his Autentico Organization (AO) remained one of the few visible critics of Castro. The AO newspaper, *Opinion Nacional*, went out of business in early December.[750] The CIA sent an officer using the pseudonym Peter N. Licari to Havana on 27 December to meet with Varona about aid to *Opinion Nacional* and other matters.[751]

---

749 NARA, JFK files, CIA January 1994 five brown boxes release, CIA Memorandum for the Record, Subject: CIA record of 9 December 1959 meeting in Pawley's office. Handwritten at the top: "Recd: 16 Dec 59."
750 Hugh Thomas, *Cuba, The Pursuit of Freedom* (New York: Harper and Rowe, 1971) p. 1223.
751 DIR 07733 to HAVA. RIF 104-10174-10050. Peter N Licari may be one of the many pseudonyms used by Gerry Droller, whose Miami pseudonym was Frank Bender. See RIF 104-10167-10018 and RIF 104-10260-10410.

The CIA also dispatched a covert contract agent—a political organizer already assigned to work on the Democratic election campaign in 1960—to Havana (20 January to 4 February) to survey the general situation. He was Henry P. Lopez and he had been assigned the CIA pseudonym Edward G. Tichborn. He was specifically tasked with investigating how to unify the non-communist opposition to Fidel Castro into a political organization."[752]

Licari met with Varona at his home on the morning of December 29.[753] One of the subjects they discussed was the Pedraza force in the Dominican Republic. An information report summarized Varona's view in this way:

> Varona is worried about a possible invasion of Cuba by General Jose Eleutario Pedraza Carrera. (Headquarters comment: Pedraza is at the moment residing in the Dominican Republic, where he is reportedly in command of an anti-Castro group.) Varona is bitterly anti-Pedraza and has averred that he and his followers would join with the Castro brothers in repelling any invasion led by Pedraza.[754]

This negative view of Pedraza was shared at CIA HQS, where senior officers had their own growing concerns about the counterproductive effects of the Batista supporters' activities in the Dominican Republic. The botched invasion in August had been a public relations success for Castro and a disaster for everyone working against Castro—especially for those still inside Cuba.

When he met with Licari in December, Varona said that the "Batista supporters" should leave the U.S. because their presence allowed Castro "to point his finger" at them, making it impossible for his Autentico Organization or any other opposition group to do anything "internally in Cuba."[755] Varona did say that an effective step to take would be to arrange for "appropriate publicity to discredit and destroy the popular image of Fidel Castro."

---

752 11/23/59, CIA Memo for the Record, by Horace Davis, Acting Chief, Political Action Division, 24 November 1959, Subject: Consultant for Cuba—Edward G. Tichborn (P); 104-10174-10052; 5/20/60, CIA Memorandum for Chief, Covert Action Staff, from Horace Davis, Chief, Political Action Division, Subject Edward G. Tichborn. 104-10174-10029.
753 CIA Havana to HQ, IN24556, December 31, 1959; see NARA, JFK files, CIA microfilm, reel 10B, at the same general location as Varona and many others, but the name of the person whose personnel file this is, is still protected.
754 12/31/59, CIA Information Report, TDCS-3/423,158, Subject: Comments of Cuban opposition figure on the present situation in Cuba. RIF 104-10260-10413.
755 12/31/59, CIA Information Report, TDCS-3/423,158, Subject: Comments of Cuban opposition figure on the present situation in Cuba. RIF 104-10260-10413.

THE CIA DECISION TO "REMOVE" CASTRO FROM POWER

A CIA memo written by Evalina S. Vidal, who attended the debrief of Tichborn, passed on this interesting observation of Castro's handling of defections:

> Fidel Castro seems to become most upset and almost panicked by defections. Possessing a "Messiah-type complex" he cannot bear the thought of someone leaving the fold. Rather than let such defections pass on unnoticed, he feels compelled to give reasons and make excuses. This then blows the matter up perhaps out of proportion and quickly becomes a matter of public knowledge.[756]

This news from Havana painted a depressing picture in which the only tool available seemed to be defecting. For the time being, the prospects for unifying anti-Castro leaders inside Cuba were dim. At CIA HQS, however, work was in progress to fashion some new tools for use in Cuba. First among them was a plan by Western Hemisphere Division (WHD) Chief J. C. King for "the elimination of Fidel Castro."[757]

NIXON AND A DRAMATIC COVERT PLAN TO GET RID OF CASTRO

By his own claim, Nixon had been "the strongest and most persistent advocate for setting up and supporting" a covert effort to remove Castro from power.[758] As previously discussed in Chapter Eleven, Nixon described the group that supported this view as including FBI Director J. Edgar Hoover, Director of Central Intelligence Allen Dulles, and William Pawley. Nixon sided "strongly" with Allen Dulles in presenting this view to the NSC.[759] Nixon also made moves of his own. In October, he reportedly proposed helping the anti-Castro exiles with arms.[760] In December, he called for a "dramatic" new covert program against Castro. That program got underway in December, at the same time that Nixon,

---
756 2/2/60, CIA Memo for the Record, by Evalina S. Vidal, February 2, 1960, Subject: Debriefing of Edward G. Tichborn. 104-10174-10038.
757 12/11/59, CIA Memorandum From Chief, Western Hemisphere Division, via Deputy Director (Plans), for Director of Central Intelligence, Subject: Cuban Problems. 104-10315-10007.
758 Richard Nixon, "Cuba, Castro and John F. Kennedy," *Reader's Digest*, November, 1964, p. 288.
759 Richard Nixon, **RN** (New York: Grosset and Dunlap, 1978, pp. 202-203.
760 Hugh Thomas, ***Cuba, The Pursuit of Freedom*** (New York: Harper and Rowe, 1971) p. 1243.

Dulles, and Pawley attended a number of key meetings during which the outlines of the new covert program to overthrow Castro were worked out.

The diminution of the "missile gap" threat took place at this time—as Cuban-American relations reached the breaking point. The end of the gap helped to further dissipate restraints on policy, which was now fundamentally revised. A new covert Cuban policy emerged that had two essential parts. First, it called for a political-military operation to overthrow the Cuban regime, and second, it called for the "elimination" and "disappearance" of Fidel Castro. At CIA, planning for this policy was—with a quick fingers makeover—approved in early December 1959.

The political-military operation was itself a two-stage program. In this case it was to build and then to use a covert commando force. A review of this plan a year and a half later for President Kennedy described it in this way:

> A. The selection, recruitment and careful evaluation (including medical, psychological, psychiatric and polygraph) of approximately thirty-five Cubans, preferably with various military experience, for an intensive training program which would qualify them to become instructors in various paramilitary skills, including leadership, sabotage, communications, etc.
>
> B. The instructor cadre would, in turn, in some third country in Latin America, conduct clandestinely a training of additional Cuban recruits who would be organized into small teams similar to the U.S. Army Special Forces concept, and infiltrated with communicators, into areas of Cuba where it had been determined numbers of dissidents existed who required special skills and leadership and military supplies.[761]

Bissell recalls that the initial plan called for an instructor cadre of just twenty men. They, in turn, were to train "a group of 100 to 150 Cuban

---

[761] This review was conducted a year later after the Bay of Pigs operation failed. See FRUS, 1960-1963, volume X, Cuba, document #169, First Meeting of General Maxwell Taylor's Board of Inquiry on Cuban Operations Conducted by the CIA, 23 April 1961. The commanders included at least CINCCARIB LTG Ridgley Gaither, and CGUSARCARIB MG Charles Dasher.

THE CIA DECISION TO "REMOVE" CASTRO FROM POWER

agents" who would then be infiltrated into Cuba.[762] Central to the CIA's concept of operations at this time was the requirement that the members of the instructor cadre would never be committed to Cuban soil. Only the members of the second group, the "paramilitary leadership groups"—or "agents," as Bissell called them—would be covertly infiltrated into Cuba. In conjunction with this plan, the CIA began to survey isolated areas suitable for training the instructor cadres, and to brief U.S. military commanders in the Caribbean on the details of these plans.[763]

In Eisenhower's absence, Vice President Nixon chaired the 10 December NSC meeting:

> The vice president felt that Congress at the next session would make a massive assault on our Latin American policy as a result of incidents in Panama and Cuba. The general line will be that the U.S. is not paying sufficient attention to Latin America. ...The vice president said it was his impression that Cuba was being driven toward communism more and more.

CIA Deputy Director of Operations Dick Bissell reported that there was only one top official left in the Cuban government without a communist affiliation.[764]

At the same time, planning for the elimination of Castro became part of the new policy. This covert operation became an integral component of any plan for military action inside Cuba—no matter how these plans changed with the passage of time. As we have seen, the idea of assassinating Castro had been on the minds of Cuban anti-communists since early 1959. By the end of that year, Castro had thoroughly purged the anti-communists, driving them underground, into exile, or into prison. With communist control of Castro's revolution now irreversible, the CIA began planning to take him out. On 11 December 1959, the WHD chief, J. C. King, wrote the memo that got the ball rolling. King recommended, among other things, that the CIA give "thorough consideration" to the "elimination" and "disappearance" of Fidel Castro. The

---

762 Richard Bissell, *Reflections of a Cold Warrior* (New Haven: Yale University Press, 1996), p. 154.
763 FRUS, 1960-1963, volume X, Cuba, document #150, First Meeting of General Maxwell Taylor's Board of Inquiry on Cuban Operations Conducted by the CIA, 23 April 23 1961.
764 FRUS, 1958-1960, volume VI, Cuba, document #408; Memorandum of Discussion at the 428th Meeting of the National Security Council, Washington, 10 December, 1959.

concurrence of the Deputy Director of Plans (DDP), Dick Bissell, was attached in a brief note to King's memorandum.[765]

> SECRET
>
> 11 December 1959
>
> MEMORANDUM FOR: Director of Central Intelligence
> VIA: Deputy Director (Plans)
> SUBJECT: Cuban Problems.
>
> This memorandum requests approval by the Director of the recommendations contained in paragraph 3.
>
> 3. Recommended Action:
>
> d. Thorough consideration be given to the elimination of Fidel Castro. None of those close to Fidel, such as his brother Raul or his companion Che Guevarra, have the same mesmeric appeal to the masses. Many informed people believe that the disappearance of Fidel would greatly accelerate the fall of the present Government.
>
> J. C. King
> Chief, Western Hemisphere Division
>
> cc: DDCI
>
> CONCUR: 12 DEC 1959
> Richard M. Bissell, Jr.
> Deputy Director (Plans)
>
> The recommendation contained in paragraph 3 is approved:
>
> Director of Central Intelligence
> Date 12 DEC 1959
>
> SECRET

Composite DCI Memo RE "Removal of Castro" Approved; 21/11/59; 104-10315-10007.

---

765 12/11/59, CIA Memorandum From Chief, Western Hemisphere Division, via Deputy Director (Plans), for Director of Central Intelligence, Subject: Cuban Problems. 104-10315-10007. See also, *Alleged Assassination Plots Involving Foreign Leaders*, United States Senate, Interim Report of the Select Committee to Study Governmental Operations (Washington DC: US Government Printing Office, 1975), p. 92.

THE CIA DECISION TO "REMOVE" CASTRO FROM POWER

The record also shows that when King's recommendation, with Bissell's concurrence, reached the desk of Allen Dulles, the Director of Central Intelligence, he penciled the words "removal from Cuba" over the word "eliminate," and the word "removal" over the word "disappearance," and then approved the recommendation.[766] Dulles was not the only senior U.S. policy-maker adept at the art of prestidigitation—a rhetorical sleight of hand. With his pen and quick fingers, Dulles *disguised* the true nature of this super-sensitive plan. Such Orwellian double-speak was common during the Eisenhower Administration whenever the subject of assassinating political leaders came up. The same sleight of hand occurred during the 1960 discussions to get rid of Patrice Lumumba in the Congo. In this manner, those involved in such discussions could say afterward that they had never even discussed the assassination of so-and-so, let alone approved of it.

The use of the word "assassination" was banned from high level White House meetings—even though all present understood that this was what was being discussed. Lying about it afterward had been sanctioned in March 1954 with the promulgation of the National Security Council Directive 5412 on covert operations. Those few officers of the government who knew the truth were supposed to deny it.[767] NSCD 5412 also required that all covert operations had to be constructed in a manner that that lying about them was "plausible."

Given the darkening contours of U.S. policy, ongoing Cuban exile activities in the Dominican Republic and underground activities in Cuba were matters of keen interest at the CIA. Through an FBI Cuban exile source, Francisco Cajigas, the CIA learned that Trujillo said he was "holding the Pedraza force until the United States' position is known."[768] A few weeks later, Senator James Eastland would ask if it was possible to have Trujillo attack Castro.[769] As previously noted, Pawley had promised

---

766 *Alleged Assassination Plots Involving Foreign Leaders*, United States Senate, Interim Report of the Select Committee to Study Governmental Operations (Washington DC: US Government Printing Office, 1975), p. 92.
767 "...if uncovered the U.S. Government can plausibly disclaim any responsibility for them..."; NSC 5412, NARA, RG 273
768 NARA, JFK files, CIA January 1994 five brown boxes release, CIA Memorandum for the Record, Subject: Cuban Political Matters, date: 12, 15, and 16 December 1959.
769 FRUS, 1958-1960, volume VI, Cuba, document #441; Memorandum of a Telephone Conversation Between Senator James O. Eastland and the Assistant Secretary of State for Inter-American

he would have the U.S. position by 15 December. He returned to Washington to talk matters over with Vice President Nixon and the CIA—and to settle some scores.

When Pawley arrived back in Washington, he discovered that Allen Dulles was opposed to the activities of the Trujillo-Pedraza force and that other anti-Castro plans were being developed at the CIA. Pawley met first with Vice President Nixon, dining with him on a busy 15 December evening. They presumably discussed all aspects of Cuban policy. Nixon and Dulles were preparing to call for a new covert Cuban policy at the NSC meeting the next day. The dinner with the vice president was only the beginning of Pawley's evening. Immediately after dinner Pawley met with Cuban exile leader Emilio Nunez Portuondo and summarily banned him from having anything to do with the plans he had learned about. Pawley explained to his CIA contacts that he "was quite perturbed" about the "many wild and dangerous statements" Nunez had been making about the invasion efforts Pawley and Trujillo had been discussing, and that Nunez was "trying to destroy" these efforts.[770]

Nunez and Pawley apparently had a major falling out during their encounter that evening. Pawley told Nunez he wanted to "drop him as head of the revolutionary movement."[771] Nunez accused Pawley of putting Nunez' brother's name on the list of Cubans who would form a post-Castro junta "with the hope of having the brother killed."[772] While Pawley was engaged in this nasty encounter with Portuondo, Pawley's associate Fabio Freyre was meeting with a CIA officer at the Mayflower Hotel. The CIA meeting with Freyre was at the request of the CIA's Western Hemisphere Division chief, J. C. King.[773] During the meeting, Freyre delivered a lengthy report to the CIA officer.

Freyre reported mainly on his own Accion Democratica Christiana, saying it had 1,500 well-organized men in Camaguey Province, with

---

Affairs (Rubottom), Washington, January 28, 1960.
770 NARA, JFK files, CIA January 1994 five brown boxes release, CIA Memorandum for the Record, Subject: Telephone Conversation with Mr. Pawley, 11:45 a.m., 31 December 1959.
771 NARA, JFK files, CIA January 1994 five brown boxes release, CIA Memorandum for the Record, Subject: Cuban Political Matters, date: 12, 15, and 16 December 1959.
772 NARA, JFK files, CIA January 1994 five brown boxes release, CIA Memorandum for the Record, Subject: Telephone Conversation with Mr. Pawley, 11:45 a.m., 31 December 1959.
773 NARA, JFK files, CIA January 1994 five brown boxes release, CIA Memorandum for the Record, Subject: Meeting of [CIA employee] and Fabio Freyre, 16 December 1959.

3,000 in reserve, another 400 in Santa Clara, and 750 in Miami. Freyre spoke of the anticipation that Castro would "set a trap and provoke an uprising by falsifying a beachhead, since he knows that something serious is being organized around General Pedraza." Freyre said he was using extreme caution and he had sent someone to Cuba to "determine the arms needs for the army." He said that maps of clandestine airstrips in Cuba were being prepared; a budget was being prepared; and, finally, General Pedraza was "ready to come to Miami." At length, Pawley joined the meeting, having already met with Nixon and Nunez. Nixon probably knew, and probably told Pawley, that the idea of a new invasion from the Dominican Republic was out. Pawley had an interesting piece of news about Pedraza: even though he had a valid passport, the State Department had "instructed the Immigration and Naturalization Service to pick him up if he enters the United States."[774]

Whatever details Pawley had not learned from his dinner with Nixon, he would learn soon enough—by 9:00 a.m. the next morning (16 December)—from Director of Central Intelligence Allen Dulles.[775] Undoubtedly, Pawley met with Dulles to discuss the new covert Cuban policy the vice president was planning to surface at the NSC meeting that very day and it is likely that Dulles explained to Pawley why the U.S. would have no part in the activities being planned with Pedraza. Once the NSC meeting was under way, Dulles quickly announced that an attack from the Dominican Republic against Cuba would be "unfortunate." The CIA chief's opposition ended whatever chance there had been for using Pedraza's invasion force. Dulles was also critical of the anti-Castro groups forming in Florida, saying they were disorganized.

At this NSC session, Nixon seized this opportunity to make a major statement on Cuban policy. According to the record, "The vice president did not believe that Cuba should be handled in a routine fashion through normal diplomatic channels."[776] In other words, covert action was called for, and Allen Dulles was already putting together a plan. With

---

774 NARA, JFK files, CIA January 1994 five brown boxes release, CIA Memorandum for the Record, Subject: Meeting of [CIA employee] and Fabio Freyre, 16 December 1959.
775 NARA, JFK files, CIA January 1994 five brown boxes release, CIA Memorandum for the Record, Subject: Cuban Political Matters, date: 12, 15, and 16 December 1959.
776 FRUS, 1958-1960, volume VI, Cuba, document #410; Memorandum of Discussion at the 429th Meeting of the National Security Council.

Nixon in charge of the meeting, there was sure to be no opposition to Dulles. The vice president announced that the U.S. needed to come up with some "dramatic things" to do about the Cuban problem "in order to indicate that we would not allow ourselves to be kicked around completely." These were fighting words for Nixon, and his use of this kind of phrase was well known.

Nixon's call for a non-routine, non-diplomatic Cuban policy gave Dulles the opening to argue for a new covert action plan against Castro. Dulles could not go into the details in an NSC meeting, but he did reveal the basic idea. The minutes indicate that the CIA chief made the following statement:

> Mr. Dulles felt the question of whether anti-Castro activities should be permitted to continue or should be stopped depended on what the anti-Castro forces were planning. We could not, for example, let the Batista-type elements do whatever they wanted to do. However, a number of things in the covert field could be done which might help the situation in Cuba.[777]

As discussed above, one of these covert programs involved the training of Cuban special forces teams for infiltration into Cuba. Another one of the "things" Dulles no doubt had in mind was the "removal" of Castro from power, a plan he had approved just a few days earlier. This subject was far too sensitive for the NSC. But in the NSC meeting, the vice president did make clear his concern that he did not want to give his political opponents the issue of a failure in Cuba to use in the 1960 election. Nixon expected action—"dramatic" covert action—to overthrow Castro.[778]

Nunez Portuondo's intense dislike of Pawley was shared by another Cuban, Francisco Cajigas. He, too, remembers the thespian events of that evening. He told the FBI that he "fears and dislikes Pawley because of some earlier transactions in Cuba in which both were involved."[779] Cajigas had been a wealthy Cuban businessman in those days and was probably referring to business dealings he had had with Pawley during

---

[777] FRUS, 1958-1960, volume VI, Cuba, document #410; Memorandum of Discussion at the 429th Meeting of the National Security Council.

[778] Richard Nixon, *Six Crises* (New York: Warner Books, 1979 ed.), p. 416.

[779] NARA, JFK files, CIA January 1994 five brown boxes release, CIA Memorandum for the Record, Subject: Cuban Political Matters, date: 12, 15, and 16 December 1959.

THE CIA DECISION TO "REMOVE" CASTRO FROM POWER

Batista's rule.[780] Cajigas' FBI contact, Jack Gilespie, did not like Pawley either. The CIA summary of a Gilespie phone call makes this point clear:

> Gillespie expressed personal distrust of Pawley, and said that he had discussed Pawley with H. Graham Morison, former Assistant Attorney General, now a prominent Washington attorney. Morison spoke adversely of Pawley, whom he characterized as a great opportunist.[781]

Gillespie also said that Cajigas had discussed the Pawley-Nunez encounter that had occurred on the night of 15 December. According to Cajigas, Nunez "mentioned several names, including Julio Sanchez and Juan Gerard, who were to be members of a junta." It was the latter name that made the evening so unforgettable for Cajigas. Juan Gerard "was the first man on the list given to Pawley by Trujillo," Cajigas said, and he "was hanged from his balcony on the night of 15 December."[782]

---

780 FRUS, 1958-1960, volume VI, Cuba, document #599; Memorandum From the Assistant Secretary of State for Inter-American Affairs (Mann) to the Secretary of State, 28 October 1960, Subject: President's Inquiry Regarding Cuban Opposition Groups.
781 NARA, JFK files, CIA January 1994 five brown boxes release, CIA Memorandum for the Record, Subject: Cuban Political Matters, date: 12, 15, and 16 December 1959.
782 NARA, JFK files, CIA January 1994 five brown boxes release, CIA Memorandum for the Record, Subject: Cuban Political Matters, date: 12, 15, and 16 December 1959.

CHAPTER NINETEEN:
THE EXFILTRATION OF ARTIME AND THE END OF CATHERINE TAAFFE AND "THE DRAGON LADY"

Like other anti-Batista leaders who were also anti-communist, Manuel Artime's time to break with Castro had arrived. Artime had joined Castro's revolution late as a protégé of a rebel commander, Sori Marin, in the Sierra Maestra.[783] As discussed in Chapter Fourteen, Marin had appointed Artime as "commander of the rural commandoes," and under Castro, Artime followed Marin into agricultural work and eventually became an official of the Agrarian Reform Institute (INRA).

Back on 23 October 1959, Manuel Artime had resigned his position in INRA and had circulated this news in an open letter to Castro in which he

---
783 Fabian Escalante, *The Secret War: CIA Covert Operations Against Cuba, 1959-62* (New York: Ocean Press, 1995), p. 32.

also accused the Cuban leader of surrendering to "international communism."[784] Artime then returned to Oriente Province to recruit students and peasants and organize them to fight against Castro. Artime joined forces with Sergio Sanjenis in founding the Movement of Revolutionary Rescue (MRR). Sanjenis stayed behind to lead the movement in Cuba while Artime prepared to build it outside of Cuba. Three of his friends in Oriente —a lawyer, a shopkeeper and a pharmacist— who belonged to the Agrupacion Catolica Universitaria (Catholic University Group), raised the money for Artime's exfiltration from Cuba.[785] In November, two padres from that same group escorted Artime, disguised as a priest, to the U.S. Embassy in Havana to seek assistance for his exfiltration.

There followed nearly two months of on-again-off-again CIA plans for the exfiltration of Artime and his deputy, Roberto Varona, the brother of Antonio Varona. As always, Stewart (Merton in the cable traffic) and AMCOO (the CIA cryptonym for Delia Failde) worked as a team on these risky CIA exfiltrations. Neither they, nor Bernard Barker, who had helped on some of these operations, had the embassy cover that provided the diplomatic protection enjoyed by most of the CIA Station in Havana. Once this exfiltration was over, no one in this group would be able to safely remain in Cuba.

THE TWO PADRES AND ARTIME DRESSED AS A PRIEST

On the morning of 6 November 1959, Manuel Artime and two Catholic padres called on the air attaché office in the American Embassy in Havana and asked for an interview. In a private interview with David Morales (Zamka) and Jack Stewart (Merton), the two padres reported the following chain of events:

> First Lieutenant Manuel Francis Artime, the number two man for the Agrarian Reform Institute for Oriente Province, has decided to defect from the Castro regime

---

784   Fabian Escalante, *The Secret War: CIA Covert Operations Against Cuba, 1959-62* (New York: Ocean Press, 1995), p. 37.
785   12/22/59, Miami WHD Representative to Chief WHD, RIF 104-10162-10173.

and had planned to leave Cuba with the assistance of the Spanish Ambassador aboard the Spanish vessel *Guadalupe* which was to have called at Havana on 6 November but at the last moment was re-routed by the company and will not come here. Artime had written a letter to Fidel Castro which was to have been delivered as soon as he had safely departed aboard the vessel. The letter denounces communist influence within the agrarian program and contains specific accusations against Castro, Raul, Che Guevara, Nunez Jimenez, et al. It also denounces Fidel for his brutal treatment of Huber Matos.[786]

The two padres then left the room and returned to Artime, who was himself disguised as a priest.

The Havana Station cable reporting the request for assistance in this exfiltration told CIA HQS that no assurances had been given to Artime at that time. One of the padres had indicated that he would take care of hiding Artime and his assistant, Roberto Varona, for the time being. The Havana cable stated that the publication of Artime's letter would be a "major blow" to Castro, and that a thermofax copy of the letter which Artime had given to Morales would be dispatched by pouch to HQS.[787] Artime told Stewart and Morales that "under no circumstances did he wish to take asylum in an embassy for he was certain that Castro would never permit him to leave Cuba alive."[788]

The CIA Station advocated that "every possible assistance" be promptly given to the clandestine departure of Artime as "a search will soon be on to locate him." The Station offered this plan to HQS:

> The AMCOO vessels have not been coming to Havana on a regular basis. If HQS agrees that KUBARK (CIA) assistance should be given to Artime, Merton (Stewart) could fly to Tampa and endeavor to arrange with AMCOO for an early visit to Havana of one of her ships. Unless she can justify the visit commercially this might require en-

---

786 11/6/59, HAVA 2856 to DIR CIA. RIF 104-10162-10194.
787 11/6/59, HAVA 2856 to DIR CIA. RIF 104-10162-10194. For the 11/6/59 Havana Dispatch, see RIF 104-10162-10198.
788 11/6/59, HAVA 2856 to DIR CIA. RIF 104-10162-10194. For the 11/6/59 Havana Dispatch, see RIF 104-10162-10198.

tering into a charter agreement. HQS may have other ideas such as a black flight.[789]

On the evening of 6 November, Patrick Karnley, a pseudonym for the CIA's Western Hemisphere representative in Miami, Bernie Reichardt, telephoned AMCOO. She agreed to arrive in Havana by air on 8 or 9 November to "supervise" Artime's exfiltration via a ship scheduled to depart Havana around 11 November. AMCOO said that when she arrived she would call on Jack Stewart "to plan the operation."[790]

On 10 November, AMCOO arrived in Havana from Tampa. She and Stewart made arrangements to board two "bodies," Manuel Artime and Roberto Varona, the next day on the *S. S. Veramar*, whose captain was Ivan H. Jones. In various memoranda associated with this double exfiltration, Roberto Varona is confused with his brother Manuel Antonio Varona. The Havana Station asked HQS to provide pseudonyms for both Artime and Roberto Varona.[791] This detail, as we will see shortly, was *crucial* to the survival of these kinds of CIA exfiltarions from Cuba.

Then the exfiltration hit a glitch. On 12 November the Havana Station reported that AMCOO had been unable to place Artime and Varona on board due to the "premature" sailing of the *Veramar*. The operation had failed to take place according to plan and had to be rescheduled for the week of 21-22 November.[792]

On 16 November, HQS sent a cable to the Havana Station stating that they had discussed the Artime-Varona defection with the State Department. The State Department approved of the exfiltration to the U.S., but stipulated that Artime had to be out of the country before any KUCAGE (the CIA's Psychological and Paramilitary Operations Staff) exploitation of his letter to Castro. The HQS cable to Havana floated several ideas on how the letter might be clandestinely distributed using the station's assets in Cuba—all of which would be abandoned within days.[793]

---

789   11/6/59, HAVA 2856 to DIR CIA. RIF 104-10162-10194.
790   11/6/59, DIR 0139 to HAVA. RIF 104-10162-10444.
791   11/10/59, HAVA 2875 to DIR CIA. RIF 104-10162-10442.
792   11/12/59, HAVA 2878 to DIR CIA. RIF 104-10162-10437.
793   11/16/59, DIR 02874 to HAVA. RIF 104-10162-10435.

THE EXFILTRATION OF ARTIME AND THE END OF CATHERINE...

In the meantime, Artime threw an unexpected curve to his Havana case officer, David Morales.[794] On 17 November, the Havana Station reported that Artime had asked to be relocated to Mexico as soon as possible after his debriefing in Florida. His reason was that he was "not interested in becoming associated with Diaz Lanz." Artime said that he had "friends" in Mexico with whom he wanted to "organize an anti-Castro group there." The Station also said it had looked into the possibility of its Havana assets publishing and distributing the Artime letter. The Station was told that the letter was "too hot to handle." The only alternative was for the Station to do it itself.[795]

On 18 November, Robert Reynolds, who worked in the Cuban section in the CIA's Western Hemisphere Division (WH/III/MEXI-CARIB), decided the time had come to include the Mexico City Station in the loop. In a cable to Havana with the Mexico Station as an info addressee, Reynolds said that inasmuch as Artime wanted to go to Mexico, it would be best for the KUCAGE exploitation of his letter to Castro to take place in Mexico. Reynolds directed the Havana Station to stop and discourage its Havana assets from publicizing the letter "at least for the present."[796] A sealed photo copy of the letter was sent to the Mexico City Station on 24 November.[797]

Meanwhile, the planned exfiltration of Artime and Varona hit yet another glitch. The exfiltration failed to materialize on the new 21-22 November target date and the plan had to be sent back to the drawing board again. As a result, three communications took place in quick succession: HQS told the Havana Station that AMCOO would return to Havana on 1 or 2 December to contact Stewart[798]; the Havana Station asked HQS for authorization for Stewart and Barker to go to Miami to discuss air exfiltration possibilities with contacts there[799]; and HQS then authorized the Miami trip.[800]

---

794 00/00 CIA PRQII on Artime; Morales is identified as the "CO." RIF104-10162-10195.
795 11/17/59, HAVA 2909 to DIR CIA. RIF 104-10162-10186.
796 11/18/59, DIR 03177 to HAVA, from Reynolds, WH/III/MEXI-CARIB. RIF 104-10162-10184.
797 11/24/59, Havana Dispatch to Chief of Station [redacted]. RIF 104-10162-10181.
798 DIR 04636 to HAVA, referenced in 11/30/59, DIR 04637 to HAVA. RIF 104-10162-10428.
799 HAVA 2959 to DIR CIA, referenced in 11/30/59, DIR 04637 to HAVA. RIF 104-10162-10428.
800 DIR 04584 to HAVA, referenced in 11/30/59, DIR 04637 to HAVA. RIF 104-10162-10428.

WHERE ANGELS TREAD LIGHTLY

The situation was clearly getting out of hand. And so, HQS decided to take a step back and determine the best order in which to consider proposals and developments—and to put Bernard Reichardt in Miami in charge of the flow of decisions from HQS to Miami and Havana. On 30 November, HQS told the Havana Station to hold off on everything until AMCOO and Stewart had a chance to meet and discuss the exfiltration on 1-2 December. HQS directed that this meeting had to take place *before* Stewart and Barker went to Miami. HQS explained that if AMCOO could handle the sea exfiltration soon, then the problems of coordinating an air exfiltration with the FBI and State Department could be avoided. If AMCOO could not do this soon, then the trip to Miami would make sense.

The 30 November HQS cable made it crystal clear that it had security concerns about Barker, whose loose talk in two previous instances had led to flaps. HQS indicated that its security concerns did not preclude the Stewart-Barker Miami trip, but then added three caveats: 1) HQS did not want Barker to make direct contact with Reichardt, "even much less with AMCOO"; 2) Hence, in Miami, Stewart alone would be permitted to contact Reichardt and first clear with him any contacts Barker wanted to make; and 3) HQS would give Reichardt instructions on a continuing basis on how to handle any proposals and developments.[801] Not surprisingly, on 4 December, HQS cabled the Havana station that on its orders Reichardt had told Barker to return to Havana and report to his case officer. Barker was back in Havana that evening.[802]

AMCOO's activities suddenly go dark in the record. We never find out if she met with Stewart in Havana as scheduled on 1-2 December. A week passes without a record indicating what was happening. The record resumes on 8 December, when CIA HQS asked the station in Havana for an update of the ongoing plans to exfiltrate Artime. HQS asked, "Has any reaction been noted on the part of INRA or other Cuban officials to his month-old disappearance?[803] On 11 December, the Havana Station responded with yet another new plan to exfiltrate Artime and Varona—that ended up *not* taking place. It was supposed to happen during the weekend of 12-14 December and was to be coordi-

---

801 11/30/59, DIR 04637 to HAVA. RIF 104-10162-10428.
802 12/4/59, DIR 05461 to HAVA. RIF 104-10237-10100.
803 12/8/59, DIR 05909 to HAVA. RIF 104-10162-10178.

THE EXFILTRATION OF ARTIME AND THE END OF CATHERINE...

nated by one of the padres [possibly padre Balbino[804]] via his Spanish Embassy contacts. The "channel" was to be an "unidentified" American using a boat or plane from the Matanzas area to Florida.[805]

However, in yet *another* strange twist, at 7:00 p.m. on 15 December, Artime and Varona did leave Havana on the *Veramar* after all. The CIA Station explained that the exfiltration had not been handled by padre Balbino and his Spanish Embassy contacts. Instead, out of nowhere AMCOO made a sudden "unexpected" appearance in Havana. She handled the operation. The Station requested that Artime be met on 16 December at the Delfa Line docks in Tampa and that Karnley (Reichardt) reimburse Artime $400 which he had been instructed to pay the boat captain. The Station also said it assumed that the Artime letter to Castro, together with a note that Artime wrote for the local press, could be given to brother Balbino once Artime left the U.S.[806] HQS concurred that same day,[807] and Jack Stewart[808] sent Artime's draft papers to the CIA Station in Mexico City.[809]

The CIA Station suggested that Artime be taken first to CIA HQS and debriefed there.[810] But Bernard Reichardt (the CIA Western Hemisphere representative in Miami) took Artime and Varona to Miami where Varona remained. Artime, after being debriefed by Reichardt, went to Mexico City.[811] Much of the debrief centered on Artime's claim that during a major INRA meeting in October, Castro had announced that he was planning the complete communization of Cuba—a remark that CIA HQS told the Havana Station it was "most anxious" to confirm.[812] In the debrief, Artime held his ground, although he hedged a little, saying that some of Castro's comments about this may have taken place during "recesses" at the meeting.[813]

---

804 12/15/59, HAVA 3042 to DIR CIA. RIF 104-10162-10188.
805 12/11/59, HAVA 3023 to DIR CIA. RIF 104-10162-10193.
806 12/15/59, HAVA 3042 to DIR CIA. RIF 104-10162-10188.
807 12/15/59, DIR 06822 to HAVA. RIF 104-10162-10190.
808 Stewart had not been transferred to Mexico City in November 1959, as the State Department's *Foreign Service Register* indicates (see Note to the 2017 Edition in the Introduction to this volume).
809 12/15/59, Havana Dispatch to COS [redacted]. RIF 104-10162-10192.
810 12/16/59, HAVA 3054 to DIR CIA. RIF 104-10162-10187.
811 1/19/60, Memo from J.C. King to Director of Security, Request for Assistance in the Cases of Manuel Francis Artime and Roberto Blas de Varona y Garcia. RIF 104-10110-10259.
812 11/21/59, DIR 03764 to HAVA. 104-10162-10430.
813 1/19/60, Memo from J.C. King to Director of Security, Request for Assistance in the Cases of Manuel Francis Artime and Roberto Blas de Varona y Garcia. RIF 104-10110-10259.

HOW THE *VERAMAR* RAN AGROUND

Although Artime and Varona were out of danger, the same was not true for AMCOO and the *Veramar* Captain, Ivan H. Jones. The first piece of troubling news came from a Tampa area source of AMCONCERT-1, whose real name was Francisco Varona "Pancho" Alonso—no relation to the brothers Antonio Varona and Roberto Varona. A Cuban government spy net in Tampa with informants on the Tampa docks had learned that two people had been disembarked from the *Veramar* and had then been taken away in an official U.S. immigration car. The Havana Station cable reporting this news to CIA HQS gave no indication that the real names of the "two people" were known.[814] As late as 9 January the Havana Station was under the impression that Castro's intelligence would be unable to link Artime and Varona to the *Veramar* and AMCOO (Delia Failde).[815]

The Mexico City Station found out otherwise and reported their disappointing discovery on 12 January. Artime had told the Mexico Station what had taken place when he and Varona arrived in Tampa. Artime said that they had been interviewed by the Immigration and Naturalization Service (INS) in the presence of Captain Jones and two members of the *Veramar* crew who were communists. Artime stated that he had *used his true name* during this interview. The Mexico Station pointed out that this information negated the assumption that Cuban intelligence would be unable to link Artime and Varona to the *Veramar* and AMCOO.[816]

Robert Reynolds, a senior officer in the CIA's WH/3/MEXI-CARIB branch, did some digging around to find out more about what had happened on board the Veramar in Tampa. Reynolds penned a long note at the bottom of the 12 January Mexico City cable. He said that Bernie Reichardt had been at the dock side but not on the ship where the INS interview had taken place. Reynolds had also discovered that on 28 December—12 days after the *Veramar* arrived in Tampa—the Cuban Consul in Tampa, a Mr. Dechard, had confronted AMCOO and asked her for the names of the "exfiltrees." "She ducked," Reynolds reported, "and denied knowledge." When Dechard went to the INS "they stalled," and

---

814 12/31/59, HAVA 3130 to DIR CIA. RIF 104-10162-10426.
815 1/9/60, HAVA 3170 to DIR CIA. RIF 104-10240-1046.
816 1/13/60, MEXI 4922 to DIR CIA. RIF 104-10240-10042.

THE EXFILTRATION OF ARTIME AND THE END OF CATHERINE...

Dechard threatened to write a letter to the INS regional director. "So far, he hasn't," Reynolds added.[817]

AMCOO "ducked" the question; 1/13/60, MEXI 4922 to DIR; 104-10240-10042.

---

817 1/13/60, MEXI 4922 to DIR CIA. RIF 104-10240-10042.

So far did not last long. Two days later the Chief of Alien Affairs at CIA HQS, William J. Cotter, received a phone call from the INS District Director in Miami. He said that the Cubans had become "suspicious" of the *Veramar* and that the boat owner was "in hot water."[818] The INS District Director said he had been asked by the CIA representative in Miami (Reichardt) to arrange for the INS to write a letter saying "they had inspected the vessel on its *several arrivals* at Tampa and that it carried no passengers." [Emphasis added] The District Director said that the Service could not comply with such a request and Cotter agreed that they should not do so. Cotter added that they should also tell Reichardt that "his superiors in Washington would be in contact with him in regard to this matter."

Cotter then called Robert Reynolds at the Cuban desk. Reynolds said that he was not aware of this "most recent" development, but then he added this:

> ...however, he [Reynolds] did mention that the boat in question has, in fact, been impounded in Cuba since December 1959. He went on to point out that we want to do everything we can to help out the owner of the vessel since the cause of her trouble was in acceding to our requests to exfiltrate individuals. Mr. Reynolds readily admitted that the Immigration Service should not have been requested to provide such a letter, and he doubted that Bernie Reichardt would have made such a request. Mr. Reynolds stated that he will telephonically contact Reichardt and get the complete story.[819]

Reynolds told Cotter that he would keep him advised, and there were additional conversations with Cotter. However, there were other CIA officers that Reynolds would need to keep advised about this problem.

On 19 January the Chief of the CIA's Western Hemisphere Division (WH/D), J. C. King, wrote a memorandum to Cotter's boss, the Agency's Directory of Security, Sheffield Edwards. King asked for Edwards' "assistance" in the "cases" of Artime and Varona. What he really wanted,

---
818   1/14/60, CIA MFR, from William Cotter, Chief, Alien Affairs Staff. RIF 104-10110-10256.
819   1/14/60, CIA MFR, from William Cotter, Chief, Alien Affairs Staff. RIF 104-10110-10256.

however, was to go over Cotter's head to get a letter from the INS—not exactly the same as Reichardt had asked for, but an untruthful letter nonetheless. The story of the exfiltration in King's memo was more accurate. Instead of her CIA cryptonym, AMCOO, King used the name Delia Failde. And she was not the *owner* of the *Veramar*—a small freighter that King acknowledged the CIA had used on *previous occasions* for the same purpose. King correctly described Delia Failde as the *operator* of the shipping line. King explained that the matter had not been coordinated with the Security Office because the arrangements had been made on a "crash basis" by Reichardt in Miami "in the last minute rush of urgent preparations arising from the extremely short notice received of the operation by this Division."[820]

King told Edwards that the *Veramar's* captain, crew, and register were Honduran. As the result of suspicions that the vessel had been used for exfiltration purposes, the captain and his crew had been put in jail after a return trip to Havana. The crew was then released but the captain remained in jail. The *Veramar* and other "interests in Cuba" of the vessel's owner, Mario E. Redondo, had been confiscated by the Cuban government:

> It is understood that *various* instances of "counter-revolutionary activity" were responsible for the confiscation, of which the precipitating one was doubtless his ownership of the *Veramar*. Since the operator of the *Veramar*, the aforementioned Delia Failde, has other shipping interests in the Cuban trade, she is understandably *most anxious* to clear the way for a continued pursuit of these interests. In this regard she has indicated that it is of the utmost importance to her to obtain a letter from the INS showing that Subjects (Artime and Varona) were "stowaways" discovered by the captain only after the *Veramar* was on the high seas bound for Tampa. This, incidentally, is the story of the captain to the Cuban government, and there is no indication that he has deviated therefrom. [Emphasis added]

---

820 1/19/60, Memo from J.C. King to Director of Security, Request for Assistance in the Cases of Manuel Francis Artime and Roberto Blas de Varona y Garcia. RIF 104-10110-10259.

King concluded by telling Edwards that it would be "greatly appreciated" if his office would request the INS to prepare a letter indicating that Artime and Varona "were in fact stowaways."[821]

King did not say how the CIA had learned what "story" the Honduran captain Jones had told the Cubans. Presumably, it could have come from a source of the CIA Station in Havana. However, it is interesting to note that King's memo made the dubious statement that there was no indication "that the identities of the exfiltrees are known" to the Cubans. It is more likely that just the opposite was true: that the exfiltration operations of Delia Failde and Mario Redondo had been forever blown by a colossal intelligence failure.

Reynolds' hand-written note at the bottom of the 12 January Mexico City cable described the interview of Artime on board the Veramar as a "routine procedure." *The Havana Station, which had requested pseudonyms for the exfiltrees, should have made absolutely sure that Artime knew that he had to use his pseudonym in just such a routine procedure.* The compromise of Artime's true name in front of the alleged communist crew had enormous implications, and was the reason that the Mexico City Station had immediately alerted HQS to the problem. One thing is certain: when the word from the Cuban spy net in Tampa reached Havana, the crew would have been asked if they remembered the names of the two passengers.

On 3 January, CIA HQS authorized the Mexico City Station to pass up to $100 to Artime for the following three weeks "or until the captain of the *Veramar* is released from jail."[822] He was still in jail when Artime arrived in Mexico City on 8 January. There is no indication in the record that a letter was obtained from the INS with the stowaway "story." Whether or not that happened, the *Veramar* captain was still in a Cuban jail at the end of March 1960.[823]

---

821   1/19/60, Memo from J.C. King to Director of Security, Request for Assistance in the Cases of Manuel Francis Artime and Roberto Blas de Varona y Garcia. RIF 104-10110-10259.
822   1/3/60, DIR 09665 to MEXI. RIF 10410163-10168.
823   3/24/60, CIA Memo to Chief, CI/OA, from Deputy Director of Security (Investigations and Support), Subject: C-82064, #210838. RIF 104-10163-10215.

THE END OF "THE DRAGON LADY" AND CATHERINE TAAFFE

Here again we take notice of how many American female spies appear in the Cuban story. We also note some uncanny similarities in the details of their lives that leave us wondering: did more than one character belong to a single person in real life? Readers can judge for themselves the possible significance of the striking parallel dramas of Catherine Taaffe and Delia Failde—two women who had *no fear of tramping in places where angels would tread lightly.*

In this regard, we will briefly reexamine the records of these two women throughout the period of the Artime-Varona double exfiltration. But we do so with this caveat: the eventual declassification of more records will need to take place before we can be certain whether or not they were the same person.

Catherine Taaffe and Delia Failde constantly move in and out of the CIA's exfiltration stories in 1959. The CIA acknowledges that there were many such operations beyond those discussed in this volume. It would not be surprising if Agency exfiltrations from Cuba extended well back into the Batista dictatorship. The records of these kinds of operations reveal how risky they were, both for the people being exfiltrated and for those operatives who participated in them—especially those operatives who did not have diplomatic cover. The movements of the two women—Catherine Taaffe and Delia Failde—in helping high profile military and political leaders get to safety outside of Cuba, appear, in retrospect, extraordinarily parallel. The Artime exfiltration is a good example of this phenomenon.

That story really began on 23 October 1959 when Artime resigned his INRA post and returned to Orient Province to recruit students and peasants and, along with Sergio Sanjenis, to organize them into the Movement of Revolutionary Rescue (MRR) to fight against Castro. The date of Artime's resignation was not a major news event—unlike the leaflet drop over Cuba by Diaz Lanz and Sturgis the same day, or the death of Camilo Cienfuegos. Not surprisingly, the Artime resignation can be found in the writings of the former chief of the Cuban State Security Department (G-2) Fabian Escalante.[824]

The day after Artime's resignation, 23 October 1959, Catherine Taaffe left her home base at the Bretton Hall Woods Hotel in New York City and went to Miami. She would not return to New York for nearly two months—her longest absence from home for the entire year. Taaffe returned to her home in New York on 17 December 1959. On the previous day, Artime had stepped off of the *Veramar* in Tampa, Florida. In other words, Taaffe's exit and return to New York form the precise bookends for the story of Artime's exfiltration from Cuba.

In between those bookends the following sequence of events took place. Upon arriving in Miami on 24 October, Taaffe checked into the Skyways Motel. She met briefly with a source of hers and was in Cuba by nightfall.[825] After her return to Miami on 27 October, we have a fairly consistent record of her activities in Miami up to 6 November—the date that Artime and the two padres walked into the U.S. Embassy and met with Stewart and Morales. Then, a dark hole appears in Taaffe's record between 6 and 11 November.

Interestingly, the day that dark hole began, 6 November, was the *same* day that Bernard Reichardt telephoned AMCOO (Delia Failde) and asked her to come to Havana to meet with Jack Stewart. They met on 10 November and planned to put Artime and Varona on the *Veramar* the next day. By chance, the FBI received a tipoff on 10 November that an unidentified "top level official in the Castro government" had defected."[826] The entire text of this FBI document is still classified. But, as discussed earlier in the chapter, 10 November was the day that the *Veramar* sailed too early for AMCOO and Stewart to place Artime and Varona on board.

The very next day, 11 November, Taaffe popped back up again in Miami for a meeting with Enrique Cabre, a long time paid source of hers

---

824 Fabian Escalante, ***The Secret War: CIA Covert Operations Against Cuba, 1959-62*** (New York: Ocean Press, 1995), p. 37.
825 1/19/60, Memorandum from SAC NYO to DIR FBI, Subject: Catherine Taaffe, RA-Cuba; FBI 8/29/2008 FOIA Release to Jim Lesar, pp. 253-254.
826 11/10/59, FBI Memo from F. A. Frohboss to A. H. Belmont, Subject: Unknown Subject; Report of Defection of Top Level Official in Castro Government. FBI 109, HQ 12-210, Vol. 22, p. 115.

THE EXFILTRATION OF ARTIME AND THE END OF CATHERINE...

working in INRA.[827] Cabre told Taaffe about new plans of former Batista followers for an attack on Cuba. Cabre would likely have known about Artime's disappearance from INRA since 23 October.

The next development in the simultaneous dramas of Failde and Taaffe occurred on 2 December. This is the date when AMCOO was *supposed* to come to Havana to meet with Stewart. Recall how important it was for her to be there: HQS had told the Havana Station that all bets were off on any new proposals for the Artime exfiltration until that meeting took place. As stated above, however, we never find out what happened. We have no record of where AMCOO was on 2 December. Her record just goes dark. On the other hand, Catherine Taaffe showed up in Havana on 2 December—*the precise date that AMCOO (Failde) was supposed to show up there.*

Taaffe stood in the FBI office (Legat) in the embassy on 2 December and asked for visas for two children, whose parents were Cuban refugees in the U.S. at that time. Although Taaffe did not talk about this trip in her reports to the FBI New York Office, we know about it because the FBI Legat reported his meeting with Taaffe to FBI HQS. This particular trip to Cuba would be the third of four that Taaffe made during her long Miami sojourn between 24 October and 17 December.

AMCOO reentered the picture suddenly and "unexpectedly" on 15 December to place Artime and Varona on the *Veramar*. Two days later, on 17 December, Catherine Taaffe was back in her home in New York. She telephoned the New York office of the FBI that day, and reported that she had made *several* trips to Cuba, the most recent being her 7-11 December trip.[828] That trip actually took place from 6 to 8 December. *But there was much more that was wrong with her telephone report to the New York office than the dates of her latest trip.*

For three weeks in October and November, the U.S. had lobbied against a proposed British sale of Hawker Hunter airplanes to Cuba.[829] When it became public knowledge that Britain had turned down the

---

827 11/17/59, Letter from John Edgar Hoover to Office of Security, Department of State, Subject: Foreign Political Matters—Cuba, Internal Security—Cuba; FBI 8/29/2008 FOIA Release to Jim Lesar, pp. 188-190.
828 12/28/59 AIRTEL from SAC NYO to DIR FBI, Subject: Anti-Fidel Castro Activities IS—Cuba, Foreign Political Matters—Cuba; FBI 8/29/2008 FOIA Release to Jim Lesar, pp. 208-212.
829 FRUS, Cuba, Vol. VI, documents 368, 369, and 386.

deal, Taaffe had stepped in. According to a later statement she gave to the FBI, Taaffe confessed that she had gone to Cuba on 6 December to sell Cuba "some twenty Hawker Hunter Mark 5 Airplanes."[830] In that same statement, she also confessed that on 5 January she had returned to Cuba again in an attempt to buy sugar for Cargill, Inc., of New York.[831] Apparently, the Cubans would use the money from the sugar deal to buy the Hawker Hunters.

Taaffe was playing a very dangerous game. She had been telling the FBI all year how bad Castro was. She had penetrated his regime and had recruited and paid several informants for information. In her 17 December telephone call to the FBI New York Office, Taaffe told a *big* lie. She said that her contact in Cuba for the Hawker Hunter deal was Raul Castro and that she had accepted his authorization to purchase the planes in order to "tie up the money that the Cuban government has in Switzerland."[832] The truth was that a low level shyster, George Valdes Amble, *not* Raul Castro, was Taaffe's contact in Cuba during both of her 6-8 December 1959 and 5-15 January 1960 trips to Cuba.

Valdes had been a member of the Castro underground during the revolution. According to the FBI, during the time of Taaffe's recent two trips to Cuba, Valdes was "involved in various business schemes involving pesos, sugar and airplanes." During Taaffe's January 1960 trip, Valdes added something more ominous to the equation than sugar for planes. He approached Taaffe to recruit her into a plot that involved the kidnapping and murder of former Cuban Senator and Batista supporter Rolando Masferrer for the purpose of creating a propaganda stunt against the U.S.[833] Taaffe said she had concluded that Valdes "was a crook." Taaffe also "implied" to a Miami associate of hers, Jack Ahlstead, that she had planned to use the plot to embarrass the Cuban government.[834]

---

830   2/11/60, Statement of Catherine Taaffe to the FBI, in 3/14/60 Report of William B. Hollman, Miami; RIF 124-90090-10120.
831   2/11/60, Statement of Catherine Taaffe to the FBI, in 3/14/60 Report of William B. Hollman, Miami; RIF 124-90090-10120.
832   12/28/59 AIRTEL from SAC NYO to DIR FBI, Subject: Anti-Fidel Castro Activities IS—Cuba, Foreign Political Matters—Cuba; FBI 8/29/2008 FOIA Release to Jim Lesar, pp. 208-212.
833   2/11/60, Statement of Catherine Taaffe to the FBI, in 3/14/60 Report of William B. Hollman, Miami; RIF 124-90090-10120.
834   3/14/60, Synopsis, Report of William B. Hollman, Miami; RIF 124-90090-10120.

THE EXFILTRATION OF ARTIME AND THE END OF CATHERINE...

We will set forth a more detailed account of the Masferrer plot in Volume II. Here we will mention only how it ended. The Cubans involved were arrested in Miami after Taaffe alerted the CIA and FBI to the plot. On 12 February 1960, two angry pro-Castro thugs entered Taaffe's Miami hotel room, held her down, and using a sharp object branded her arm with the number 26—the number for Castro's 26 July Movement.[835] Taaffe was able to avoid prosecution, but her usefulness to *any* U.S. agency was now over.

Meanwhile, in January 1960, things ended badly for Delia Failde too. According to the CIA's operational notes on Manuel Artime, AMCOO's (Failde) war name was "the Dragon Lady."[836] Recall the 14 January phone call from the INS District Director in Miami to CIA HQS. He had told HQS that the owner of the *Veramar* was "in hot water."[837] He was referring to AMCOO. Robert Reynolds of WH/3 had also referred to Failde as the owner. But we know that Failde was the *operator*, not the owner. And we know that it was she, the operator, who was in hot water. She was the one constantly going in and out of Cuba and whose face was most directly associated with the *Veramar*—and, now, with the CIA's exfiltrations from Cuba.

The usefulness of Delia Failde, like Catherine Taaffe, was over. Whether they were the same woman or two different women, there is no record that either of them played any further role in getting people out of Cuba. Both had stomped fearlessly *where angels would tread lightly*. But by early 1960, Taaffe had no more tales to tell and the Dragon Lady was out of fire.

---

835 2/17/60, AIRTEL from SAC Miami to DRI FBI, Subject: Juan Fernandez de Castro Rodriguez, et al; Rolando Masferrer Rojas—Victim; Kidnapping—Conspiracy; IS—Cuba; (OO: Miami). RIF 124-90090-10105.
836 00/00 CIA handwritten notes from debrief of Artime. RIF 104-10162-10197.
837 1/14/60, CIA MFR, from William Cotter, Chief, Alien Affairs Staff. RIF 104-10110-10256.

CHAPTER TWENTY:
ROLANDO CUBELA, JUANITA CASTRO AND TONY SFORZA

The first attempt to recruit Rolando Cubela occurred shortly after Castro came to power in 1959. Carlos Tepedino, who had himself been recruited by Jack Stewart in 1957, facilitated the situation by arranging a "fishing trip" to put Cubela and Stewart in contact. That plan failed when Castro sent Cubela to Spain as Cuba's military attaché in March 1959.[838] In 1961, Stewart tried to defect Cubela again, this time in Mexico, but that approach failed too.

Some most important operations of the Havana Station had been handled by Phillips, not just because he was good at what he did, but also because he was operating in the open without diplomatic cover. His success was impressive but the risks were also greater. One slip could mean life in prison, or worse, death at the hands of Castro. Concerns over security ended the CIA's psychological warfare sleuth's role in Cuba

---

[838] 00/3/59, CIA Havana Dispatch HKH-1855, from Andrew F. Merton, Subject: Rolando Cubela Secades, New Cuban Military Attaché to Spain, RIF 104-10215-10443.

at the end of 1959. As the CIA built up its Cuban operations at HQS and in Miami, there would be plenty for Phillips to do in the coming months. We will get to those anti-Castro operations in the next volume of the present work.

Back in Havana, the departure of Phillips left big shoes to fill. All the more so because the looming and inevitable break in Cuban-U.S. relations would free Cuban intelligence to focus more keenly on the Americans remaining on the island, some of whom would be CIA "stay-behind" agents. The person who came closest to replacing Phillips' skills as a recruiter and case officer in Cuba was a man named Tony Sforza. The Agency placed Sforza in Havana's gambling casinos just months before the break in relations. The details concerning Sforza's CIA pseudonyms—Frank Stevens, Henry Sloman, and Enrique—are located in Appendix Three. Information about Sforza's CIA cryptonym, AMRYE-1, is located in Appendix One, and will be more fully discussed in a future volume of this work.

NOVEMBER 1959: CUBELA AND TEPEDINO IN MEXICO CITY

On 24 November 1959, the CIA Station in Havana notified HQS that Carlos Tepedino would be accompanying a Cuban delegation to a Soviet exhibition in Mexico City. The Havana cable stated that Tepedino was willing to cooperate with "any friend of Andrew F. Merton in Mexico."[839] As discussed in Chapter Two, Merton was a pseudonym for Jack Stewart. The cable noted that Tepedino was an "anti-commie revolutionary" that Merton had known for eighteen months.

The Havana Station asked the Mexico Station to contact Tepedino daily during the trip for debriefings. The cable noted that it might be possible for Tepedino to attend a dinner for the Soviet First Deputy Premier, Anastas I. Mikoyan, but that in any event, Tepedino would be able to get the details "from his intimate friend Rolando Cubela," who would be attending the gathering as an official member of the Cuban delega-

---

839   HAVA 2940 to DIR CIA. RIF 104-10183-10085.

tion. The contact plan was for a Spanish-speaking case officer to make a phone call to Cubela and mention the name "Ricardo Alvarez," in order to set up a meeting with Tepedino. Tepedino was to alert Cubela to this procedure upon his arrival in Mexico City on 25 November.[840]

Tepedino knew Stewart by his true name, as most everyone did who knew him in Havana. It was Stewart who sent Tepedino to Mexico to gather information about the Soviet exhibition. Not only did Tepedino attend the event, but he also succeeded in becoming a member of the Cuban commission that arranged for the transfer of the Soviet exhibition to Cuba. A CIA biography on Tepedino stated that he had obtained "valuable" detailed information for Stewart during this trip.[841]

MARCH 1961: CUBELA, TEPEDINO AND STEWART IN MEXICO CITY

When Stewart left Cuba in early 1960, the CIA Deputy Chief of Station in Havana, Arthur Avignon, took over as Tepedino's case officer. When Cubela and Tepedino were attending a student conference in Switzerland in September 1960, Tepedino's step-father called him and warned him to never come back to Cuba. So Tepedino went to the U.S., using his temporary student visa.[842] It was about this time that the Havana CIA Station Chief, Jim Noel, asked Tony Sforza to come to Cuba. Sforza was a CIA officer working in Argentina at the time, and his job in Cuba would not be covered by diplomatic immunity, as Phillips' had not been. The coming break in relations with Cuba was only months away and there would be no embassy and no CIA Station in Havana.

In November 1960, Sforza took over as the case officer for Francisco Wilfredo "Pancho" Varona Alonso, whom we discussed in Chapter Three in connection with the history of the Directorio Revolucionario (DR). Pancho had been recruited by Stewart in 1957, and had been handled by Emilio

---
840 HAVA 2940 to DIR CIA. RIF 104-10183-10085.
841 6/28/65, CIA Contact Report, Participants: Carlos Tepedino, [redacted] and Harold P. Swenson. 104-10183-10424.
842 6/28/65, CIA Contact Report, Participants: Carlos Tepedino, [redacted,] and Harold P. Swenson. 104-10183-10424.

Americo Rodriguez until Sforza arrived in Cuba. Sforza posed as a gambler named "Frank Stevens," and Pancho reported to Sforza as "Enrique."[843]

Meanwhile, Tepedino was still in New York City when the U.S. and Cuba broke relations on 31 December 1960. Tepedino lost his jewelry business in Cuba and had become a partner in a new jewelry business, Corleta Inc., of New York City. In order to secure a permanent visa, Tepedino had to first exit and then return to the U.S., so he spent the first half of March 1961 handling this task in Mexico City. It so happened that Cubela was attending a Latin American peace conference in Mexico City at the same time. When Tepedino discovered this he immediately contacted Cubela and "began to convince him of the error of his ways."[844] Once again, Tepedino made arrangements with Stewart to defect Cubela.

On the night of 9 March 1961, in the Skyroom of the Hilton Continental in Mexico City, Jack Stewart interviewed Rolando Cubela for two and a half hours in the presence of Carlos Tepedino. On 22 March Stewart a detailed memorandum about his interview with Cubela, as well as Tepedino's contacts with Cubela.[845] Tepedino had met with Cubela three times and had briefed Stewart on the results. Tepedino told Stewart he had been brutally frank with Cubela but was unable to make "much of a dent." Tepedino encountered extreme sensitivity regarding reports that senior Cuban government leaders were putting money into Swiss banks. Cubela emphatically denied that this had occurred. Cubela's intense emotional display left Tepedino with the impression that Cubela might commit "una locura":

> ...a crazy action—Tepedino meant that Cubela is capable of picking up a gun and taking matters into his own hands, as he is commonly believed to have done in the assassination of Lt. Colonel Antonio Blanco Rico, Batista's chief of the Military Intelligence Service.

---

843 6/18/69, CIA Memorandum for Special Agent in Charge (Kane) from Chief of Station WH/Miami, Anthony R. Ponchay (Jake Esterline), RE: Charles Govea and Francisco Wilfredo "Pancho" Varona (Alonso). RIF 104-10109-10162.
844 3/22/61, CIA Dispatch from COS Mexico City to Chief WH Division, Subject: Interview with Rolando Cubela Secades, with 3/17/61 MFR by Andrew F. Merton, Subject: Interview with Rolando Cubela. RIF 104-10215-10122.
845 3/22/61, CIA Dispatch from COS Mexico City to Chief WH Division, Subject: Interview with Rolando Cubela Secades, with 3/17/61 MFR by Andrew F. Merton, Subject: Interview with Rolando Cubela. RIF 104-10215-10122.

Cubela also told Tepedino that Fidel Castro would not run away if his government was overthrown, but rather he would die fighting to the bitter end. Cubela, however, did not believe that the Cuban government would be overthrown.

Stewart assumed that his identity was known to Cubela, probably from Havana, where a similar meeting had been previously arranged but had fallen through.[846] So Stewart began the conversation by referring to the "fishing date" they had been unable to keep. Cubela quickly recalled the incident and the conversation seemed to begin in a relaxed manner. After some "light talk" about music and girls, Tepedino began to steer the conversation toward serious matters. Cubela immediately pushed back and said he was only there to talk in "general terms."

At that moment, Tepedino stated that Cubela was anti-communist, and Cubela agreed. Cubela then said that U.S. Cuban policy was to blame for the communists' ultimate takeover of the 26 of July Movement, and thus, control of the country. He said that because Fidel could not get support from the U.S. he had been "forced" to seek it from the communists. Stewart asked him for the names of other friends in the Cuban government who also felt that the 26 of July Movement had been "lost to the communists." Cubela mentioned Jose "Pepe" Llanusa, Asef (first name unknown), and Raul Diaz Arguelles, the same names he had given to Tepedino. When asked what he thought of anti-Castro figures, Cubela said that he preferred Manolo Ray, although he was not much of a leader. He dismissed all other anti-Castro leaders as representatives of the old politics.

Stewart repeated his offer to help Cubela "in any way within my power." They parted with a handshake and a Cuban-style abrazo (embrace). However, Cubela had a distinctly negative reaction to this remark by Stewart. According to Tepedino, Cubela later turned to him, shrugging his shoulders in a manner of saying, "So I need help from him?"[847] This was the second failed attempt to defect Cubela. Subsequently, when

---

846 3/22/61, CIA Dispatch from COS Mexico City to Chief WH Division, Subject: Interview with Rolando Cubela Secades, with 3/17/61 MFR by Andrew F. Merton, Subject: Interview with Rolando Cubela. RIF 104-10215-10122.
847 9/00/62, Richard M. Fallucci, TFW/FI, Summary of Contacts with AMWHIP and AMLASH. RIF 104-10102-10050.

both Cubela and Sforza were in Cuba, Sforza would pursue the defection of Cubela.

MARCH-APRIL 1961 IN CUBA

On 17 March 1961, Tepedino, still in Mexico City, received a strange call from Cubela in Havana:

> [Cubela] ordered two car springs be given to Manuel "Manolito" Perez, a member of the Cuban G-2 and on the Cuban UN delegation for delivery to Cubela. Tepedino was uncertain whether Cubela wanted the springs or wanted to alert him to Perez's G-2 connection.[848]

This phone call was followed by numerous reports referring to the possible defection of Cubela. There was an unsubstantiated rumor that Cubela had been "arrested" while attempting to flee Cuba. This event was said to have been a Cuban trap, with Cubela witting, and that it resulted in the arrest of several anti-Castro individuals.[849]

In fact, there was a CIA operation in play at the end of March to defect Cubela and exfiltrate him using the boat exfiltration activity codenamed "FLAME." With Stewart and AMCOO out of the picture, the point person this time was Henry Sloman—a pseudonym for Tony Sforza. "Henry" was the recipient of several warnings from CIA HQS and the JMWAVE Station in Miami to use extreme caution in this sensitive operation. He received this strict warning on 29 March:

> Message...#64: For Henry: "We believe police are aware of Cubela desire to defect and of his departure plans. Police are probably alerted to the area of FLAME (boat exfiltration activity). Exercise extreme caution in your involvement with Cubela's exfiltration and FLAME group."

---

848   3/24/61, MEXI 7686 to DIR CIA. RIF 104-10215-10235.
849   10/24/64, CIA Memorandum RE Weaknesses and Derogatory Information on Rolando Cubela. RIF 104-10215-10235. DWAIQ #64 was a signal plan operator for contact in [FLAME] boat infiltrations and exfiltrations. He was also AMGLEN-9, a stay-behind FI [foreign intelligence] operator.

Sforza received another warning the next day: "For Henry: FYI: Cubela told friends he was being followed. Suggest you ignore him for the present unless you can circumvent surveillance."[850]

It appears that the exfiltration of Cubela was temporarily put on hold, as something much bigger was looming: the Bay of Pigs invasion. We will get to a more detailed examination of the Bay of Pigs in a subsequent volume of this work. Here we will address a smaller but critically important element that took place within that larger story. The setting for this particular piece is the home that Tony Sforza lived in at the time of the Bay of Pigs. The details of his residence in the home enable us to definitively link Tony Sforza to the pseudonyms "Frank Stevens" and "Henry Sloman." These details also reveal that the original owner of the home was the Aspuru family. Carlos Tepedino's father might have lived there for a time prior to when Sforza was living there.[851]

Sforza probably had a pretty good idea of when the Bay of Pigs invasion was going to happen. When it did, Sforza was hiding in the Aspuru home. Years later, in 1969, Jake Esterline, by that time the CIA chief of station in Miami, wrote about how Sforza got away with this in April 1961:

> The night of the Bay of Pigs invasion, the Cuban Internal Service sent agents to the ASPRU [sic] home to pick up "Frank" [Sforza]. One colored and one white servant were at home at that time and they told the DSE (Securidad Estado Cubana) agents that "Frank" was "a gay blade" and would not be home until early the next morning. The DSE left the residence leaving behind a note for "Frank" to report to their headquarters the following morning. In this context, it should be noted that "Frank's" cover in Cuba during the period in question was that of a professional gambler; a cover which served him well during most of his service there.[852]

---

850 3/30/61, WAVE 5065 to DIR CIA. RIF 104-10215-10235.
851 Pancho's biographical sketch of Tepedino stated that Sforza stayed in Tepedino's father's home. While it may be true that Tepedino's father occupied this home before Sforza lived there, Sforza himself referred to this dwelling as the "Aspuru home," the name "Aspuru" having probably been misspelled in the 6/18/1969 Esterline memo about Sforza. See note below.
852 6/18/69, CIA Memorandum for Special Agent in Charge (Kane) from Chief of Station WH/Miami, Anthony R. Ponchay (Jake Esterline), RE: Charles Govea and Francisco Wilfredo "Pancho" Varona (Alonso). RIF 104-10109-10162.

WHERE ANGELS TREAD LIGHTLY

This information and other significant details about the history of Tony Sforza in Esterline's 1969 memorandum were assembled in response to a public tirade by Pancho Varona against Sforza at that time.

> Agency found it useful to use this friendship as a means of controlling Mr. VARONA when he became unmanageable.
>
> f. Re paragraphs 9 and 10 of your memorandum of 11 June 1969:
>
> We know that Mr. VARONA has written at least one article for VIDA LATINA. We have no information however, to the effect that he is being at all successful in re-establishing and/or revitalizing the old "Autentico" Party. Given his unfavorable reputation in the Cuban community, it is unlikely that he would enjoy any success in this endeavor.
>
> g. Re paragraph 11 of your memorandum of 11 June 1969:
>
> It should be noted that Mr. Osorio DAVILA, presently living in Miami, is the brother of a prominent Communist in Cuba today and should be viewed in that light. "Frank's" recollection of the situation involving servants and the ASPRU home, which he took over with the servants does not jive with Mr. VARONA's report. There were two white and two black servants in the house. The night of the Bay of Pigs invasion, the Cuban Internal Service sent agents to the ASPRU home to pick up "Frank." One colored and one white servant were at home at that time and they told the DSE agents that "Frank" was "a gay blade" and would not be home until early the next morning. The DSE left the residence leaving behind a note for "Frank" to report to their headquarters the following morning. In this context, it should be noted that "Frank's" cover in Cuba during the period in question was that of a professional gambler; a cover which served him well during most of his service there.

Esterline Memo RE Sforza hiding in "ASPRU" home, 6/18/69; 104-10109-1016.

ROLANDO CUBELA, JUANITA CASTRO AND TONY SFORZA

Esterline devoted eleven pages to refute Pancho's charges against Sforza. The long list of Pancho's allegations included the "fumbling" of the Juanita Castro defection, and possessing information that could have aided in the assassination of Castro. Esterline characterized Pancho's charges as another "vituperative" attempt to "strike at 'Frank' who he apparently blames for his downfall with the Agency."[853]

The importance of the 1969 Esterline memo cannot be understated. In the process of dismissing Pancho's rants, Esterline's memo gives away a great deal of important information about Sforza. By itself, the memo helps establish that Tony Sforza's cover in Cuba was as a gambler named "Frank Stevens." (See Appendix Three) The Esterline memo also reveals that "Frank" was Pancho Varona's case officer at the time, and that Pancho addressed him as "Enrique." Without the Esterline memo, it would be more difficult to understand how the evidence from three important CIA documents—that originated at the time of the Bay of Pigs—substantiate the story about the home in which Sforza was living and *hiding* when the invasion failed.

The first of these three CIA documents is a one-page biography of Tepedino, written on 17 June 1962, and attributed to Pancho Varona. The note at the bottom states that Tepedino's "father is known *as* Sloman. Sloman remained in hiding in his [Tepedino's father] home 18-21 April 1961."[854] The first part of that note is untrue and misled the present author during research for this volume during the summer of 2014. As Charmaine Sforza-Flick pointed out to the author in 2014, Tepedino's father, Francesco Antonio Tepedino, was not *her* father [see note below].[855] Her father did use the pseudonyms Frank Stevens and Henry Sloman, as well as "Enrique," the Spanish name for Henry.

---

853 6/18/69, CIA Memorandum for Special Agent in Charge (Kane) from Chief of Station WH/Miami, Anthony R. Ponchay (Jake Esterline), RE: Charles Govea and Francisco Wilfredo "Pancho" Varona (Alonso). RIF 104-10109-10162.
854 6/17/62, JMWAVE "Biographical Data Sheet" on Carlos Tepedino based upon information from AMCONCERT-1 (Francisco Wilfredo "Pancho" Varona Alonso). RIF 104-10183-10073.
855 At first I incorrectly tied Sforza to Carlos' step-father, Francesco Antonio Tepedino, based on the information in Pancho's memo. After I met Charmaine Sforza-Flick at a conference in September 2014, I looked into the memo in more detail. I discovered that Pancho did not speak English and that a translator would have to have been involved in producing the document. The translator could not have been Sforza because he would have known that he was not Tepedino's father. Jefferson Morley later pointed out to me when we examined the memo closely that there is the hint of a hand edit above the word "as" which might be the word "to." This would change the meaning to: Tepedino's "father was known to Sloman," instead of "known as" Sloman. I now believe Morley was correct on that point.

WHERE ANGELS TREAD LIGHTLY

The second part of the biography on Tepedino (attributed to Pancho), which stated that Sloman (Sforza) hid in Tepedino's father's home from 18 to 21 April, might only be partly true. In the 1969 Esterline memo, Sforza refers to this dwelling as the "Aspuru home," and Tepedino's father is not mentioned at all.

Pancho Bio of Tepedino; incorrect note at bottom; 6/17/62; 104-10183-10073.

ROLANDO CUBELA, JUANITA CASTRO AND TONY SFORZA

The two JMWAVE cables that followed the biographic report (attributed to Pancho) repeat the second part of the note at the bottom of the report. An 18 June 1962 JMWAVE cable stated that Sloman "hid five days in the home of Tepedino's father."[856] And, finally, an 8 July 1962 JMWAVE cable stated that "Enrique [Sforza], known by Tepedino's father, hid in the home of [Tepedino's] father."[857] What we can surmise from these three 1962 JMWAVE documents is that Francesco Antonio Tepedino—Carlos Tepedino's step-father—may have occupied the Aspuru home for some period of time prior to the time Sforza lived there. However, we can be certain of this: Sforza *did* hide from Cuban DSE agents in this home and his gambling cover helped him to get away with it.

Rolando Cubela was not the only important Cuban that Tony Sforza was interested in recruiting and defecting. He also had his sights set on Juanita Castro, Fidel's sister. In this endeavor, Sforza would succeed, using the pseudonym "Enrique."

THE UNEXPECTED OFFER

On 10 July 1962, a memorandum from the Chief of Task Force W (TFW), William Harvey, to the Deputy Director of Plans (DDP), Dick Bissell, stated that "some time ago" TFW had targeted Fidel Castro's sister, Juanita Castro, in connection with TFW *efforts to split the Cuban leadership.*[858] [Emphasis added] The CIA's defection and use of Juanita, or "Juana," became project "AMSTRUT." A 1978 CIA report assembled in response to a list of questions posed by the House Select Committee on Assassinations (HSCA) included an explanation for the AMSTRUT operation. The report stated that AMSTRUT was the "operation and net of assets" involved in the defection and recruitment of Fidel Castro's sister, Juanita Castro, and subsequently, the "initiation of her anti-Castro radio broadcasts."[859]

---

856 6/18/62 WAVE 4746 to DIR CIA. RIF 104-10215-10107.
857 7/8/62 WAVE 5457 to DIR CIA. RIF 104-10295-10016.
858 7/10/62, Memorandum from William Harvey, Chief TFW, to Deputy Director of Plans; found in 00/00, "CIA DDCI Documents," p. 67. RIF 104-10310-10020.
859 5/26/78, DIR 229921 to Mexico City; RIF 10410065-10102.

WHERE ANGELS TREAD LIGHTLY

The first approach in the recruitment of Juanita Castro was made through AMSTRUT-1, the wife of the Brazilian ambassador to Cuba, Vasco Leitao da Cunha. Juanita Castro was assigned the CIA crypt AMSTRUT-2. Information on the correct identifications of these two CIA cryptonyms is provided in Appendix One. An 18 June 1969 memorandum from the CIA Miami Chief of Station, Jake Esterline (using the pseudonym Anthony R. Ponchay), revealed that Sforza had "certain responsibilities" with respect to Juanita Castro:

> "Frank" [Sforza] was fundamentally responsible for the defection of Juanita Castro although Mr. Varona (Pancho) furnished the lead. The "Frank"/Juanita Castro relationship is now *quasi-legendary*. He did not fumble the very difficult handling of this controversial person.[860]
>
> [Emphasis added]

When Sforza arrived in Cuba in late 1960, he soon discovered that Pancho Varona had been a good friend of the Vasco da Cunha family for a number of years, from the time when Vasco Leitao was the Brazilian ambassador to Cuba. The ambassador had given Pancho asylum during the Batista period. For the last three months before Castro came to power, the Brazilian Embassy had also given asylum to Fidel's sister, Juanita Castro. During her asylum there, Juanita Castro became very close to the ambassador's wife, Virginia Leitao. Sforza told Pancho to introduce him to the da Cunha family as "Frank Stevens."[861] Not long after the Bay of Pigs invasion, Juanita received a call from Virginia.[862]

The remainder of this section is based on a translation of pages 274-277 from Juanita Castro's 2009 autobiography ***Fidel and Raul—My Brothers—The Secret History***:

In her 2009 autobiography, Juanita Castro said that the call from Virginia took her by surprise. Virginia asked her to stop by the ambas-

---

860 6/18/69, CIA Memorandum for Special Agent in Charge (Kane) from Chief of Station WH/Miami, Anthony R. Ponchay (Jake Esterline), RE: Charles Govea and Francisco Wilfredo "Pancho" Varona (Alonso). RIF 104-10109-10162.
861 6/18/69, CIA Memorandum for Special Agent in Charge (Kane) from Chief of Station WH/Miami, Anthony R. Ponchay (Jake Esterline), RE: Charles Govea and Francisco Wilfredo "Pancho" Varona (Alonso). RIF 104-10109-10162.
862 That call was very likely made at the request of Tony Sforza using the pseudonym "Enrique," the name he used as Pancho Varona's case officer.

sador's residence that afternoon, as she had something she needed to share with her. Juanita recalled that moment:

Anything that Virginia asked, for me it was more than an order. I always held great affection for her and Vasco, her husband, in whose embassy I sought asylum until after the triumph of the Revolution and we forged a friendship that will last until we pass away.

When Juanita arrived, Virginia said, "These have been terrible days, Juanita. It is especially disappointing to realize that all of our ideals, for which we all fought and supported Fidel to make a real change in Cuba, are lost."

Virginia quickly came to the first point: her husband Vasco had been assigned as the new Brazilian ambassador to the Soviet Union and Virginia wanted Juanita to be the first to know. Juanita remembers that the impact of this news felt like a bucket of cold water had been emptied over her head. Virginia then came to the real message:

> I thought a lot about all the activities to which you devote yourself, Juanita. I have seen your struggle for the revolution and the suffering during those three months as an asylee in the embassy until the triumph of Fidel, and have lived with you these past two years since the ascension to power. All this has led me to deliver a message from friends who know your work and want to help.

Juanita said that if it had been anyone else besides Virginia she would have cut off the conversation, as "It was so bad that no one could hear it." Virginia continued, "Juanita, fear not, these people are in the front line. Very important people want to meet you and make an approach."

Juanita replied, "Of whom are we speaking, Virginia? Tell me the extent of this. That kind of work is not acceptable and you know how risky it is to work with people who oppose the regime." Virginia said, "I know, and that is why they, who have followed all your steps, have asked me to speak with you."

Virginia got up from the couch where they were sitting and motioned for them to go out to the balcony to continue the conversation. "This is the CIA, Juanita." Juanita asked, "You are involved with them, Virginia? And what can I do for the CIA, Virginia?" Virginia answered:

> Much, Juanita, much. Basically, what you are doing now, but with organization and with goals to achieve, the re-

> sources that solve many problems for people who need to leave Cuba. Anyway, I know a lot of things. But that is exactly what "they" want to talk to you personally about. For obvious reasons, it cannot be here in Cuba. We need to go to another country to reduce the risks.

Virginia explained that the da Cunhas were going to Brazil for a few weeks to receive instructions before going on to Moscow. So about two weeks hence, she said, would present the perfect opportunity to meet with "them" in Mexico City. Virginia suggested that it would not raise any suspicion if Juanita would make the trip to visit her sister Emma, who was living there.

Finally, Virginia explained that if upon hearing the "proposal" Juanita decided not to accept it, it would be "as if the talks never existed."

When leaving the residence of the ambassador that afternoon, Juanita Castro recalls how she quietly reflected on the situation:

> However, the name had sounded impressively sharp: "CIA," "the CIA." Fidel considered the CIA the biggest enemy of the regime and the revolution, and it was the CIA who was looking for me! And the person who was taking me to them was nothing more and nothing less than the wife of the Brazilian ambassador, and a person who had been a faithful follower of Fidel. She was a brave and righteous woman, who deeply knew the situation in Cuba.

"Did I feel remorse for betraying Fidel by accepting to meet his enemies? No, for one simple reason: I did not betray him. It was he who betrayed me. He betrayed the thousands of us who suffered and fought for the revolution that we thought was generous and fair and would bring peace and democracy to Cuba."

JUNE 1961: THE FAILURE TO EXFILTRATE CUBELA AND ORTA FROM CUBA

Sforza undoubtedly knew he had to escape from Cuba. Before leaving, he apparently tried once more to exfiltrate Cubela. In a later November 1961 JMWAVE dispatch to HQS, Sforza reported that in April

1961 he had begun preparations to exfiltrate two Cuban government officials.[863] One was Cubela and the other may have been June Cobb's former boss, Juan Orta, whose CIA cryptonym was AMDOFF-1.[864] In a news interview with the *Miami Herald* before his death, Jake Esterline revealed that Juan Orta had been recruited to assassinate Castro by slipping poison pills into his drink. Santo Trafficante had reportedly selected Orta to carry out the poison pill plot.[865] Orta changed his mind a few days before the Bay of Pigs invasion and took asylum in the Venezuelan Embassy in Havana.

Another stay-behind CIA agent, Emilio Rodriguez, (the same case officer who handed off Pancho to Sforza) reported, "Rolando Cubela very probably will defect in Operation ASTA... Expect Cubela's arrival at Marathon on 8 June 1961."[866] That did not materialize, but an 8 July 1962 JMWAVE cable confirms that Sforza had made an unsuccessful attempt to exfiltrate Cubela from Cuba in June 1961.[867]

Sforza succeeded, however, in making arrangements to meet Juanita Castro in Mexico City. On 10 June 1961, AMRYE-1, Tony Sforza, aka Henry Sloman, arrived at Key West on a fishing boat. CIA HQS told the JMWAVE Station that they wanted to debrief Sforza for several days at HQS area "before he plans to take a vacation."[868] According to Juanita Castro, two weeks later Sforza was in Mexico City meeting with her.

JUANITA CASTRO BECOMES "DONNA"

This section is based on a translation of pages 284-291 from Juanita Castro's 2009 autobiography *Fidel and Raul—My Brothers—the Secret History*.

On 23 June 1961 Juanita Castro's plane landed in Mexico City. No one other than Virginia Leitao da Cunha and the CIA knew the real reason for Juanita's trip to see her sister Emma, who was about to give birth.

---

863 11/7/61, JMWAVE Dispatch to Chief, Western Hemisphere Division. RIF 104-10267-10104.
864 3/28/61, bell 3417 to OPIM WAVE. RIF 104-10215-10120.
865 9/7/76, CIA MFR Subject: John Roselli, RIF 104-10133-10008.
866 6/8/61, RIMM 5842 to DIR CIA. RIF 104-10215-10235.
867 7/8/62, WAVE 5457 to DIR CIA. RIF 104-10295-10016.
868 6/12/61, BELL to OPIM WAVE. RIF 104-10180-10134.

Once Juanita arrived at Emma's home, she immediately contacted Virginia, who had arrived from Brazil on time for the meeting. Virginia asked that they first meet in her hotel suite and then go to the "appointment" together. Juanita took a taxi to the newly opened Hotel Maria Isabel, the most luxurious in the Mexican capital at the time.

After an affectionate greeting in Virginia's suite, the two went to Enrique's (Sforza's) room, which was in the same hotel. Juanita recalls, "I knew from the start that Enrique was not his real name." Sforza thanked them for accepting the invitation and said it had not been easy to arrange. He then asked Juanita to describe the situation in Cuba. This was her response:

> Well—I began to explain—these last years after the triumph of the revolution have certainly not been easy. All that the government has been doing is aimed at destroying democracy in Cuba and establishing a totalitarian system. I worry about myself and other people with whom I interact, and we consider ourselves true revolutionaries. Every day we see that more and more members of the Communist Party are placed in key government positions, and the non-communists who helped overthrow the Batista regime are being eliminated. For us this is a betrayal of the principles for which we fought to have a democratic system.

Juanita recalls that Sforza said little while he watched her and listened to her account of the many issues brought up: her opinions on foreign interventions, land reform, increased political prisoners, and the failed invasion at the Bay of Pigs. This discussion continued for a couple of hours.

Virginia then said it was time to leave and that they would reconvene. They said their goodbyes and left, and afterward Juanita asked Virginia what she thought about the meeting. Virginia reassured her that her answers were "very accurate" and explained that "they" needed to understand her strengths and how she would interact when facing other people. Juanita returned to Emma's home thinking to herself, "Emma could not have imagined the meetings I was having on this trip."

ROLANDO CUBELA, JUANITA CASTRO AND TONY SFORZA

Two days later the second meeting took place in Sforza's hotel room. He began the meeting this way:

> Juanita, we are interested in having you participate in some of our operations in Cuba. We believe it is nothing new to you, because we know of your activities to help many of your countrymen. So we need to know if you agree. This is who you will be. Do you understand this?

Juanita replied that she understood it "perfectly" and that she was aware of the risks. She said "all this is worth the sacrifice to try anything to help my country to the best of my ability. I cannot remain indifferent to the injustices, persecutions and all that is happening there."

When Sforza told Juanita that now was the time to state any doubts that she had, this was her response:

> Well, there is something very important to me. I want to make clear that agreeing to collaborate with you does not mean I will participate in any violent activity against my brothers, nor against any official of the regime. I will not encourage any homicide, and that has to be made very clear. That's my most important condition. I would say that is the only condition. And if you do not accept it, it will be like none of this happened.

Sforza reassured her that they were not asking her to take part in any conspiracy:

> We leave that well clarified. You are enormously valuable to the freedom of Cuba in other ways such as helping many who are in danger there. Many of our men are working beyond safety; some might be discovered or have already been. Your mission is to protect and move them from one place to another, offering maximum safety, to seek accommodation in homes that are safe... ...there are three important things to survive and succeed in any mission. The first is discretion: any failure could betray you and we might not be able to help you at that time. The second is an ally: this mission will require another

person to work with you; and the third is trust: the loyalty of your partner must be foolproof.

Juanita later said she had not yet realized that she was with one of the "experts" that the CIA had assigned to the Cuban case. She recalled that "years later I learned that his name was actually Tony Sforza, and that he was a key element of Operation Mongoose and had been infiltrated into Cuba, where he passed for a gambler in the casinos under the name of Frank Stevens." Juanita said that Sforza spoke perfect Spanish and that his accent was "perfectly pure."

Juanita asked Sforza how communications would be handled. Sforza then asked her if she knew how to operate a shortwave radio. She replied, "No, but if it's necessary I will learn." Sforza promised that his people in Cuba would make sure to get her the equipment she would need and the instructions to operate it. He then said she had to choose a password to identify herself when communicating. He asked her to name any melody. "Fascination," she replied. Sforza said that was fine and explained, "You will have to listen to transmissions every day at seven in the evening. When you hear 'Fascination' you must be ready to receive the message." Sforza asked her to name another melody. She chose the opening of "Madame Butterfly," and he explained that after "Fascination" was played in the phone call, the "Madame Butterfly" melody would be a signal that there was no message. Sforza then explained,

> In a few days, before you return to Havana, we will have the material you need to manually decode the messages you receive. We must take care as this is your own life. What will there be to say that if you are caught with the manual in hand. ...I'll be honest: if it is discovered you will be lost.

Juanita asked if there was anything else she needed to know. Sforza said that she would need a code name and that their suggestion was "Donna." Juanita agreed, saying she found the name interesting and easy to remember.

Sforza told Juanita that her first mission would be to take messages and money to hideouts in Havana that would fit inside cans of food so as not to arouse suspicion. The meeting ended with Juanita declining

ROLANDO CUBELA, JUANITA CASTRO AND TONY SFORZA

Sforza's offer of money to defray her expenses. The next day Virginia handed Juanita a briefcase full of cans of food, some with messages in them and some without. The next day Juanita said goodbye to her sister, Emma, and returned to Havana without incident: "Nothing happened, and I reached my home safely, but not alone, because now I had Donna."

Juanita Castro was a huge catch for Tony Sforza. Before she left Cuba at the end of 1963, Juanita would prove to be valuable to ongoing CIA operations on the island. Later, after she left Cuba, her anti-Castro radio programs were a propaganda disaster for her brother, Fidel.

In the summer of 1962, Tony Sforza became the point person in the JMWAVE Station to get a new effort underway to defect Rolando Cubela (see Chapter Twenty One). When CIA agents were meeting with Cubela in Helsinki and Paris during July and August, a "friend" of AMSTRUT-1 (Virginia Leitao) in Cuba reported that Cubela's wife had been making indiscreete remarks about her husband—including that he did not intend to return to Cuba. Her comments found their way to Raul Castro.[869] Raul visited Cubela's mother to ask if the rumor was true.[870] Cubela was warned by the CIA and he sent a message to Raul to convince him that the rumor was false. Juanita may have been Virginia's source.

Juanita would be able to make regular trips to visit her sister Emma in Mexico City. During the missile crisis in October 1962, Juanita would travel there to provide her JMWAVE case officer with information about anti-Castro groups working inside Cuba, including Manuel Ray's People's Revolutionary Movement (MRP).[871] In Mexico City, the CIA Station would be able provide a secure safe house for the use of JMWAVE case officers to debrief and train her.[872]

---

869 8/22/62, WAVE 7444 to DIR. RIF 104-10295-10008; See also
870 10/24/64, CIA Memorandum RE Weaknesses and Derogatory Information on Rolando Cubela. RIF 104-10215-10235.
871 10/5/62, WAVE 9496 to DIR CIA. RIF 104-10192-10251.
872 4/8/63, MEXI Dispatch to CH/WHD. RIF 104-10414-10402.

CHAPTER TWENTY ONE:
THE RECRUITMENT OF ROLANDO CUBELA

The previous chapter began with a brief summary of four CIA attempts to approach, recruit and/or defect Rolando Cubela. All were unsuccessful. The first attempt occurred in early 1959 and the last one was in June 1961. Jack Stewart was the case officer for the first two attempts and Tony Sforza was the case office for the last two attempts. After the failure in June 1961, there was another "planned defection" of Cubela (not discussed in the previous chapter) that failed in Paris in August 1961.[873] Cubela may have been attending the French National Student Union Cultural Festival that was taking place there at that time.

From the beginning, Cubela's close friend Carlos Tepedino had been intimately involved in helping to defect him. Tepedino became so dissatisfied with the way the CIA "handled" the planned defection in Paris that he gave up on the CIA altogether. Afterward, Tepedino began to share what he knew about Cubela with the FBI. And that is where matters stood in the summer of 1962. Then, in June, Tepedino received

---

873   3/00/59, CIA memo, section entitled the "AMLASH Operation. Note: the date on the RIF sheet, 3/00/59, is obviously incorrect. The CIA memorandum was prepared in response to the Church Committee Report; the correct date should be 8/30/77. RIF 104-10065-10094; see also 104-10103-10359.

news that his friend wanted to defect to the U.S. This chapter begins with that news from Cubela and then closely examines a crucial moment in the history of the plots to overthrow Castro that took place in Helsinki and Paris.

Before proceeding, the reader should be reminded of the reason that this chapter and the previous one have been included in this volume. (I would encourage you to go back to the Introduction and reread the section about Chapters 20 and 21.) The reason is because we know what is coming at the end of 1963: a "dark operation" to make it *appear* that the Kennedy brothers' plan to overthrow Castro was turned back on them by Fidel and into the assassination of President Kennedy instead. Many people in and out of the U.S. government were fooled by this false scenario. But that does not make it less false. It just helps to make that dark operation more successful.

We understand that this "turnaround" scenario is false. This knowledge informs us as we look back at the history of the attempts to overthrow Castro. It becomes a useful lens. In this and future volumes, it will be the magnifying glass through which we will peer, searching for clues to the conspiracy and the fingerprints of the people and their accessories connected to the plot.

THE BIG NEWS FROM THE ECHEVARRIA FAMILY ABOUT CUBELA

On 15 June 1962, the JMWAVE Station in Miami cabled CIA HQS with big news. AMCONCERT-1, Francisco Wilfredo "Pancho" Varona Alonso, had learned the news from Lucia Bianchi, the sister of the Directorio Revolucionario (DR) martyr Jose Antonio Echevarria. Lucia told Pancho that her parents had arrived in Miami on 9 June. They had just been seen off at the Rancho Boyeros Airport in Havana by Rolando Cubela. Lucia's mother told her that Cubela wanted to defect and to enter the U.S.[874] Cubela would be headed to Helsinki to attend the World Youth Conference taking place there. He said that on his return trip he

---

874 6/15/62, WAVE 4672 to DIR CIA. RIF 104-10215-10110.

THE RECRUITMENT OF ROLANDO CUBELA

would pass through Paris and call his friend Carlos Tepedino, whom he planned to ask for assistance with his entry to the U.S.

The JMWAVE cable to HQS proposed that the CIA should encourage the defection for KUTUBE (foreign intelligence) and KUCAGE (paramilitary and psychological warfare) exploitation. The Station asked for HQS concurrence to have Pancho contact Tepedino and offer financial assistance to Cubela for his entry into the U.S. CIA HQS immediately swung into action that same day. HQS asked the Mexico City Station to run traces on Tepedino in preparation for using him in a defection approach to Cubela.[875]

At the same time, William Harvey, Chief of Foreign Intelligence (FI), sent a priority cable back to the JMWAVE Station stating that HQS was "greatly interested" in the possible defection of Cubela.[876] Harvey indicated that there had been reports during the previous year from several sources suggesting that Cubela was disillusioned with the Castro regime and that he wanted to defect. On 22 May 1962, the CIA Station in Berne, Switzerland, had learned from the local FBI representative there that Cubela wanted to flee Cuba and would attempt to get permission to visit some European country. If he was successful, the cable from the Bern Station stated, Cubela would defect and "announce his dissatisfaction with the present government of Cuba."[877]

On 17 June 1962 at the JMWAVE Station, Pancho Varona gave a summary of what he knew about Carlos Tepedino's history. [Tony Sforza had become Pancho's case officer in the fall of 1960 and had remained so up through June 1962.] As Pancho's English was poor, someone else probably translated and typed an oral statement furnished by Pancho. This one-page biographical *report* stated incorrectly (see the details mentioned in the previous chapter) that Henry Sloman (Sforza) was Tepedino's father.[878] Pancho told the translator that Tepedino's parents were (Francesco) Antonio Tepedino and Amada Gonzales, who had been friends of his wife's family for twenty-five years.[879] While that was techni-

---

875   6/15/62, DIR 17410 to MEXI. RIF 104-10215-10111.
876   6/15/62, DIR 17466 to WAVE. RIF 104-10215-10108.
877   5/22/62, BERN 9140 to DIR CIA. RIF 104-10215-10112.
878   6/17/62, JMWAVE Biographical report on Carlos Tepedino by Pancho Varona. RIF 104-10183-10073.
879   His wife, Norma Ugarizza Varona, may possibly have been descended from the Spanish line of

WHERE ANGELS TREAD LIGHTLY

cally true, Pancho neglected to clarify that only the mother was a biological parent of Carlos. Carlos' father, Ignacio Lopez, had died in 1950, and his mother had remarried Antonio Tepedino.[880]

Pancho's biography of Tepedino also neglected to mention that Carlos Lopez Gonzales was married to Labrador Caridad Romay and had a two-year-old daughter, Maria Loretta, at the time Ignacio Lopez died. Understandably, Carlos' mother's name became Amada Tepedino Gonzales when she remarried. However, it seems unusual for a twenty-nine year old man with a wife and child to become legally adopted by his step-father.[881] In any event, Carlos decided against continuing in school and followed his adoptive father's avocation for jewelry work. In this field, he worked with his step-brother Antonio until the latter died in a car accident in New York on 7 November 1961.[882]

On 18 June 1962, JMWAVE cabled HQS some of the details from Pancho's profile of Carlos Tepedino, as well as his history with Cubela and Echevarria in the revolution against the Batista regime.[883] The cable did not repeat the confusion about Tepedino's father that was present in Pancho's biographical profile of Carlos Tepedino. That confusion may have been an innocent mistake, but Pancho also had an ulterior motive. Pancho's profile of Tepedino was constructed to enhance his family ties with the Tepedinos and therefore to underscore his importance in being the best contact to handle Tepedino. The 18 June JMWAVE cable shows that the station had bought into this idea by suggesting to HQS that Pancho could visit or call Tepedino to "establish the bona fides" of a CIA representative and "lay on a plan" for the defection approach to Cubela. But Tepedino would never let that happen.

On 19 June, the Mexico City Station weighed in with numerous traces on Tepedino. The Mexico Station said he was a CIA contact in Havana and had been part of a previous unsuccessful attempt to defect Cubela. The cable said that Jack Stewart was certain that Tepedino would coop-

---

the Ugarizza family that married into the Aspuru Spanish line in the middle of the 19th century and settled in Latin America.
880   00/00, CIA PRQ-I on Carlos Tepedino Gonzalez. RIF 104-10247-10198.
881   00/00, CIA PRQ-I on Carlos Tepedino Gonzalez. RIF 104-10247-10198.
882   6/17/62, JMWAVE Biographical report on Carlos Tepedino by Pancho Varona. RIF 104-10183-10073.
883   6/18/62, WAVE 4746 to DIR CIA. RIF 104-10215-10107.

THE RECRUITMENT OF ROLANDO CUBELA

erate in any way desired. Further, Stewart had no objection to Pancho using his (Stewart's) name to establish Pancho's intelligence service bona fides.[884] On 21 June CIA HQS forwarded the details, reported by the Mexico Station, on to JMWAVE. The HQS cable added that they would use Tepedino in a direct approach to Cubela in Europe and have a staffer contact and brief Tepedino before the trip. The cable said that Pancho could be used to set up the contact between Tepedino and the staffer.[885]

Apparently, the JMWAVE Station did not know that Tepedino had already told the FBI office in Miami that Cubela planned to go to Paris following the Youth Congress in Helsinki, and that Cubela wanted Tepedino to meet him there.[886] Tepedino had told the FBI that he had been in close contact with Jack Stewart in Havana. Tepedino also told the FBI that after Stewart was transferred to Mexico City, he (Tepedino) was in contact with Arthur Avignon (the deputy chief of Station) at the embassy in Havana. Tepedino also mentioned the failed defection attempt in Mexico City in 1961. On 27 June 1962, FBI Director Hoover sent a letter to the CIA reporting all of this information. Tepedino was furnishing these details to the FBI at the same time that CIA HQS and the JMWAVE Station were planning a defection approach to Cubela. This surprise letter from Hoover motivated the JMWAVE station to get in contact with Tepedino immediately.

On 29 June, the CIA notified its Station in Helsinki that a defection attempt of Cubela was in play.[887] On 6 July, HQS notified JMWAVE that Tepedino's operational approval had been granted and that a "staffer" would contact Tepedino ASAP about the "Cubela Op." HQS requested that Pancho "write" to Tepedino to let him know that "Mr. Harvey Thompson" would be coming to New York to meet him ASAP. Pancho was authorized to use Stewart's name to establish his bona fides with Tepedino. Then came another surprise.

---

884 6/19/62 MEXI 1111 to DIR CIA. RIF 104-10183-10072.
885 6/21/62, DIR 18354 to WAVE. RIF 104-10215-10103.
886 6/27/62, FBI letter to the Director, Central Intelligence Agency, Subject: Rolando L. Cubela Secades,, Internal Security—Cuba; with enclosure of 6/18/62 FBI Miami memorandum RE possible defection of Cubela. RIF 124-10290-10100.
887 6/29/62, DIR 20741 to several stations. RIF 104-10215-10092.

THE SURPRISE CUBELA POSTCARD TO TEPEDINO

On 8 July 1962, the JMWAVE Station sent a priority cable to CIA HQS with the details of two back-to-back phone calls involving Pancho and Tepedino.[888] Pancho had been doing some digging around. On 6 July, Pancho told the JMWAVE Station that he had just had a conversation with the father of Lucia Echevarria—Antonio Echevarria's sister. Her father told Pancho that Tepedino had received a postcard from Cubela. On the afternoon of 6 July, the JMWAVE Station set aside HQS' instruction that Pancho write to Tepedino. Rather, the station instructed Pancho to immediately call Tepedino. When Pancho made the call, Tepedino confirmed that he had received a postcard from Cubela but *refused* to give Pancho any details about it.

One can only wonder at the extent of embarrassment Pancho felt when Tepedino refused him. The preceding two weeks of cables between HQS and JMWAVE had assumed that Pancho was the right person to use to get to Tepedino. Tepedino told Pancho to call back later in the evening, purposely leaving him with no alternative but to tell the Station what had happened. Obviously, the Station had to ensure that the second phone call occurred; only this time they made sure that Sforza was present in the room when Pancho placed the call.

Pancho must have felt even more humiliation when, for a second time, Tepedino refused to tell him *anything* about the details of Cubela's postcard. Evidently, Tepedino feared that sharing such details with Pancho might endanger Cubela's security. Sforza then took the phone away from Pancho and introduced himself as Enrique—a pseudonym well known to Tepedino's father. Enrique (Sforza) had tried unsuccessfully to exfiltrate Cubela in early June 1961 and Tepedino was more than willing to talk with Sforza.

Tepedino confided that he had actually traveled to Miami on 9 June to talk with Lucia's parents, and that on 30 June he had received a postcard from Cubela. The postcard, mailed from Vienna, said that Tepedino "should not fail to meet Cubela in Paris in August." Sforza told

---

888 7/8/62, WAVE 5457 to DIR CIA. RIF 104-10295-10016.

THE RECRUITMENT OF ROLANDO CUBELA

Tepedino that he had been pursuing the defection of Cubela since 12 June and had planned on contacting Tepedino when they determined his (Tepedino's) location. Tepedino confessed that he had contacted the FBI in Miami and explained that his reason for doing so was his "dissatisfaction" with the CIA's previous attempt to defect Cubela in Paris in 1961. This failure may have taken place during the French National Student Union Cultural Festival in August 1961.[889]

In the phone call with Tepedino, Sforza said that he was "very interested" in the operation to defect Cubela. He added that Cubela might not return from Helsinki to Cuba via Paris and asked Tepedino if he would be interested in going to another country. Tepedino replied he would travel anywhere to assist Cubela but said he would be away in Canada for a few days beginning on 7 July. The JMWAVE cable to HQS conveyed that Tepedino knew Stewart by his true name and that Pancho would call Tepedino after his return from Canada on 10 July to inform him that "Harvey Thompson" would make contact with him.

On 13 July, Pancho alerted Tepedino to await the call from "Harvey Thompson," as planned.[890] The man behind the "Harvey Thompson" pseudonym was from the Foreign Intelligence section of Task Force W (TFW/FI). TFW was the Agency's Cuban operations task force. And the man who called and then approached Tepedino in New York City was Richard M. Fallucci.[891] Further, the pseudonym had changed to "William Thompson," which is the version of the pseudonym that CIA HQS sent to the station in Finland, along with his expected arrival date of 26 July.[892] That pseudonym would remain Bill Thompson afterward.[893] It is interesting to combine the two pseudonyms, as "William Harvey Thompson" might betray the egotistic hand of the Chief of TFW, William Harvey.

---

889 3/00/59, CIA memo, section entitled the "AMLASH Operation. Note: the date on the RIF sheet, 3/00/59 is obviously incorrect. The CIA memorandum was prepared in response to the Church Committee Report; the correct date should be 8/30/77. RIF 104-10065-10094; see also 104-10103-10359..
890 7/13/62, WAVE 5688 to DIR CIA. RIF 104-10183-10064.
891 6/28/65, CIA Contact Report, Participants: Carlos Tepedino, [redacted] and Harold P. Swenson. 104-10183-10424.
892 7/20/62, DIR 24592 to Helsinki. RIF 104-10215-10080.
893 See, for example, RIFs 104-10183-10054; 104-10102-10010; and 104-10102-10050.

CUBELA DECIDES TO RETURN TO CUBA TO ASSASSINATE CASTRO

Fallucci, using the name "Thompson," visited Tepedino in New York City on 13 July.[894] (The certain identification of Fallucci with this pseudonym is due to an inadvertent gift from a redactor who removed Fallucci's name from the text of a cable but forgot to remove it from the RIF sheet.[895]) The two men then traveled separately to Helsinki: Fallucci arriving on 26 July, and Tepedino arriving on 30 July. Upon arrival, Tepedino, as instructed, used the name "William Thompson" to make contact again with Fallucci. When they located Cubela on 1 August, Tepedino met with him for seven hours, after which Fallucci joined Cubela and Tepedino for dinner in a private room at "The White Lady" restaurant located some distance from the center of town. The meeting lasted until shortly after midnight. They met again the next evening in Tepedino's hotel, The Vaakuna. At this meeting, they decided it was best not to meet again in Helsinki; rather, they would continue their talks in Stockholm and Paris.

After the meeting and dinner with Cubela and Tepedino, Fallucci produced a detailed account of the Helsinki discussions.[896] He also cabled HQS on 3 August with a more succinct account.[897] Fallucci was surprised to discover that Cubela was "firmly determined" to go back to Cuba in an effort to overthrow the regime, and said that defection would mean just another man outside of Cuba on the American dole. He insisted that effective action "had to come from within." Cubela said his plans included sabotage, demolition, and the *assassination of Fidel*, key communist leaders and even the Soviet ambassador. Cubela was adamant. He declared that he was not the type to sit tight and that he preferred "violent action." He claimed that he had two captains, two majors and several others inside Cuba who would help him.

Cubela "reluctantly" conceded that he needed U.S. support. Fallucci's report stated that he had made no commitments to Cubela. How-

---

894   7/13/62, DIR 23130 to WAVE. RIF 104-10183-10063.
895   7/20/62, DIR 24592 to Helsinki. RIF 104-10215-10080.
896   9/00/62, Richard M. Fallucci, TFW/FI, Summary of Contacts with AMWHIP and AMLASH. RIF 104-10102-10050.
897   8/3/62, HELS 1609 (IN 39865) to DIR CIA. RIF 104-10215-10073.

ever, Fallucci did tell Cubela that the kind of schemes that he envisioned certainly had their place, but that a lot of coordination, planning, information collection, etc., were necessary prerequisites to "ensure the value and success of such plans." Cubela said he agreed with this, but Fallucci wrote afterward that he was not so sure how much of this "argument" Cubela would be willing to buy.[898]

Fallucci told HQS he was very concerned that Cubela was under extreme emotional strain, was not trustworthy "yet," and that he would be difficult to control in operational situations. Cubela spoke emphatically of his "complete distrust" of security among the contract Cubans at JM-WAVE and demanded that there be "absolutely no contact or even their knowledge of his cooperation" with the U.S. Fallucci told HQS that he promised Cubela maximum security on that point. Cubela then expressed his willingness to be debriefed on "all fields." Fallucci told HQS that this should be done by a U.S. Spanish speaking case officer who was intimately familiar with the Cuban scene.[899]

As Fallucci made his notes on the meetings in Helsinki, he wrote this interesting evaluation of Tepedino:

> AMWHIP (Tepedino)... has a tendency to interpret AMLASH's (Cubela's) remarks and feelings subjectively, and to attempt to guide us a bit too much; it might be wise to eliminate [this] in later portions of the talks in Paris. AMWHIP has no clandestine training to speak of... ... However, to his credit, he responds quickly to directions in this area, and follows rather well suggestions for aiding the security of the meetings. His remark about the advisability of keeping his old friend AMCONCERT-1 (Pancho Varona) out of the operation or from <u>any</u> knowledge thereof, is gratifying.

Tepedino told Fallucci that he was truly surprised when Cubela said he wanted to go back to Cuba. Tepedino had been sure, as Fallucci had been, that Cubela "would defect, period." Later, Cubela confided to Tepedino that he feared that a public defection statement would jeopar-

---

898   9/00/62, Richard M. Fallucci, TFW/FI, Summary of Contacts with AMWHIP and AMLASH. RIF 104-10102-10050.
899   8/3/62, HELS 1609 (IN 39865) to DIR CIA. RIF 104-10215-10073

dize his friends in Cuba for no good reason.[900] In Helsinki, the plan to defect Cubela had turned into a recruitment instead.

STOCKHOLM AND PARIS

Cubela stayed in Helsinki until the end of the Youth Festival for cover purposes. The group met up again in Stockholm on 10 August. Tepedino and Cubela both stayed at the Palace Hotel. Fallucci stayed at the Carlton, where "talks of a general nature" were held during several dinners. Not a whole lot of new information came from these discussions, other than the observation that Cubela appeared "genuinely interested" in getting Cuba out of its present predicament—with some help from the U.S.

The three men were together again in Paris by 15 August. Cubela and Tepedino were at the Hotel Franklin and Fallucci stayed at the Hotel Roblin. Cubela asked Tepedino about the meeting time with "the man from Washington" who had not yet met up with the group. Fallucci told Tepedino that in the future he and Cubela would call this man "Jaime," as they could not readily pronounce his "first true name"—Earl.

The Spanish-speaking case officer from CIA HQS who came to Paris to handle the final interviews of Cubela had used a number of different pseudonyms over a period of many years. In his reports during the summer of 1962, Fallucci identified this man as Wallace A. Growery—the same Wallace A. Growery who had been the Deputy Chief of Station in Havana from 1956 to 1958. His true name was Earl J. Williamson. He had used the minor variation "William Williamson" in Havana, where he had been a case officer for Manolo Ray, the chief of the underground in Havana. (At that time and afterward, Ray would refer to Williamson by another pseudonym, "Alfredo Fernandez.") When he became Cubela's case officer in 1962, Williamson was a "special assistant" in William Harvey's Task Force W (TFW), the Agency's Cuban operations staff—using *yet another* pseudonym—"Alfonso L. Rodriguez." And if that is not

---

[900] 9/00/62, Richard M. Fallucci, TFW/FI, Summary of Contacts with AMWHIP and AMLASH. RIF 104-10102-10050.

THE RECRUITMENT OF ROLANDO CUBELA

complicated enough, the same "Alfonso L. Rodriguez" was the Deputy Chief of Station in Mexico City *at the same time* he was working in Cuba. The complete references for the identification of these three pseudonyms with Earl Williamson are set forth in Appendix Four.

On 15 August, Tepedino and Fallucci met the Paris Chief of Station, "Peter J. Kymingham," a pseudonym for Jack "Red" Stent, aka Jack Stevens. This we know because a CIA person was kind enough to scribble the true name above the pseudonym in cables from 1963 and 1964.[901] The three men discussed the arrangements for the next day, when Cubela would meet Growery for the first time. On that day, Cubela and "Jaime" had their first two meetings, which were, for the most part, held in the absence of Tepedino and Fallucci. On 17 August Cubela's training in secret writing began and Growery had a third session with Cubela that lasted for several hours. The same sequence of events took place on 18 and 19 August.

On 20 August, Cubela, Fallucci, Williamson (aka Growery, aka Jaime), and Stent were driven to the U.S. Army Air Corps Support Element at St. Andres in southern France. There, Cubela received a demonstration and instruction in the use of plastic explosives. In the afternoon they were driven to the outskirts of Paris so that Cubela could alight and take a separate taxi back into town. During a conversation over drinks that evening, Cubela said he was satisfied with the demonstrations but was interested in having smaller explosives with more power and a remote control to detonate them. A final debriefing of Cubela by Growery took place on 22 August.

On 22 August, the JMWAVE Station cabled a disturbing piece of news to CIA HQS. The Miami station had learned from the station in Rio de Janeiro that AMSTRUT-1, Virginia Leitao da Cunha, had visited the "Miami area." She told the CIA that she had received a letter from a "friend" in Cuba. Virginia may have called on the person who recruited her in Cuba, Tony Sforza, and it is possible that the letter she had received from Cuba was from her best friend there, Juanita Castro. The letter reported that Cubela's wife, Mirth Novoa Delgado de Cubela, "was

---

[901] 10/21/63, PARI 1122 to DIR CIA. RIF 104-10215-10369; 1/30/64, DIR 98245 to WAVE. RIF 104-10216-10144; see also RIF 104-10120-10010.

telling friends that he does not intend to return to Cuba from Helsinki."⁹⁰² The JMWAVE cable suggested that Cubela be warned about his wife's "indiscretion."

On that same day, 22 August, Cubela made a phone call to his mother in Havana to find out what was going on. She told Cubela that she had been visited earlier in the week by Raul Castro, who inquired as to where Cubela was and when he would return.⁹⁰³ Tepedino commented that there was no chance now of a reconciliation of Cubela with his wife as she was too talkative about her anti-regime views and her determination to leave Cuba. Cubela commented that the newspaper publicity concerning his activities in Helsinki would help the "loose talk" in Miami (probably referring to the Echevarria family and Pancho Varona) about his plan to defect.⁹⁰⁴ Cubela then contacted Cuban Embassy personnel in Paris and sent word to Raul that he was following his current itinerary. Cubela added that he wanted a refresher course in the army when he returned home.⁹⁰⁵ On 29 August, Cubela returned to Cuba via Prague without incident.

---

902   See details in 10/24/64 CIA Memo on Cubela derogatory information. RIF 104-10215-10235; and the matching 8/22/62, WAVE 7444 to DIR CIA, RE AMSTRUT-1 received letter from freeing in Cuba saying Cubela does not intend to return from Cuba. RIF 104-10295-10008.
903   9/00/62, Richard M. Fallucci, TFW/FI, Summary of Contacts with AMWHIP and AMLASH. RIF 104-10102-10050.
904   See details in 10/24/64 CIA Memo on Cubela derogatory information. RIF 104-10215-10235; and the matching 8/22/62, WAVE 7444 to DIR CIA, RE AMSTRUT-1 received letter from freeing in Cuba saying Cubela does not intend to return from Cuba. RIF 104-10295-10008.
905   9/00/62, Richard M. Fallucci, TFW/FI, Summary of Contacts with AMWHIP and AMLASH. RIF 104-10102-10050.

AFTERWORD

Seven years have passed since the sequel to ***Oswald and the CIA*** was published in 2008. The boundaries were much narrower in the original 1995 edition, but even in that book, the pre-assassination movements of Oswald and manipulation of his CIA files foreshadowed what came at the end of the 2008 sequel: conspiracy. I argued in the sequel, and I am still convinced today, that the gloves of the person most likely behind that part[906] of the plot fit best on the hands of James Jesus Angleton, the Agency's counterintelligence chief.

As I waded into these dark waters then, my instincts told me to step back. With millions of new records released and tens of thousands still withheld, I needed a lot more time to investigate—and some time off. And so, I turned to an investigation of parallel paradigms in ancient mysticism. I returned to the JFK case in 2011.

It is not uncommon to view Dealey Plaza as *the* crime scene in the assassination of President Kennedy. Of course, it is. But I believe that the crime scene in this case extends beyond Dealey Plaza, where the president was shot; and Parkland Memorial Hospital in Dallas, where the president is said to have expired; and Bethesda Naval Hospital in Maryland, where

---

906 Jefferson Morley, "The Oswald File: Tales of the Routing Slips; Six Weeks Before the President's Murder, the CIA Didn't Tell All That it Knew," ***Washington Post***, 2 April 1995. "The routing slips that shed new light on the CIA's handling of information about Oswald before the assassination were found by John Newman, a 20-year veteran of U.S. Army Intelligence…"

the president's autopsy took place. I am convinced that the "crime scene" also includes the millions of records at the National Archives and Research Administration (NARA) facility, now located in College Park, Maryland. The "crime scene tape" was eventually extended to this facility, so to speak, by the passage of the JFK Assassination Records act in 1993. The records at NARA can also help us to find the criminals.

When I returned to active investigation of this case, I knew straight away that I had to make a critical decision: all in or stay out. I also knew that *all in* meant to do more than a new book. It meant perhaps three, four or even more volumes. It also meant testing hypotheses, making mistakes, and readjusting the investigation to follow the evidentiary trail. That is what is supposed to happen in murder investigations.

In this investigation, however, we are attempting to look inside a very dark box. The people involved in the design of the plot, even if they were only a few, were very sophisticated in propaganda and deception operations. In his book, **The Craft of Intelligence**, former Director of Central Intelligence Allen Dulles wrote about the "collateral effect" of a successful deception operation. Dulles often used the term "black operation," which is similar to the term used in this volume, "dark operation."

Dulles explained the "collateral effect" this way: once a "single piece" of the enemy's deception has succeeded in its purpose, "then almost anything that happens can be taken as one of his tricks."[907] This is what happened when British and French intelligence failed to believe some half-burned documents "from the complete plans of the German invasion of France through Belgium, for which Hitler had already given marching orders." British and French officials felt that "the whole thing was a German deception operation." The point that Dulles was driving at was this: "Often the very fear of deception has blinded an opponent to the real value of the information which accidents or intelligence operations have placed in his hands." The burned documents had fallen into British and French hands by accident, when a German plane landed in the wrong place.

---

907   Allen W. Dulles, Craft of Intelligence: *The Craft of Intelligence—America's Legendary Spy Master On the Fundamentals of Intelligence Gathering For a Free World* (Guilford, Connecticut: The Lyons Press, 2006), p. 147.

AFTERWORD

It is worthwhile pondering how Dulles' point might apply to the Kennedy assassination. As stated in the Introduction to this work, in this case a very significant "single piece" of deception succeeded in its purpose:

> The plot to assassinate President Kennedy was designed to deceive both people in the government and the public at large. A convincing trail of evidence was established to make it *appear* that the Kennedy brothers' plan to overthrow Castro had been turned around and used against them by Fidel himself, resulting in the assassination of President Kennedy.[908]

We should heed Dulles' advice and not fear that "almost everything" is a successful deception operation. We should, as Dulles advises us, realize that accidents in intelligence operations happen. Such accidents have occurred in this case too. They have placed important clues into our hands.

There is an unstated corollary principle in the game of deception that Allen Dulles was kind enough to give us. Once a "single piece" of a black operation has been compromised, the entire fabric of that operation can potentially unravel.

When talking about the assassination of President Kennedy, David Atlee Phillips, the CIA's most adept psychological warfare and propaganda operator, enjoyed standing dangerously close to the edge of the truth without going over the cliff. He observes:

> Allen Dulles was a keeper of many secrets which perforce had to be shared with a few others, a very few others. Among those secrets, there were a few marks on the dark side of the ledger: Dulles had been the senior case officer for two attempts to assassinate foreign leaders.

One of them was Castro, and Phillips avers that it is "obvious" that the revelation of that information "would have provided the Warren jurors with a possible motive for a Castro involvement in Kennedy's assassination."

---

[908] For more on this, see Peter Dale Scott, ***Deep Politics II: Essays on Oswald, Mexico, and Cuba*** (Skokie, Illinois: Green Archive Publications, 1995), p. 64. Scott also proposed (see p. 69), a hypothetical "turn around" scenario. According to this hypothesis, the trigger event was originally a shooter team, "in effect licensed by the CIA to kill Castro," that "might then have returned from Cuba and killed the president instead."

Yet Phillips tells us that *what appears to be so is not so.* Like the cat that swallowed the canary, Phillips then states flatly, "I know of no evidence that Fidel Castro, or the Soviets, encouraged Oswald." And why would Phillips be in a position to make such a statement? "I should add," he says, "that I was an observer of Cuban and Soviet reaction in Mexico City when Lee Harvey Oswald contacted their embassies."[909]

In other words, in the course of telling us about a big secret—that Dulles' operation appeared to give Castro a motive to kill JFK—Phillips lets us in on a bigger "unpopular" secret: the big secret was false.

Getting Chief Justice Earl Warren to believe that it was true was one of the most successful deception operations in history.

---

909   David Atlee Phillips, *Secret Wars Diary—My Adventures in Combat, Espionage Operations and Covert Action* (Stone Trail Press, 1989), pp. 162-166.

APPENDIX ONE:
SELECTED CIA CRYPTONYMS

AMAPACHE-2: Iglesais Pons, **JMWAVE** FI asset, arrived Key West 6/16/61 on boat PANMAJA; 104-10236-10328.

AMBALD: Cuban engineer in U.S., talks with Carlos Franqui in 3/65; 104-10216-10337.

AMBALD-2: Works for CIA Paris Station, circa March 1965; 104-10216-10340.

AMBANG: Paramilitary operation of internal resistance in Cuba, originally called **AMCOBRA**, rolled up by Castro in 1964; 104-10308-10135.

AMBANG-1: Manuel Ray Rivero, discussed **AMSMILE-1** with Sidney P. Di Ubaldo, 6/10/64; 104-10274-10274, 104-10308-10135.

AMBUNNY-1: Was a Female candidate, at suggestion of Sidney P. Di Ubaldo, for French-English-Spanish speaking secretary to be sent to Paris in

1965 to penetrate the **UNSNAFU-19** office"; met with Carlos Tepedino (**AMWHIP-1**) and Norris W. Damicone; 104-10183-10437; 104-10183-10439.

AMBANG-4: Rogelio Cisneros; 104-10165-10022.

AMBARK-1: Hernandez (fnu), used as informant in the Federation of University Students (FEU) when he was active member in 10/58; attended Havana Medical School; knew Frank Belsito by true name; 104-10226-10108.

AMBIDDY-1: Manuel Artime Buesa, prominent Cuban exile in the Bay of Pigs invasion, in 1963 moved to Nicaragua as leader of operation **AMWORLD**; 104-10240-10327, 104-10241-10018.

AMBLEAK-1: Estaben Jacquin Blanco Sanchez; Blanco was a Rescate (Revolutionary Democratic Rescue) official who helped another Rescate official, Frank Paez, who served as a cutout to couriers going into Cuba. Blanco also conducted business with Paez on behalf of Antonio Varona*; 104-10061-10115; *1/23/63, 104-10167-10361.

AMBOAR: Possibly Mitchell Werbell III [did covert work for Batista in Cuba in 1959, later worked in the Dominican Republic]; 104-10182-10126.

AMBRILL-1: in 12/60 in Cuba, **AMBRILL-1** was a source of Edward D. Knapman; 104-10169-10270.

AMBRUSH: Intel Section of the FRD (Cuban Democratic Revolutionary Front); 104-10061-10115.

AMBUCKLE-1: A CIA source on Dr. Miro Diaz Cruz and the Rainforth Foundation; 104-10236-10204.

AMBUD: Cuban Revolutionary Council (CRC), Cuban exile organization formed on 22 Mar 1961; 104-10308-10024.

SELECTED CIA CRYPTONYMS

AMBUD-1: Jose Miro, first Prime Minister of Cuba under Castro, who left Cuba and headed the Cuban Revolutionary Council (CRC) exile group; 104-10308-10265.

AMCALL-1: Reynold Gonzalez Gonzalez, labor leader of MRP; 104-10271-10234; 104-10217-10397; 104-10217-10144.

AMCANOE: Project of U.S. contacts for a resistance group in Cuba, incl. support of Unidad de Liberacion Nacional (ULN); 104-10308-10029, Church Committee testimony of Harold Swenson, 10 May 1976, p. 17.

AMCANOE-1: Eduardo Garcia Molina; Swenson, CH SAS/CI was concerned about a penetration of the **AMCANOE** group; Swenson described **AMCANOE** and **AMLASH** as SAS/EOB positive intelligence ops against Cuba*; 104-10308-10029; 157-10014-10048; *157-10014-10048 (P. 40).

AMCANOE-3: Antonio "Tony" Ramirez Mendez; ["planning utilize ... good professional approach in working with Cuquito (**AMTURVY-1**); "**AMHALF-2** (gender is male) mechanism" (use of diplomatic car) to be used to get **AMCANOE-3** inside Uruguayan Embassy for asylum, 9/14/63*]; 104-10308-10029; 104-10077-10045; *104-10308-10182 AND 104-10103-10349.

AMCANOE-7: Benjamin Acosta Valdez; 104-10308-10029.

AMCANOE-9: Juan Amestoy Dominguez; 104-10308-10029104-10308-10029.

AMCAPE-1: Tad Szulc, New York Times journalist involved in **AMTRUNK** project, suspected by CIA of being hostile foreign agent; 104-10103-10097, 104-10103-10363, 104-10102-10234.

AMCARBON-1: Al Burt, Miami Herald journalist used as source and "operational support" for CIA's **JMWAVE** station; 104-10072-10289, 104-10308-10135.

AMCARBON-3: Donald Dean Bohning, Latin American editor of Miami Herald and CIA source; 104-10310-10251, 104-10106-10653.

AMCHEER: enter before **AMCHIRP**, a group of approximately 100 older, non-political Cubans, who received training from Dave Morales at **JMWAVE** as reserve intelligence personnel—80 had been trained by April 1961. 104-10310-10020.

AMCHIRP-1: 11/60 associated with Operation Unity and **AMPAN-1**; 104-10296-10043.

AMRASP: Frente Revolucionario Democratico (FRD), aka Cuban Democratic Revolutionary Front; it became **AMIRON** after the 11/60 Orrison security compromise; 104-10220-10418; 104-10220-10385.

AMCIGAR: FRD Executive Committee; it became **AMPORT** after the 11/60 Orrison security compromise; 104-10220-10418; 104-10220-10379.

AMCLATTER-1: Bernard Leon Barker, Cuban policeman working for CIA in Cuba, reprimanded for unoperational behavior in the "Mendizabal affair"*; Cuban exile and contract agent for CIA, worked with E. Howard Hunt and Frank Sturgis in Miami and later the three were part of the Watergate burglars; *104-10237-10101; 104-10308-10265, 104-10164-10186, 180-10144-10221.

AMCLATTER-5: Alberto de Jesus Alberty Garcia; in October-November 1959 temporarily taken out of the **AMCLATTER** net due to "Mendizabal affair"*; 104-10164-10186; *104-10237-10101.

AMCLATTER-6: In 10/59 Alberto Bayo operation ("Mendizabal affair") against Venezuelan President Marcos Perez Jimenez for Cuba, **AMCLATTER -1** (Barker) disclosed sensitive information (about Jack Stewart and others including aliases they used) in front of **ODENVY** (FBI) informant (possibly Catherine Taaffe) endangering **AMCLATTER-1** and **AMCLAT-**

TER-6; **AMCLATTER-6** is female who went to Miami and had name of an (redacted) FBI agent as emergency contact*; 104-10215-10416; 104-10215-10417; 104-10215-10055; 124-10205-10370 (FBI report); *104-10237-10101.

AMCOG: A "complex" operation, 5/11/65, 104-10070-10079; **JMWAVE** planning to split up **AMCOG** net into smaller compartmented groups, 12/13/63, 104-10076-10443. The **AMCOG** people identified below belonged to Varona's Rescate Movement (Revolutionary Democratic Rescue); see Fabian Escalante, *The Secret War*.

AMCOG-1: Brother of **AMCOG-2** and **AMCOG-3**

- Nephew of Ramon Grau San Martin (former President of Cuba), circa 5/6/65, 104-10181-10460 and 104-10181-10461; uncle is aka "the Doctor," 12/9/63, 104-10073-10101.
- Possibly aka "Pancho" who, besides AMCOG-3, was one of 'the old man's (President Ramon Grau San Martin) two nephews"; 104-10073-10101.
- **AMCOG-1's** "brother and sister, **AMCOG-2 and 3**," were imprisoned in Cuba, which demanded a million dollar ransom for their release; **AMCOG-1** went to Mexico to meet **AMPOON**-1 to get the latest "sitrep" on his brother and sister; **JMWAVE** proposes a "multiple phase provocation and psych play which allows for pitching **AMPOON**-1; 104-10181-10460.
- **AMCOG-1** "should play straight" with **AMPOON-1** [Manuel Vega Perez, aka "Marcos, diplomatic attaché to Cuban Embassy in Mexico City] re ransom," 7/11/62, 104-10181-10454.
- **AMWEE-1** is temporary case officer for **AMCOG-1**, 5/6/65, and **AMCOG-1** is knowledgeable of certain "phases" of **AMCOG-3** case, and familiar with two CIA staff officers, knows various field agents and knows true name and vital data of **PBPRIME** (U.S.) contact agent **AMPAL-1**, 104-10181-10460; as of 5/6/65.

AMCOG-2: Mrs. (Maria) Leopoldina Grau Alsina de Aguero, aka "Polita"

- Niece of Ramon Grau San Martin, circa 5/6/65, 104-10181-10460 and 104-10181-10461; uncle is aka "the Doctor," 12/9/63, 104-10073-10101.
- Sister of **AMCOG-1** and **AMCOG-3**, 12/9/63, 104-10073-10101.
- Wife of Jose Aguero; 104-10073-10101.
- Her CIA 201 file indicates she was granted a Provisional Operational Approval OA on 17 March 1961 for her use as a source of intelligence in her brother's net; 104-10103-10183.
- Rescate (Revolutionary Democratic Rescue) contact, sent by Antonio Varona to work with Alberto Cruz Caso, his brother Ramon, and Manuel de Jesus Campanioni Souza (an associate and friend of Santo Trafficante) to plot Castro's assassination in the Havana Libre Hotel using poison pills; Fabian Escalante, *The Secret War* (pp. 132-133); see also document at end of Shackley Deposition to SSCIA, 157-10014-10046.
- Arrested by Cuban authorities circa 1/20/65, 124-90135-10117.
- **AMCOG-2** knew too much about **AMFAUNA-1** "for the latter's good," 5/11/65, 104-10070-10079.
- **AMCOG-2's** female friend, Elvira Diaz Biarte, had moved into **AMCOG-3** house and taken over as warder (on behalf of DSE) of **AMCOG-1's** uncle, Ramon Grau San Martin, circa 5/6/65, 104-10181-10460 and 104-10181-10461; uncle is aka "the Doctor," 12/9/63, 104-10073-10101. The ailing former Cuban President (Ramon Grau San Martin) was being coerced to remain in the **AMCOG** residence while his nephew, **AMCOG-3**, and niece, **AMCOG-2**, were being held in a Cuban prison for a ransom of one million dollars. 104-10181-10460.

AMCOG-3: Ramon Grau San Martin

- Brother of **AMCOG-2** and **AMCOG-1**; 12/9/63, 104-10073-10101.

SELECTED CIA CRYPTONYMS

- CIA 201 file indicates Ramon Grau Alsina was employed by the CIA as head of an intelligence gathering net at the time of his arrest on 21 January 1965; he was convicted of espionage on behalf of the CIA; 104-10103-10183.
- **AMCUTLER-2**, "Carmina," received exfiltration instructions [circa 1/30/61] from **AMCOG-3**, 104-10075-10150.
- **AMCOVE-12** is subsource for **AMCOG-3**, 11/30/63, 104-10075-10320.
- **JMWAVE** (after not receiving letters from **AMLASH-1**) asks **AMCOG-3** "determine soonest whereabouts" of "pro-regime" doctors, including Julio Martinez Paez (former Health Minister of Castro regime); 104-10215-10205.
- 1/28/64 **AMCOG-3** reported: "According to what **AMCOG-5** tells me, Oswald was in Havana between 2 and 7 October 1963. A lady saw him in shirt sleeves, wearing good shoes and smoking American cigars accompanied by Clemente Morera, an employee of Terminales Nambisas who belongs to the DSE. He (Oswald) was seen by the sister of Commandante Miranda," her name is possibly "Ofelia Miranda," a source for **AMCOG-5**; 104-10021-10047.
- Ramon was arrested by Cuban authorities along with his sister circa 1/20/65, 124-90135-10117.

AMCOG-5: Oswald was in Havana between 2 and 7 October 1963," Oswald "was seen by the sister of Comandante Miranda," her name is possibly Ofelia Miranda, a source for **AMCOG-5**, 104-10021-10047.

AMCONCERT-1: Francisco Wilfredo "Pancho" Varona; associated with **AMCOO***; a friend of E. D. Brand in 1960**; Henry Sloman (Tony Sforza, Pancho's case officer****) says "Coco" (Jorge Nobregas) failed to pick up **AMCONCERT-1** at exfiltration point in 1961***; *104-10162-10178; **104-10103-10128; ***104-10267-10104; ****104-10109-10162 and 104-10113-10074.

AMCOO: is Delia Failde, the "Dragon Lady"*; identity compromised in marginalia**; operator of boat *Veramar****; *104-10162-10197; **104-10240-10042;***104-10110-10259.

AMCOOP-1: Miguel Xiques Marcias; began contact with Cuban intelligence net circa 8/60 and is cutout for **AMDOODLE-1***; alleges Cuban underground told to stand down on 17 April 1961**; is a man who met with underground leader in Cuba known as "Rene"***; 104-10061-10115, p.59, 104-10061-10115, p.56; *104-10180-10161; **104-10296-10119; ***104-10168-10149.

AMCORE-2: Luis Conte Aguero; Phillips is case officer, 1/26/61*; Robert Trouchard is case officer, circa 1962**; William S. Wibalda is **JM-WAVE** cut-out to **AMCORE-2*****; *104-10165-10104, 104-10165-10285, 104-10112-10101; **104-10244-10018;***104-10165-10104; 104-10166-10327.

AMCOVE: An "operation centered around an FI (Foreign Intelligence) net in Cuba"; 104-10308-10017.

AMCOVE-1: Alejandra Sanchez; 104-10308-10017.

AMCRAG-1: and Operation Tilt (exfiltration of four Soviet officers from Cuba)*; **AMLASH-2** sent letter to Cuco Leon (**AMWORM-1**) who gave it to **AMCRAG-1****; *104-10057-10102; **104-10216-10411.

AMCROAK-1: Bernardo Milanes Lopez, 201-738660, Castro's mother's doctor, recruited by Tony Sforza in Madrid in 1963,* and was part of Operation Raphael, a plot to assassinate Fidel, Raul, and Che; part of the **AMTURVY** net; later, Tony Sforza learned from Cubela's father that Milanes ended up in the La Cabana prison where he and Cubela were the principal medical doctors for the prisoners there, 7/29/69**; 104-10308-10020, 104-10308-10021; 104-10308-10325; 104-10308-10326; 104-10506-10031; *104-10076-10042; **104-10216-10027.

SELECTED CIA CRYPTONYMS

AMDIP-1: Manuel Antonio Varona; was **AMHAWK-1** before the Orrison security compromise.

AMDIP-3: "Tandi"; 104-10193-10258.

AMDENIM-1: Alberto Fernandez Hechevarria, collected tribute from sugar companies for Castro when he was in Sierra Maestra; first head of Castro's Sugar Institute; later a Cuban exile whose boat *Tejana* was used in CIA infiltrations and exfiltrations from Cuba; a long time close associate of Catherine Taaffe and Wallace Quinn, boat dealer in Miami; in 1962 he emerged as the external leader of Union Revolucionaria*; 104-10172-10152, 104-10172-10086; *104-10172-10152.

AMDENIM-4: possibly Larry Laborde, 104-10264-10051 and microfilm, Reel 53, Folder E.

AMDENIM-11: possibly Eddie "Bayo" Perez, of the "Bayo-Pawley Affair," see 104-10171-10351 and 104-10312-10172 and CIA Card Index 104-10425-10075.

AMDENIM-14: Antonio ("Tony") Cuesta Vallee, prominent Cuban exile, involved in Comandos L and other militant anti-Castro organizations; 180-10143-10175, 104-10244-10126, 104-10244-10077.

AMECRU-1: Alonso Pujol, business partner of Tony Varona; **AMSIGH-2** was a CIA contact for Pujol*; 104-10061-10115, 104-10233-10423; 104-10217-10140.

AMEER: Add Travis not aware **AMEER** identity on 10/21/60, 104-10240-10165, might break with the FRD as of 10/5/60, 104-10165-10252; 10/20/60, **AMEER** rep in NYC, Manuel Cobo, abandons **AMEER** to join Varona, 104-10168-10348, 3/27/61 **AMEER** protests Manuel Ray complex in AMBUD (the CRC), 104-10297-10052; in August 1960 Artime was asked to come to Miami to fix the "AMEER problem" 104-10269-10008; NEWMAN COMMENT: this profile may possibly fit with Aureliano Sanchez Arango, the Foreign Minister the former government of Carlos Prio Soccaras; for example on 10/7/60, he withdrew from the FRD, 104-10168-10398, see also 104-10168-10207.

AMEMBER-1: Julio Lobo, richest sugar magnate in Cuba and later an exile and financial backer of several anti-Castro groups; 104-10102-10176; 104-10308-10121, 104-10103-10158, 180-10142-10307.

AMFAT: a group of Cuban men trained by David Morales at JMWAVE to serve as future CI officials and Cuban government officials; 61 of them trained in Guatemala with Brigade; they accompanied the brigade to the invasion, two were lost, nine were caught, and the rest got out. 104-10310-10020.

AMFAUNA: Network of in-Cuba agents, nearly all women, providing military, political, and economic reporting; 104-10308-10120, 104-10070-10079.

AMFAUNA-1: is a Cuban male, aka "Julio,"*; most in this net are female; 104-10308-10120; *104-10070-10079.

AMFAUNA-7: on 7/30/63, **AMFAUNA-7** asked **AMFAUNA-1** to advise CIA about A-7's plans to assassinate Castro and to request financial support, 104-10308-10120.

AMFAUNA-14: Was successfully exfiltrated with **AMWEE-2** by **AMHICH** team on 11/22/63 *; both associated with **AMCUTLER-2**, "Carmina," ** who received exfiltration instructions from **AMCOG-3**; 104-10079-10305; *104-10073-10101; **104-10075-10150.

AMFAUNA 25: "El Grande"; 104-10073-10101.

AMFAUNA-27: "Edgardo"; 104-10073-10101.

AMFLAME-5: Luis Puig Tabares, 201-329604; 104-10308-10120.

SELECTED CIA CRYPTONYMS

AMFOX-1: Stay-behind CIA agent in Cuba, was still reporting in 1973, but WH Division believed he had been doubled (BOP History VOL III); 104-10301-10001.

AMGLEN-1: Jesus A. Valdez Cardenas; 104-10061-10115.

AMGLEN-9: Inactive W/T operator associated with **AMTURVY-1**; 104-10266-10123.

AMGOSH-1: 104-10226-10169 handwriting over crypt **AMGOSH-1** is "Frau Marsal Barbaressa Lorenzo," who in 180-10142-10305 was a former Havana Station contact for Manuel Antonio Varona. However, 104-10226-10290 indicates **AMGOSH-1** is a man, a former rebel army officer who quit in January 1959, and founded the Democratic Insurrection Organization (OID). **AMGOSH-1** is contact for Margot Pena, former head of Sierra Maestra terrorist group in Bayamo during Castro revolution, during last four months of which she worked with MRR terror group. 104-10226-10169; 104-10296-10003, 104-10296-10003.

AMGUPPY-1: Becomes **AMLOON-1**, former vice president of the Colomos organization, that had four specific groups in Camaguey Province in 1960"; 104-10172-10072.

AMHAWK-1: Manuel Antonio (Tony) de Varona, former Cuban Prime Minister (1948-1950). Later a Cuban exile leader in the Cuban Revolutionary Council; became **AMDIP-1** after the Orrison security compromise (see above); 104-10308-10042; 104-10167-10339; 180-10143-10183.

AMHIM-2: Agustin Alles Soberon, worked under **AMHIM** project and also for **Juanita Castro's** radio program; 104-10104-10041, 104-10104-10038, 104-10104-10049, 104-10104-10051.

AMHINT-1: Alberto Muller Quintana; 104-10181-10346; 104-10181-10347.

AMHINT-2: Manuel Salvat Roque, cousin* of Oscar Echevarria Salvat, 201-263473; 104-10181-10346; 104-10181-10347; *104-10181-10341.

AMHINT-24: Victor Espinoza Hernandez, 201-285147, knows "Alonso" well but not on good terms; 104-10263-10078.

AMHINT-53: Luis Fernandez Rocha; used to be **AMTOPIC-2***; *104-10213-10085; 104-10171-10268 with 104-10308-10170.

AMHINT-56: Juan Francisco Blanco Fernandez, participated in DRE raids on Cuba; 104-10215-10161, 104-10215-10402, 104-10215-10145.

AMHOBO-1: 11/30/62, Cuban national, who publishes newsletter, compiling press and **AMBUD** and **AMSPELL** reports, believes Cuba can only be liberated through U.S. intervention, can be expected to keep issue alive in spite of case officer instructions to the contrary, 104-10298-10137; 10/11/61, Dave Phillips received a letter forwarded from his Washington address from **AMHOBO-1**, who complained that "all telephone numbers have been cut off." 104-110267-10008. [Newman comment: Phillips is possibly **AMHOBO-1**'s case officer.]

AMICE: see **AMTRUNKS**.

AMING-4: Manuel Salvat Roque; 104-10181-10373.

AMIRE-1: Emilio Americo Rodriguez; his CIA crypt, very carefully guarded by the Agency through all of the rounds of declassification, was accidentally compromised on p. 6 (entry of 6/61) of a list of CIA derogatory information on Rolando Cubela; his **JMWAVE** pseudonym was Peter J. Digerveno *; likewise his true name was very carefully protected, but a redactor failed to keep it off of a single RIF sheet **; so too was the fate of his security number with his initials ***; 104-10215-10235; *104-10161-10341; **104-10161-10373; ***104-10129-10022 and 104-10236-10182.

SELECTED CIA CRYPTONYMS

AMJAG: Justo Carrillo, Montechristi group; used to be in **AMWAIL** group; 104-10102-10176.

AMJAVA-4: Rafael Quintero; 104-10241-10010 with 104-10241-10014.

AMJUTE-1: Arnesto N. Rodriguez, father of Emilio Americo Rodriguez—**AMIRE-1**; 104-10072-10207.

AMLAME-1: Luis Puig Tabares; 201-329604, 104-10308-10120.

AMLASH-1: Rolando Cubela Secades, second in command of Revolucionario (DR) during Batista regime; Rolando Cubela Secades, Cuban doctor and FEU officer recruited by CIA in July-August 1962 in Finland and France; role of Richard M. Fallucci and Wallace Growery (Earl Williamson) as first case officer*; CIA history of derogatory information and weaknesses of Cubela**; CIA history of **AMLASH** operation***; CIA biographic data on Cubela****; Carlos Tepedino's (**AMWHIP-1**) extreme influence on Cubela*****; 124-10290-10100; 104-10295-10016; 104-10215-10080; *104-10102-10050; **104-10215-10235; ***104-10065-10094; ****104-10103-10187 and 104-10102-10010; *****104-10215-10107.

AMLASH-2: Jorge Robreno Marieges, aka "El Mago"; 104-10234-10165.

AMLASH-3: Alberto Blanco Ramirez, aka "El Loco," 201-759879; 104-10216-10346; 104-10054-10018; 104-10234-10237; 104-10216-10318; 104-10234-10343; 104-10103-10185

AMLAW-3: Carlos Lechuga; 104-10179-10107 with 104-10274-10337.

AMLEO-3: Jose Ricardo Rabel Nunez, 201-249386; **AMLEO-3** along with Gilberto Fondora and Miguel Ramos were crew of JURE mother vessel *Venus*; 9/3/65 **AMLEO-3** caught trying to exfiltrate his family using Venus*; **AMLEO-3's** sister's uncle is Emilio Nunez Portuondo**; Dave Phillips was emergency contact for AMLEO-3 debrief in Mexico circa 11/15/63***;

104-10102-10231; *104-10087-10130; **10410087-10130; 104-10308-10059, 104-10103-10349, 104-10103-10362; ***104-10290-10442.

AMLILAC: Commando group involved in infiltrations into Cuba; 180-10144-10221, 104-10215-10394.

AMLOON-1: was **AMGUPPY-1**, former vice president of the Colomos organization, that had four specific groups in Camaguey Province in 1960"; 104-10172-10072.

AMLOUT-1: Raul Castro; 104-10103-10349; 104-10308-10234.

AMNORM: Nino Diaz; 104-10262-10034; 104-10193-10095.

AMOT: Cubans in Miami (outside group) controlled by **JMWAVE** station who gathered information on Cubans, primarily from debriefing of Cuban refugees; 104-10308-10209, 104-10308-10214, 104-10235-10109.

AMOT-2: Joaquin Sanjennis Perdomo (brother of Sergio Sanjennis*); 104-10079-10014 with 104-1061-10115; *157-10005-10125 (Sturgis deposition).

AMPACK-1: Carlos Tepedino (**AMWHIP-1**) was a contact of Andrew Merton (Jack Stewart) in Havana through **AMPACK-1**; 104-10215-10106.

AMPALM-1: Oscar Echevarria y Salvat, 201-263473; circa 1960, **AMPALM-1** case office was Edward D. Knapman*; 104-10271-10039; *104-10164-10201.

AMPALM-2: Laureano Batista Falla, 201-268277; 12/13/59 operational approval request to use **AMPALM-2** through **AMCRACKLE** in PP operation publishing attacks on communism in Cuba, and to be handled directly by station for FI purposes*;104-10271-10039; *104-10164-10030.

AMPALM-3: Roberto Ortiz Batista Falla, 201-268277; 104-10271-10039.

SELECTED CIA CRYPTONYMS

AMPALM-4: Angel Fernandez Varela, 201-273100; 104-10271-10039; 104-10061-10115, 104-10308-10113, 104-10229-10340.

AMPALM-5: Jose Ignacio Augusto Rasco y Bermudez, 201-274330; 104-10271-10039.

AMPALM-6: Maria Rafael Calleja y Morales Lopez, 201-273312; also a member of **QDCOVE** group*; 104-10271-10039; *104-10192-10158.

AMPALM-7: Ramon Dominguez y Sanchez, 201-274066; 104-10271-10039.

AMPALM-8: Alberto Francisco Hildalgo Garcia, 201-274067; 104-10271-10039.

AMPALM-9: Otto Ernesto Lanz Ruano, 201-274068; 104-10271-10039.

AMPALM-10: Angel Sebastian Ros Escala, 201-271573; also a member of **QDCOVE** group*; 104-10271-10039; *104-10192-10158.

AMPALM-11: Fernando de Jesus Figuerdo Clarens; 104-10271-10039.

AMPAN-1: In 3/60 **AMPAN-1's** brother works in Castro's office and reports on June Cobb; Olien (Jim Noel) handles **AMPAN-1** in 3/61; 11/60 **AMPAN-**1 is giving a lot of weapons to several anti-Castro groups; associated with Operation Unity and **AMCHIRP-1**; accompanied Peter N. Licari to meet **AMHAWK** (Antonio Varona) on 12/29/59*; 11/4/60 **AMIRE-1** was **AMPAN-1** cutout to Havana Station, 104-10180-10188**; 11/23/60, Havana Station aware that **AMRUNG-1** appointed **AMPAN-1** as chief of action and sabotage for Havana area and provide him with plastic, 104-10265-10060***; Havana Station attempting to develop sea or air exfiltration capability through **AMPAN-1******; 3/1/61, George D. Scorgory was case officer for **AMPAN-1** and **AMIRE-1*******; 104-10177, 104-10180-10176; *104-10174-10049; **104-10177-10158; ***104-10180-10176; ****104-10162-10193; *****104-10180-10176 and 104-10180-10177.

AMPAN-2: 6/17/60, **AMPALP-1**, **AMIRE-1**, and **AMPAN-2** are three net chiefs in stay behind plan in Havana, 104-10180-10140; in October 1963, when **AMFAUNA-14** was interrogated by the DSE, she "deliberately protected" the address for the home of **AMPAN-2**, "not knowing whether this was a real or a factitious person, 104-10073-10101.

AMPAN-4: **AMPAN** boat, 104-10193-10321; 12/8/60, **AMPAN-4** ship, 104-10274-10020; Manuel Ray arrived in Florida via **AMPAN-4** boat on or about 11/10/60, 104-10274-10172.

AMPANIC-14: Juan de Jesus Arbelo Zabaleta, 104-10061-10115.

AMPARCH-1: Probably Edward D. Knapman—was exfiltrated from Cuba on 6/8/61 with Tony Sforza (**AMRYE-1**)*, both had been stay-behind agents; both went on to work in the FI branch at **JMWAVE**, where Knapman was the chief** and Sloman (Sforza) worked for him***; in 12/60 in Cuba, **AMBRILL-1** was a source of Kanpman's****;*104-10180-10134; **104-10231-10102; ***104-10231-10246; ****104-10169-10270

AMPATRIN-1: Jack Malone; a CIA Havana source and close associate of **AMDENIM-1** (Alberto Fernandez)*; Jack Malone was the general manager of Robert Kleberg's King Ranch in Cuba**; *104-10172-10425; **104-10172-10152.

AMPOON-1: Manuel Vega Perez, aka "Marcos," diplomatic attaché to the Cuban Embassy in Mexico City; 104-10276-10072 with Reel 17 Folder Q, and also with 104-10276-10010; 104-10276-10220; 104-10276-10003.

AMQUACK-1: Che Guevara, killed in Bolivia in 1967; in 1965 Victor Espinosa told the FBI he learned of a plot to assassinate Fidel Castro, his brother **AMLOUT-1**, and Che Guevara **AMQUACK-1***; 104-10308-10005, 104-10308-10046; *104-10103-10327.

AMRIPE-2: Jose (pseudonym); 104-10077-10045.

AMQUIP-1: possibly Vidal (fnu), **AMWAIL-3** went to Venezuela in 3/30 to recruit him; 104-10162-10042.

AMROD: CIA operations against the Cuban intelligence service. One such operation involved planting false papers on Cuban cultural attaché Teresa Proenza, to make it look like the Vice-Minister of Defense had betrayed the Soviet missile buildup in Cuba to the Americans; 104-10052-10208, 104-10065-10174; 1993.07.19.18:07:44:460150; 104-10513-10091.

AMRUNG/AMYUM complex: Stanley Zamka (David Morales) works the complex inside Cuba and Bender (Droller) works the complex outside of Cuba; 104-10193-10367.

AMRUNG-1: Rogelio Gonzalez y Corzo*; pseudonym "Francisco,"**; *104-10296-10001; *104-10240-10154.

AMRYE-1: Tony Sforza, aka Henry J. Sloman; was exfiltrated from Cuba on 6/8/61*, had been stay-behind agent in Cuba, went on to work in the FI branch at **JMWAVE**, where Edward D. Knapman was the chief** and Sloman (Sforza) worked for him***; *104-10180-10134; **104-10231-10102; ***104-10231-10246; (see Chapter Twenty and Chapter Twenty Two of this book).

AMSAIL-1: Carlos Fernandez Trujillio, head of CRC Mexico City Delegation, **AMSUPER -1**, Dimas Figuerdo, works for **AMSAIL-1***; Met Bernard Barker 17 July 1963, 104-10052-10130; associated with or might be identical with **AMCHEER-22**, 104-10297-10037; 7 April 1961 reported on **AMLEO-3**, Jose Ricardo Rabel Nunez, 104-10290-10442; 5/13/63 **AMSAIL-1** is principal link to all Cuban refugees in Mexico, handling debriefings, dispersing funds, and mailing propaganda to Cuba [see Trouchard in **JMWAVE** PW: 104-10245-10062], good prospect for penetration of Cuban Embassy; **AMSUPER-1** one works with **AMSAIL-1** in Mexico City, 104-10512-10025; becomes **LICOMET-1** In Mexico City by

March 1965, 104-10217-10169; Jack Stewart (Merton) may be case office in March 1962, 104-10229-10375; *104-10512-10026, 104-10512-10025, and 104-10245-10062.

AMSHALE-1: Antonio Veciana Blanch, 201-312966; 104-10181-10192; 104-10102-10176.

AMSIGH-2: Mente; 104-10077-10045.

AMSLAW-1: Pedro Julio Martinez Fraga y Fernandez; 104-10061-10115.

AMSMILE-1: In discussion 6/10/64 with Sidney P. Di Ubaldo, described as anti-**AMBANG-1** (Manuel Ray); 104-10274-10274.

AMSPORT-1: Marcelo Artime; 104-10215-10190 with 104-10215-10185.

AMSTOW-1: Filipe, the principal agent of the **AMRYE-1** (Sforza) net in 6/61, made arrangements to exfiltrate **AMCONCERT-1** ("Pancho" Varona); 104-10267-10104; 104-10267-10099.

AMSTRUT: The operation and net of assets involved in the defection and recruitment of **AMSTRUT-2** and, subsequently, her anti-Castro radio broadcasts; 104-10065-10102.

AMSTRUT-1: Virginia Vasco Leitao da Cunha, in 1961 wife of Brazilian ambassador to Cuba*; made first approach to Juanita Castro, **AMSTRUT-2****; *104-10295-10008 with August 62 entry in 104-10215-10235; ** Juanita Castro, *Fidel and Raul—My Brothers.*

AMSTRUT-2: Juanita, "Juana," Castro, sister of Fidel Castro*; approached by Virginia Vasco Leitao soon after Bay of Pigs and recruited by Tony Sforza circa 6/25/61 in Mexico City**; safehouse for **AMSTRUT-2** in Mexico City for debriefings by **JMWAVE** officers***; CIA Mexico Station phone taps on **AMSTRUT-2** family members living in Mexico City****; **AMSTRUT-2** radio program criticizing her brother Fidel re 1966 trial of

SELECTED CIA CRYPTONYMS

Cubela*****; **AMSTRUT-2** payments to ALPHA-66 in August and September 1969******; *1993-.07.22.09:37:48:180620 (name Juana Castro compromised by marginalia, compare to identical cable in 104-10104-10042, in which same space in text is **AMSTRUT-2**, and name Juana Castro compromised on RIF sheet; **Juanita Castro, *Fidel and Raul—My Brothers*; ***104-10414-10402; ****104-10188-10043; *****104-10234-10147; ******1993-.07.22.09:37:48:180620 with 104-10104-10042.

AMSUPER-1: Dimas Figueredo: see **AMSAIL-1**.

AMTHUG-1: Fidel Castro; 104-10179-10235; 104-10076-10087; 104-10308-10004.

AMSTUFF-1: associated with **AMSTOW** and **AMTURVY**; 104-10267-10104.

AMTIKI-1: Juan A. Paula Baez; 104-10061-10115; worked with **AMBUD** (CRC) finances, and appeared in JMWAVE PW (psych warfare) traffic and WH/4/PA memoranda*; 104-10235-10120; *104-10231-10228 and 104-10227-10358.

AMTOPIC-2: Luis Fernandez Rocha; used to be **AMHINT-53**; 104-10213-10085.

AMTRUNK: Operation for military overthrow of Castro's government in 1963, aka Plan Leonardo, promoted within White House circles but distrusted by CIA. Aka "Plan Leonardo"; 104-10213-10262.

AMTRUNK-1: Jorge Volsky; 104-10102-10229; 104-10102-10226.

AMTRUNK-2: Possibly Enrique Cayado Rivera; see 104-10247-10342.

AMTRUNK-3: Possibly Antonio Garcia Perez, see 104-10247-10342

AMTRUNK-9: Modesto Orlando Orozco Basulto; 104-10102-10226.

AMTRUNK-10: Ramon Thomas Guin Diaz; recruited by **AMICE 27***; 104-10102-10226; *104-10103-10112.

AMTRUNK-11: Carlos Predaza Aguilar; 104-10102-10226.

AMTRUNK associated cryptonyms:

- **AMICE-14:** Miguel A. Diaz Isalgue; Harold Noemayr as "Roger Fox" is case officer for Isalgue*; 104-10102-10266; *104-10183-10372.
- **AMICE-27:** Nestor Antonio Moreno Lopez, 201-312091; 104-10102-10232.
- **AMLEO-3:** 104-10102-10226
- **AMCAPE-1:** Tad Szulc; 104-10102-10226.

AMTURVY: An operation "designed for the purpose of conducting sabotage operations against Cuba. It consisted of a net of 13 **AMTURVY** assets whose primary function, apart from sabotage, was the preparation of target studies and analysis of sabotage operations"; 104-10506-10031.

- **AMCROAK-1:** Bernardo Milanes Lopez, 201-738660, Castro's mother's doctor, recruited by Tony Sforza in Madrid in 1963,* and was part of "Operation Raphael," a plot to assassinate Fidel, Raul, and Che; part of the **AMTURVY** net; 104-10308-10020, 104-10308-10021; 104-10308-10325; 104-10308-10326; 104-10506-10031; *104-10076-10042.

AMTURY-1: Alturo Maria Jesus Varona; 104-10267-10104; 04-10506-10030; 104-10506-10031.

AMTURVY-4: Enrique Diaz Fernandez; 104-10267-10104; 104-10506-10030; 104-10506-10031.

AMTURVY-13: Mario Salabaria Aguiar, brother of Julio Salabarria, Mario is the key figure in Operation or "Plan" [or Operation] Rapahel,

SELECTED CIA CRYPTONYMS

a plot to assassinate Castro; 104-10506-10030; 104-10506-10031 [10030 has the clearest marginalia: "WHAT WAS OPERATION RAPHAEL?"; see also Esterline 6/18/1969 memo, 104-10109-10162.

AMUPAS-1: Viola June Cobb, a CIA FI asset* in Cuba and the U.S; her crypt was changed to **LICOOKY-1** in Mexico City**; Tom Hazlett, aka Shryock, aka Bill Mannix is Cobb's case office in Mexico City***; *104-10218-10163; 104-10218-10185; 104-10174-10123; **104-10175-10117; ***104-10175-10428 and 104-10266-10024.

AMWAIL-1: Justo Carrillo Hernandez, leader of Agrupacion Montecristi and a founding member of the Frente Civico Revolucionario (FRD), forerunner of the CRC; 104-10103-10158; 104-10168-10054; 104-10240-10164.

AMWARBLE: Possibly Andres Diaz Rojas; June 1959, the CIA Station in El Salvador dispatched a list of ten documents and news clippings concerning communist activities to HQS for delivery to Pedro Diaz Lanz and Andres Diaz Lanz in Cuba; 104-10167-10297.

AMWORM-1: Marginalia possibly compromises a part—"Cuco" de Leon"* of a true name, Miguel Angel Leon aka "Cuco"; possibly associated with **AMWHIP-1, AMLASH-2** and **AMWORLD****; *104-10216-10355; **104-10216-10356.

AMWHIP-1: Carlos Tepedino Gonzalez, born Carlos Lopez Gonzalez*, recruited by Jack Stewart (Merton) in Havana and very close friend of to Cubela and financial backer of the Directorio Revolucionario (DR) in 1957-1958**, arranged the March 1961 meeting between Andrew Merton (Jack Stewart) and Cubela***; helped Tony Sforza and Richard Fallucci recruit Cubela in Helsinki and Paris in July-August 1962****; *104-10247-10198 (PRQ-I); **104-10215-10107 and 104-10183-10424; ***104-10215-10122; ****104-10295-10016 and 104-10102-10050.

QDBIAS: Pedro Diaz Lanz; 104-10061-10115; 104-10260-10168; 104-10260-10178.

QDCHAR: Marcos Diaz Lanz (Pedro's brother); 104-10177-10039; 104-10260 10061.

QDDALE: William Pawley; 104-10061-10115; 104-10265-10299.

QDCOVE: Possibly Ricardo Lorie*; had a radio show which part of Phillips' group of propaganda radio broadcasts were targeting Cuba; Ricardo Lorie had a program**; associated with Artime MRR activities in Cuba during 1960***; *104-10260-10122; **104-10193-10095; ***104-10162-10234.

CITASTE: Allen Dulles, aka "Ascham"*; *104-10310-10001; 104-10049-10323; 104-10315-10036; 104-10315-10037; 104-10177-10113.

APPENDIX TWO:
SELECTED CIA PSEUDONYMS

MANUEL ARTIME

- JAVIER 104-10193-10382
- MR. IGNACIO 104-10240-10314

BERNARD BARKER

- SPENCER O. TERTELING, 104-10194-10059

TRACY BARNES

- PLAYDON [SEE HSCA NAMES LIST 104-10061-10115]

RICHARD BISSELL:

- JOHN L. KANE; 104-10185-10384, 104-10185-10060

WHERE ANGELS TREAD LIGHTLY

JUNE COBB:

- JOYCE H. PINEINCH; 104-10175-10117
- CLARINDA E. SHARP; 104-10175-10365

COL. AL COX:

- ROBERT REYNOLDS [SEE APPENDIX SIX]
- ROBERT ROGERS, 104-10261-10017
- [POSSIBLY PAUL J. MANSON (CH MASH/WAVE) SEE WEYDEN P. 290 AND MANSON DOCS: 104-10240-10164 [1/28/60], AND [PROBABLY] MANSON INITIALS ON DISPATCH SIGNED BY CORBUSTON: 104-1016510344 [4/27/61], AND CORBUSTON BOTTOM RIGHT AND MANSON BOTTOM LEFT ON WAVE 6194, 5/12/61: 104-10231-10369]
- VINCENT IS C/O PSEUDO OF MANSON FOR USE WITH MANOLO RAY: 104-10179-10075

KEN M. CROSBY [Seymour Hersh, *The Dark Side of Camelot*, 1998 ed., pp. 161-162]:

- PATRICK I. KARNLEY ["FREDDIE" TO ARTIME DURING EXFIL]: 104-10240-10358]: 104-10110-10213, 104-10110-10206, 104-10061-10115
- BERNANRD REICHARDT: 104-10061-10115

ROSS LESTER CROZIER:

- RON CROSS; 104-10143-10180
- ARTHUR G VAIVIDA #112569 SAME AS ROSS CROZIER; 104-10114-10070 AND 1993.08.10.16:29:28:780038
- HAROLD R. NOEMAYR; 104-10114-10007 (ALSO #112569)
- ROGER FOX; 104-10181-10325

SELECTED CIA PSEUDONYMS

NORRIS W. DAMICONE:

- [POSSIBLY:] AL MARIN; 104-10183-10437 WITH 104-10183-10439

LAWRENCE DEVLIN, CONGO, LEOPOLDVILLE STATION CHIEF:

- VICTOR S. HEDGMAN; 157-10014-10080
- GUTHMAN; 104-10185-10057; 104-10185-10058
- [PROBABLY:] WALTER D. HESTON; 104-10182-10194

GERARD DROLLER:

- FRANK BENDER; 104-10193-10351
- WALLACE A. PARLETT; 104-10160-10195; 104-10271-10158
- DRECHER (HUNT: *GIVE US THIS DAY*, P. 24)

RAY DUBOIS AKA WIESINGER:

- RAY ADAMS; 104-10296-10062; 104-10165-10039
- CHARLES B. WIESINGER; 104-10296-10062

ALLEN DULLES:

- ASCHAM; 104-10310-10001; **CITASTE**: 104-10049-10323; 104-10315-10036; 104-10315-10037; 104-10177-10113 [NOTE: THE DIGRAPH CI IS A "PROBABLE"]

ANN ELIZABETH GOLDSBOROUGH EGERTER

- BETTY EGGETER; 104-10015-10043; 104-10322-10043; 104-10015-10042
- SUSAN PURCELL; 180-10131-10333 AND 104-10246-10017 (BETSY WOLF WRITE-UP OF INTERVIEW WITH SUSAN PURCELL)

WHERE ANGELS TREAD LIGHTLY

JAKE ESTERLINE:

- ANTHONY R. PONCHAY; 104-10109-10162
- JACOB ENGLAND; 104-10220-10017

DELIA FAILDE:

- "DRAGON LADY"; 104-10162-10197
- [POSSIBLY:] CATHERINE TAAFFE—BOTH NAMES MAY BE PSEUDONYMS—SEE CHAPTER 19 FOR A DISCUSSION OF THE POSSIBLE CONNECTION BETWEEN THESE TWO WOMEN

RICHARD M. FALLUCCI (TFW/FI)

- WILLIAM "BILL" THOMPSON, AND "HARVEY" THOMPSON; SEE 104-10215-10080 (THE REDACTOR FORGOT TO REMOVE FALLUCCI'S NAME FROM THE RIF SHEET] 104-10102-10010 AND 104-10102-10050, AND 104-10183-10064
- AMWHIP WILL CONTINUE TO WRITE TO "ALIAS THOMPSON AND TO PHONE ME ALIAS BREITHEIM ON **737-8294**," 104-10183-10048; ALFREDO "ALFRED" FERNANDEZ, HAS WASHINGTON, D. C. PHONE NUMBER **737-8294**, 104-10275-10176;

[THE POSSIBILITY THAT FALLUCCI IS, OR, WORKS WITH, SIDNEY P. DI UBALDO:]

- SIDNEY P. DI UBALDO IS AKA JOHN BREITHEIM: MET AMSMILE-1 6/10/64, 104-10274-10274; MEETING WITH AMWHIP-1 5/21/65; RE AMBUNNY: 104-10183-10439;
- [POSSIBLY ALSO:] MR. WILLS; 104-10183-10413 (IGLESIAS WANTS TO SEE HIM IN MADRID)

SELECTED CIA PSEUDONYMS

DESMOND FITZGERALD:

- JAMES CLARK—AS A REP OF GPFOCUS; 104-10521-10019; 104-10102-10010
- CHESTER D. DAINOLD 104-10195-10142; 104-10182-10034

CARLOS LOPEZ GONZALEZ:

- CARLOS TEPEDINO GONZALEZ (LEGAL NAME CHANGE); 104-10247-10198
- "FRANCISCO"; 104-10183-10413

DAVID U. GROVES:

- DOUGLAS J. FREAPANE; 104-10128-10329

WILLIAM K. HARVEY: [#32814: RIF 1993.07.20.14:27:51:590280, WILLIAM KING HARVEY—OS/SAG FILES FOR HSCA STAFF; HARVEY, W.K. SECURITY FILES]

- WILLIAM WALKER, #32814, ALIAS ISSUED MAY 62 USED UNTIL REASSIGBNED JUNE 1963; 104-01310-10013
- DANIEL M. PRESLAND; 104-10298-10045, 104-10274-10121

THOMAS J. HAZLETT: [104-10266-10155] [CHIEF CUBAN OPS MEXICO CITY STATION 56-4/62, 104-10086-10394] [C/O FOR JUNE COBB, 104-10266-10022]

- CLYDE K. SHRYOCK; 104-10175-10428
- BILL MANNIX; 104-10266-10024

WHERE ANGELS TREAD LIGHTLY

HENRY HECKSHER:

- NELSON RAYNOCK; 104-10241-10131 [HECKSHER IS ARTIME'S COLE AMERICAN CONTACT]; 104-10240-10320 [ARTIME CASE OFFICER IS NELSON RAYNOCK]
- HENRY BOYSEN; 104-10241-10184
- JAMES E. BECKHOFF; 104-10101-10066, 104-10211-10346

RICHARD HELMS:

- THOMAS LUND; 104-10088-10058
- KNIGHT

E. HOWARD HUNT: (SEE APPENDIX FIVE FOR DOCUMENTS AND RIF NUMBERS)

- EDWARD J. HAMILTON (ALSO EDUARDO AND EDWARDO)
- WALTER C. TWICKER
- TERRENCE C. CRABANAC

GEORGE E. JOANNIDES:

- WALTER D. NEWBY; 104-10304-10000

COLONEL WENDELL G. JOHNSON:

- T. F. PASSAVOY; 104-10227-10145; 104-10232-10003; 104-10227-10143; 104-10227-10345]

WILLIAM M. KENT: 104-10303-10003, 104-10163-10181; (WILLIAM KENT NAME COMPROMISED IN ORRISON AFFAIR: 104-10414-10124, P. 345)

- ROBERT K. TROUCHARD; TROUCHARD IS CASE OFFICER FOR CONTE AGUERO: 104-10244-10018

SELECTED CIA PSEUDONYMS

- OLIVER H. CORBUSTON; CORBUSTON = GUPTON AND FORMS DRE IN 1960: 104-10181-10325
- DOUGLAS GUPTON AKA GEORGE WITNER; 104-10406-10273; KENT = GUPTON = WITNER: 104-10140-10325

OTHER FACTORS IN THE CASE FOR CORBUSTON/GUPTON/TROUCHARD = KENT:

- THE CORBUSTON/GUPTON/TROUCHARD/KENT FILES END IN AUGUST 1961—THE EXACT POINT IN TIME WHERE THE TROUCHARD FILES BEGIN
- TROUCHARD WAS A FORMER CASE OFFICER FOR BERNARD BARKER; DURING THE SUMMER OF 1960 BARKER WAS HIRED AND SENT TO JMWAVE TO TAKE THE LOAD OFF WILLIAM KENT (104-10163-10181)
- THE GROUP OF THE DRE THAT FLED TO MIAMI IN THE FALL OF 1960 WAS HANDLED AND ORGANIZED INTO A UNILATERAL ASSET OF THE JMWAVE STATION BY CORBUSTON/GUPTON/KENT
- WHILE THE JMWAVE FILES DURING TROUCHARD'S ASSIGNMENT THERE NEVER MENTION KENT'S NAME IN THE CLEAR, KENT'S INTELLIGENCE MEDAL WRITE-UP BETRAYS HIS ASSIGNMENT AT JMWAVE AND QUOTES A FITNESS REPORTS THAT MATCHES TROUCHARD'S FITNESS REPORTS—ESPECIALLY HOW HE "SHONE" WITH HIS ABILITY TO RESOLVE DIFFICULT PROBLEMS HANDLING PARTICULARLY UNRULY AND INCOMPATIBLE GROUPS, "ACCOMPLISHING THE IMPOSSIBLE BY SATISFYING EVERYBODY CONCERNED."

J. C. KING:

- OLIVER G. GALBOND; 104-10218-10153; 104-10061-10115

WHERE ANGELS TREAD LIGHTLY

WARREN E. FRANK: (See 104-10103-10024)

- WALTER H. GEBAIDE; 104-10271-10039, 104-10164-10201, 104-10164-10198 and 104-10271-10039 (MRR and AMPALM C/O)
- EDWARD D. KNAPMAN; 104-10164-10198 and 104-10065-10359 (handwriting);
- FRANK BOOTH; 104-10171-10401
- JOE CRESPI; 104-10166-10440

MARCOS DIAZ LANZ:

- MARIANO JIMENEZ Y GOMEZ; (180-10144-10222)

ELVIO RIVERO LIMONTE:

- SANTIAGO SANZ; 104-10171-10401

HENRY PRESETON LOPEZ:

- EDWARD TICHBORN; 104-10119-10229; 1993.08.03.18:55:08:960027 (p. 258 of 316)
- FRED MORSE; 104-10174-10036

MIGUEL ANGEL LEON

- CUCO; 104-10267-10104 (SEE SLOMAN COMMENT); 104-10216-10352; 104-10076-10088
- DOMINGO BELTRAND; 104-10267-10099

ELOY GUTTIEREZ MENOYO:

- LAZARO CRISTOBAL FLORIAN MARTINEZ MENDEZ; 124-90135-10190

SELECTED CIA PSEUDONYMS

DAVID SANCHEZ MORALES ("EL INDIO"):

- STANLEY R. ZAMKA, AKA DELGADO; 104-10261-10040
- DR. GONZALES; 180-10142-10307

LEE R. MYLCHRAINE (POSSIBLY):

- GERALD N. ASKREN; 104-10246-10021; TDY MEXI, RTN HQS 5/8/64

JORGE NOBREGAS HERIA:

- COCO; 104-10267-10099

JAMES (JIM) NOEL:

- WOODROW C. OLIEN; 104-10167-10383
- JIM NOBLE: PETER WYDEN, *BAY OF PIGS* (114-116)

JUSTIN O'DONNEL:

- OLIVER B. ALTMAN: 104-10310-10215
- MICHAEL J. MULRONEY: *Alleged Assassination Plots Involving Foreign Leaders*, United States Senate, Interim Report of the Select Committee to Study Governmental Operations (Washington DC: US Government Printing Office, 1975), pp. 32-45.

MANUEL VEGA PEREZ:

- MARCOS; 104-10276-10220; 104-10276-10003

DAVID A. PHILLIPS:

- MICHAEL M. CHOADEN; 104-10128-10329
- KNIGHT [*GIVE US THIS DAY*]

- "DOUGLAS" NAME FOR PHILLIPS USED BY LUIS CONTE AGUERO FOR MICHAEL C. CHOADEN, SEE 104-10166-10440 (10/31/67); ALSO RE AMIGGY-1, C/O CAN ESTABLISH BONA FIDES BY IDENTIFYING SELF AS "MIGUEL" AND SAYING HE FRIEND OF "DOUGLAS," SEE 104-10231-10224 (3/2/61)
- BOB LEE, AND ROBERTO (104-10072-10234, WHEN PITCHING AMSESS ON 9/24/64)
- JOHN D. NADLEMAN (1954-1955: PP/OPS STAFF, PP/INFO COORD DIV, PP/CRTV) 104-10128-10086; 104-10128-10120; 104-10136-10358
- [POSSIBLY:] NEIL T. PICKWORTH, INTERVIEWED AND ASSESSED AMCORE-2—CONTE AGUERO—ON HIS ARRIVAL IN MAY 1960; AMCORE-2 KNOWS PREVIOUS CONTACT OF MICHAEL CHOADEN AS "DONALD BARTON" AND JOHN P. HASSELLSTROM AS "FRED MARTINS", AND KNOWS BINAURAL AS "RICHARDO BOLFORT" AND WILLIAM S. WIBALDA UNDER TRUE NAME; 104-10244-10018; SEE NEIL T. PICKWORTH MEMO ON DRE: 104-10171-10033

NESTOR SANCHEZ:

- MATTHEW H. ONTRICH [C/O FOR AMLASH]; COMPARE 104-10215-10241 TO P. 87 OF 104-10057-10270, SEE ALSO 104-10215-10238
- NICHOLAS SANSON, THIS PSEUDO IS KNOWN TO AMWHIP (CARLOS TEPEDIN0), IN PARIS 63-64; 104-10521-10019

WINSTON SCOTT (MEXICO CITY STATION CHIEF)

- WILLARD C. CURTIS (SEE JEFFERSON MORELY, *OUR MAN IN MEXICO*)

COLONEL SEVERS:

- COLONEL ERIKSON S. NICHOLS, AMERICAN AIR ATTACHE IN U.S. EMBASSY HAVANA; 104-10167-10057

SELECTED CIA PSEUDONYMS

ANTHONY L. SILEO (ASSISTANT ATTACHE U.S. EMB HAVANA IN 1958)

- GEORGE D. SCORGORY: HE AND OLIEN MET AND TALKED WITH AMLASH-3 ABOUT CUBELA'S PLAN TO ASSASSINATE CASTRO: 4/13/66 CIA BACKGROUND REPORT ON CUBELA, 104-10102-10010; (ALBERTA BLANCAS RAMIREZ IN MADRID ON 9/15/64 104-10183-10187. THE DAY AFTER THAT MEETING, MADRID STATION SENT A CABLE (1705) TO HQS AND WAVE SAYING THAT OLIEN AND SCORGORY HAD MET AMLASH-3 ON 9/15/64 AND DISCUSSED THE AMLASH-1 PLAN TO ASSASSINATE AMTHUG, 104-10234-10428; A DIFFERENT CIA REPORT OF THE 9/15/64 MEETING WITH ALBERTO BLANCO RAMIREZ SAYS THE TWO WERE [JAMES NOEL] AND ANTHONY SILEO: THEREFORE SILEO MUST BE SCORGORY 104-10103-10187 [AND OLIEN WE KNOW FROM ELSEWHERE IS JAMES NOEL]
- ANDRES SANDERS: THE DAY BEFORE THAT 9/15/64 MEETING, SCORGORY, USING THE ALIAS ANDRES SANDERS, TALKED WITH AMLASH-3 (MADRID 1681), 104-10183-10187

ANTHONY SFORZA:

- ENRIQUE; 104-10295-10016 AND 104-10109-10162 AND 104-10113-10070; [HID IN HOME 18-21 APR 61: 104-10183-10073 AND 104-10295-10016]
- HENRY J. SLOMAN, AKA ENRIQUE [BEST COPY IS 104-10295-10016; 104-10183-10065]
- FRANK STEVENS (AND ENRIQUE): 104-10109-10162
- ALFRED SARNO; 6/25/75 DEPOSITION: 157-10005-10250

JACK STEWART:

- ANDREW F. MERTON; 124-10290—10098 AND 124-10290-10100; 104-10295-10016; 104-10183-10085; 104-10215-10103
- JACK STEWART AKA JACK WARREN: 104-10183-10424; 104-10127-10207; 104-10171-10118.

WHERE ANGELS TREAD LIGHTLY

HAROLD SWENSON: [104-10131-10005]

- HAROLD SAFELY; 104-10216-10413, 104-10183-10428
- PHILLIP TOOMEY:
- "THOMPSON"; 104-10265-10128

EARL WILLIAMSON (MADRID A/COS BY 12/31/64: MADR 2694, 104-10216-10236) [SEE APPENDIX FOUR]

- WALLACE A GROWERY AND **"JAIME"**: 10/23/62 MET WITH AMWHIP IN NYC: AMLASH-1 HAD NOT PROVIDED AN ADDRESS AT WHICH HE WAS TO RECEIVE MAIL FROM **"JAIME"** (EARL WILLIAMS 104-10215-10343; [SAME DOC:] AMWHIP-1 TALKED WITH WILLIAMSON LAST AUGUST: 104-10215-10343; **"JAIME"** IS IDENTIFIED AS WALLACE GROWERY IN FALLUCCI'S SUMMARY OF CONTACTS WITH CUBELA—THE REASON CUBELA AND TEPEDINO USED THE NAME **"JAIME"** WAS BECAUSE THEY COULD NOT PRONOUNCE WILLIAMSON'S TRUE FIRST NAME (EARL): 104-10102-10050
- ALFONSO RODRIGUEZ AND ALFREDO FERNANDEZ: IN CUBA DURING THE LATE 1950S, MANUEL RAY KNEW RODRIGUEZ AS ALFREDO FERNANDEZ BUT USED HIS TRUE NAME RODRIGUEZ IN ALL OF THEIR PERSONAL MEETINGS, AND RAY RECOGNIZED AND REMEMBERED "HAVING MET [REDACTED NAME] (THE TEXT INDICATES THIS PERSON'S PSEUDONYM WAS GROWERY] IN CUBA YEARS AGO"; THE NAME EARL WILLIAMSON FITS PERFECTLY IN THE SPACE: 104-10179-10135; WILLIAMSON WAS STILL USING THE ALFREDO FERNANDEZ PSEUDONYM WHEN MEETING WITH MANUEL RAY IN NYC 20-22 JULY 1962: 104-10274-10194.
- FOR SIGNATURE OF WALLACE A. GROWERY ON 8/15/57, HAVANA STATION, VARONA PRQ-II, SEE 104-10261-10024
- EARL WILLIAMSON WAS DCOS, HAVANA STATION—FIRED BY AMBASSADOR SMITH; *WINDS OF DECEMBER*: A BILL

SELECTED CIA PSEUDONYMS

WILLIAMSON WAS DEPUTY COS IN HAVANA. WILLIAMSON HAD BEEN EXTREMELY CLOSE TO THE PLOTTERS OF THE 9/5/57 NAVAL UPRISING AT CIENFUEGOS, AND HAD BEEN TRANSFERRED OUT OF CUBA A FEW MONTHS BEFORE THE END OF 1958. SIMILARLY, HUGH THOMAS (***CUBA—THE PURSUIT OF FREEDOM***, P. 961) IDENTIFIES THE CIA DCOS AS "WILLIAM WILLIAMSON," WHO "HAD TOLD THE CONSPIRATORS THAT ANY GOVERNMENT SET UP AS A RESULT OF A SUCCESSFUL UPRISING WOULD BE RECOGNIZED BY THE U.S. (P. 961). MANOLO RAY'S CIA CRYPTONYM WAS AMBANG. THE 5/29/59 CIA PRQ-II ON HIM CONFIRMS THAT GROWERY WAS PRESENT AT ALL THREE MEETINGS BETWEEN RAY AND THE CIA STATION. AT THAT TIME RAY WAS THE HEAD OF UNDERGROUND IN HAVANA. IT IS POSSIBLE THAT WILLIAMSON CHANGED HIS FIST NAME FROM EARL TO WILLIAM FOR HIS MISSION IN CUBA.

- ALFONSO RODRIGUEZ; AKA ALFREDO FERNANDEZ WHEN MEETING WITH MANUEL RAY—104-10179-10135; AKA ALFONSO FERNANDEZ WHEN MEETING WITH ELVIO RIVERO LIMONTE—104 10171-10401; SEE APPENDIX FOUR FOR MORE ON THE ALFONSO RODRIGUEZ PSEUDONYM

TRUE NAME UNKNOWN:

- PETER N. LICARI; SEE 104-10167-10018;"LICARI/BENDER" 05/26/60 MIAM 115 TO DIR CIA; 104-10260-10410: 3/17/60, HAVA 3782 TO DIR CIA; "TIME RIPE FOR RTN TRIP TO HAVA AS "REPRESENTATIVE OF THE GROUP" TO VARONA

TRUE NAME UNKNOWN: (SEE APPENDIX FIVE FOR DOCUMENTS AND RIF NUMBERS)

- SAMUEL G. ORRISON
- DUDLEY J. PACHUKE

AMLASH NET:

JORGE ROBRENO MARIEGES (AMLASH-2):

- "EL MAGO," 104-10234-10165

JOSE ALBERTO IBARRA MARTIN (AMLASH-3):

- ALBERTO BLANCO RAMIREZ; 104-10234-10344 AND 104-10234-10237 AND 104-10216-10113
- "EL LOCO" AND "EL LOCO BLANCO"; 104-10234-10344 AND 104-10234-10237

PARIS STATION

JOHN STENT (STATION CHIEF):

- "RED" STENT; 104-10216-10144
- PETER J. KYMINGHAM; 104-10120-10010; 104-10216-10144
- JOHN STEVENS; 104-10521-10019
- JACK STEVENS; 104-10102-10010
- [POSSIBLE:] PAUL K. STOCKWOOD; 104-10216-10035; 104-10215-10358 [STOCKWOOD MAY HAVE BEEN LATER PARIS COS]

ROBERT OWEN:

- "ROBERTO"; 104-10521-10019

RICHARD LONG:

- "DICK"; 104-10521-10019

APPENDIX THREE:
THE PSEUDONYMS OF TONY SFORZA

Pulling together the various pseudonyms for Tony Sforza can be done with eight sources: six CIA records, Sforza's deposition to the Church Committee, and the public records of Sforza.

The six CIA documents include two 1962 JMWAVE documents generated during the 1962 CIA attempt to defect Roland Cubela—one was information about Carlos Tepedino furnished by Francisco Wilfredo "Pancho" Varona Alonso (1), and the other was a cable from JMWAVE to CIA HQS about the Cubela defection story (2). The CIA documents also include three CIA memoranda from the 1969 fallout that resulted from the accusations Pancho made about "Frank" (Sforza) in the media; these three include one from Kane to the Station Chief in Miami, Jake Esterline, about the problem (3); another from Kane to CIA HQS, where there was apparently some difficulty figuring out who Frank really was (4); and, finally, Esterline's reply memo, after speaking with "Frank (Sforza)," to Kane (6). And, finally, this group of CIA records also includes a 1962 Task Force W memo about U.S. domestic alias documentation which has a CIA HQS security number for Frank Stevens in the clear (5).

Here are the citations for all eight sources:

(1) 6/17/62 JMWAVE bio sheet on Tepedino with a note at the bottom about Henry Sloman hiding in his home during the Bay of Pigs.[910]
(2) 7/8/62 JMWAVE cable to HQS CIA.[911]
(3) 6/11/69 Charles Kane memo to Esterline.[912]
(4) 6/11/69 Charles Kane memo to CIA HQS.[913]
(5) 7/20/62 Task for W memo.[914]
(6) 6/18/69 Jake Esterline memo to Charles Kane.[915]
(7) 6/25/75 Testimony of Sforza to the Church Committee.[916]
(8) Public records of Joseph Anthony Sforza from 1923 to 1985.[917]

LINKING HENRY SLOMAN TO FRANK STEVENS AND ENRIQUE

These three identities share the identical he "hid in his home" story. Henry Sloman hid in his home the night of the Bay of Pigs—sources (1) and (2). Frank Stevens, aka Enrique, did this too—source (6). When Sloman spoke with Tepedino on the phone he was introduced as Enrique—source (2).

---

910 6/17/62, JMWAVE "Biographical Data Sheet" on Carlos Tepedino based upon information from AMCONCERT-1 (Francisco Wilfredo "Pancho" Varona Alonso). RIF 104-10183-10073.
911 7/8/62 WAVE 5457 to DIR CIA. RIF 104-10295-10016.
912 6/11/69, Memorandum for Chief of Station, WH/Miami from Charles W. Kane, Special Agent in Charge. RIF 104-10113-10074.
913 6/11/69, Memorandum for CIA Headquarters, Subject: Security Support—Project [xx] NOM, #518 334, FSD/1, From Charles W. Kane, Special Agent in Charge, Miami Field Office. 104-10113-10070.
914 7/20/62, Memorandum for Chief TFW, From Deputy Director of Security (Investigations and Operation Support. RIF 104-10129-10032.
915 6/18/69, CIA Memorandum for Special Agent in Charge (Kane) from Chief of Station WH/Miami, Anthony R. Ponchay (Jake Esterline), RE: Charles Govea and Francisco Wilfredo "Pancho" Varona (Alonso). RIF 104-10109-10162.
916 6/25/75, Testimony of Alfred J. Sarno to the Senate Select Committee on Intelligence Activities (Church Committee). RIF 157-10005-10250.
917 In June 1951, the year that Sforza—according to his (using the Alias Alfred Sarno) deposition to the Church Committee —joined the CIA, Anthony Joseph Sforza (age 28), Maria Cynthia Berge de Sforza (age 26), Sandra Evelyn Sforza (age 4), and Diana Delores Sforza (age 10 months), arrived in New York City on the S.S. Uruguay from Buenos Aires, Argentina. Source: Ancestry.com public records.

LINKING TONY SFORZA TO FRANK STEVENS

First, Sforza and Frank had both served in Argentina—sources (3) and (8). Second, Sforza and Frank then both served in Cuba—sources (6) and (7). Third, Frank worked in the Cuban program at JMWAVE—sources (3), (6) and (7). Fourth, both Sforza and Frank were the subject of HQS security number 53472—sources (4) and (5).

```
                                        Miami Field Office
                                        11 June 1969

MEMORANDUM FOR: Headquarters
SUBJECT       : Security Support - Project[**]OM
                #518 334    F SD/1

    1. Enclosed herewith is a copy of a self-explanatory memorandum
to Chief of Station, WH/Miami dated 11 June 1969, and one copy each
of enclosures (a) and (b) mentioned in this memorandum.

    2. The person referred to as "Frank" in the enclosed memorandum
is understood to be the SUBJECT of Headquarters file #53 472.

    3. Other than to accept any information volunteered in the
future by Charles GOVEA and/or Francisco Wilfredo VARONA (Alonso),
this office intends to take no action in this matter.

                                        CHARLES W. KANE
                                        Special Agent in Charge

CC: Hdqs File #53 472
    Hdqs File on Francisco Wilfredo
                 VARONA (Alonso)

Enclosures:
    Memo to COS, WH/Miami dated 11 June 1969
    w/encs. (a) and (b)

                    CIA HISTORICAL REVIEW PROGRAM
                      RELEASE AS SANITIZED
                             1998
```

Kane Memo RE "Frank's) HQS number: #53 472; 6/11/69; 104-10113-10070.

WHERE ANGELS TREAD LIGHTLY

~~SECRET~~

**CIA HISTORICAL REVIEW PROGRAM
RELEASE AS SANITIZED
1998**

20 JUL 1962

21440
214442

MEMORANDUM FOR: Chief, TFW

ATTENTION: Mr. George Ladner, Security Officer, TFW
GH 5607

FROM: Deputy Director of Security (Investigations and Operational Support)

SUBJECT: ALIAS DOMESTIC DOCUMENTATION
[10] Driver's Permits)
[08]

1. Reference is made to your recent memo in which you requested numerous items of alias documentation for several TFW personnel. Among the documents requested were backstopped [10] Driver's Permits for four individuals.

2. Attached are the four [10] Driver's Permits for the designated individuals:

NAME	LICENSE NUMBER
[03]	[08]
SFORZA, Anthony	[08]
BELSITO, Frank J.	[08]
DUBOIS, Rene E.	[08]

3. In order for the Driver's Permits to be completely validated, they should be signed, of course in alias, in the designated space.

4. When these permits are no longer needed, they should be returned to this office for appropriate disposition.

5. No further action is contemplated by this office.

FOR THE DIRECTOR OF SECURITY:

cc - PSD 214 442 [03]
PSD 53472 (Sforza)
SSD 34551 (Belsito)
SSD 62319 (Dubois)

Attachment:
Four [10] Driver's Permits
PSD 214 442

Victor R. White

GIKAS/mg
20 July 1962
CLOSED

TFW Domestic Alias Memo: Sforza is 53472; 104-10129-10032.

NOTES:

- Source (5), the 20 July 1962 Task Force W memo, was about U.S. domestic alias documentation for four people. It was created at exactly the time that the 1962 Cubela defection operation was in play. The first name that is still withheld belongs to Emilio Americo Rodriguez (AMIRE-1).
- Information about Sforza's CIA cryptonym, AMRYE-1, is located in Appendix One, and will be more fully discussed in a future volume of this work.
- Sources (3) and (4) are memoranda written by Charles W. Kane, the Special Agent in Charge of the CIA Miami Field Office, and source (6) was a memorandum written by Anthony R. Ponchay, a pseudonym for Jake Esterline, Chief of Station, WH/Miami. All three memoranda were written in June 1969 in response to a media rant by Francisco Wilfredo "Pancho" Varona Alonso. Pancho had made several accusations against Tony Sforza.

APPENDIX FOUR:
EARL J. WILLIAMSON, WALLACE A. GROWERY, AND ALFONSO L. RODRIGUEZ

LINKING ALFONSO L. RODRIGUEZ TO WALLACE A. GROWERY

On 19 June 1963, Alfonso L. Rodriguez was working for Henry Hecksher in the Security Office in the SAS—the Special Affairs Staff, which handled the CIA's Cuban mission at that time. Rodriguez wrote a memorandum for record that day concerning Manuel (aka "Manolo") Ray Rivero.[918] Ray was a Cuban-born engineer best known for his May 1960 creation of the anti-Castro group called Revolutionary Movement of the People (MRP). From mid-1957 through 1958 he was the head of the

---

918 6/19/63, MFR by Alfonso Rodriguez, SAS/SO, Subject: Manolo Ray, RIF 104-10179-10135.

underground Civic Resistance Movement, which engaged in sabotage and propaganda activities against the Batista regime.[919]

At the end of his 6/19/63 memo, Alfonso Rodriguez revealed these details about how Ray had come to know his true identity:

> b. Ray has known me as *Alfredo Fernandez*, but because of operational limitations (false identity documents, reservations in true name) it became necessary for him to call me in my true name. He was not, however, told that this latter name was in fact true. In all our personal meetings he continued to call me "*Fernandez.*"
>
> c. Ray recognized and remembered having met [redacted: 7 or 8 letters]   [redacted: 10 letters] (*Growery*-P) in Cuba years ago. [Emphasis added]

In the first redacted space, either "William" or "Earl J." fits perfectly, and in the second redacted space "Williamson" fits perfectly. The last two lines of text suggest two things: first, "Growery" is a pseudonym for the author, Alfonso Rodriguez; and second, Alfonzo Rodriguez is also a pseudonym for the true name of the author that was hidden by the redactor.

We are looking for a CIA officer working in Cuba who was handling Manolo Ray in 1957-1958 and who had the pseudonym "Growery." On 29 May 1959, the CIA Havana Station chief, Jim Noel, using the pseudonym Woodrow C. Olien, forwarded the Personal Record Questionnaire (PRQ)-II for AMBANG—the CIA cryptonym for Manolo Ray.[920] The PRQ-II reveals that Noel had first met Ray in October 1958, when he was head of the Civic Resistance movement in Havana. It also reveals that Noel and Wallace A. Growery had three "clandestine" meetings with Ray before 1 January 1959, and that Growery and Sherwood P. Rochon had functioned as case officers for Ray. Rochon is either the true name or a pseudonym for the chief of station before Noel.

Ray was also a member of Castro's 26 July Movement,[921] and the Civic Resistance Movement had itself been created by the 26 July Movement

---

919   Hugh Thomas, ***Cuba, The Pursuit of Freedom*** (New York: Harper and Rowe, 1971) p. 945.
920   5/29/59, Havana Dispatch from COS Havana, Woodrow C. Olien, to Chief, WHD, Subject: AMBANG PRQ Part II. RIF 104-10179-10087.
921   Hugh Thomas, ***Cuba, The Pursuit of Freedom*** (New York: Harper and Rowe, 1971) p. 953.

to attract businessmen and professionals.[922] Ray met Castro personally for the first time in September 1958.[923] During the time of the three clandestine meetings with Noel and Growery, Ray returned to the Sierra Maestra to meet Castro again to discuss the latter's desire to dissolve the Civic Resistance Movement and incorporate it formally into the 26 July Movement.[924]

We know for certain that Growery was working with the Havana underground and the 26 July Movement for two consecutive Havana Station chiefs. From this much we can assume that Growery was probably a senior officer of the Havana Station.

---

[922] John Dorschner and Roberto Fabricio, *The Winds of December* (New York: Coward, McCann & Geoghegan, 1980), p. 132.
[923] Hugh Thomas, *Cuba, The Pursuit of Freedom* (New York: Harper and Rowe, 1971) pp. 1007-1008.
[924] 12/16/58, CIA HAVA 0693 to DIR CIA; RIF 104-10180-10062.

```
                    DESENSITIZED
                    SECRET

    PERSONAL RECORD QUESTIONNAIRE
    PART II - OPERATIONAL INFORMATION          169
                                               DISPATCH NO. HMM-A-5222
```

SECTION I — CONTACT AND DEVELOPMENT

1. INDICATE HOW, WHEN, WHERE, WHY, AND BY WHOM SUBJECT WAS FIRST CONTACTED OR DEVELOPED.

Woodrow C. Olien met Subject in October 1958 when the latter was head of the Civic Resistance Movement in Habana. Three clandestine meetings were held with Subject prior to 1 January 1959, which, in addition to Olien and Wallace A. Growery, were also attended by Ignacio Mendoza, a member of NRC (civic resistance) who originally introduced Subject to Olien. Subsequent to 1 January 1959 Subject was given an important post within the revolutionary government and Olien has seen him only twice since then and on a social basis. Subject believes Olien to be a political officer of [99].

2. INDICATE WHETHER SUBJECT COULD BE TURNED OVER QUICKLY AND IN A SECURE MANNER TO ANY RESPONSIBLE CASE OFFICER FOR HANDLING. IF SO, INDICATE TO WHOM.

Subject is not an agent who can be turned over to another case officer. However, there would be no problem in introducing Subject to another member of the Station in his [99] capacity.

3. LIST OTHER CASE OFFICERS WHO HAVE HANDLED SUBJECT OR WHOM HE KNOWS OR HAS KNOWN. GIVE NAMES BY WHICH THEY HAVE BEEN KNOWN.

Subject knew Sherwood P. ROCHON, Olien's predecessor, but also as an [99] officer. He had also met Wallace A. Growery.

AMBANG-1 (Ray) PRQII: Woodrow C. Olien, Sherwood P. Rochon, and Wallace A. Growery; 5/29/69, 104-10179-10087.

LINKING GROWERY WITH WILLIAM WILLIAMSON AND EARL J. WILLIAMSON

Having established that Alfonso L. Rodriguez was both Alfredo Fernandez and Wallace A. Growery, we look next for his true name. According to researchers John Dorschner and Roberto Fabricio, the deputy chief of the CIA Havana Station (DCOS), whose name was Bill Williamson "had been extremely close to the plotters of a naval uprising in Cienfuegos."[925] On 5 September 1957, a group of young navy officers at the naval base in Cienfuegos—who were supporters of the 26 July Movement—launched a coup to overthrow Batista. The revolt, which failed after just one day, had been known about beforehand by the American Embassy. However, though the ambassador did know of the projected revolt, he did not know what the number two man at the CIA Station was up to at the time of the revolt. Later, during the trial of the naval conspirators, the ambassador found out that the CIA deputy chief, Williamson, "had told the conspirators that any government set up as the result of a successful rising would be recognized by the U.S."[926]

Williamson and his boss, the CIA Station chief, were also the Havana case officers for Antonio Varona. Hugh Thomas' work on Cuba has this interesting bit of information on Williamson's first encounter with incoming Ambassador Earl Smith:

> In his first weeks (at the embassy) ...Smith asked him to investigate communist strength in Cuba, but he seems to have refused and, walking out of Smith's office, muttered: "We don't care what you think." This man was shortly removed but other members of the U.S. Embassy (many of them being new) remained hostile to Batista...[927]

A PRQ-II for Varona (AMHAWK) indicates that he was "first introduced to James R. Palinger and Wallace A. Growery" by a contact of Palinger's

---

925 John Dorschner and Roberto Fabricio, *The Winds of December* (New York: Coward, McCann & Geoghegan, 1980), p. 70.
926 Hugh Thomas, *Cuba, The Pursuit of Freedom* (New York: Harper and Rowe, 1971) p. 961.
927 Hugh Thomas, *Cuba, The Pursuit of Freedom* (New York: Harper and Rowe, 1971) pp. 964-965. See also Earl E.T. Smith, *The Fourth Floor—An Account of the Castro Communist Revolution* (New York: Random House, 1962), p. 34.

in May 1957.[928] Although the name "Palinger" appears at the bottom of several CIA Havana Station documents, the initials "SPR" are clearly visible at the top of several of them. Those initials very likely stood for Sherwood P. Rochom whose name appears in a 1959 PRQ-II for Manolo Ray as a case officer, as discussed above.[929] From this information we know for certain that Rochom and Palinger were the same man, but, without more information, we cannot be certain if either name was a true name or both were pseudonyms.

---

928 00/00, (probably circa 1960), CIA PRQ-II for AMHAWK. RIF 104-10167-10346.
929 5/29/59, Havana Dispatch from COS Havana, Woodrow C. Olien, to Chief, WHD, Subject: AMBANG PRQ Part II. RIF 104-10179-10087.

> PRQ Part II – Operational Information

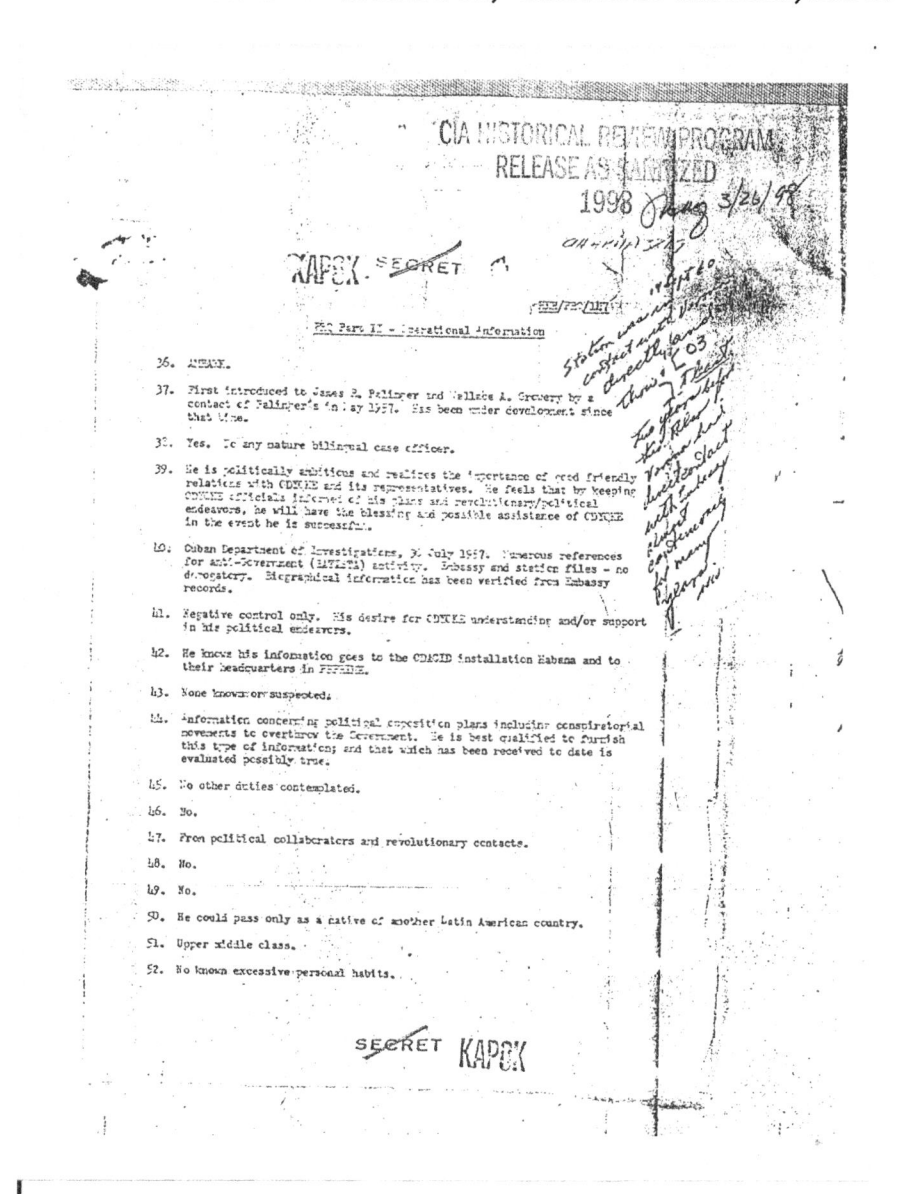

36. AMTRUNK.

37. First introduced to James R. Palinger and Wallace A. Growery by a contact of Palinger's in May 1957. Has been under development since that time.

38. Yes. To any mature bilingual case officer.

39. He is politically ambitious and realizes the importance of good friendly relations with CDYKEE and its representatives. He feels that by keeping CDYKEE officials informed of his plans and revolutionary/political endeavors, he will have the blessing and possible assistance of CDYKEE in the event he is successful.

40. Cuban Department of Investigations, 31 July 1957. Numerous references for anti-Government (LITLETA) activity. Embassy and station files – no derogatory. Biographical information has been verified from Embassy records.

41. Negative control only. His desire for CDYKEE understanding and/or support in his political endeavors.

42. He knows his information goes to the CDAGID installation Habana and to their headquarters in FFYBDE.

43. None known or suspected.

44. Information concerning political opposition plans including conspiratorial movements to overthrow the Government. He is best qualified to furnish this type of information and that which has been received to date is evaluated possibly true.

45. No other duties contemplated.

46. No.

47. From political collaborators and revolutionary contacts.

48. No.

49. No.

50. He could pass only as a native of another Latin American country.

51. Upper middle class.

52. No known excessive personal habits.

AMHAWK-1 (Varona) PRQII: James R. Palinger, Wallace A. Growery; Circa 1960, 104-10167-10346.

WHERE ANGELS TREAD LIGHTLY

Williamson's story before Castro came to power is distinguished by the extraordinary feat of double duty as a deputy chief of station (DCOS)—both in Havana and Mexico City. Howard Hunt did something similar in the summer and fall of 1960, doing double duty in Mexico City and Miami (not as a COS or DCOS) with the Cuban exiles. But Williamson did it for two years. We have established through multiple sources that he was the deputy at the Havana Station from at least May 1956 to the latter part of 1958. In addition, two separate studies on the history of the Mexico City Station—both originated by Anne Goodpasture—list Alfonso L. Rodriguez as the Deputy Chief of Station from July 1956 to July 1958.[930]

It is not impossible, though it is quite unlikely, that there were two different people named Alfonso L. Rodriguez working for the CIA in Havana and Mexico City at the same time. Rodriguez places himself, in the 1963 memo discussed above, in Havana as Manolo Ray's case officer at the time he is listed as the DCOS in Mexico City. Why would Williamson, aka Rodriguez, want to be working in both of these cities at the same time during mid-1956 to mid-1958?

The answer is that Fidel Castro, Raul Castro, Che Guevara, and many other members of the 26 July Movement, were exiled in Mexico City from July 1955 to November 1956.[931] Williamson, aka Rodriguez, was therefore present for the last six months of the exile of Castro and his closest confidants in Mexico City. During 1957-1958, the action was in Cuba, where Williamson, aka Rodriguez, aka Growery, was working with the 26 July underground in Havana. If this is true, Williamson would not have been physically in both places at once. He would have been a senior case officer traveling between the two cities with the same mission: contact with the growing anti-Batista forces.

As discussed in Chapter Twenty One, Wallace Growery was the Spanish-speaking officer from CIA HQS who became Cubela's case officer

---

930   See 11/16/78, Anne Goodpasture, Mexico City Station History, Excerpts, p. 500. 104-10414-10124; also 2/10/77, Background on Mexico Station Support Assets (Coverage of Soviet and Cuban Embassies), p. 8 (of 11 pages). 104-10427-10044; and 00/00/00 "Background of Mexico Station Support Assets (Coverage of Soviet and Cuban Embassies), evidently written by Anne Goodpasture and located in a 104-page CIA record entitled, "Copy 2 of a duplicate file entitled, 'Goodpasture,'"; 104-10086-10394.
931   Robert E. Quirk, **Fidel Castro** (New York: W. W. Norton, 1993), pp. 87-118.

in Paris during August 1962. Growery arrived in Paris around 15 August and departed on 25 August. The present author has searched for documents that indicate the location of Task Force W (TWF) Special Assistant Alfonso Rodriguez during this period; thus far, four documents have been located that were written by him in July and August of 1963, but none are in the strike zone: they are dated 12 July, 13 July, 25 July, and 30 August.[932] The reason for this hole is straightforward: Rodriguez, in his own 19 June 1963 memo, stated his pseudonym was Wallace Growery. Growery was debriefing Cubela in Paris at this time. His true name, Wiliamson, was probably used in the CIA IG report of his 17 August 1962 cable from Paris to CIA HQS.[933]

Alfonso Rodriguez continued to work in the security office of the Special Affairs Staff (SAS/SO) up to the fall of 1964. A cryptic memo on 15 September 1964 appears to be instructions on how to contact Ray in Puerto Rico—possibly meaning Rodriguez was being reassigned.[934] And he was: On 31 December Wallace A. Growery resurfaced at the Madrid Station as the Deputy Chief of Station (DCOS). In a dispatch he sent to CIA HQS, he said that Carlos Tepedino had contacted QUSPORT-1 who had said Cubela wanted to meet in Paris to discuss plans for a coup against Castro.[935] On 3 June 1965, the CIA learned through an FBI source that the DCOS had had an affair with a Cuban girl named "Tota." Although the true name of the DCOS that appeared in the text was redacted, later someone scribbled it in, and it is clearly Earl Williamson.[936]

---

932 See respectively, RIFs 104-10179-10156; 104-10274-10362; 104-10274-10194; and 104-10298-10264.
933 The CIA Inspector General's (IG) *Report on Plots to Assassinate Fidel Castro*, 23 May 1967, RIF 1994.03.08.14:54:36:690005, p.85 (Williamsson fits into the redaction).
934 9/15/64, CIA MFR, apparently by Alfonso Rodriguez on how to get in touch with Manuel Ray in Puerto Rico. RIF 104-10180-10363.
935 12/31/64, Dispatch from Madrid Deputy Chief of Station, Wallace A. Growery, CIA. RIF 104-10216-10237.
936 6/3/65, CIA Memo for Record, RIF 104-10103-10327.

SECRET

3 June 1965

MEMORANDUM FOR THE RECORD

SUBJECT:

RETURN TO CIA
Background Use Only
Do Not Reproduce

1. Mr. Papich (of the FBI) telephoned to report that Victor Domindador ESPINOSA Hernandez, accompanied by an officer from I &NS, talked to the FBI in New York City on 2 June 1965.

2. ESPINOSA said he had just returned to New York on 29 May after having spent 26 days in Paris and a day in Spain. In Paris he had heard from Cuban exiles and Cuban citizens of a plot to assassinate Castro, his brother, and Che Guevara. He said that the following Cuban citizens knew of the plot:

Rolando CUBELA, a next door neighbor of Castro

(possibly identical with Major Rolando L. CUBELA y Seçades);

Alberto BLANCO; and

Major Warren ALMEIDA Bosque

3. ESPINOSA said that in Spain he had heard from Cuban exiles that our Chief of Station, Earl Williamson, knew of this plot to some extent, but the anti-Castro Cubans do not trust him for he was compromised by a Cuban girl known as "TeTa."

4. ESPINOSA said that he wanted to talk to someone from CIA and that he had tried to see us through I &NS in New York, but our people did not want to see him, consequently I &NS took him to see the FBI.

FBI Memo: marginalia compromise of Earl Williamson as Madrid DCOS; 65/3/65, 104-10103-10327.

In 1967, Earl J. Williamson was the Acting Chief of the Cuban Operations Group in the Western Hemisphere Division (WH/COG). Dave Phillips was the chief of WH/COG at that time.[937] In 1975, Alfonso Ro-

---

[937] 5/20/68, cable from WH/COG/PP to JMWAVE. RIF 104-10166-10042.

driguez shows up as the Director of Training in the Operations Staff at CIA HQS. On 23 April, he sent a memo "to whom it may concern" that discussed reviews of the Zapruder film of Kennedy's assassination by officers and a training instructor in the Office of Training in 1965 and 1969.[938]

In the above story from 1956-1975, all of the characters—Williamson, Rodriquez, Growery and Fernandez—are missing from 1959 to 1961. It is very likely that Williamson was using yet another pseudonym during this time. We are most likely hunting for a case officer closely connected to Ray and Varona during that period. We will attempt to identify that name in Volume II of this work.

---

938 4/25/75, RE a 4/23/75 memo to whom it may concern from Alfonso Rodriguez, Director of Training. RIF 1993.08.06.09:18:39:840005.

APPENDIX FIVE:

THE PSEUDONYMS OF E. HOWARD HUNT: WALTER C. TWICKER, TERRENCE S. CRABANAC, AND EDWARD J. HAMILTON

8/31/59: **HUNT** HAD RECORDED HIS SAFE COMBINATION ON THE BOTTOM OF HIS PEN HOLDER AND IT WAS DISCOVERED DURING A MARINE GUARD SECURITY SWEEP AT THE CLOSE OF BUSINESS ON 8/31/59. SEE 104-10120-10326 AND 104-10119-10128

8/31/59: **HUNT** STATEMENT IN DEPT OF STATE REPORT FROM THE AMERICAN EMBASSY IN MONTEVIDEO (11/17/59) EXPLAINING HIS VERSION OF THE SECURITY VIOLATION. 104-10119-10130.

WHERE ANGELS TREAD LIGHTLY

11/4/59: ONE-DAY SUSPENSION IMPOSED ON *HUNT* FOR THE SECURITY VIOLATION. 104-10120-10326

11/9/59: MEMO IN REPLY TO MR. *HUNT* FROM ELMER R. HIPSLEY, CHIEF DIVISION OF PHYSICAL SECURITY, OFFICE OF SECURITY, AMERICAN EMBASSY [21-24 NEWMAN: = URUGUAY] *HUNT* IS SAID TO HAVE ACCEPTED RESPONSIBILITY. SEE 104-10120-10326 AND 104-10119-10128.

11/20/59: *HUNT* MEMO TO JOSEPH J. JOVA, ACTING CH PERSONAL OPERATIONS DIV, APPEALS HIS PUNISHMENT OF A ONE-DAY SUPENSION ON GROUNDS THAT THERE WAS NO POSSIBILLITY OF COMPROMISING CLASSIFIED MATERIALS. SIGNED "***E. HOWARD HUNT***, FIRST SECRETARY OF EMBASSY. 104-10120-10326 SEE ALSO ***HOWARD HUNT*, AMERICAN SPY**, 2007, P. 99.

11/30/59: *HUNT'S* APPEAL RE THE ONE-DAYS SUSPENSION FOR HIS SECURITY VIOLATION IS DENIED. 104-10120-10326

2/8/60: MONT (REDACTED 21-24 AND 16-24 = URUGUAY) 3530 TO DIR: ACCORDING TO AMBASSADOR [WOODWARD] PRESIDENT NARDONE HAS STATED THAT DURING HIS PRIVATE TALK WITH PRESIDENT EISENHOWER HE INTENDS TO REQUEST PRESIDENT EISENHOWER TO CANCEL [REDACTED PSEUDO FOR *HUNT*] TRANSFER PERMIT REMAIN IN PRESENT CAPACITY]. [NEWMAN COMMENT: A 2/4/63 CIA SECURITY APPRAISAL OF *HUNT* BY L. L. THOMPSON STATES: INFORMATION CONTAINED IN SUBJECT'S FILE INDICATES POSSIBILITY THAT HE ATTEMPTED TO CANCEL HIS TRANSFER FROM [URUGUAY] BY POLITICAL MANEUVERING. THE PRESIDENT OF [URUGUAY] REPORTEDLY INDICATED HIS INTENTION, IN PRIVATE CONVERSATION WITH PRESIDENT EISENHOWER, TO REQUEST CANCELLATION OF SUBJECT'S TRANSFER FROM MONEVIDEO. 104-10119-10098]

THE PSEUDONYMS OF E. HOWARD HUNT: WALTER C. TWICKER...

3/3/60: **HUNT** INTERPRETS FOR EISENHOWER-NARDONE MEETING IN MONTEVIDEO URUGUAY: MY INTEREST IN IKE DIMINISHED FURTHER AFTER PRESIDENT NARDONE PERSONALLY ASKED EISENHOWER TO ALLOW ME TO STAY ON. EISENHOWER DEFERRED THE DECISION TO AMBASSADOR WOODWARD ASKING, "WE HAVE A REQUEST BY THE GOVERNMENT TO KEEP **MR. HUNT** IN POSITION. HOW DO YOU FEEL ABOUT IT?" OF COURSE, WOODWARD'S REPLY WAS "WE WOULD PREFER SOMEONE ELSE, SIR." SOON THEREAFTER, I RECEIVED NOTICE FROM THE EMBASSY WATCH OFFICE THAT MY FATHER HAD DIED, SO I FLEW HOME TO HELP MY MOTHER WITH THE FUNERAL, BURYING HIM IN THE HUNT FAMILY PLOT BESIDE MY INFANT BROTHER. ...HUNDREDS OF PEOPLE SHOWED UP AT HIS FUNERAL TO PAY THEIR RESPECTS. FROM *AMERICAN SPY*, *HOWARD HUNT*, 2007, P. 110.

EARLY MARCH 1960: **HUNT** RECALLS: SHORTLY AFTER THE EISENHOWER [NEWMAN COMMENT: THE TEXT READS NIXON BUT THIS IS PROBABLY A MISTAKE AS HUNT IS LIKELY REFERRING TO THE EISENHOWER-NARDONE MEETING—NIXON HAD BEEN IN URUGUAY IN MAY, 1958 DURING THE PRESIDENCY OF FISCHER] TOUR LEFT, I RECEIVED A CABLE FROM WASHINGTON, WHICH I HAD BEEN EXPECTING EVER SINCE WOODWARD'S ARRIVAL, RECALLING ME TO WASHINGTON. THE MISSIVE WAS SIGNED JOINTLY BY TRACY BARNES AND MY NEW BOSS, RICHARD BISSELL, WHO HAD TAKEN OVER CLANDESTINIE SERVICES FROM FRANK WISNER... I FLEW TO WASHINGTON FOR MEETINGS ABOUT MY NEW POSITION. TRACY BARNES, NOW PRINCIPAL ASSISTANT TO BISSELL, EXPLAINED THAT I WAS NEEDED FOR AN IMPORTANT NEW PROJECT THAT WAS SIMILAR TO THE ONE I HAD WORKED ON FOR HIM DURING THE OVERTHROW OF JACOBO ARBENZ. ...I'M REASSEMBLING MOST OF THE TEAM FROM PB/SUCCESS. IT'S EXTREMELY SENSITIVE. EISENHOWER INSISTS ON COMPLETE DENIABILITY." "AND WHO IS THE TARGET?" I ASKED. "CASTRO," BARNES REPLIED LACONICALLY. "WE'RE TAK-

ING DOWN FIDEL CASTRO." I LET OUT A BREATH. "FINALLY." FROM *AMERICAN SPY, HOWARD HUNT*, 2007, PP. 111-112. SEE ALSO *GIVE US THIS DAY*, 1973, P. 22.

AFTER VISITING WITH ESTERLINE WHO SENT *HUNT* TO **DRECHER** [= **DROLLER**]: **DRECHER** GREETED ME EFFUSIVELY, SAID THINGS WERE ROLLING AT A GREAT RATE AND I WAS NEEDED URGENTLY TO TAKE OVER FIELD MANAGEMENT OF THE CUBAN GROUP. JUST GO BACK TO YOUR STATION AND GET READY TO MOVE OUT. YOUR REPLACEMENT'S BEEN SELECTED AND WILL BE THERE BEFORE YOU LEAVE. *GIVE US THIS DAY*, P. 24.

THE FOLLOWING DAY I FLEW BACK TO MY STATION AND INFORMED MY AMBASSADOR [WOODWARD] THAT I WAS BEING TRANSFERRED IN THE IMMEDIATE FUTURE AND WOULD BE REPLACED BY AN OFFICER WHO HAD SERVED WITH HIM... OVER THE NEXT FEW WEEKS THERE WERE NUMEROUS CABLE EXCHANGES WITH PROJECT HQS HAVING TO DO WITH MY COVER AND ACTIVITIES IN SAN JOSE. THEN CAME A MESSAGE TELLING ME THAT COSTA RICA WAS OUT; FIGUERES HAD BEEN UNABLE TO SECURE GOVERNMENT ASSENT, AND SO MY CUBAN GOVERNMENT-IN-EXILE GROUP WOULD BE BASED IN MEXICO CITY. *GIVE US THIS DAY*, P. 29.

4/00/60: IN APRIL I [*HUNT*] LEFT MY FAMILY AND FLEW TO MADRID, SPAIN, WHERE I HAD BEEN ORDERED TO UNDERTAKE THE DEFECTION OF THE CUBAN MILITARY ATTACHE, COLONEL RAMON BARQUIN. *GIVE US THIS DAY*, P. 30.

5/00/60: MEXI STATION HISTORY: *SAMUEL G. ORRISON* WAS (IN 1960) A 45-YEAR-OLD US CITIZEN WHO HAD SERVED AS A CAREER AGENT IN MEXICO FROM 1951 TO MAY 1960. HE WORKED EXCLUSIVELY ON CA PROJECTS, USING COMMERCIAL COVER. ...HE RESIGNED IN MAY 1960 AND MOVED TO HOUSTON, TEXAS. 104-10414-10125.

THE PSEUDONYMS OF E. HOWARD HUNT: WALTER C. TWICKER...

6/23/60: MEMO FROM DEP DIR SEC INVEST AND SUPPORT FRED HALL TO DEP DIR SECURITY, SUBJECT *HOWARD HUNT*: SUBJECT IS TO GO ON PCS BASIS TO MEXICO UNDER COMMERCIAL COVER AS A WRITER. HE WILL BE THE POLITICAL ACTION MAN FOR THE PROJECT IN MEXICO AS A REPRESENTATIVE TO THE FRD. SUBJECT SHOULD BE CLEAN OTHERWISE. PRIOR TO HIS PCS ASSIGNMENT TO MEXICO, SUBJECT IS GOING TO CUBA FOR A WEEK OR SO ON A SORT OF OREINTATION BASIS. 104-10119-10120.

6/28/60 [APPROX]: *HUNT* RECALLS OF HIS TRIP TO CUBA: THAT NIGHT I DINED WITH A GIRL WHOSE NAME HAD BEEN GIVEN ME BY **KNIGHT** [**PHILLIPS**]. ATTRACTIVE AND IN HER TWENTIES. **VIOLETA** WAS THE MOTHER OF A SMALL CHILD WHOSE FATHER HAD BEEN KILLED IN THE MOUNTAINS WITH CASTRO. ...IN THE MORNING I FLEW BACK TO TAMPA AND TOOK A CONNECTING FLIGHT TO WASHINGTON WHERE I PREPARED A REPORT ON MY IMPRESSIONS. WHEN IT CAME TO RECOMMENDATIONS RELATED TO THE PROJECT I LISTED FOUR: 1. ASSASSINATE CASTRO BEFORE OR COINCIDENT WITH THE INVASION (A TASK FOR CUBAN PATRIOTS)... *GIVE US THIS DAY*, PP. 37-38.

1ST WEEK OF JULY: 7/26/60 SO MEMO TO FILE, SUBJECT *HUNT*: HE WILL SERVE AS POINT OF CONTACT FOR POLITICAL ACTION TYPES CONNECTED WITH THE PROJECT. SINCE THE FIRST WEEK OF JULY 1960 HE HAS BEEN UTILIZED IN THIS SAME CAPACITY IN MEXICO CITY. 104-10120-10350.

7/6/60: *HUNT* RECALLS: **BENDER** [NEWMAN = **DROLLER**] AND I MET DR. RUBIO IN HIS MAYFLOWER HOTEL (WASHINGTON D.C.). ... IT SOON BECAME APPARENT TO ME THAT FOR RUBIO THE INTERVIEW WAS A FUTILE EXERCISE, AND TO CONCEAL MOUNTING EMBARRASSMENT I LEFT THEM AND SPOKE WITH RUBIO'S NEPHEW, FABIO FREYRE... RUBIO WAS CLEARLY DISSATISFIED, AND AS WE LEFT THE HOTEL **BENDER** SAID TO ME, "THESE GUYS DON'T UNDERSTAND THEIR CUBA IS PART OF THE PAST; EVEN

AFTER CASTRO IT WON'T BE THE SAME. NOW I SUPPOSE RUBIO WILL TELL PAWLEY HE DIDN'T GET ANYWHERE WITH ME, AND PAWLEY WILL BEEF TO NIXON OR JAKE OR KING. THEN I'LL HAVE TO DO IT ALL OVER AGAIN." HAILING A TAXI, WE DROVE BACK TO QUARTERS EYE. **NEXT [7/8 APPROX] MORNING WE FLEW TO NEW YORK** WHERE I WAS INTRODUCED TO THE JUST-FORMED NUCLEUS OF THE GOVERNMENT-IN-EXILE. ...AURELIANO SANCHEZ ARANGO [FOREIGN MINISTER IN THE GOVERNMENT OF CARLOS PRIO SOCCARAS] WAS COMPLETING A STUDY OF THE CUBA SUGAR SITUATION FOR THE DEPARTMENT OF STATE. JUSTO CARRILLO [PRESIDENT OF THE BANK FOR INDUSTRIAL AND AGRICULTURAL DEVELOPMENT UNDER PRIO AND CASTRO] STALKED ABOUT GESTICULATING AND ORATING TO THOSE WHO WOULD LISTEN. MANUEL ANTONIO ("TONY") DE VARONA [PRIME MINSTER UNDER PRIO] SHOUTED INTO A TELEPHONE. ... ALL THREE CUBANS STORMED AND RANTED, BUT **BENDER** AND I HELD THE LINE. THE IMPORTANT THING, I SAID, WAS TO RELOCATE IN MEXICO AND BEGIN THE ARDUOUS WORK OF ENGENDERING LATIN AMERICAN SYMPATHY FOR THE EXILE CAUSE. ... OVER THEIR GRUMBLING WE DRAFTED A PRESS ANNOUNCEMENT OF THE FRD'S FORMATION THAT INCLUDED A MANIFESTO FOR CASTRO'S DEFEAT. ON THAT POINT, AT LEAST, WE AGREED. *GIVE US THIS DAY*, PP. 45-46,

7/11/60 [APPROX]: HUNT RECALLS: I FLEW TO MIAMI AND LODGED IN ONE OF THE MANY MOTELS I WAS TO KNOW OVER THE NEXT TEN MONTHS. AN OFFICER ESCORTED ME TO OUR OPERATIONAL HQS IN CORAL GABLES. HQS PROVED TO BE AN OFFICE BUILDING CONVERTED FOR OUR USE AND DISGUISED AS AN ELECTRONICS FIRM WORKING ON GOVERNMENT CONTRACTS. ... HERE, FOR THE FIRST TIME, I MET **DOUGLAS GUPTON** [NEWMAN = WILLIAM KENT], AN AGGRESSIVE AND BILINGUAL YOUNG OFFICER WHO HANDLED FIELD PROPAGANDA FOR KNIGHT [NEWMAN = **PHILLIPS**]. **GUPTON** WAS ALREADY ORGANIZING, GUIDING AND SUBSIDIZING THE SAME EXILE

GROUPS THAT VARONA HAD WANTED TO BRING UNDER FRD DIRECTION AND CONTROL. HE ALSO SUBSIDIZED A NUMBER OF HAVANA NEWSPAPERS THAT NOW HAD "IN EXILE" ADDED TO THEIR NAMES. ... OVER COFFEE IN A LUNCHEONETTE ON CORAL GABLES "MIRACLE MILE" I MET AND TALKED WITH MANUEL ARTIME FOR THE FIRST TIME. ... HIDDEN BY THE HAVANA STATION DURING A NATIONWIDE SEARCH FOR HIM, ARTIME HAD BEEN EXFILTRATED TO MIAMI WHERE HE FORMED HIS MOVEMENT FOR REVOLUTIONARY RECOVERY. ...THAT NIGHT I MET JOSE IGNACIO RASCO AT MY HOTEL. ... HE HANDED ME A LIST OF REQUESTS HE HAD MADE OF JIMMY [SMITH AKA ENZEL], NONE OF WHICH HAD BEEN FILLED, AND I PROMISED TO SEE WHAT COULD BE DONE. ...**NEXT MORNING** AT THE CORAL GABLES OFFICE I TAXED JIMMY WITH NONPERFORMANCE AND TOLD HIM NOT TO PROMISE WHAT HE COULD NOT OR DID NOT INTEND TO DELIVER. *GIVE US THIS DAY*, PP. 46-48.

BENDER ARRIVED IN MIAMI, WE LUNCHED TOGETHER. ... LATER I WAS TO DISCOVER THAT BENDER'S SYMPATHIES WERE ATTRACTED BY ENGLISH-SPEAKING CUBANS. ... DURING THE SAME MEETING WE DISCUSSED FINAL ARRANGMENTS FOR MEXICO CITY OPERATIONS. ... IT WAS NOW LATE JULY. [PP. 47-50]. ... [**BENDER'S**] FONDNESS FOR KIBITTZING PROVED HIGHLY EMBARRASSING TO BENDER ON ONE OCCASION. UNKNOWN TO ME, HE HELD A CONFERENCE WITH A CUBAN—EITHER YABOR OR LORIE—IN A MOTEL ROOM NEAR THE MIAMI AIRPORT. HIS ROOM HAD A CONNECTING DOOR MADE OF INSUBSTANTIAL MATERIAL, AND IN ADDITION THE LOWER EDGE WAS TRIMMED FOR CARPET CLEARANCE. THE OCCUPANT OF THE ADJOINING ROOM WAS A VACATIONING STENOGRAPHER WHOSE BROTHER WORKED FOR THE FBI. HEARING A DISCUSSION NEXT DOOR BETWEEN TWO ACCENTED VOICES SHE TOOK DOWN THE CONVERSATION IN SHORTHAND AND TURNED OVER A TRANSCRIPT TO THE FBI, CONVINCED SHE HAD OVERHEARD TWO FOREIGN CONSPIRATORS. HER DOCUMENT WAS DUELY LAID AT CIA'S

DOORSTEP AND **BENDER**, AFTER MUCH EMBARRASSMENT, WAS ABLE TO GET OFF WITH ONLY A REPRIMAND. *GIVE US THIS DAY*, P. 64.

8/00/60: MEXI CITY STATION HISTORY: IN AUGUST 1960, **_ORRISON_** WAS RECRUITED AGAIN BY E. HOWARD **_HUNT_** TO WORK ON CIA PROJECTS ON A PART-TIME BASIS ON BUSINESS TRIPS MADE BETWEEN HOUSTON AND MEXICO CITY. 104-10414-10124.

8/00/60: **_HUNT_** RECALLS: MY FAMILY WAS ARRIVING IN THE STATES. MEETING THEM IN NEW YORK I BROUGHT THEM TO WASHINGTON WHERE WE EXCHANGED DIPLOMATIC PASSPORTS FOR ORDINARIES AND OBTAINED RESIDENT VISAS FROM THE MEXICAN CONSULATE. IN AUGUST ... WE FLEW FROM WASHINGTON TO MEXICO CITY. *GIVE US THIS DAY*, P. 50.

8/8/60: MASH 0463 **CORBUSTON** [NEWMAN = WILLIAM KENT] ACTING TO DIR PRI MEXI FOR **_TWICKER_**: AMHAWK [NEWMAN = VARONA] ARR MIAMI 18 AUG DUE DEATH FATHER IN LAW. 104-10167-10047.

8/10/60: MASH 0400 TO DIR AMHAWK STAYED BEHIND AFTER 9 AUG **BENDER** AMCIGAR [NEWMAN = FRD EXECUTIVE COMMITTEE] MTG TO ARGUE FOR MORE MONEY AND AMRASP [NEWMAN = FRD] NEEDS LEADER. ...FINANCING SYSTEM FROM MEXI WORKED OUT BETWEEN **_TWICKER_** AND JUAN PAULA SEEMS ADEQUATE AND SPEEDY ENOUGH. ... IT COMMON TALK MIAMI THAT AMRASP HARD UP. 104-10167-10051.

8/15/60: DIR 45292 TO MEXI INFO MASH: PLS ADVISE **_TWICKER_** ADDRESS AND TELEPHONE WHICH COULD BE GIVEN AMRASP COMMITTEES CONTACTS IF NECESSARY. 104-10171-10205.

8/17/60: MASH 0452 TO PRI DIR INFO PRI MEXI FOR **_TWICKER_**: **GUPTON** MET AMRASP COORDINATOR SOSA 17 AUG. SOSA

THE PSEUDONYMS OF E. HOWARD HUNT: WALTER C. TWICKER...

FEELS NEED TIGHTENING UP SECURITY AND ENFORCING DISCIPLINE. BEGAN ACTIVITIES BY ELIMINATING SURPLUS EMPLOYEES AND LOITERERS AMRASP MIAMI OFFICES. RE AMRASP STATEMENT INVITING EXILE GROUPS JOIN …SUGGEST ***TWICKER*** URGE AMCIGAR REISSUE STATEMENT FOR MEXI PRESS. 104-10269-10012.

8/24/60: DIR 47036 TO PRIORITY MEXI (***TWICKER***); REQUEST ***TWICKER*** RERAISE SUBJ WITH AMHAWK TAKING FIRM POSITION DISAPPROVAL INDEPENDENT ESTABLISHEMENT COMMO FACILITY BY AMCIGAR AT THIS TIME. …WH COMMENT: STATION HAS DISCOVERED PURCHASE OF TRANSMITTER BY AMHAWK HENCHMEN FOR DIRECT COMMO BETWEEN MEXICO AND CUBA. AMBIDDY-1 CONFIRMED INTENT AND ***TWICKER*** POINTED OUT SECURITY HAZARDS. 104-10171-10216.

8/25/60: MEXI 6163 TO DIR FROM ***TWICKER***: 23 AUG MEM AMWAIL SAID AMRASP SHOULD KEEP EYE ON NEW ANTI-CASTRO GROUP NOW FORMING. 104-10271-10265.

8/25/60: DIR 47226 **BERNARD REICHARDT** TO MEXI 25 AUG AMHAWK TELEPHONED FROM MEXI TO ALONSO PUJOL IN NEW YORK TO ASK HIM TO GET IN TOUCH **LICARI** TO CHECK ON AUG REPORT. REQUEST ***TWICKER*** IMPRESS ON AMHAWK SERIOUSNESS SECURITY IMPLICATIONS SUCH CALL USING **LICARI** NAME FOR ANY REASON MUCH LESS ROUTINE ADMIN MATTER. 104-10168-10077.

8/25/60: MEXI 6182 TO DIR FROM ***TWICKER***: STATION LEARNED THAT [08] HAS [24] HOME WHERE AMHAWK STAYING. ***TWICKER*** TOLD AMWAIL TO WARN AMHAWK AND REMIND AMCIGAR THAT TELEPHONE SECURITY ESSENTIAL FOR ALL. 104-10171-10211.

8/25/60: DIR 47344 TO MASH MEXI (***TWICKER***): HQS NOT AWARE AMHAWK EFFORTS ESTABLISH QUOTE NEW POLITICAL GROUP

UNQUOTE. CAN MASH/*TWICKER* SHED MORE LIGHT ON THIS? 104-10171-10212.

9/1/60: MASH 0591 TO DIR MEXI FOR *TWICKER*: SINCE DEPARTURE AMCIGAR FOR MEXI, AMRASP MIAMI FUNCTIONING WITH MEASURE OF EFFECTIVENESS UNDER ABLE GUIDANCE AMRASP COORDINATOR. FRUSTRATING AND HAMPERING FACTOR HAS BEEN SUFFICIENT AUTHORITY NOT GRANTED TO COORDINATOR. AN EVEN GREATER OBSTRUCTION HAS BEEN PRESENCE OF AMEER IN MASH AREA. RETURN OF ENTIRE AMCIGAR TO MASH AREA LIKELY MULTIPLY OBSTRUCTION SIX FOLD. FEEL IT IMPERATIVE AMCIGAR BEGIN EXTENSIVE AND EFFECTIVE SELLING JOB IN LA SOONEST. 104-10269-10008.

9/1/60: MEXI 6231 TO DIR FROM *TWICKER*: [MARGINALIA: MASH AMRASPERS SPECULATE AMHAWK SEEKING TO USE HIS PRESTIGE/AUTHORITY IN HIS AMRASP POSITION TO ESTABLISH NEW POLITICAL GROUP "RESCATE."] 104-10168-10090.

9/3/60: MEXI 6235 TO DIR FROM *TWICKER*: [REF DIR 48334] CANNOT BUT AGREE REF [C/S COMMENT: CONCERNED AMCIGAR'S POSSIBLE NEED FOR RELOCATION] THINKING. ...AMCIGAR PROBABLY REACT ADVERSELY ANY FOREIGN BASE THAN MIAMI. THUS IF MEXI NO LONGER SUITABLE AS BASE, BEST RESULTS FROM AMCIGAR CAN PROBABLY BE OBTAINED IF AMCIGAR RECONSTITUTED IN MIAMI AREA. 104-10171-10170.

9/10/60: MEXI 6304 TO DIR FROM *TWICKER*: PLANNING NEEDED AND URGENT FULL-SCALE AMCIGAR MEETING MIAMI O/A 17 SEPT 60. 104-10168-10047.

9/10/60: MEXI 6308 TO DIR FROM *TWICKER*: FOLLOWING EARLIER MEETING WITH AMWAIL *TWICKER* MET AGAIN WITH AMHAWK AND PRESENTED NEW ORGANIZATIONAL PLAN. 104-10168-10048.

THE PSEUDONYMS OF E. HOWARD HUNT: WALTER C. TWICKER...

9/12/60: DIR 00105 TO OPIM MEXI *TWICKER* PRI MASH REF MEXI 6310 [IN 11178]: PUZZLED WHY AMHAWK AMWAIL CANNOT BE MIAMI FOR 16 SEPTEMBER AMCIGAR MEETING. SUGGEST YOU PRESSURE THEM STEP UP THEIR ITINERARY. 104-10171-10162.

9/12/60: MEXI 6311 TO DIR FROM *TWICKER*: PRIOR MEETING DESCRIBED MEXI 6308 *TWICKER* HAD PLANNED GIVE AMHAWK ROUGH TIME ON SECURITY BREACHES, LOOSE-MOUTHEDNESS ETC; HOWEVER IN VIEW CURRENT RAPPORT PREFER NOT RAISE SUBJECTS PRIOR TO AMCIGAR MEETING IN MIAMI. 104-10167-10028.

9/14/60: MEXI 6330 FROM *TWICKER*: PLACING **ORRISON** IN CONTACT WITH AMHAWK BROTHER TO BEGIN WORKING WITH AMRASP MEXI DELEGATION. 104-10171-10160.

9/21/60: DISPATCH FROM CH, WHD TO CHIEF OF BASE, JMASH FOR *TWICKER*; SUBJECT BACKGROUND ON "COMMITMENTS" TO AMHAWK BY OLIEN A. HAVA 641, 13 SEPT 60 B. MEXI 6309, 10 SEPT 60: WITH REFERENCE TO AMHAWK'S STATEMENT TO *TWICKER* THAT ODYOKE HAS NOT LIVED UP TO THE "PACT SIGNED BY HIM AND OLIEN" [NEWMAN = JIM NOEL HAVANA STATION CHIEF], AND AFTER RECEIVING THE CABLES LISTED IN REF A, WE BELIEVE AMHAWK REFERRED TO THE SPECIFIC COMMITMENTS HE SAID THE OPPOSITION NEEDED FROM ODYOKE [= USG] (HAVA 3708). 104-10168-10037 [NEWMAN COMMENT: THERE IS ANOTHER COPY WHICH HAS HANDWRITING ON THE LAST PAGE: "THIS WAS DISCUSSED WITH MR. NOEL WHO SAID THERE WERE NO OTHER COMMITMENTS. MT."]] 104-10167-10383.

9/24/60: MEXI 6394 TO DIR FROM *TWICKER*: *TWICKER* RETURNING WASH 27 SEPT 60 VIA EAL 302 FOR FINAL CONSULTATION PRIOR RELOCATING MIAMI O/A 3 OCT. PAULA AND AMWAIL WIFE LEAVING MEXI BY SEPARATE CARS ON 25 SEPT. ARRANGE-

MENTS COMPLETED **ORRISON** HANDLE AMRASP DELEGATION MEXI. 104-10171-10045.

9/26/60: SO MEMO TO FILE FM E. J.M. S..., SUBJECT *HUNT*: HE WILL SERVE AS POINT OF CONTACT FOR POLITICAL ACTION TYPES CONNECTED WITH THE PROJECT. SINCE THE FIRST WEEK OF JULY 1960 HE HAS BEEN UTILIZED IN THIS SAME CAPACITY IN MEXICO CITY. DOCUMENTATION... STATE OF MASS DRIVERS' LICENCE... PROVIDENCE R.I. ADDRESS. ... ON ABOVE DATE (9/26/60) SO PROJECT JMARC CALLED AND REQUESTED SB/2 TO CONCUR IN THE ISSUANCE OF ALIAS DOCUMENTATION FOR THE SUBJECT. ...SUBJECT WILL BE USED IN THE MIAMI FLORIDA AREA AS A FREE LANCE WRITER FOR THE DURATION OF THE PROJECT. 104-10120-10350.

9/26/60: MEXI 6405 TO DIR FROM *TWICKER*: ON 24 SEPT *TWICKER* AND **ORRISON** USING OPNL ALIASES MET INDIVIDUALLY WITH FOLL MEMBERS AMRASP DELEGATION: DR. ROLANDO ROJAS, ROBERTO DE VARONA, SERGIO LOPEZ MESA (SON-IN-LAW MIRO CARDONNA) AND JULIAN ARIAS. ...*TWICKER* TOLD EACH MAN THAT **ORRISON** WAS HIS REPRESENTATIVE IN MEXI... ... THEY CLEARLY UNDERSTAND **ORRISON** IN CHARGE AND FULLY BACKED BY *TWICKER*/**BENDER**. 104-10171-10156.

9/27/60: MEXI 6412 TO DIR FROM *TWICKER*: NEW FUINCTIONAL RESPONSIBILITIES AMRASP MEXI DELEGATION ASSIGNED... EACH MAN RESPONSIBLE TO **ORRISON** FOR ACCOMPLISHMENT... **ORRISON** TO FUND ALL ACTIVITIES LOCALLY, CHARGING JMNET. 104-10171-10154.

9/29/60: MASH 0846 TO DIR: AMCIGAR MINUS AMEER [SNACHEZ ARANGO] MET WITH US AFTERNOON 27 SEPT AND REPORTED: AMHAWK APPOINTED GENERAL COORDINATOR WITH WIDE AUTHORITY... FINANCE –AMWAIL [JUSTO CARRILLO]... PUB

THE PSEUDONYMS OF E. HOWARD HUNT: WALTER C. TWICKER...

RELATS AMEER... PLANNING PROP AMPALM-5 [JOSE IGNACIO RASCO]...DEFENSE AMBIDDY ...SPECIFIC DATES AND DETAILS LEFT FOR NEXT *TWICKER* AMCIGAR MTG WEEK 3 OCT. 104-10261-10023.

9/30/60: MEMO TO CH SUPPORT BRANCH 3 [SECURITY OFFICE] SUBJ: ***HUNT, EVERETTE HOWARD JR***: THIS DATE CHRIS GIKAS SB/2 CALLED FOR A BACKSTOPPED ADDRESS FOR [24]. I CALLED WFO RONEY WHO ADVISED THAT 331 1ST ST. N.E. WAS OKAY. NAME ***EDWARD J. HAMILTON***. ...HE IS GOING TO FLORIDA. WILL USE [24] AND RENTAL CAR FOR 1 WEEK THEN APPLY FOR FLA LICENSE. NOT USING 331 1ST ANY LONGER. 104-10120-10317.

10/3/60: ***HUNT*** RECALLS: ON 3 OCTOBER 1960, THE FRD EXECUTIVE COUNCIL ABANDONED MEXICO, AND AS WE FLEW EAST ACROSS THE GULF, IT SEEMED AS THOUGH WE COULD HEAR A SIGH OF RELIEF FROM LOS PINO [THE MEXICAN WHITE HOUSE]. *GIVE US THIS DAY*, P. 58.

10/5/60: MASH 0936 TO DIR: FIRST *TWICKER*/AMHAWK MEETING SINCE LATTER ASSUMED POST OF GENERAL COORDINATOR... *TWICKER* WILL MAINTAIN NORMAL CONTACTS WITH AMHAWK AND OTHER AMCIGAR MEMBERS... **GUPTON** AND **ENZEL** WILL CONFINE CONTACTS TO DEPARTMENTAL CHIEFS WITH WHOM THEY HAVE BEEN WORKING... 104-10167-10350.

10/6/60: MEXI 6502 TO DIR: PROBLEM [= LOOSE LIPS] OF ROBERTO DE VARONA BECOMING ACUTE... **ORRISON** REPORTED... RECOMMENDS *TWICKER* FRANK DISCUSSION AMHAWK THIS PROBLEM DETERMINE IF AMHAWK WILL AGREE SENDING ROBERTO EXTENDED LATIN AMERICAN TRIP. ... STATION COULD HAVE [08] ADVISE ROBERTO TO LEAVE COUNTRY OR WOULD BE SUBJECT ARREST AND DEPORTATION. REQUEST HQS, MASH VIEWS. 104-10171-10106.

WHERE ANGELS TREAD LIGHTLY

10/6/60: MASH 0953 (MEIGS ACTING) TO DIR REF DIR 04465: PER **PARLETT** (**BENDER**) PHONE REQUEST *TWICKER* ASKED AMHAWK PREPARE STANDBY STATEMENT EVENT AMEER [AMEER = SANCHEZ ARANGO SEE 104-10220-10418] MAKES OPEN CHARGES. STATEMENT WOULD SAY THAT AMEER WAS EXPELLED FROM AMCIGAR FOR TREATING WITH MASFERRER AND DENY THAT AMPALM-5 GUILTY OF ANY DEFALCATION. PAULA HAS SIGNED RECEIPTS SHOWING AMEER ACCEPTED AMCIGAR FUNDS. AMCIGAR MEMBERS SO ENRAGED OVER AMEER'S ATTITUDE AND THREATENED ACTION THAT FOR ALL PRACTICAL PURPOSES AMEER NO LONGER MEMBER AMRASP/AMCIGAR. 104-10168-10394. [[NEWMAN: AMCIGAR IS THE EXECUTIVE COMMITTEE OF AMRASP—FRD SEE 104-10220-10418.]

10/6/60: MASH 0959 MEIGS ACTING TO DIR: *TWICKER* WOULD LIKE **ORRISON** COME MIAMI 10 OCT FOR OPNL/FINAN MEETING WITH *TWICKER*/**SADORUS**. 104-10171-10104.

10/6/60: CIA SETS UP LIVE WASH ADDRESS FOR *HUNT* AS *EDWARD J. HAMILTON* 104-10120-10316.

10/8/60: MASH 0991 MEIGS ACTING TO PRI DIR: 6 OCT AMPALM-5 REQUESTED MEETING WITH **GUPTON**. PURPOSE WAS DISCUSS ANTI CASTRO BOOKLET. ... DURING CONVERSATION A-5 INDICATED THAT DESPITE REORGANIZATION NO CHANGES MADE IN PROP COMM. AMHAWK DECIDED MESTRE TO CONTINUE AS HEAD. ... MASH WILL TRY THROUGH *TWICKER* PRESSURE AMHAWK AMCIGAR HANDLE PUBLICATION BOOKLET THROUGH PROP COMM... 104-10168-10381. MASH 0992 TO DIR: ... IF **MESTRE** NOT AGREEABLE, MASH HAS ALTERNATIVES TO PROBLEM: THROUGH *TWICKER*, HAVE AMCIGAR SEND **MESTRE** EXTENDED TOUR LA. IN ABSENCE, APPOINT SUITABLE SUBSTITUTE WITH FULL AUTHORITY. ...THROUGH *TWICKER* MASH PLANS REMIND AMHAWK OF AGREEMENT REACHED WITH **BENDER** WHEREBY **GUPTON** RETAINS CONTROL AND FUNDING AMRASP APPILI-

ATES. 104-10168-10378. MASH 0993 MEIGS ACTING TO PRI DIR REF A. MASH 0775 (22 SEPT) B. DIR 02420: AMHAWK APPARENTLY INTERESTED MOUNTING PM OPS AS POLITICAL FAVOR HIS CONTACTS CUBAN EXILE COMMUNITY WHO NOT WILLING AFFILIATE AMRASP BUT DESIROUS UTILIZE AMHAWK CLAIMS ACCESS ARMS… 104-10171-10394.

10/15/60: MASH 1090 TO DIR: DURING 13 OCT MEETING WITH **CORBUSTON** AMHAWK SAID BENDER GROUP DEALINGS WITH AMRASP AFFILIATES CONSTITUTED INTERFERENCE IN INTERNAL AFFAIRS AMRASP AND STRONGLY EMPHASIZED HE HAVE FULL CONTROL AFFAIRS. … **CORBUSTON** AGREED KEEP HANDS OFF AFFILIATES UNTIL RETURN *TWICKER* AND *TWICKER* AMHAWK DISCUSSION THIS SUBJECT. … MASH PROPOSES HAVE *TWICKER* TAKE STRONG STAND WITH AMHAWK ON QUESTION AFFILIATES AND TRY MAKE AMHAWK ABIDE BY AGREEMENT REACHED WITH **PARLETT**. 104-10167-10337.

10/21/60: MASH 1191 TO DIR: ON 21 OCT *TWICKER* REQUESTED THAT AMHAWK/AMCIGAR MAKE UNEQUIVOCAL STATEMENT AS FOLLOWS: NEITHER AMHAWK NOR ANY MEMBER AMCIGAR CONSIDERS THAT HIS CURRENT POSITION WITHIN AMRASP HAS ANYTHING TO DO WITH ANY POSITION IN THE POST-CASTRO CUBAN GOVT… 104-10168-10345.

11/1/60: DIR 89… **G. DROLLER** WH/4/PA TO MEXI MASH: REF DIR 04368: RE PARA 3 REF. ASSUMING YOU FIND **ORRISON** ROLE IN STATION AMRASP DELEGATION WORKING ARRANGEMENT SATISFACTORY. THUS WE PROCESSING **ORRISON** CONTRACT. 104-10171-10127.

11/5/60: MASH 1455 TO DIR: ON 3 NOV AMHAWK TOLD *TWICKER* THAT AMHAWK HAD RECEIVED INFORMATION THAT MANOLO RAY WANTED TO LEAVE CUBA AND WAS TO BE EXFILTRATED CLANDESTINELY BY **BENDER** GROUP. 104-10179-10403.

11/9/60: MASH 1528 TO DIR: RE PROBLEM OF AMRASP "AFILIADOS": ON NOV 8 *TWICKER* TOLD AMHAWK THAT HENCEFORTH **CORBUSTON** WOULD ASSUME FULL RESPONSIBILITY FOR PAYMENT OF SALARIES, MAINTENANCE, TRAVEL, RENT, ETC. 104-10168-10294.

11/21/60: MASH 1774 TO DIR: PURSUANT HQS AGREEMENT 18 NOV *TWICKER* OBTAINED AMHAWK CONCURRENCE FUND MANOLO RAY GROUP (MRP) SUM OF 7,500 DOLLARS, VIA COMPTROLLER PAULA. 104-10179-10348.

11/22/60: DIR 12777 TO MEXI MASH: MEXI STATION AUTHORIZED ADVANCE **ORRISON** UP TO $15,000 MONTHLY FOR JMNET/AMRASP ACTIVITIES MEXI. … **ORRISON** IS AUTHORIZED TRAVEL MASH OR HQS MONTHLY COORDINATE ACTIVITIES. 104-10171-10112.

11/22/60: CONTACT REPORT BY **WALLACE A. PARLETT** [= **DROLLER**]: AS PREARRANGED, **ORRISON** CAME TO MIAMI FROM MEXICO ON 14 NOVEMBER. **ORRISON** IS—UNDER THE SUPERVISION OF THE MEXICO STATION—THE CASE OFFICER FOR JMARC MATTERS IN MEXICO AND, IN THIS CONNECTION, HE HANDLES THE AMRASP BRANCH OFFICE IN OUR BEHALF. **ORRISON** WAS INTRODUCED TO THIS COMPLEX BY *HAMILTON*, BUT WHETHER OR NOT **ORRISON** IS KNOWN AS A **BENDER** MAN OR A *HAMILTON* MAN, OR WHATEVER ELSE, HAS BEEN LEFT UNSPOKEN. SINCE IT BECAME CLEAR THAT THE AMRASP MEXICO BRANCH WAS PRIMARILY A PROPAGANDA INSTRUMENTALITY, *HAMILTON* AND THE UNDERSIGNED, AFTER CONSULTATION WITH COS/JMASH, FELT IT ADVISABLE TO BRING **ORRISON** TOGETHER WITH THE JMASH PROPAGANDA OFFICES AND SUBSEQUENTLY WITH WH/4/PROP SECTION IN WASHINGTON. *HAMILTON* UNDERTOOK TO ARRANGE FOR THE SCHEDULIING OF THESE MEETINGS. 104-10171-10432.

THE PSEUDONYMS OF E. HOWARD HUNT: WALTER C. TWICKER...

11/24/60: JMASH 1841 TO DIR: AMHAWK QUERIED **_TWICKER_** RE PAY FOR NEW PILOTS (**INCLUDING FIORINI** [= FRANK STURGIS]) BROUGHT IN BY PEDRO DIAZ LANZ WHEN HE JOINED AMRASP. FEEL POLTICAL ADVANTAGES KEEPING DIAZ SATISFIED AND CO-OPERATIVE WELL WORTH ABOVE RELATIVELY MINOR EXPENDITURE. [MARGINALIA: FULLY CONCUR—**DROLLER**. 104-10260-10145.

11/29/60: THE _"ORRISON AFFAIR"_: ORRISON VISITED THE STATION OFFICES IN MIAMI AND HEADQUARTERS IN NOVEMBER 1960 FOR A BRIEFING ON ASPECTS OF HIS JOB. HE THEN SPENT THANKSGIVING IN HOUSTON WITH HIS FAMILY, AND ON ALL OF THESE TRAVELS HE CARRIED TWO LARGE BRIEFCASES OF CLASSIFIED CIA PAPERS. ORRISON ARRIVED IN MEXICO CITY FROM HOUSTON ON PAN AM AIRLINES AT 1115 HOURS ON TUESDAY, 29 NOVEMBER 1960. HE PICKED UP HIS STATION WAGON AT THE AIRPORT PARKING LOT, WHERE HE HAD STORED IT, THEN DROPPED OFF A TRAVELING COMPANION, AND PROCEDED TO HIS OFFICE AT [08]. HE PARKED THE STATION WAGON [08]. ORRISON WENT IN THE BACK SEAT OF THE STATION WAGON AND OPENED THE TWO BRIEFCASES, AND EXTRACTED SOME PAPERS PERTAINING TO HIS PERSONAL BUSINESS. HE CLOSED THE BRIEFCASES, COVERED THEM WITH A SUITBAG, AND LAID THEM ON THE FLOOR IN THE REAR OF THE STATION WAGON. HE THEN GOT OUT AND LOCKED THE DOORS AND WINDOWS OF THE STATION WAGON. SOME 30 MINUTES LATER, ORRISON RETURNED TO THE STATION WAGON AND, AFTER GLANCING TO THE REAR TO NOTE THE SUITBAG WAS IN PLACE, PROCEDED TO HIS APARTMENT. WHEN HE PICKED UP THE SUITBAG, THE BRIEFCASES WERE MISSING. EXAMINATION OF THE STATION WAGON REVEALED THAT A SMALL WINDOW IN FRONT HAD BEEN FORCED OPEN. ORRISON RETURNED TO THE ATOYAS AREA AND DROVE AROUND FOR ABOUT A HALF HOUR, THEN WENT BACK TO HIS APARTMENT AND TELEPHONED HIS MEXICO CITY STA-

TION CONTACT [03] TO REPORT THE BAD NEWS. [03] THEN ADVISED SCOTT [= MEXI STATION CHIEF]… BY 1800 HOURS THAT EVENING, NO TRACES OF THE MISSIING DOCUMENTS HAD BEEN FOUND. SCOTT SENT A CABLE TO HEADQUARTERS AND MIAMI, NOTIFYING THEM OF THE LOSS. …AMONG THE MISSING PAPERS WERE THE TRUE NAMES OF THE FOLLOWING CIA EMPLOYEES: JOSEPH BAKER, GERARD **DROLLER**, JACOB D. ESTERLINE, DAVID A. **PHILLIPS**, [03], STANNARD K. SHORT, [03], PHILLIP TOOMEY, E. HOWARD HUNT, AND WILLIAM KENT. THE FOLLOWING OFFICIAL CRYPTONYMS AND PSEUDONYMS WERE COMPROMISED: **AMCIGAR, AMGUPPY-1, AMHAWK-1 AND 2, AMRASP, AMWAIL, AMWAIL1 THROUGH 12, JMASH, SAMUEL G. ORRISON** (PSEUDO FOR [04], AND *WALTER C. TWICKER*. 104-10414-10124.

12/2/60: FROM DIR (**DROLLER**) TO JMGOLD: AS SEEN FROM HERE MRP POSTURE VIS-À-VIS ODYOKE, **BENDER** GROUP, AND AMRASP APPEARS TO BE IN STATE OF FLUX. IN HIS FIRST DISCUSSION WITH BENDER RAY DEVELOPED A POSITION WHICH WAS NOT ANTI-AMERICAN … BUT WHICH LEFT QUESTION WIDE OPEN WHETHER RAY'S PHILOSOPHY WOULD BE COMPATIBLE WITH LONG RANGE ODYOKE HEMISPHERIC INTERESTS. 104-10274-10012.

12/6/60: GOLD 2038 TO DIR: IN *HAMILTON*/AMDIP [NEWMAN = VARONA SINCE THE SECURITY COMPROMISE] 5 DEC DISCUSSION PROVISIONAL GOVT AMDIP AGREED THAT NOT ONLY PROVISIONAL PRESIDENT BUT ALL CABINET MEMBERS INELIGIBLE FOR SUCCEEDING ELECTIVE OFFICE. FYI: DOCUMENT AUTHORED BY CONTE AGUERO AND EDITED BY MANUEL RAY WOULD MAKE CABINET MEMBERS INELIGIBLE FOR ELECTIVE OFFICE. …AGREED THAT MIRO CARDONA PROBABLY BEST AVAILABLE MAN FOR PROVISIONAL PRESIDENT AND AS SUCH SHOULD NOT BE BROUGHT INTO AMIRON [NEWMAN: WAS AMRASP BEFORE SECURITY COMPROMISE] SINCE PREFERABLE

THAT PROV PRESIDENT NOT BE IDENTIFIED WITH ANY GROUP. 104-10165-10240

12/6/60: GOLD 2062 TO DIR: FOLL SUMMARIZES 6 DEC *HAMILTON*/AMJAG MTG: **AMJAG** [NEWMAN = AMWAIL/1, JUSTO CARRILLO] ...VOLUNTEERED INFO THAT MIRO AND RAY HAD FALLEN OUT, MIRO DEPRECATED RAY AS YOUTHFUL "PERSONALISTA" AND SAID THAT RAY WAS DISILLUSIONED WITH "YOU PEOPLE" BECAUSE ALLEGED PROMISES MADE BY BONSAL AND UNNAMED "HIGH EMBASSY OFFICIAL" HAD NOT BEEN HONORED BY **BENDER** GROUP.

WHEN *HAMILTON* EXPLAINED CIRCUMSTANCES INCLUDING RAY'S REFUSAL TO ACCEPT MONETARY ASSISTANCE MIAMI AMIRON AND HIS OPPOSITION TO THE 1940 CONSTITUTION, **AMJAG** EXPRESSED HIMSELF AS DISILLUSIONED WITH RAY WHO, HE SAID, WAS ACCUSTOMED TO THROWING AROUND MILLIONS IN CUBA AND HAD TREMENDOUS PRESIDENTIAL AMBITIONS. **AMJAG** CONCERNED OVER ALLEGED AGITATION IN CAMPS AND DESIROUS SPENDING XMAS WITH TROOPS IN COMPANY AMPORT [NEWMAN FRD EXCOM, WAS AMCIGAR BEFORE SECURITY COMPROMISE], POINTED OUT NECESSITY OF AMPORT AGREEING ON UNIFIED POSITION TO PRESENT TO TROOPS PRIOR DEPARTURE. 104-10193-10335

12/7/60: WAVE 2095 TO DIR: IN REVIEWING WITH *HAMILTON* POSSIBLE BASES FOR PROVISIONAL GOVT AMLOON-1 (RICARDO RAFAEL SARDINAS DANCHEZ) EXCLUDED HIMSELF FROM ANY PARTICIPATION, STATING THAT HE DESIRED ONLY TO RETURN TO HIS FINCA, HIS LAW OFFICE AND PRESIDENCY OF COLONOS. ... AMLOON-1 ON POINT OF RESIGNING OVER WHAT HE CONSIDERS FIDELISTA INTRIGUING BY AMJAG [JUSTO CORRILLO HERNANDEZ] BUT ALLOWED HIMSELF BE PERSUADED MORE VALOR AND UTILITY IN REMAINING. 104-10168-10220.

12/7/60: DIR 15428 G. **DROLLER** TO PRI WAVE REF A. WAVE 2038 B. WAVE 2041: IN VIEW PARA 3 REF B CONTE AGUERO PERHAPS NOW READY DO BUSINESS AMIRON. …IF ABOVE FEASIBLE FEEL WE SHOULD DRIVE WEDGE BETWEEN AGUERO AND RAY …REQUEST _CRABANAC_ WHO FULLY FAMILIAR THINKING IN REF PARA 1 ABOVE EXPLORE AND ADVISE SOONEST. WH COMMENT REF A: _HAMILTON_ AMDIP DISCUSSION RE PROVISION GOVERNMENT ON 5 DEC. 104-10165-10233; SEE ALSO 104-10274-10021.

12/9/60: WAVE 2142 TO DIR REF DIR 14634: DURING INITIAL EXPLORATORY MTG WITH QDBIAS [NEWMAN: PEDRO LANZ] 8 DEC _HAMILTON_ WAS IMPRESSED WITH MAN'S SINCERITY AND POTENTIAL. QDBIAS ENTHUSIASTIC OVER REF TRIP BUT WANTED VERY CAREFUL PREPARATION IN ORDER AVOID ANY POSSIBLE FAILURE. … QDBIAS SPEEDING UP WORK ON A/C WHICH CAN BE READY O/A 15 DEC. PLANE CAN ACCOMMODATE NUMBER NAMED WAVE 2351 (IN 12988). C/S COMMENT REF: HQS APPROVED PLANNING DIAZ-LANZ PROPAGANDA "FLIGHT OF TRUTH" AS PROPOSED HQS BY _TWICKER_. 104-10260-10141.

12/10/60: MEXI 6904 TO OPIM DIRREF DIR 15781 [OUT 51484]: DEBRIEF **PACHUKE** [NEWMAN = WAS **ORRISON** BEFORE HE LOST THE TWO SUITCASES] CONTINUING. LONGAN [NEMWAN: POSSIBLY SHOULD BE LANGAN OF WH/4/SECURITY] PLANS TAKE **PACHUKE** WASH FOR LCFLUTTER [= POLYGRAPH] ETA 12 DEC 60. 104-10168-10213 [NEWMAN: FULL PSEUDO WAS **DUDLEY. J. PACHUKE** SEE 101-10171-10060].

12/16/60: MEXI 6944 TO DIR RE DIR 16758: ONLY POSSIBLE LOCAL REPLACEMENT **DOUGLAS J. FREAPANE**. STATION AND **FREAPANE** BOTH FEEL WOULD BE BURNING A LONG TERM STATION ASSET TO PUT **FREAPANE** IN DIRECT CONTACT. IF **PACHUKE** PASSES LCFLUTTER RE LOYALTY SUGGEST HE HAS LEARNED LESSON HARD WAY AND BE ALLOWED CONTINUE FUNCTION

THE PSEUDONYMS OF E. HOWARD HUNT: WALTER C. TWICKER...

UNTIL SUITABLE HQS REPLACEMENT FOUND. IF HQS DOES NOT AGREE SUGGEST SENDING LINGUIST TDY. 104-10171-10117.

12/21/60: DIR 17970 L. NAPOLI TO JMWAVE MADD PANAMA CITY RAND GUATEMALA: PER TELECON 19 DEC *CRABANAC* WAS TOLD THAT PASSPORT NOT VISAED AND WOULD REQUIRE 7-8 DAYS TO PROCESS. LEARNING THIS *CRABANAC* CANCELLED REQUEST FOR PASSPORT ADVISING SUBJ WOULD LEAVE BLACK. WH COMMENT RE WAVE 2369: REQ FALSE DOCUMENT FOR AMBIDDY-1'S TRAVEL; IF NOT AVAILABLE SUBJ WOULD TRAVEL BLACK. 104-10240-10111. [NEWMAN: AFTER THE SECURITY COMPROMISE THE *WALTER C. TWICKER* PSEUDO WAS CHANGED TO *TERRENCE S. CRABANAC*.]

12/24/60: J.D. ESTERLINE MEMO FOR C/WH/4/PA **DROLLER**. RE CUBAN OPPOSITION GROUPS AND MANOLO RAY'S NEW POLITICAL POSTURE: I ASSUME THAT A DEAL [WITH VARONA] COULD BE IN PROGRESS WHICH WE ARE NOT AWARE OF. I WOULD SUGGEST, THEREFORE, THAT THIS NEW DEVELOPMENT AND THIS MEMORANDUM BE REVIEWED CAREFULLY WITH *HAMILTON* WHEN YOU NEXT SEE HIM. 104-10167-10072.

12/28/60: BELL 0047 TO OPIM MEXI REF MEXI 6944: **PACHUKE** WILL RETURN MEXI NEAR FUTURE TO SETTLE ACCTS WITH APPROPRIATE STATION OFFICER. ADVISE AMIRON MEXI CONTACTS THAT HE NO LONGER AVAILABLE WORK WITH THEM. 104-10171-10115.

12/29/60: CONTACT REPORT FROM **WALLACE A. PARLETT** [= **DROLLER**] SUBJ: MEETING WITH AMBRONC-1 (EDUARDO MARTIN Y ELENA) AT *CRABANAC'S* COCONUT GROVE APARTMENT, 21 DECEMBER 1960: EUSTACE C. KEATOR, USING THE ALIAS COLONEL RODERICK, ACCOMPANIED ME TO THE MEETING. THE PURPOSE OF MY TALK WITH AMBRONC-1 WAS TO ASSESS HIS ATTITUDE TOWARD THE PROCEDURES IN ESTABLISHING A PROVISIONAL GOVERNMENT IN CUBA. THIS PURPOSE WAS NEVER

MENTIONED EXPLICITLY AND THE ENTIRE DISCUSSION WAS HANDLED INTENTIONALLY IN A LOW KEY. ... I WAS PREOCCUPIED WITH HOW A PROVISIONAL GOVERNMENT COULD BE ESTABLISHED. ... AMBRONC-1 REPLIED THAT THE 1940 CONSTITUTION SHOULD BE THE BASIS FOR ANY FUTURE GOVERNMENT. ... AMBRONC-1 THEN TOLD ME ABOUT HIS MEETING WITH AMBANG-1 (MANUEL RAY), AND LET IT BE KNOWN THAT HE WAS RATHER IMPRESSED WITH HIS HONESTY AND SINCERITY. I ASKED HIM WHETHER HE HAD EXAMINED AMBANG-1'S POLITICAL BELIEFS. HE ASSURED ME HE HAD NOT. 104-10274-10003.

12/31/60: WAVE 2621 TO BELL: CITING AMBIDDY-1'S PLANNED RETURN TO CUBA, AMPALM-5 ON 30 DEC TOLD *CRABANAC* HE ANXIOUS EMULATE AMBIDDY [=ARTIME] AND CITED PREVIOUS REQUEST TO **BENDER** WHICH ADMITTEDLY NOT ANSWERED. AMPALM-5 WAS TOLD HIS REQUEST WOULD RECEIVE CONSIDERATION ONCE HE HAD COMPLETED ALL PREREQUISITES AS HAD AMBIDDY, I.E. ACCEPTABLE INFILTRATION AND POLITICAL PLANS, TRNG AT CAMP AND REVIEW OF TARGET SITUATION. COMMENT: THIS TO BE EXPECTED AS ALL AMPORT [**NEWMAN: FORMERLY AMCIGAR**] MEMBERS KEENLY AWARE THAT MORE FACE CAN BE MADE IN CUBA THAN IS BEING LOST IN MIAMI. FEEL ONE WAY DISCOURAGE THE OLDER AND PHYSICALLY UNFIT IS FOLLOW THRU ON POSTPONED XMAS TRIP COMMITMENT, SHOW CAMP RIGORS AND QUELL SENTIMENT. THUS, REQUEST DEFINITE DATE FOR AMPORT BLACK FLIGHT TO TRAV. 104-10220-10379—MARGINALIA OVER AMPORT READS "FRD EXEC COMMITTEE"—AND 104-10240-10103.

1/6/61: BELL 0297 [BISSELL] TO PRIORITY WAVE, REF MEXI 7023: SUGGEST *CRABANAC* LOOK INTO PARA 3 REF MATTER WHILE TDY MEXI. ADDITIONAL TRAFFIC RE ROBERTO DE VARONA BEHAVIOR AVAILABLE WAVE. AFTER FACTS ASCERTAINED ASSUME *CRABANAC* WILL ATTEMPT REMEDY SITUATION VIA APPROPRIATE CHANNEL. SUGGEST *CRABANAC* TDY HQS IMMEDIATELY AFTER MEXI TRIP.

THE PSEUDONYMS OF E. HOWARD HUNT: WALTER C. TWICKER...

WH COMMENT: MEXI 7023 STATED LITAINT-2, 5, LITAMIL-1, AND 2 DISGUSTED SCANDALOUS ACTIVITIES ROBERTO DE VARONA & OTHERS MEXI DELEG AND WILL ATTEMPT CONVINCE AMIRON MIAMI DO AWAY WITH MEXI GROUP SOONEST. 104-10171-10444.

1/13/61: BELL 0807 [BISSELL—*HOWARD HUNT* IS AUTHOR OF THIS CABLE] TO MEXI, REF MEXI 7056: APPROVE PROCEDURE DEVELOPED IN COS/*CRABANAC* TALK 12 JAN: **CRABANAC** WILL TRAVEL MEXI APPROX ONCE EACH MONTH REVIEW ACCOUNTING, PROVIDE FUNDING AND OPNL ORIENTATION MEXIDELEG. MEXIDELEG FUNDING TO BE T/A WAVE. DURING *CRABANAC* ABSENCE MEXI UNDERSTAND MEXIDELEG CONTACT TO BE VIA CARLOS FERNANDEZ TO **MERTON** [NEWMAN = JACK STEWART]. 104-10171-10119.

1/13/61: *HUNT* MEMO: I ARRIVED IN MEXICO CITY ON THE NIGHT OF 10 JANUARY AND WAS MET BY **ANDREW F. MERTON** [= STEWART]. **MERTON** HAD NO MEANS OF CONTACT WITH THE DELEGATION AND SO I WAS FORCED TO HAVE AS MY FIRST CONTACT SENORA [06] (SENORA [06] AND I HAVE KNOWN EACH OTHER FOR MANY YEARS. ... AT NOON ON 12 JANUARY I INFORMED COS, MEXICO CITY OF THE DELEGATION SITUATION AND OF THE ACTION I HAD TAKEN TO ASSURE THE EFFICIENT COMPLETION OF ITS WORK. WE AGREED THAT **ANDREW F. MERTON** SHOULD BE INTRODUCED BOTH TO SENORA [06] AND TO FERNANDEZ AS "**JACK WARREN**." SENORA [06] IS TO CONTACT **MERTON** ONLY UNDER EMERGENCY CIRCUMSTANCES, BUT FERNANDEZ WILL MEET ROUTINELY EACH THURSDAY WITH **MERTON** TO ADVISE HIM OF DELEGATION MATTERS AND TO RECEIVE ADDITIONAL FUNDING INCREMENTS. 104-10171-10118.

2/2/61: AMPALM-5 PRQII: SUBJECT FOUNDED A CHRISTIAN POLITICAL MOVEMENT IN CUBA IN OPPOSITION TO CASTRO REGIME. IN APRIL 1960 HE FLED CUBA. HIS ORGANIZATION WAS ALREADY IN CONTACT WITH CIA AND HE WAS PLACED IN CON-

TACT WITH **WALLACE A. PARLETT** [= **DROLLER**]. HE AGREED TO COOPERATE WITH PRIVATE AMERICANS WHO WOULD ASSIST A CUBAN LIBERATION MOVEMENT. SUBJECT COULD BE TURNED OVER TO ANY C/O KNOWLEDGABLE OF CUBAN AND CARRIBBEAN POLITICAL NUANCES, IF INTRODUCED BY **WALLACE A. PARLETT** OR *TERENCE S. CRABANAC*. SUBJECT IS AN OFFICIAL OF AN OVERT ORGANIZATION WITH HEADQUARTERS IN AN AMERICAN CITY. 104-10519-10227.

2/12/61: MADD1404 **PONCHAY** [= ESTERLINE] SENDS TO BELL: *CRABANAC* RETURNING WAVE O/A 13 FEB. WILL ACT AS ESCORT OFFICER FOR AMDIP-1, AMBIDDY-1 AND DR. ANTONIO MACEO ON BLACK FLT TO TRNG AREAS. ...**CRABANAC** WILL MAKE ARRANGEMENTS WITH MACEO ON RETURN MIA. PURPOSE TRIP, OUR JUDGMENT, SHOULD BE EXPLAIN TO TROOPS CURRENT STATUS AMPORT, FACT THAT AMIRON NOT DISSOLVED BUT ON CONTRARY ENLARGED. 104-10240-10215.

2/16/61: WAVE 3725 TO BELL: IF MEXIDELEG ACCTG READY SUGGEST **MERTON** [= STEWART] BRING SAME TO JMWAVE FOR REVIEW AND DISCUSSION AS *CRABANAC* UNABLE TDY MEXI FORESEEABLE FUTURE. ADVISE ETA TO ASSURE *CRABANAC* WAVE AREA. 104-10171-10382.

2/17/61: BELL 1751 TO MEXI WAVE REF WAVE 3725: NO OBJECTION HERE IF YOU CONCUR. WH COMMENT REF: SUGGESTED **MERTON** BRING JANUARY **AMIRON** MEXIDELEG ACCOUNTING TO WAVE FOR REVIEW AND DISCUSSION AS **CRABANAC** UNABLE TDY MEXI FORESEEABLE FUTURE. 104-10171-10381 [NOTE: AMIRON = FRD].

2/17/61: WAVE 3746 TO BELL REF BELL 1613: C/S COMMENT REF: *CRABANAC* AUTHORIZED TO TELL AMDIP-1 THAT IF HE CAN GIVE *CRABANAC* SPECIFIC REFS TO INDIVIDUAL OFFICERS IN TRAIN-

ING AND SPECIFIC REASONS WHY THEY NOT COMPETENT. 104-10167-10223.

3/2/61: WAVE 4122 TO BELL: IN EVENT HQS CONTEMPLATING CONTINUED FINANCIAL AID TO LORIE SUGGEST CONSIDER FOLL FACTORS: *CRABANAC* IN GOOD FAITH TOLD ARTIME, UPON RETURN FROM JMRYE, THAT **BENDER** HAD TERMINATED UNILATERAL AID TO LORIE... 104-10240-10300.

3/7/61: MEXI 7525 TO WAVE INFO BELL: REF ACCOUNTING READY [MARGINALIA: "FEB MEXI DELEGATION ACCOUNTING"] C/S COMMENT REF: *CRABANAC* ETA MEXI 9 MAR REVIEW MEXI DELEG ACCTG. [MARGINALIA: "NOTE: WAS TO HAVE BEEN REVIEWED BY *HUNT* ON HIS PLANNED TRIP TO MEXI AND HQS."] 104-10171-10435.

5/10/61: BELL 0489 TO MEXI REF MEXI 7938 (IN 43759): REQUEST STATION CONTACT **PACHUKE** STATING DOING SO AT HIS REQUEST. ADVISE WE HAVE NO FURTHER CONTEMPLATED USE HIS SERVICES FROM HQS STANDPOINT. SUGGEST YOU HAVE HIM EXECUTE SECRECY AGREEMENT AND QUITCLAIM AFTER SETTLING ANY OUTSTANDING REIMBURSABLE EXPENSES HE HAS INCURRED. CHARGE JMATE. WH COMMENT REF: MEXI AGREES TERMINATION **DUDLEY J. PACHUKE** AND SUGGESTS CLEARANCE BE MAINTAINED. 104-10171-10057.

APPENDIX SIX:
AL COX AND ROBERT REYNOLDS

THE BACKGROUND OF AL COX

On 6 August 1945 the *Enola Gay* dropped the first atomic bomb on Hiroshima, Japan. At the time E. Howard Hunt was serving in the Office of Strategic Services (OSS) in China. He volunteered to go with a team to Nanjing, a city known for the terrible atrocities committed by the Japanese army there. In his autobiography, ***American Spy***, Hunt identifies the commander of the team that landed at Nanjing airfield as "Colonel Al Cox."[939] The OSS, which was formed on 13 June 1942, was dissolved on 9 September 1945. In 1948, the U.S. created a covert psychological and paramilitary operations organization known as the Office of Policy Coordination (OPC). It was merged with the CIA in 1951. Hunt went to work for the OPC and was assigned the job of setting up training courses in covert political and psychological warfare. Al Cox also went to work for the OPC. Hunt reports that Cox was assigned to Taiwan to advise

---

[939] E. Howard Hunt, *American Spy: My Secret History in the CIA, Watergate and Beyond* (Hoboken: John Wiley and Sons, Inc., 2007) pp. 27-28. RIF 104-10301-10004.

Chiang-Kai-shek's "shaky" nationalist government and that later "Cox became the president of Civil Air Transport, the CIA-owned and operated nationalist airline."[940]

In 1958, Al Cox was working in the CIA's Political and Psychological Staff (PP) as a senior officer under the chief of the Paramilitary Division (PMD—which later became the Paramilitary Group, PMG). According to Volume III of the *CIA's Official History of the Bay of Pigs Operations* by Jack B. Pfeiffer, Cox wrote a proposal to the chief of the PP Staff at the time when the Agency's fears about Castro's movement were increasing. Pfeiffer states that Cox had a "rather different idea," and suggested that instead of trying to "whip Castro," the "wisest move for the Agency would be to join Castro."[941]

Cox believed that, since Batista was doomed, the CIA should find a way to reverse Castro's hostility toward the U.S. that had resulted from the American support of Batista. In his 25 August 1958 memo to the chief of PP Staff about how to accomplish this, Cox offered this course of action:

> A practical way to protect the United States interests in this matter would be to make secret contact with Castro, assure him of the U.S. sympathy with some of his objectives, and to offer him support. The individual chosen to make the contact should be of such background that it is clear that he speaks with the authority of the U.S. government. Obviously the support must be given covertly so as not to endanger U.S. relations with Batista. The most effective means of help to Castro would be arms and ammunition. Air dropping this equipment might be dangerous from the security aspect. Allowing a shipload of equipment manned by a Cuban crew to evade our Coast Guard would probably be a better method. The most secure means of help would be giving

---

940 E. Howard Hunt, *American Spy: My Secret History in the CIA, Watergate and Beyond* (Hoboken: John Wiley and Sons, Inc., 2007) pp. 45-48.
941 12/59, Jack B. Pfeiffer, *CIA Official History of the Bay of Pigs Operations*, Volume III, p. 8. RIF 104-10301-10004. Note: Pfeiffer suggests that C/PMD sent the proposal forward; see fn below showing Pfeiffer's fn 15 on p. 348 shows that the proposal was originally a memo sent *from* Cox to the Chief of PP PMD.

the money to Castro, who could then purchase his own arms. A combination of money and arms would be best.[942]

Citing a fall 1958 Agency report that Castro was "definitely" not a communist, Pfeiffer noted that not all CIA reporting "out of the Cuban area" was biased against Castro.[943]

By the end of 1958, the CIA's Western Hemisphere Division (WHD) asked the PMD to establish a small contingency task force capable of making air drops into Cuba to dissidents "who were both anti-Castro and anti-Batista." Two Agency representatives, one of them from PMD, were sent to Havana to locate these dissidents.[944] On 31 December 1958, Alfred Cox (PP/PMD) reported this to WHD:

> A Helio Courier was already in place in Key West with a backup Helio in Washington; a sterile C-54 had been requested from Europe; and the Office of Logistics would have an arms load rigged for a drop by 2 January 1959.[945]

There are more memoranda from this period on the subject of Castro authored by Cox.[946] A year later, on 21 January 1960, a meeting was held at CIA HQS to talk about propaganda and to identify and discuss "the principal" future leaders of Cuba. The meeting was attended by Dick Helms, J. C. King, and Jake Esterline, and Al Cox attended as "one of the senior officers in paramilitary [group]."[947] At that time, the CIA was gearing up a new branch (WH/4) dedicated exclusively to toppling the Castro regime. Proposals were discussed at an 11 February 1960 staff meeting attended

---

942 8/25/58, Memo for Chief, PP STAFF by Alfred T. Cox, Chief, PP Paramilitary Division, Subject: U.S. Course of Action in Cuba; *CIA Official History of the Bay of Pigs Operations*, Volume III, pp. 8-9, and fn 15, p. 348. RIF 104-10301-10004.
943 12/00/79, Jack B. Pfeiffer, *CIA Official History of the Bay of Pigs Operations*, Volume III, p. 8. RIF 104-10301-10004.
944 12/00/79, Jack B. Pfeiffer, *CIA Official History of the Bay of Pigs Operations*, Volume III, pp. 13-14. RIF 104-10301-10004.
945 12/31/58, Memo for Bob Dahlgren from Alfred T. Cox and Colonel C. H. Heinlein, Subject: Support Arrangements; 12/59, Jack B. Pfeiffer, *CIA Official History of the Bay of Pigs Operations*, Volume III, fn 23, p. 349. RIF 104-10301-10004.
946 1/30/59, Memo for Chief WHD and Chief FI Staff from Alfred T. Cox, Subject: Research Project on Castro Movement; *CIA Official History of the Bay of Pigs Operations*, Volume III, fn 28, p. 350. RIF 104-10301-10004.
947 12/00/79, Jack B. Pfeiffer, *CIA Official History of the Bay of Pigs Operations*, Volume III, pp. 44-46. RIF 104-10301-10004.

WHERE ANGELS TREAD LIGHTLY

by Tracy Barnes, Jake Esterline, Al Cox, Dave Phillips and Jim Flannery.[948] Pfeiffer reports on another Cox memo from October 1960.[949]

ENTER: ROBERT REYNOLDS

When the new Cuban Branch in the CIA emerged officially in March 1960, the Deputy Chief's name was Robert Reynolds. There is no mention of the name "Al Cox" in WH/4 documents. Many years after his retirement from the Agency, in 2001, Reynolds attended a conference of Americans and Cubans, including Fidel Castro, on the Bay of Pigs. Reynolds furnished this biographical statement:

- Began his CIA Latin America career in 1949 and served in Mexico, Argentina, Bolivia and Brazil
- From 1957 to March 1960 was the CIA's Caribbean desk officer monitoring the Cuban revolution
- March-September 1960 served as deputy to Jacob Esterline, the CIA's task force chief
- *CIA chief of Miami base (the largest CIA station in the world) from September 1960 to October 1961*
- Retired from CIA and the Foreign Service in 1968

I have added emphasis to the fourth bullet which discusses Reynolds' tenure as the chief of the CIA's JMWAVE Station in Miami.

The formation of WH/4 at CIA HQS was followed by the creation of a forward operations base in Coral Gables. This base was later relocated to Miami, and initially given the cryptonym JMASH.[950] The base expanded exponentially over the summer and fall of 1960 and, after the Orrison security compromise in November 1960 (See Appendix Five), the JMASH cryptonym was changed to JMWAVE.[951] Reynolds thus be-

---

948 12/00/79, Jack B. Pfeiffer, *CIA Official History of the Bay of Pigs Operations*, Volume III, pp. 46-47. RIF 104-10301-10004.
949 10/12/60, Memo for Chief WHD from Alfred T. Cox, Subject: Recruitment of American Volunteers; *CIA Official History of the Bay of Pigs Operations*, Volume III, fn 106, p. 362. RIF 104-10301-10004.
950 12/00/79, Jack B. Pfeiffer, *CIA Official History of the Bay of Pigs Operations*, Volume III, pp. 84. RIF 104-10301-10004.
951 12/00/79, Jack B. Pfeiffer, *CIA Official History of the Bay of Pigs Operations*, Volume III, p. 100. RIF 104-10301-10004. See also the "Orrisson Affair" in Appendix One (Selected CIA Cryptonyms) of this book.

came the base chief a few months after the move to the Miami complex and was there before, during and after the cryptonym change.

At this point it is important to pay attention to the Church Committee deposition of the man who replaced Reynolds as chief of the JM-WAVE Station. His name was Theodore G. "Ted" Shackley, and on 19 August 1975 he testified before the Church Committee using the pseudonym "Halley." Shackley told the committee that the name of the man who headed JMWAVE before his arrival was "Mr. Al Cox, who has since died." Then the following exchange took place:

> Mr. Barron: Was that team the equivalent of the JMWAVE Station?
>
> Mr. Halley: Yes. Mr. Cox was the head, then, of what would be the equivalent of the JMWAVE Station.
>
> Mr. Barron: Was he the head of JMWAVE until the point when you replaced him, or until the point you became the chief of the JMWAVE Station?
>
> Mr. Halley: That is correct. He was head of that unit until such time as I replaced him.[952]

Shackley had already arrived at the JMWAVE Station before he replaced Cox, and that happened because Cox was fired by William Harvey.

The chief of Task Force W (TFW), William Harvey, had pressed Shackley to go to Miami as JMWAVE's chief of operations. Harvey said that taking this job was the "brass ring" that held out the prospect of becoming the station chief. Shackley wrote that he agreed to go. In his autobiography, *Spymaster—My Life in the CIA*, he described the arrangement put into place when he arrived at the JMWAVE Station:

> My reception at the Miami Station was correct but cold. Station chief Al Cox was on leave, according to what his secretary told me. It was agreed then that his deputy, Bob Moore, would handle the day-to-day traffic of the station, while I, in the capacity of operations, would organize and prepare for the future. What followed were four and a half intensive days of breakfast, lunch, and dinner meetings, lots of quick chats over a *café cubano*

---

952 8/19/75, Shackley deposition to the Church Committee, p. 9. RIF 157-10014-10046.

with contract agents and Cuban personalities, and conferences with station officers, particularly Dave Morales and Tony Sforza, who were fluent Spanish speakers and had seen service in Havana. Morales, who was chief of paramilitary, was frequently accompanied by his assistant, Tom Clines.[953]

It is possible that Cox's leave began close to the time Reynolds gave for the end of his duty as the chief of JMWAVE—October 1961. It is clear that there was no other station chief between Cox and Shackley. We know that the deputy chief, Bob Moore, filled in until William Harvey fired Cox.

Cox returned to Miami but spent most of his time at his home instead of at work. Unfortunately for Cox, that was the situation when William Harvey came to visit the station. Shackley had persuaded William Harvey to come to the station for a review of the March operations schedule:

> On the designated date, I picked Harvey up at Miami International Airport. Seeing me as his only greeter, he grumpily asked, "Where is Cox?" Startled somewhat by the question, I told Bill that Cox was probably at home, as he had not been in the office in the last two days. "What is the problem with this guy?" asked Bill. I said he might have been trying to cope with a major medical issue. Cox's secretary, I added, was very devoted to him and spent a lot of her working time caring for him at his residence.

Instead of going to the operations review, Harvey left Shackley when they got to the station and went to Cox's home. Three hours later Harvey found Shackley in his office and gave him this report:

> He said he had found Cox at home in bed and had relieved him on the spot as chief of station. Harvey said he had already sent a cable to Helms outlining this development and telling Helms that, as of that time, I was the acting chief of station. The "acting" label lasted until May 1962 when I was officially confirmed as chief of station, JMWAVE."[954]

---

953   Ted Shackley, *Spymaster—My Life in the CIA* (Dulles, Virginia: Potomac Books, 2005), p, 51.
954   Ted Shackley, *Spymaster—My Life in the CIA* (Dulles, Virginia: Potomac Books, 2005), p, 55.

Memoranda from late January and early February 1962 suggest that Cox's firing occurred in late January (rather than early February) and that he was immediately transferred back to his original unit in PP at CIA HQS.[955]

From all of the known references to Cox in Pfeiffer's Volume III (of the CIA Bay of Pigs history) and elsewhere, we discover a hole from February 1960 to late January 1962. Into this gap Reynolds' assignment at JMWAVE fits perfectly. Not long after he returned to HQS, Al Cox wrote an interesting report about how his unit in PP/PMG had penetrated WH/4:

> Stringent security precautions were placed on JMARC including the *exclusion of the PP Staff* and other Agency components from all cable and dispatch traffic and from access to correspondence between the project and the office of the DDP. In point of fact such restrictive measures were somewhat meaningless insofar as keeping awareness of the project's activities away from PP/PMG. The A/DDP/granted permission to PP/C/PMG to read daily project traffic (with Esterline's knowledge and permission). Esterline personally knew the majority of the PP/senior officers and in no time *he had drafted six or seven of these including the Deputy Chief PMG for assignment to JMARC*. This of course was valuable as a built-in penetration of JMARC in the best FI and CI tradition.[956]
> [Emphasis added]

JMARC, the CIA cryptonym for the WH/4 anti-Castro operation, was changed after the Orrison security compromise in November 1960 to JMATE.[957] In any event, it appears reasonable to suggest that Cox (as Robert Reynolds) was one of these six or seven offi-

---

955   1/23/62 Memo to Al Cox, Re Pedro Margolles y Duenas and a Cuban plot to assassinate President Kennedy. RIF 104-10506-10026; and 2/16/62, Memorandum for Al Cox, Subject: Missing Memoranda. RIF: 104-10233-10232.
956   Alfred T. Cox, Subject: Paramilitary Ground Activities at the Staff Level, 15 September 1955 – 31 December 1961; 12/00/79, Jack B. Pfeiffer, *CIA Official History of the Bay of Pigs Operations*, Volume III, fn 16, p. 353. RIF 104-10301-10004.
957   12/00/79, Jack B. Pfeiffer, *CIA Official History of the Bay of Pigs Operations*, Volume III, n. p. 46. RIF 104-10301-10004; See also Appendix Five of this book for the "Orrison Affair."

cers—and probably the deputy chief of PP/PMG. Esterline gave Reynolds his job as the deputy chief of WH/4.

On a visit to Cuba in 2001 for the scholarly summit with Fidel and Raul Castro mentioned above, Robert Reynolds allegedly told his Cuban interlocutors, "Me and my staff were all Fidelistas."[958] This statement, if Reynolds made it as alleged, is not inconsistent with Cox's position that the CIA should have considered secretly both arming and financing Fidel Castro to heal the latter's anti-U.S. attitude due to their support for Batista.

---

958 01/09/12, Humbarto Fontava, "How the U.S. 'Bullied' Poor Little Castro," TOWN HALL.com.

APPENDIX SEVEN:
THE PSYCHOLOGICAL AND PARAMILITARY OPERATIONS STAFF

We will build upon the information in this Appendix in the forthcoming volumes of this work. Below is a list of subordinate offices of the PP staff and a chart indicating some of the history of four men who worked in PP:

PP/PMG (Paramilitary Group)
PP/PA (possibly Political Action)
PP/EAD (?? Division)
PP/CRTV (Cinema, Radio and Television)
PP/Information Coordination
PP/SRD (?? Division)
PP/IOD (possibly International Organizations Division)
PP/ADMIN
PP/SECURITY

HISTORY OF CIA PSYCHOLOGICAL WARFARE

Army COL Al Cox was Howard Hunt's CDR in OSS (China)		
11/49 Hunt in Office of Policy Coordination (OPC) Group II: Political and Psychological Warfare		Al Cox was advisor to Chiang Kai-shek
	Cox heads CIA's Civil Air Transport	
54 Phillips in PP/CRTV	8/53 Hunt is CH PP/Staff/FE	
	6/54 Hunt is CH PP/Staff/FE	
4/55 Phillips in PP/OPS Staff 8/55 Phillips in PP/Ops/Info Coord Div		
8/58 Phillips in "PP activities" for Havana COS		58 Al Cox in PP/PMG
4/60 Phillips CH/WH/4/PP; William Kent* with Phillips	4/60 Hunt: WH/4/PA	4/60 Cox is D/CH WH/4
9/61 Phillips is CH/Covert Action Mexico City Station	6-11/61 Hunt in DCI office	9/60-10/61 Cox CH/JMASH/JMWAVE; in 1960 Kent is JMWAVE chief of Psych Warfare Branch, and reconstitutes DR remnant into DRE

*William Kent is Robert Trouchard; Al Cox is Robert Reynolds

APPENDIX EIGHT:
RESEARCH METHODOLOGIES

I have spent many years visiting the National Archives and using the Mary Ferrell website. I would like to share some research strategies I have developed over that time that go beyond the first stage of searching by name or event.

HOW TO MAXIMIZE YOUR RESEARCH TIME ON MFF AND NARA

The Mary Ferrell Foundation (MFF) provides JFK researchers with an extraordinary opportunity to access records. The data base and website far surpass anything available elsewhere—due to the genius and hard work of Rex Bradford. The system that Rex has designed enables the researcher to see the entire document before making a decision to download it for digital storage and/or to print a hardcopy. You cannot do this at National Archives (NARA) in College Park, where you must select boxes from finding aids and fish through them. While it is true that you can, from the comfort of your home, search the NARA JFK Records data base, you cannot see the document. You see only the Record Identification Form (RIF). These RIF sheets, made with the human hands of redactors who are brought in periodically to review the documents, are notoriously inadequate in what they actually tell you about the document. I estimate that there is a better than a fifty percent chance that from the RIF sheet alone you cannot determine whether or not you want the document.

With these considerations in mind, below are some research strategies I have developed to 1) speed up the process of getting to the documents you need in any given moment, and 2) get around the countless mistakes made by the creators of the RIF sheets that do not tell you what you need to know. These strategies go beyond the usual method of merely entering a name or a subject to see what pops up. But I will start with that strategy just the same.

ENTERING A NAME OR SUBJECT

Just entering a name or subject in the *search all documents box* will get you further on MFF than NARA. We owe Rex Bradford a huge thank you for providing this faculty. Placing quotation marks around this entry in the *search all documents box* is a good way to block hundreds or thousands of other documents from popping up on your screen. Let's say you are searching for Dave Phillips. Refine this strategy by entering "Dave Phillips" "David Phillips" "David A. Phillips" "David Atlee Phillips"; you may also use the AND feature: "Dave" AND "Phillips". You may also use the "OR" feature: "Dave Phillips" OR "David Phillips." For instructions on how to work with these basic strategies go to *How to Search* on the Search page of the MFF website.

1. THE CENTER RIF BLOCK SEARCH STRATEGY

To employ this useful technique you need to understand *what* the RIF numbers themselves tell you about *where the documents are located* physically and in cyber space. The RIF number is made up of 13 dig-

RESEARCH METHODOLOGIES

its divided into three groups separated by two dashes: 000-00000-00000. Think of this three-tiered system as something like a library building: a stack on a floor, and then the books in that stack that have an additional set of numbers. That's how RIF numbers really work.

The first three numbers [**000**-00000-00000] tell you the *main location* of the document. This is usually an institutional location such as FBI files (124) or CIA files (104), or Senate Select Committee on Intelligence on Intelligence Activities (157) or House Select Committee on Assassinations (180).

The second block of five numbers [000-**00000**-00000] is the most important and what you really want to pay attention to. This set of numbers represents, metaphorically, the stack where the librarian placed books that are in some way similar. When searching for records on the MFF website, the system is even more precise than that. It tells you *where* similar documents on a person or subject were placed on a particular day for the first time. The same document may have come into the entire collection from different sources and at different times. Therefore a single document may have been placed in the collection multiple times. This phenomenon is reflected in the *center* RIF block. Documents on Phillips may be in several locations—and are best identifiable by their different *center* RIF block [000-**00000**-00000] locations.

The final block of five numbers [000-00000-**00000**] is related to the document itself rather than its location. However, this block is inextricably bound to the center RIF block which precedes it.

Now let's suppose you are on MFF and have happened upon a couple of documents that you consider very important. Let's say they are cables and dispatches between CIA HQS and its Station in Havana or JMWAVE in Miami. You determine that the information or story they are discussing is exactly what you have been looking for. Yet from the documents you are looking at this story is incomplete. You notice that they contain references to previous cables at the top and even a small comment at the bottom of the cable describing what a previous cable was talking about. You enter the indicated cable numbers in the MFF *search all documents box* and nothing comes up.

This situation can happen for a number of reasons. If the document was old with smudges in the wrong places you can still find it. The first strategy is to take advantage of what I call the "center RIF block" strategy. Look at the most important document you have and enter its RIF number in the *RIF search window* (on the right side of the gray tool bar). Hit the enter key once on your computer and MFF will then present a *search results window* for your document. It will have a title, some text, the RIF number and a date. Now, let's say hypothetically that the RIF number you entered was 104-10165-10167. Do not open it up (as you already have it). You will see that the *RIF search window* is now empty. Enter the next RIF number: 104-10165-10168. Tap the enter key on your computer and see what pops up in the introduction window to the document.

You now make a decision between two alternatives. You notice that from the information on the introduction window that this document is unrelated to what you are looking for. Place your cursor on the blue colored back button (top left of your MFF screen) and left click it. The number 104-10165-10168 is still in the *RIF search window*. Place your cursor just to the right of the last number—8. Hit the *backspace key* on your computer and enter the next number—9, and then press enter on your keyboard. This time you find it is exactly the document you wanted or a document closely related to it. Open it up and download it as a PDF file if you like. Save it to a directory on your hard drive or thumb drive. If you went through the step of downloading it as a PDF file, a few clicks of the blue back space key will take you back to the point where the RIF number 104-10165-10169 is in the *RIF search window* again. This time you have to hit the backspace key twice to remove the 69 and replace it with 70 to see the next document in this center RIF block series (10165). The entire procedure can be done in a matter of seconds once you get the hang of it.

Don't forget to work up and down from your starting point. In this case it was 10168. So the next number up is 10169 and the next number down is 10167. Sometimes I will work up and down ten or even thirty numbers to ensure I have scooped up all of the high value documents. *Do not be surprised to see that the vein you are mining is interwoven with a separate stream of documents—so that the stream you want appears in every other or every third document in a particular center RIF-bloc series.* Once you have

RESEARCH METHODOLOGIES

practiced this technique you can fly through hundreds of documents very quickly. This technique has saved me thousands of hours of precious research time over the last fifteen years.

Finally, remember that what you are looking for may also be (and probably will be) located in one or more different center RIF block series. It is valuable to have handy several center RIF blocks for those people or subjects you are researching. Make sure that in the most important cases you type and arrange these center RIF numbers in a file to save in the relevant directory or subdirectory of your hard drive or thumb drive for future reference. You will thank yourself many times for having done so.

2. THE DAY BY DAY SEARCH STRATEGY

When all else fails, there are other strategies that, while they take longer, will still bear fruit—and sometimes, luckily, the very answer you have been looking for. Look at the date on the document you want to follow up on. Let's say it says 10 March 1962. In the *search all documents* window, type in that date as 03/10/62 (you do not need quotation marks). See what else pops up on that date. Sometimes the offices who are communicating with each other will respond on the same day, or the next day, or 2-4 days later. Consider yourself lucky if there are less than 15 hits. Sometimes (especially as you are working just before or after the assassination) there may be 100-200 hits or more for a single day. Again, when I have to resort to this strategy I will generally work forward and backward from the date I begin with. [Note: there might be a new feature added to the website that will make this strategy even more useful.]

3. THE MICROFILM SEARCH STRATEGY

Another slow but sometimes very successful strategy is the microfilm search strategy [see the CIA microfilm section on MFF]. This technique usually involves extra steps and takes extra time because single folders may contain 100-200 pages of documents, and they may be very heavily redacted and of poor quality, in terms of readability. The documents inside these folders will not have RIF numbers—there is only one RIF number for the entire folder. Once you find a document that looks promising, pray that the date is legible and, even better, that you can see the cable or dispatch number *or* the HQS IN or OUT number associated with it.

Once armed with this information, it's back to the first strategy—entering a name or number. If that pops up a document that does have a RIF number, then it's off to the races with the center RIF block strategy. If necessary, combine that with a day-by-day hunt.

4. THE REDACTION CROSS CHECK STRATEGY

The same document may have been redacted on different dates by different redactors. For example, in one document I saw this: "We heard from the [xxxx] Station that…"; in a duplicate I saw this: "We heard from the Rome [xxxxxxx] that…" From this it is obvious the document refers to the "Rome Station." This happens more often than you might think. Hunting for every copy of each document to cross check every redaction is impossible. But you should consider doing it for the most important pieces of information you are trying to find.

Do not forget to cross check the redaction in the text of the document against the title on the RIF sheet. Failure to do so will sometimes result in missing a huge opportunity. I have found on many occasions that the name of the person being hidden by redactions in the text is just lying there in the open on the RIF sheet. For example, when trying to identify the name for Cubela's first case officer in his 1961 recruitment in Helsinki, I discovered a document where, as usual, the name was redacted, but, in this case, someone forgot to redact it on the RIF sheet too.

5. THE HANGMAN STRATEGY

In redacted documents prior to the establishment of the Assassination Records Review Board, redactions were most often single words or two words of a name or place name. In such instances it is often easy to determine the exact number of letters, including punctuation, inside of the redacted space. For instance, if you suspect an identity is being withheld—either a true name or pseudonym—and you know something about their history, you might play "hangman" and fill in the spaces

On several occasions this technique has helped me uncover the true name of a person behind several pseudonyms. If you know enough about the assignment history of one or more of the false names, breaking into just one of them makes recovery of the remaining ones easier.

6. CHECK THE MARGINALIA

This is extremely important, even if at first the handwriting and scribbles are very hard to read. There are many instances of individuals who worked on temporary duty during declassification reviews—who, 1) did not know enough about the history of the case to know whether or not to redact an item, or 2) did not feel they had enough time to give attention to little scrawls at the margins. For example, the use of this technique in this volume uncovered the identities of the CIA chiefs of station in Paris and Madrid, and the cryptonym (AMSTRUT-2) for Castro's sister, Juanita Castro.

7. FILL IN BARELY LEGIBLE DOCUMENTS

Documents in terrible shape can sometimes be partly or nearly fully recovered. This process takes both time and considerable knowledge of the case. These documents may not have been withheld because it was assumed they would be impossible to read, as some are. The circumstance of some of these documents sometimes leaves one wondering if they were intentionally rendered illegible (though there is no proof that this is so). The rule of thumb is this: something is better than nothing if the document is important. This method helped me identify the cryptonym (AMCROAK-1) for Bernardo Milanes Lopez, the doctor of Castro's mother, recruited by Tony Sforza, and "Operation Raphael."

8. MAINTAIN A "FOR FUTURE REFERENCE" FILE

The above strategies will work. When they do you will see a lot of important documents that you were not necessarily looking for. These are gems. Do not, in the joy of your moment of discovery, simply pass these documents by. You will punish yourself later by spending an inordinate amount of time trying to find them again. When you see a gem, there is no need to download it right away. Just open up your "for future reference file" (that you have placed on your hard drive or thumb drive) and enter the RIF and 3 words about why it is important and then move on. I have learned this lesson the hard way.

9. DOUBT AND DOUBLE CHECK IMPORTANT ITEMS

When you discover something new and you determine that it is important, make a concerted effort to find an independent source to back it up—two more sources would be even better. Do not put in stone something you have seen in only one document. Beware: *there are mistakes in CIA and FBI records*. As discussed in the Afterword, once recognized, mistakes can be extremely valuable to your research.

BIBLIOGRAPHY

Belsito, Frank, J., *CIA: Cuba and the Caribbean—CIA Officer's Memoirs* (Reston VA: Ancient Mariner Press, 2002)

Beschloss, Michael, *The Crisis Years: Kennedy and Khrushchev, 1960-1963* (New York: Edward Burlingame Books, 1991)

Bethel, Paul, *The Losers* (New York: Arlington House, 1969)

Bissell, Richard M., *Reflections of a Cold Warrior: From Yalta to the Bay of Pigs* (New Haven: Yale University Press, 1996)

Calhoun, Jack, *Gangsterismo: The United States, Cuba, and the Mafia: 1933-1966* (New York: O/R Books, 2013)

Canfield, Michael, and Alan J. Webberman, *Coup D'état in America* (New York: The Third Press, 1975)

Castro, Juanita, *Fidel and Raul—My Brothers—The Secret History* (Doral, Florida: Santillana USA Publishing Company, Inc, 2009)

Corn, David, *Blond Ghost: Ted Shackley and the CIA's Crusades* (New York: Simon and Schuster, 1994)

Dorschner, John, and Roberto Fabricio, *The Winds of December* (New York: Coward, McCann & Geoghegan, 1980)

Dubois, Jules, *Fidel Castro: Rebel, Liberator or Dictator?* (New York: Bobbs-Merrill Company Inc., 1959)

Allen W. Dulles, *Craft of Intelligence: America's Legendary Spy Master On the Fundamentals of Intelligence Gathering For a Free World* (Guilford, Connecticut: The Lyons Press, 2006)

Eisenhower, Dwight D., *The White House Years: Waging Peace, 1956-1961* (New York: Doubleday, 1965), p. 329.

English, T. J., *Havana Nocturne: How the Mob Owned Cuba and Then Lost the Revolution* (New York: Harper, 2008)

Escalante, Fabian, *The Secret War: CIA Covert Operations Against Cuba, 1959-62* (New York: Ocean Press, 1995)

Franqui, Carlos, *Family Portrait with Fidel* (New York: Random House, 1984)

Freedman, Lawrence, *US Intelligence and the Soviet Strategic Threat* (Boulder Colorado: Westview Press, 1977)

Geyer, Georgie Anne, *Guerrilla Prince: The Untold Story of Fidel Castro* (Boston: Little, Brown & Co., 1991)

Hinckle, Warren and William Turner, *Deadly Secrets: The CIA-Mafia War Against Castro and the Assassination of JFK* (New York: Thunder's Mouth Press, 1992)

Hunt, E. Howard, *Undercover—Memoirs of an American Secret Agent* (Berkley: Berkley Publishing Corporation, 1974)

BIBLIOGRAPHY

—Hunt, E. Howard, *Give Us This Day—the Inside Story of the Bay of Pigs Invasion* (New Rochelle, N.Y.: Arlington House, 1973)

— *American Spy: My Secret History in the CIA, Watergate and Beyond* (Hoboken: John Wiley and Sons, Inc., 2007)

Hunt, Jim, and Bob Risch, *Warrior: Frank Sturgis—the CIA's #1 Assassin-Spy* (New York: Tom Doherty Associates Book, 2011)

Lacy, Robert, *Little Man—Meyer Lansky and the Gangster Life* (Boston: Little Brown and Company, 1991)

Lazo, Mario, *Dagger in the Heart: American Policy in Cuba* (New York: Twin Circle Publishing Co., 1970 ed.)

Lopez-Fresquet, Rufo, *My Fourteen Months with Castro* (New York: World Publishing Company, 1966).

Marchetti, Victor, and John Marks, *The CIA and the Cult of Intelligence* (New York: A. A. Knopf, 1974)

Martino, John, *I was Castro's Prisoner –An American Tells his Story* (Southlake, Texas, JFK Lancer Publications, 2008 ed.)

Mellen, Joan, *The Great Game in Cuba: How the CIA Sabotaged its own Plot to Unseat Castro* (New York: Skyhorse, 2013)

Morley, Morris H., *Imperial State: The United States and Revolution and Cuba, 1952-1986* (Cambridge: Cambridge University Press, 1989 ed.)

Nixon, Richard, *RN* (New York: Grosset & Dunlap, 1978)

—*Six Crises* (New York: Warner Books, 1979 ed.)

—"Cuba, Castro and John F. Kennedy," *Reader's Digest*, November, 1964.

Patterson, Thomas G., *Contesting Castro* (New York: Oxford University Press, 1994)

Perez, Louis A. Jr., *Cuba and the United States: Ties of Singular Intimacy* (Athens: University of Georgia Press, 1990)

Perry, James David, *The Foreign Policy of John F. Kennedy, 1961*, George Washington University doctoral dissertation, September 30, 1996.

Phillips, David A., *The Night Watch: 25 Tears of Peculiar Service* (New York: Atheneum, 1977)

Prados, John, *The Soviet Estimate: US Intelligence Analysis and Soviet Strategic Forces* (Princeton: Princeton University Press, 1986 ed.)

Quirk, Robert E., *Fidel Castro* (New York: WW Norton, 1993)

Rovner, Eduardo Saenz, *The Cuban Connection: Drug Trafficking, Smuggling, and Gambling in Cuba from the 1920s to the Revolution* (Chapel Hill: North Carolina Press, 2008)

Scott, Peter Dale, *Deep Politics and the Death of JFK* (Berkley: University of California Press, paperback ed., 1996)

—*Deep Politics II: Essays on Oswald, Mexico, and Cuba* (Skokie, Illinois: Green Archive Publications, 1995)

Shackley, Ted, *Spymaster—My Life in the CIA* (Washington D.C., Potomac Books, paper ed., 2006)

Siragusa, Charles, *The Trail of the Poppy—Behind the Mask of the Mafia* (Englewood Cliffs, N.J.:Prentice-Hall, Inc.:1966)

BIBLIOGRAPHY

Smith, Earl E.T., *The Fourth Floor—An Account of the Castro Communist Revolution* (New York: Random House, 1962)

Smith, Wayne, *The Closest of Enemies: A Personal and Diplomatic History of the Castro Years* (New York: W. W. Norton, 1987)

Stockton, Bayard, *Flawed Patriot—The Rise and Fall of CIA Legend Bill Harvey* (Washington, D.C.: Potomac Books, Inc., 2006)

Szulc, Tad, *Fidel: A Critical Portrait* (New York: William Morrow & Co., 1986)

Talbot, David, *Brothers—The Hidden History of the Kennedy Years* (New York: Free Press, 2007)

Thomas, Hugh, *Cuba: The Pursuit of Freedom* (New York: Harper and Row, 1971)

Thornton, Richard C., "Exploring the Utility of Missile Superiority, 1958"; 1979 unpublished manuscript, George Washington University.

Valentine, Douglas, *The Strength of the Wolf: The Secret History of America's War on Drugs* (New York: Verso, 2004)

Webb, Gary, *Dark Alliance: The CIA, the Contras, and the Crack Cocaine Explosion* (New York: Seven Stories Press, 1999)

Wyden, Peter, *Bay of Pigs—the Untold Story* (New York: Simon and Schuster, 1979)

Docymentary Collections, Oral Histories, and other Miscellaneous Sources

National Archives and Records Administration (NARA), JFK Records
Mary Ferrell Foundation (MFF) Archives

WHERE ANGELS TREAD LIGHTLY

FOIA releases to James Lesar RE Catherine Taaffe; FBI HQS and New York Office Cuban (109) files.

Foreign Relations of the United States (FRUS), 1958-1960, volume VI, Cuba.

Jack B. Pfeiffer, *Official CIA's Official History of the Bay of Pigs Operations*, Volume III.

Alleged Assassination Plots Involving Foreign Leaders, United States Senate, Interim Report of the Select Committee to Study Governmental Operations (Washington DC: US Government Printing Office, 1975).

Anti-Castro Activities and Organizations, Appendix to Hearings before the Select Committee on Assassinations of the US House of Representatives, Ninety-fifth Congress, Second Session, Volume X, (Washington DC: US Government Printing Office, March 1979).

The CIA Inspector General's (IG) *Report on Plots to Assassinate Fidel Castro*, 23 May 1967, RIF 1994.03.08.14:54:36:690005.

Frank Sturgis Deposition to *The President's Commission on CIA Activities*, on April 3, 1975. [The RIF for the original version, 178-10002-10238, is now classified in the National Archives. I copied it there before it was reclassified. Note: the NARA RIF audit trail does not show that it was ever declassified—although it was for a short while.]

Wayne Jackson, CIA Historical Staff, *Allen Welsh Dulles as Director of Central Intelligence: 26 February 1953-29 November 1961*, Volume V, Intelligence Support of Policy.

Neil McElroy interview, 1967, *The Eisenhower Oral History Collection*, Columbia University Library.

Oral Interview of Mr. Richard M. Bissell, Jr. by Jack E. Pfeiffer, 17 October 1975.

BIBLIOGRAPHY

Oral Interview of Jacob D. Esterline by Jack E. Pfeiffer, 10-11 October 1975.

Ted Shackley (Halley) Deposition to the Church Committee (19 August 1975; RIF 157-10014-10046).

Anthony Sforza (Alfred J. Sarno) Deposition to the Church Committee (25 June 1975, RIF 157-10005-10250.

1995 June Cobb letter to John Newman.

INDEX

Agramonte, Roberto 42
Aguero, Luis Conte 146-48, 152-53, 320, 340, 344, 384, 386
Aguero, Jose 318
Aguero, Rivero 12
Aguiar, Alfredo Guerra 203
Almeida, Juan 185-87
Alsop, Joseph 240
Alvarez, Ricardo 279
Alvarez, Santiago 221
Amble, George Valdez 274
Ameijeiras, Efigenio 91
Anderson, Jack 99-100, 102-06, 136, 139
Anderson, Robert B. (Sen.) 239
Anslinger, Harry J. 114-16, 131, 134, 136-37
Aspuru (household, later occupied by Sforza) 283, 286-87, 300
Aranguren, Armando de Cardenasy 38
Arbenz, Jacobo Guzman 69, 159, 369

Armas, Castillo 145
Artime, Marcelo 330
Artime, Manuel Francisco (aka Javier, aka Mr. Ignacio) xix, xxvi, 191-93, 196-99, 202, 212, 234, 259-275, 314, 321, 334-36, 340, 373, 388, 391
Aufhauser, Alfred 105-06, 108
Avignon, Arthur 219-20, 279, 301

Baggett, Sam H. 227
Bailey, E. Tomlin 57
Barbo, Juan Pedro 33
Barletta, Amadeo Barletta 115
Barker, Bernard 88, 196, 204-05, 207, 220, 260, 263-64, 316, 329, 335, 341
Barnes, Tracy (aka Playdon) 335, 369, 396
Barquin, Ramon (Col.) 11-12, 16-20, 23, 44, 246, 370,
Barth, Lee (Rosalie Butler) 120

Batista, Fulgencio (Pres.) xi, xviii, xxv-xxvi, 1-8, 11-19, 22-24, 28-38, 42-47, 51, 57-65, 71-73, 76, 84, 90, 113-17, 143-44, 169, 192, 196n, 214-16, 221, 226, 231, 234, 244, 247-48, 256-57, 259, 271, 273-74, 280, 288, 292, 300, 314, 325, 356, 359, 362, 394-95, 400

Balbino, Padre 265

Barbaressa Lorenzo, Frau Marsal 47, 323

Bayo, Alberto 94, 161-62, 166, 316

Belmont, Alan H. 43n, 44n, 51n, 57, 58, 59n, 61n, 63n 72n, 75-76, 171n, 172n, 174n, 272n

Belsito, Frank J. 58, 59n, 84, 314, 411

Beltran, Marcelino Garcia 41-44

Beltrand, Domingo 342

"Bender, Frank" (see Droller)

Beschloss, Michael 13n, 411

Bethel, Paul 4n, 12n, 83n, 161-66, 170, 176-77, 216n, 219-20, 232-33, 411

Betancourt, Ernesto 9n

Betancourt, Romulo 68

Bianchi, Lucia (sister of DR martyr Jose Antonio Echevarria) 298

Biarte, Elvira Diaz (friend of Maria Leopoldina Grau Alsina) 318

Bissell, Richard M. 28, 146, 158, 250-53, 287, 335, 369, 388-89, 411, 416

Bonsal, Phillip A. (Amb.) 61, 149, 174n, 184, 193-95, 218-19, 222, 227, 230, 233, 237, 385

"Booth, Frank" (see Knapman) 342

Booth, John P. 61-63

Borbonet, Enrico (Maj.) 167, 246

Botano, Antonio 133-34

Bowles, Lucy Ann 101

Boyar, Monica 171-74

Bradley, Leslie 166, 170, 212

Broglie, Warren 108

Brown, Jerry G. 89n, 213n

Bryant, Charge 75

Bryer(s), Jim 186-87, 203n

Burke, Arleigh (Adm.) 6, 8, 19, 239

Byrnes (Sec. State) 65

Cabell, Charles (CIA Dep. Dir.) 88

Cabre, Enrique 197-98, 272-73

Cajigas, Francisco G. 246, 253, 256-57

Calhoun, Jack 31n, 411

Canfield, Michael viii, 6n, 86, 93, 411

Canizarea, Rafael Salas 114

Cantillo (Gen.) 17-20

Carr, Willard Hubert 19
    De La Carrera 117

Carrillo, Justo 11-12, 15, 18-19, 325, 333, 372, 378, 385

Carrington, J.C. 9

Castro, Emma (sister of Fidel Castro) 290-95

Castro, Fidel xiv, xvi-xxvi, 1-2; weapons for Castro during revolution: 3-6, 394-395; CIA failure to block Castro's assumption of power: 15-20; Castro's secret plan to communize Cuba: 28-30; Castro and DR: 35-39; Castro

INDEX

avoided by Catherine Taaffe: 77-79; Castro's April 1959 visit to the U.S.: 141-160; Castro and the 1959 Cuban invasions of the Caribbean: 161-163, 174-178; Castro thwarts Dominican invasion of Cuba: 211-222, 225-227; Castro and INRA: 189-199; Castro's complete victory in Cuba: 229-242

Castro, Juan Fernandez 275n.

Castro, Juanita (Juana) (sister of Fidel Castro) xix, 285-295, 307, 323, 330-31, 409, 411

Castro, Raul 3n, 7, 24, 27-28, 33, 82, 85-86, 93, 158, 164, 173, 176-77, 179-82, 185, 198-99, 229-30, 232, 237, 261, 274, 281, 288, 291, 295, 308, 320, 326, 330-32, 362, 400, 411

Chomon, Faure 24, 35-38

Cienfuegos, Camilo 31, 51, 79, 82, 91, 164, 167, 170-74, 180, 211-12, 226, 232, 234-35, 271

Clark, Robert 23-24

Clark Walter 23-24

Cobb, Arthur Tom 99

Cobb, Jasper E. 99, 101

Cobb, Jasper E. Jr. 99

Cobb Jessie Lois 101

Cobb, Viola June (aka Joyce H. Pineinch, aka Clarinda E. Sharp) xviii, 71, 97-109, 111-28, 129-40, 141, 146-48n., 152-57, 173, 291, 327, 333, 336, 339, 417

Contreras, Lopez 68-69

"Corbuston, Oliver H." (see Kent) 39, 336, 341, 374, 381-82

Corn, David 411

Cotter, William J. 268-69, 275n

Cox, Al (aka Robert Reynolds, aka Robert Rogers) xix, 3n., 263, 266-268, 270, 275, 336, 393-400, 402

Crozier, Ross Lester 39, 336; (aka Ron Cross) 336; (aka Arthur G. Vaivida) 336; (aka Harold R. Noemayr) 39, 332, 336; (aka Roger Fox) 39, 332, 336

Corzo (Col.) 246

Cubas, Jorge 237-38

Cubela, Mirth Nova Delgado (wife of Rolando Cubela) 307

Cubela, Rolando xix, xxi-xxii, 30-39, 90, 202, 277-87, 290-91, 295, 297-308, 320, 324-25, 331, 333, 345-46, 349, 353, 362-63, 408

Dahlgren, Robert K. 207, 395n.

Damicone, Norris W. 314, 337

Dasher, Charles (MGen.) 250n.

Davis, Horace 248n.

Dechard (Cuban Con.) 266-67

Dejoie, Luis 161

Delay, Frank P. 196n.

Devereau (Capt.) 182-83

Diaz Brull, Sergio 185, 187, 201, 212

Diaz Lanz, Marcos xix, 90-91, 94n., 162, 180, 181n., 184, 187, 201-03, 208n., 209, 211, 334; (aka Mariano Jimenez Gomez) 342

421

Diaz Lanz, Pedro xix, 5, 6n., 85, 87, 90-91, 162, 165, 175, 177, 179, 182, 184, 186-88, 211, 220, 231-34, 263, 271, 333, 383, 386
Dodge, Harris F. 9
Dorschner, John 15n., 357n., 359, 412
Droller, Gerry (aka Frank Bender) xxiv, 158-59, 214, 247n., 329, 337, 370-71, 381-84, 386-87, 390; (aka Wallace A. Parlett) 337, 380-82, 387, 390; (possibly aka Henry Hecksher) xxiv, 340, 355
Dubois, Jules 141-45, 412
Dubois, Ray 337
Dulles, Allen W. (DCI) 7n., 12-13, 16-20, 22, 43-44, 58, 95, 145-46, 152, 208, 218, 239-43, 249-256, 310-12, 334, 337, 398n., 412, 416
Dulles, John Foster (Sec. State) 18, 25, 58, 149, 150n.

Eastland, James O. (Sen.) 253
Echegoyen, Carlos 187, 201
Echevarria, Jose Antonio 2, 30-35, 90, 298, 300, 302, 308
Edwards, Sheffield (Dir Sec.) 13n., 268-70
Egerter, Ann Elizabeth Goldsborough 337
Eisenhower, Dwight D. (Pres.) xiv, 3, 6-18, 25, 28, 44, 58-59, 95, 145, 148-51, 164-65, 188, 194-95, 217, 229, 236, 239-41, 251-53, 368-69, 412, 416

Ellis, R.B. (Adm.) 8
Emerick, Chester A. 131, 134n.
English, T. J. 22n., 23n., 24n., 114n., 115n., 412
Escalante, Fabian viii, 53n., 54n., 177, 194n., 197n., 212, 214-16, 219, 222, 225-26, 231n., 232n., 234n., 259n., 260n., 272, 317-18, 412
Esterline, Jacob D. 69, 193n., 196n., 280n., 283-91, 333, 337, 349-53, 370, 384, 387, 390, 395-96, 399-400, 417; (aka Anthony R. Ponchay) 280n., 283n., 285n., 288, 338, 350n., 353, 390

Fabricio, Roberto 15n., 357n., 359, 412
Failde, Delia (AMCOO) xix, 201-04, 260, 266-75, 320, 338
Fallucci, Richard M. (aka Harvey Thompson, aka William Thompson) 281n., 303-08, 325, 333, 338, 346
Fernandez, Alberto 43-44, 55, 63-64, 66, 74, 167, 171-74. 177, 197, 321, 328
Ferrando, Augusto (Col.) 215
"Fiorini, Frank" (see Sturgis) 4, 83, 85-86, 89, 162, 163n., 174n., 181-84, 203-04, 383,
"Fox, Roger" (see Crozier) 39, 332, 336
Franqui, Carlos 143-44, 148-49n., 160, 313, 412

INDEX

Freedman, Lawrence 10n, 240-41n., 412
Freyre, Fabio xxv, 244-47, 254-55, 371
Fuguoli, Daniel 161

Gaffney, George 98n., 126, 129, 137-40
Gaither, Ridgley (Lt. Gen.) 250n.
Garcia, Antonio, 331
Garcia, Enrique 172-73
Garcia, Jesus Alberty 316
Garcia, Johnny Abbes 214
Garcia, Miguel 39
Gardner, Arthur (Amb.) 152
Geyer, Georgie Anne 150n., 151n., 160n., 164n., 199n., 412
Giordano, Henry L. 137
Gobart, Fabio 82
Godoy, Bernie 168
Gonzalez, Amada (Carlos Tepedino's mother) 30
Gonzales, Carlos Tepedino (see Carlos Tepedino) 300, 333, 339
Gonzalez, Juan 116
Goodpaster, Andrew 18
Govea, Charles 280n., 283n., 285n., 288n., 350n.
Gray, Gordon 18, 146
Grau Alsina, Maria Leopoldina (niece of Grau San Marin) 53-54, 318
Grau San Marin, Ramon (Pres.) 45
Grau San Marin Ramon (nephew of Grau San Marin) 317-318

"Growery, Wallace A." (see Williamson) 47, 306-07, 325, 346-47, 355-59, 361-65
Guardia, Ernesto, Jr. 163
Guardia, Ruben Miro 170
Guerra, Oscar (Cons.) 83
Guevara, Che 27, 33, 82, 90, 94n., 158, 164, 166, 182, 190-91, 197, 237, 261, 328, 362
"Gupton, Douglas" (see Kent) 39, 341, 372, 374, 379-80

Hall, Loran 166, 169-70, 212, 218n.
Hamilton, Alexander xiii
"Hamilton, Edward J." (see Hunt) 340, 367, 379-80, 382, 384-87
Hardway, Dan (HSCA) viii, xv, 100-01
Haverty, James T. 72-73, 181
Healy, George W. Jr. 141, 143
Hecksher, Henry (possibly an alias for Gerry Droller) xxiv, 340, 355
Hemming, Gerry Patrick 166-70, 212-14, 235
Hemmingway, Ernest 81
Hendrickson, Paul R. 166-68
Hermsdorf, Harry (possibly a pseudonym) 99-105, 108, 124, 140, 154-55, 173
Herran Olozaga, Monina 107, 123, 128
Herran Olozaga, Rafael 71, ("Rafa" 103), 102-06, 109, 115, 118-28, 131-40

423

Herran, Olozaga, Tomas 71, 102, 115, 122, 126-27, 131-40
Herran, Pedro Alcantara 102
Herter, Christian (Sec. State) 25n., 28, 36n.., 37, 57-63, 77-79, 145, 149, 194-95, 217, 236-37, 243-44
Hevia, Carlos 42
Hidalgo, "Bebe" (or "Bebo") 4-5
Hinckle, Warren viii, 412
Hollaway, G.L. 67
Hoover, J. Edgar 25n., 28, 36n, 37, 46n., 47, 52n., 57-79, 152, 162, 182n., 184n., 211, 249, 273n., 301
Hopkins, Chris 180n., 196n.
Hormel, Charles 4
Van Horn (Maj.) 87-88
Hummel, R.A. 9
Humphrey, Hubert (Sen.) 14, 65
Hunt, E. Howard xix, 88-89, 316, 337, 340, 362, 367-91, 393-94, 402, 412-13
Hunt, Jim 88, 94n., 183n., 184n., 413

Jackson, Wayne 7n., 239n., 240n., 416
"Jimenez Gomez, Mariano" (see Marcos Diaz Lanz) 204, 342
Jimenez, Enrique Moya (Capt.) 172-76, 178, 183n.
Jimenez, Nunez 190, 192, 197, 261
Johnson, Lyndon B. (Sen., Pres.) xx, 227, 241
Johnson, Wendell G. (Col.) (aka "Passavoy") 340

Johnston, William W. 129-36
Jones, Ivan H. (Capt.) 262, 266, 270
Jones, M.A. 162n., 163n., 181n.

Kail, Samuel (Maj.) 176
"Karnley, Patrick" (see Reichardt) xxiv, 207, 262, 265, 336
Kennedy, John F. xiv-xvii, 10n., 13n., 149n., 151n., 164n., 240n., 242n., 249-50, 298, 309-11, 365, 399n., 411, 413-15
Kennedy, Robert F. xi-xxii, 298, 311
Kent, William M. 39, 88, 340-41, 372, 374, 384, 402; (aka Oliver H. Corbuston) 39, 336, 340-41, 374, 381-82; (aka Robert K. Trouchard) 320, 329, 340-41, 402; (aka Douglas Gupton) 39, 341, 372, 374, 379-80; (aka George Witner) 341
Khrushchev, Nikita 3, 10-11, 13n., 14, 238-42, 411
King, J.C. (Col.) 13, 55, 207, 245, 249, 251-54, 265n., 268-70, 341, 372, 395
Kleberg, Robert J. 9, 43-44, 194-95, 222, 227, 328
Knapman, Edward D. (aka Warren Frank, aka Frank Booth, aka Joe Crespi) 314, 326, 328-29, 342
Kostikov, Valery xx
"Kymingham, Peter" (see Stent) 302, 348

Lacy, Robert 413
Lansky, Meyer 23-24, 112-16, 413

INDEX

Leitao de Cunha, Vasco 288
Leitao de Cunha, Virginia 291, 295, 307, 330
Llanusa, Jose 66, 281
Lazo, Mario 12n., 15, 196, 237-38, 413
Lemay, Curtis (Gen.) 239
Lesar, James viii, xxiii, 23n., 36n., 60, 61n., 63n., 64-66, 68n., 69n., 72n., 73, 74n., 75n., 76n., 171n., 197n., 198n., 272n., 273n., 274n., 416
Lesnick, Max 90
Liebacher, Ernst 166-68, 214n.
Licari, Peter, N (pseudonym for true name unknown, possibility it may be Droller) 247-48, 327, 347, 375
Londregan, E.W. Jr. 46n., 47-53
Lopez-Fresquet, Rufo 29, 142-43n., 158-60, 190-91, 231n., 232, 413
Lopez, Ignacio 30, 300
Loretta, Maria 300
Lorrie, Ricardo 90-91
Luciano, Charles "Lucky" 112-14

Machado, Geraldo (Cuban Pres.) 30, 44
Mackey, James. E. Jr. 50
Madison, James xiii
Manners 74-75
Marchetti, Victor 20n., 413
Marin, Humbarto Sori 190-92, 196-97, 212, 234, 259
Marin, Luis Munoz 150
Marks, John 20n., 413
Martinez, Rolando 182

Martino, John 215, 413
Masferrer, Rolando (Sen.) 21-22, 76, 211, 221, 274-75, 380
Matos, Huber 90-91, 180, 196-97, 212, 231-33, 261
Matthews, Herb 161, 178, 188, 219
McElroy, Neil (Sec. Def.) 8, 165, 240, 416
McGill, 168-69
Medina (Lt. Col.) 69
Medina, Julio 66
Mellen, Joan 413
Menoyo, Eloy Gutierrez 215, 219, 222, 225-26, 342
Meskil, Paul 93n., 94n.
Mikoyan, Anastas I. 39, 278
Mitchell, Johnny (Capt.) 167
Morales, David 202-08, 260-63, 272, 316, 322, 329, 343, 398; (aka Stanley R. Zamka) 202-03, 260, 329, 343
Morgan, William A. 212, 214-26
Morley, Morris H. 11n., 12n., 16n., 18n., 19n., 25n., 199n., 413
Morley, Jefferson viii, 285n., 309n.
Morse, Wayne B. (Sen.) 65
"Morse, Fred" (see Henry Preston Lopez) 342
Mosquera, Tomas Cipriano 102
Murphy, Robert 8n., 13n., 19, 236n.

Nichols, Ericson S. (possibly Colonel Severs) 9, 87-94, 183, 186-87, 202-03, 344

425

Nixon, Richard M. 6n., 14-15, 62-64, 72, 146, 149-52, 163-64, 214, 236, 243, 249-56, 369, 372, 413
Noel, James (aka "Jim Knowles") 16, 88, 220, 279, 327, 343, 345, 356-57, 377; (aka Woodrow C. Olien) 48n., 327, 343, 345, 356, 358, 360n., 377

Ochoa, Delio Gomez 90, 171-77
Ochoa, Emilio 90
Ordonez, Ricardo Valazco 222
Orrison, Samuel G., and Dudley Pachuke (both pseudonyms for true name unknown) 316, 321, 323, 340, 347, 370, 374, 377-84, 386-87, 391, 396, 399
Orta, Juan 53, 92, 94, 291
Oswald, Lee Harvey viii, xix, xx, 39, 52n., 112n., 113n., 196n., 309, 311n., 312, 319, 414
Otepka, Otto 57,

Paez, Julio Martinez 71, 147, 319
Paez, Frank 314
Palinger, James R. (aka Sherwood P. Rochom) 47, 359-61
Papich, Sam 73n., 74-75
Patterson, Thomas G. 8n., 13n., 14n., 15n., 194n., 414
"Patterson, William" 83
Pawley, William D. 11-16, 152, 244-47, 249-50, 253-57, 321, 334, 372
Pedraza, Jose Eleutario 215, 221, 244-48, 253-55

Pelletier, Yanes (Capt.) 198
Pena, Margot 47, 323
Pena. Oreste 196n.
Perez, Antonio Garcia 331
Perez, Eddie "Bayo" 321
Perez, Faustino 34
Perez, Louis A. Jr. 194n., 414
Perez, Manuel "Manolito" 282
Perez, Manuel Vega 317, 328, 343
   Jimenez, Marcos Perez, (Pres.) 316
Perez, Pedro Font 153
Perry, Huley 65
Perry, James D. 10n., 240n., 242n., 414
Pfeiffer, Jack B. 394-96, 396n, 399, 416-17
Phillips, David A. xix, xxiv, (aka Jack Stewart, aka Andrew Merton, aka Michael Choaden) 37, 88-89, 100-01, 196n., 202-09, 220-25, 260-65, 272-73, 277-82, 297, 300-03, 311-12, 316, 320, 324-26, 329, 333-34, 343-44, 364, 371-72, 384, 389, 390, 396, 402, 404-05, 409, 414
"Ponchay, Anthony R." (see Esterline) 280n., 283n., 285n., 288, 338, 350n., 353, 390
Pope, Alexander xii
Portuondo, Emilio Nunez 244, 254-56, 325
Posada Franco, Maria Cecilia 131, 135
Power, Thomas 239

INDEX

Prados, John 240n., 241n., 414
Preston, Rosita 66
Preston, Roy 43
Prio, Carlos Socarras 4, 11, 42, 45-46, 63, 183, 191, 322, 372

Quarles, Donald A. (Dep. Sec. Def.) 146
Queen Elizabeth 148
Quevedo, Miguel 151
Quinn, Wallace A. 171-74, 321
Quintana, Alberto Muller 39, 323
Quirk, Robert E. 19n., 31n., 32, 33n., 34n., 35, 150n., 151n., 160n., 362n., 414

Ragano, Frank 115
Ray, Manuel "Manolo" xxv, xxvi, 3, 48, 281, 295, 306, 313, 321, 328, 330, 336, 346-47, 355-65, 381-82, 384-88
Raynock, Nelson (aka Lawrence R. Charron) 21-22, 47, 340
Rebozo, Bebe 62-63, 72
Redmond, Kenneth R. 9
Redondo, Mario E. 269-70
Reichardt, Bernard (aka Patrick I. Karnley—both names might be pseudonyms) xxiv, 207, 262-69, 272, 336, 375
"Reynolds, Robert" (see Cox) 263, 266-70, 275, 336, 393, 396-400, 402
Rico, Antonio Blanco (Col.) 33, 280
Rivers, Joe 23-24

Roca, Blas 81-82, 199
Roca, Rosalba 146-48, 152
Rodriquez, Arnesto N. (Emilio's father) 325
Rodriguez, Carlos Rafael 173
Rodriquez, Emilio Americo (aka Peter J. DiGerveno) 280, 291, 324-25, 353
Rodriguez, Felix 175n., 176n., 214n., 226n., 227n., 234n.
Rojas, Andres Diaz 186, 333
Romay, Labrador Caridad (Carlos Tepedino's wife) 300
Roque, Manuel Salvat 39, 324
Rosen, Alex 73n., 75-76
Rubottom, Roy 16, 152, 235-36, 254n.
Rovner, Eduardo Saenz 99, 102n., 114n., 115n., 132n., 133-39, 414

Sanchez (Col.) 69
Sanchez, Alejandra 320
Sanchez, Augusto Martinez 230
Sanchez, Celia 153-54
Sanchez, Nestor (aka Matthew H. Ontrich, aka Nicholas Sanson) 344
Sanjenis, Sergio xxvi, 164, 179-80, 182-84, 212, 234, 260, 271
Sanjenis, Joaquin 184
Segal, Marvin 73-75, 97
Scott, Peter Dale vii, xv, 52, 112-13, 311n., 414
Scott Winston 344, 384
Sforza, Anthony xix, (aka Henry J. Sloman, aka Frank Stevens, aka Enrique, aka Alfred Sarno)

277-95, 297, 299, 302-03, 307, 319, 320, 328-30, 332-33, 345, 349-53, 398, 410, 417
Sforza-Flick, Charmaine 285, 285n.
Shackley, Ted xxii, 318, 397-98, 411, 414, 417
Sharp, Jessie Lois (June Cobb's mother) 101
Silesi, Joe 24
Sileo, Anthony L. (aka George D. Scorgory) 345
Simo, Juan de Dios Venture 175
Siragusa, Charles 116-17, 414
Smathers, George A. (Sen.) 62-64, 72
Snapper, Isadore (Dr.) 107, 154
Somoza, Anastasio 150, 162, 167, 217
Stockton, Bayard 415
Smith, Earl E.T. (Amb.) 2, 4n., 7n., 8-9, 12, 14n., 15, 16n., 25, 27, 59, 61-63, 72, 152, 346, 359, 415
"Smith, Jim" 373
Smith, Wayne 23, 42, 76n., 415
Sourwine, J.G. 98, 104-06
Stent, Jack "Red" (aka Peter J. Kymingham, aka Jack Stevens) 307, 348
Sturgis, Frank (aka Frank Fiorini) xviii, xix, 4-6, 9, 81-95, 162-63, 167, 174-75, 179-84, 203-04, 212, 233-35, 271, 316, 326, 383, 413, 416
Symington, Stuart (Sen.) 239-41
Szulc, Tad 2, 28, 81-84, 173n., 178, 219, 315, 332, 415

Taaffe, (sometimes spelled "Taife" or "Taffee") Catherine xi- xii, xviii-xix, xxiii, 23, 36, 41-43, 55, 57, 60-69, 71-79, 82, 97-98, 171-74, 177, 197-98, 211, 259, 271-75, 316, 321, 338, 416
Taaffe, William Francis Randall Dunne (Col.) 65, 67, 69
Talbot, David viii, xx(n), xxii(n), 415
Tamayo, Rodriguez (Gen.) 221, 246
Taylor, Maxwell D. (Gen.) 250n., 251n.
Tepedino, Antonio (Carlos Tepedino's step-brother) 300
Tepedino, Carlos 30-37, 90, 202, 277-87, 297, 297-308, 314, 325-26, 333, 339, 346, 349-50, 363
Tepedino, Francesco Antonio (Carlos' step-father) 30, 285, 287
Tharp, Martha 205
Thomas, Hugh 17n., 18n., 19n., 42n., 91, 94n., 160n., 162-64, 168, 173, 175n., 176n., 180n., 188, 190n., 191n., 192, 193n., 194n., 229n., 231n., 232n., 234n., 239n., 247n., 249n., 347, 356n., 357n., 359, 415
Thompson, Robert 62
Thornton, Richard C. 8n., 10n., 11n., 19n., 415
Tichborn, Edward G. (pseudo for Henry Preston Lopez) 248-49n., 342
Tolson, Clyde 73

INDEX

Trafficante, Santo 24, 53, 92, 113-15, 170, 291, 318
Travieso, Ernesto Fernandez 39
True, Ralph 98, 100, 109, 122, 124-28, 128, 138-39
Trujillo, Raphael 65, 163, 176-78, 179, 211-27, 233, 244-47, 253-54, 257
Trujillo, Raphael Jr. 176
Turner, William viii, 412

Ugarizza, Norma (Pancho Varona's wife) 31, 299n., 300n.
Urrutia, Manuel 24-25, 36, 42, 55, 66, 79, 232

Valdes, Ramiro 82, 164, 180
Valdez, Alfredo Hernandez 45, 66
Valentine, Douglas 98n., 112, 113n., 114n., 115-16, 129n, 137-40, 415
Vallejo, Rene 173
Varona, Francisco Wilfredo "Pancho" 30-32, 204, 266, 279-80, 283n, 284-88, 298-300, 305, 308, 319, 330, 349-53
Varona, Antonio xviii, xxvi, 1n., 30, 41-55, 191-93, 202n, 212, 230n., 247-48, 260-62, 266, 314, 317-18, 321, 323, 327, 331, 346-47, 359, 361, 365, 372-74, 378-79, 384, 387-88

Varona, Roberto 193, 202n., 260-73, 266, 389
Verdaguer, Roberto 165
Vickers, Jesse 67
Vidal, Evalina S. 249
Vizzini, Sal 116

Wachter, John 72-73
Wallach 105
Warren, Earl (Ch. Jus.) xx, 312
Wiecha, Robert D. 2, 83-85, 90, 173
Wessel, Milton R. 74-76
Whilding, Alun Jones 67
Williamson, Earl J. xix, xxiv, 306-07, 325, 346-47, 355-63 (aka Wallace A. Growery) 47, 306-07, 325, 346-47, 355-65 (aka Alfonso L. Rodriguez and Alfredo Fernandez) 306-07, 338, 346-47, 356, 359, 365, (aka "Jaime") 306
Wollam, Park Fields 2, 8, 83-84, 87, 90
Webb, Gary xv, 415
White, George 114-16
Wyden, Peter 343, 415

Zicarelli, Joseph Arthur 66-67

Printed in Great Britain
by Amazon